WITH
WALT WHITMAN
IN CAMDEN

April 8—September 14, 1889

By HORACE TRAUBEL

Edited by

GERTRUDE TRAUBEL

SOUTHERN ILLINOIS UNIVERSITY PRESS
CARBONDALE, ILLINOIS

EDITOR'S PREFACE

This fifth volume of Horace Traubel's "With Walt Whitman in Camden" is the first to appear in print without the benefit of a final reading by the author. I have corrected only obvious slips and unnecessary repetitions, checking references that seemed unclear. While the manuscript was sometimes difficult to decipher, it was never in disjointed notes, but always a continuous narrative.

Here is my mother's description of H. T.'s procedure (as quoted by Sculley Bradley in his Introduction to Volume 4): "The notes of the visits to Whitman were written on small bits of paper to fit into the pocket of his jacket and were written in what he called 'condensed longhand,' in the dim light of Whitman's room. Within the hour of the words spoken, the material was put into the complete form with which you are familiar in the three published volumes. There was no vacuum of time or emotion, thus preserving the vitality of the original conversation."

Vitality, contemporaneity—these Whitman characteristics —bring him to you not just an old man reliving a memorable career, but—like most seers—looking at the events before him with flashes of prophetic insight.

GERTRUDE TRAUBEL

Germantown, Philadelphia
May, 1963

ACKNOWLEDGMENTS

First to my mother, Anne Montgomerie Traubel, whose unfaltering faith in the value of this work was responsible for the devoted preservation of the original manuscript.

Then to Charles E. Feinberg, who, with a belief in this record second only to hers, has, with encouragement and assistance made the publication possible.

Also to Arthur W. L. Basy for his translation of the letter from Gabriel Sarrazin.

Also to the men and women at the Free Library of Philadelphia and the Historical Society of Pennsylvania, who so readily met with patience and cooperation my numerous requests for assistance and information.

And to Mildred Bruning who made a labor of love out of the typing.

CONTENTS

ILLUSTRATIONS CONTAINED IN THIS VOLUME

[*Frontispiece*]

ILLUSTRATIONS

LETTERS CONTAINED
IN THIS VOLUME

(Including Other Manuscripts of Walt Whitman)

WITH WALT WHITMAN
IN CAMDEN

Monday, April 8, 1889

10.45 A.M. W. sitting up, reading papers, but not looking well, which I remarked to Ed, who said, however, W. had made no remarks confessing any bad sensations. W. talked only briefly—somewhat about the morning's news, the book, the weather, &c. He expressed some regret that no mail at all had for several days again come from Washington. Gave me advice as to work in town. Then I left.

Evening 7:00. The room darkened—sun just fully down— the night clear beyond description, and calm at last, after the tempestuous forenoon. W. on his bed—laying out flat—his cane beside him—he covered and tucked in by his knee-blanket. Ed sat on foot of bed. They had been talking. We had a fairly good talk, Ed retiring. W. kept his position, his hands folded across his stomach, his voice very clear, and head not seemingly at all troubled. I said on taking a seat, "I hope this does not mean that you are sick?" It has been rarely of late that I found him on his back of an evening. He responded: "No —nor does it: but I have had a bad day: in fact, all my days of late have been pretty bad." Then half-reflectively: "But we get along, at a slow pace, it is sure—but get there!"

It is very curious how quickly if I have a bundle in my hand he will ask like a child "What have you got there?" and how soon after my coming, if he expects anything, he will inquire "What have you got with you? What have you got for *me?*" This last he asked tonight the first thing after the talk of his

1

health. I had seen Myrick and brought back a second proof of title-page with me. He reached forth his hand in the dark. I felt for it and gave him the proof—along with this, the receipt for the three dollars which I had got from Brown today. Of the last he said: "Oh! I am glad you got there! It was very right that he should have it!" We talked then somewhat of Brown's father, who is much worse in his paralysis now than last year, when he still came down to the office and once or twice asked me of W. W. whom he had known as a boy in Brooklyn. W. exclaimed "Oh! It is sad! sad! to see anyone in such a condition!"

W.'s knowledge of the positions and names of stars is rather wide. Knowing from what I said that the night was remarkably clear he asked—"And what of the moon? How big has she got, and where now lays?" I spoke of a lustrous—to me problematical star off towards the N.W., and W. asked: "Tell me how low—and how she impresses you?" Then proceeding along a list of names to my more ignorant ear musical but irrepeatable. Always speaks of his "envy" of me in a pleasant sort of way, that I can so regale myself "with the sights of seasons and sounds of out-door things." And on my often-repeated protest—"I wish you could get out to see them for yourself—but don't forget, you saw them all and 'full measure' before I was born!"—he will laugh thoughtfully and say "True again —true again, boy!" We spoke of good hours for reading—I of midnight hours, at times: especially for L. of G.—the deeper passages. He questioning and commending me, father-like, that I "can read anywhere" after all.

We discussed again McKay's singular exclamation over Bryant's letter Saturday. W. laughed heartily at remembrance of it. But he spoke in best terms of McKay. I repeated to him the main points of a debate I one day had with Bucke while here. I contending that I had more than merely business feelings for McKay and his espousal of W., and Bucke contraverting with statement that he had not, since with McKay it was only a matter of business which others—perhaps many

2

—would have embraced if he had not. Said W. to all this: "I myself would not at all endorse such exceptions, assertions: I think it is just as you say, that Dave has proved himself genuinely my friend. I know he is a business man—that he is sharp, quick, as a man has to be who is in business, or thinks he has; but that is the worst that can be said of him." Dave was "fallible," of course—but "evidence of tricksiness," of which even W. had been warned of in him, had never been forthcoming.

I had a long talk with Ferguson today, who gave me in a general way the story of the growth of his business. W. was greatly interested in my repetition of this. This interest— when he feels it—is always evinced in his questioning me, which was here quite marked. Among other things Ferguson had said: "There is money in the newspaper business let me tell you: make a hit and you come out way on top!" Instanced the difficulties with Curtis at the start with The Ladies Home Journal of which Ferguson is to print 700,000 copies next number. W. commented: "I should think George W. Childs and Bill Singerly would say so. Yes, even the Press folks, I suppose. Isn't it Wells who owns the Press?" The Press is a sore point with W., and this reference to it drew forth the usual caustic criticism. "It seems to me that in the whole range of journals pretending to anything, the Press is the greatest mess—gives most evidence of being shovelled together. It is made up as if the head man at the eleventh (or 50th) minute had come in and said: 'Here boys, all get your shovels, set to work, shovel in and shovel out—now we must get the paper up!'—and they would set to, and the thing would get done, with what result we know. And yet somehow I read the Press— read it straight along—probably because there is nothing else to do while it is here: read even the witty paragraphs, or what they put in as witty, though I must say I always come to them with a scowling and sour temper." W. alluded to Walsh's departure for New York, "wondering much," he said, "how Walsh gets along there?—how the paper was last Sunday" explaining—"I have not seen the Herald at all since the copy

3

you brought me." That had been a "disappointment" to him—
the fiction symposium "dull beyond precedent."

Ed came in for mail—W. directed him to a couple of postals
over on the floor in the darkness, which he found. I was on my
way to Philadelphia to hear Tom Davidson's lecture on
Aquinas. W. inquisitive—greatly "tempted" by my description of D.'s reading of Scotch poetry: "I should like to hear
them without a doubt." Then said: "By the way Horace—I
see the Camden papers have been giving Moorhouse a big lift
—his sermon is there in one of them at great length." W.
never reads sermons and I knew it, but I asked him with a
laugh—"Well, what did you think of it? You read it, of
course?" His enjoyment great—"Well—well—well—I can't
say that I did! I saw that it was there!"

Further along W. said: "Now tell me, Horace—how did the
Emerson speech come off that night last week. You don't tell
me anything about it." My details few, but he evidently a good
listener. He was amused with my account of nervousness pre-
ceding. Had he ever experienced nausea before speech-
making? He said quietly: "I don't know what it is. I have
heard of stage fright—a sort of tremor—sometimes momen-
tary, sometimes fatal—have even heard of this—this sickness
at the stomach, as you call it—but as to personal knowledge of
it, or participation—that is not in the line of experience for
me—never has been." It is easy to believe this is the case. His
serenity surpasses that of any person I have known—is much
like what he says was the "necessary atmosphere" of Emerson.
I sat down this morning and wrote up a brief account of Saturday night's stroll up Second Street. W. had me tell him much
of its substance.

Tuesday, April 9, 1889

10.30 A.M. W. writing on "Epilogue." Looked rather ill—
not as much in color as is best. But cheery. We talked some

few minutes together. He gave me proof on which he had written "this pleases better" and made one or two minor alterations. Had signed sheet to see how it looked complete, name and all: then marked name out. "Now I am satisfied," he said. "I am surprised, knowing Myrick's good taste as I do, that he ever consented to pass such a page as that other." He had some of the sheets of "Epilogue" pinned to proof, but withdrew them. "I think I'll hold these—copy them, perhaps—give them to you tomorrow." "By the close of this week—at latest the beginning of next, I want to have things in such shape that they can go right along with them." The "Epilogue" comes hard out of his indisposition of the past week. As his digestion has seemed right favorable, his present cloudiness must be from the paralysis. He is inclined so to place it. I gave him a letter I received from Clifford this noon. This he read and on passing it back said: "It does me good to get a glimpse of him that way. How great is the joy of letters!" Having application for more tickets for Friday's Club meeting than I have, W. gave me his two.

Alluded to "personal" in yesterday's Press stating that the latest reports of Tennyson's sickness are but false repetition of older ones. W. then spoke of Walford's letter in Critic in which he quotes F. W. H. Myers' saying, that Tennyson has "passed out of the poet into the thinker" and that his "face expresses not delicacy, but power." W. had taken careful note of it. "But I don't think Myers hits the mark. Not that Tennyson lacks power or anything signifying power—but that power is the dominant factor. It seems to me—I should say— that Tennyson rather expresses elegance—such elegance as at least our age has nowhere else displayed—workedness, sublime care." And he went on reflectively, "And so it is, I think, while Tennyson does a good deal of good—oh! incalculable good! —he does harm too—often much harm: his mellifluosity—one may call it: it is great, overwhelming, everything in his imitators is sacrificed to accomplish that."

5

5.30 P.M. W. eating his dinner. It seems he has had a rather poor day of it, though eating quite a breakfast of buckwheat cakes and honey and now a supper of, for him, considerable proportions. But he complains of his head, says: "I look forward to a bad night"—and has by no means done the work he had desired to do today. When I asked if the "Epilogue" was finished, he replied: "Sort o' finished—yet not finished"—for he would not give it to me now, but he rather "must keep it till tomorrow, anyhow." I brought him now the third proof of the title page and he said the instant he looked at it: "That is good —that seems all right now." As to a change still of some figures from Italic to Roman which Myrick suggested, he remarked: "I am not bent on it: if he had put them that way I don't think I should have changed them. If he thinks best let him do it still."

Commented on the still "rather ominous absence" of word from Washington.

Talked explanatorily of a Truebner pamphlet I picked up from the floor. "I have a friend over there in the Truebner establishment" [he pronounced it Trubner without diphthong, and bore with my correction with a laugh and an attempt to correct himself]—"a man named Childs—Josiah Childs—I imagine him old and a Quaker: there have been letters from him. I picture him as a man of the confidential clerk kind which Dickens so delighted to talk about—the invaluable men in the big houses." The reference to Dickens reminded me of the discussion at Clifford's table between his daughter Charlotte and Dr. Bucke as to the visit of Dickens, the former stoutly defending him against the Doctor's severe disposition to brush him aside as of no importance. W.'s amusement extreme at the "audacity" of the "youngster." His own feelings towards Dickens "more kind" than the Doctor's.

He ate slowly as he talked—toast, preserves, coffee (or tea). My enthusiastic description of the day aroused him so that he flung the window sash all the way up. "I suppose Chestnut Street—Market Street—are alive—a breathing mass!" "And the way down and down—and then the river, too!" His manner rather pensive, if not sad. I asked him, "You remember Tommy?" He responded with a question: "Tommy? Tommy Logan? The great, big hearty Irishman? Oh yes!" "Well, Tommy is now engineer—seems to be in the engine house most of the time if not all." "Is that so? Oh! I know Tommy well. I used to count him one of my best friends on the river." Then he asked: "Do you know Eugene Crosby? He was up in the wheelhouse—was a night pilot. He was a very noble fellow—always very good, affectionate to me!" So we talked. He spoke of "the old days—the boys—the rides to and fro." Then questioned slowly: "The Beverly, the Wenonah—what is the other boat? they have a third?" "The Pennsylvania." "The old Pennsylvania!" Then asked after Lindell—the time of the men, Foxy, several others by name. "You know them all," he said, when I shook my head over some names he mentioned. But I did not know the *names*. I had said to Tommy as I sat there in the engine room on the return trip and talked, that he should not be surprised to see W. wheeled down on the boat some day "when the spring is really here." Tommy then pathetic in his homely description of old days with W.—hearty greetings, talks, sights: of W.'s generosities—"he'd give the boys money —the boys up there on the street—and never a word about what they would spend it for!" But W. himself when I mentioned the wheeling matter was more dubious than I have known him in a long time about getting out again.

Just a word with Tom Davidson last night after the lecture, about W. "I do not know him but I know many of his friends—his brother Tom, for one, out there in St. Louis." But W. had never heard reference to Davidson from that source. I advised with Ed, whether it would not be well to have Dr. Walsh come in and report on W. Probably will do so. W.

7

looked grand in his place there at the window, in the waning light—the flitting paleness at times, the lengthened hair, often the faraway look as with folded hands he faced the west.

Wednesday, April 10, 1889

10.45 A.M. W. reading the Record. Appearance not well, indeed, though he reports himself "about as well" as he "has been"—which is not very well, of course. Ate very little breakfast. Speaks of taking powders again—significantly showing he must feel very bad: volunteer doctoring only the resort of his extremity. "Epilogue" not yet done. "I am very dilatory. You'll pronounce me as bad as Oldach after a while. But I shall try my best to let you have it for tomorrow." Title-page he now wholly approved. As to Myrick's suggestion therewith: "I approve of the change if he thinks it advisable to make it." Not only "no mail from O'Connor" this morning, but "no mail at all," his report. Is anxious again as to O'Connor, but tries "to wait patiently." I asked him for a Sarrazin sheet for Mr. Coates, but he said: "Won't it do this evening? The bundle has got spirited away into some corner. I have plenty of them. I wanted one for Tom the other day, but could not find it."

The day out-of-doors is exceedingly mild. He sat there with his window closed and a blazing wood-fire, which he stirred from time to time, seeming unconscious that it was too warm, whereas the room was stifling. As to getting out-of-doors he is doubtful. "Oh! If I only could!" But just now, "impossible." W. asked me about the Thomas Symphony concert I attended last evening. "I read of the death of his wife. And so he was there? And everything went off well from beginning to end?" They had played Raff's "Lenore" Symphony among other things.

Evening, 8:00. W. just being helped to chair by Ed as I entered and light put on. Had lain a long while on the bed,

8

hoping to better himself of bad symptoms. Greeted me cordially. Said: "It seems to have been a wonderful beautiful perfect day out-of-doors!" And after Ed had left: "I received a letter from Kennedy, but felt so bad, I hardly looked to see what was in it—if anything, and what: did not finish it at all. I have had a dreadful bad day all through—my constipation and my cold have been the two beans in the pod. It seems to go worse than common with me nowadays."

Excused himself then as to preface. "I have put nothing final on it: my head got so bad I put aside, resigned, everything." This is "great misfortune." Our time so limited—"the days, even weeks, passing" and "I still tarrying, doing nothing." Of course not to be helped. I stayed only a few minutes. Our work is blocked by the infelicity of this attack. Though breakfasting but slightly, W. ate quite improved his late dinner between 4 and 5.

Still "no word at all from Nellie." I kissed him good-bye as I left, and said—"You must not let it slip you, Walt, how much we all think of you." And he answered as he fervently kept my hand—"I shall not, my boy—no—no—not for a minute"—and then "Goodbye! but only for a while: You'll come again—come in the morning?" Talked a little with Mrs. Davis on my way out. Ed had gone for his music lesson. While I was with Walt he opened a letter Ed brought him, which proved to be an elegant request for an autograph, immediately (except for return stamp) consigned to the woodbox.

Thursday, April 11, 1889

10 A.M. W. sitting with the Record on his lap. Had just finished breakfast. Looked rather better than yesterday, but evidently felt utterly miserable, for he said—"I don't feel myself changed, and yesterday afternoon I felt as dreadful as a fellow well could feel and stand up at all." Asked me "Did you ever see Mrs. Gilchrist's 2nd piece—her 'Confession of Faith'

9

as she calls it? I have laid a copy here aside for you." Scraping his chair across the floor to the east table where he had folded up a copy of To-day. It was a curious little way he had of preserving this for me. The article itself fine, with certain paragraphs marked in red ink by his own hand.

"And something more," he said, after giving me the package, proceeding then among the papers under the table. "But I suppose it is still hopeless. I had hoped to hit upon the Sarrazin sheets before this—but you know things have been put to rights, which means buried, lost! I think there used to be a prize offered in the Philadelphia Press for the man who will put the Jersey news where nobody can find it—and their prize man must have been let loose here, working through our women. There was a time when I could go into the other room there, and, with a little difficulty, get anything I wanted. But now nothing is in its place, or near its place, and I am utterly at sea!" "About here"—motioning toward the several confused but overflowing baskets—"everything is indiscriminately mixed with everything: there has been no taste, no tact, no selection, no nothing!" He was considerably aroused—has been much searching for this bundle, which was large enough, it would seem, not to have been hidden far. "I shall set Ed to work to-day—see what he can do towards finding what we want."

He had his window thrown up—the air outside was mellow—the fire crackling in the stove. He spoke hopelessly of the thought of getting out. "But give my love to all the ferry boys—to Ed Lindell, to Tommy—Tommy Logan—to Foxy, to Eugene Crosby." I took him a copy of fine photo-engraving from photo of Gruetzner's painting "The Connoisseurs"—I think the finest specimen of process-work of that kind I have ever seen. W. put on his spectacles and studied it a great while, with great and manifest enjoyment. "Everything is impossible—till it is possible!" he said. And yet, "nothing seems impossible to the human critter," once his mind is fairly on the track of an idea. I left the picture with W., who had "no doubt" a "few more looks" would be an enjoyment.

Evening, 7.35. Saw on approaching the house a light in W.'s room, and concluded he was better, as indeed proved to be the case. Once in the room, I found him looking much improved, and willing to talk. Higher color, clearer eye. But the room fearfully and wonderfully hot. Last night he took one of his powders. Had it acted yet? "No—I don't think it has." When I asked him if he was not relieved, he said "I don't dare to say I am, for fear I may fall back again—get shame of all my boasting." Had at last finished "preface," which he sends along without a headline, with simply date and "Camden, New Jersey, U. S. America." It is to immediately precede "A Backward Glance." Enclosed with it a sheet of instruction for general make-up of the book, (all but a few lines of this written in pencil) and then wrote in ink on envelope enclosing

best respects to
Mr. Ferguson
15 North 7th Street
to Mr. Myrick
& to the proof readers
& printers
Phila : ——

arranged just in that way. "This," he said "gets us all under way again. Now we ought to be able to go right ahead: a week done before the hour is better than a week *after:* and this is a special book, occasion, which should be achieved when the hour is struck." But the pictures had not yet turned up, nor the Sarrazin sheets—"though Eddy looked about here today some." When I spoke favorably of pictures,—"I like them, too," he exclaimed—"and all the more unfortunate then if they don't appear!"

I had this afternoon called on Jo Fels at their soap-factory on North 3rd Street, and had been taken by him through the

11

large establishment and had its mysteries more or less (some of them greatly *less*) cleared. He insisted among other things that I should take a box of soap "for Walt Whitman," which I did, much to W.'s enjoyment. He slowly unfolded one of the cakes. "It is quite providential," he exclaimed—"quite in the nick of time—hits the nail square on the head. Look here" uncovering a corner of the table, on which some change had been laid out—"Just last night I put that there for Eddy—told him I wanted soap: and somehow, providence made the rascal forget to go for it today!" He kept the cake a long time at his nose—then laid it down—then took it up again—then once more laid it down. At this last Ed came in with a letter which W. took. "See here Ed," he called out, as E. was about to go (E. thereupon coming back near W.'s chair) "What do you think of that?—a present of soap!" And as Ed said—"The room is full of it—I smelt it the minute I opened the door"— W. laughingly followed—"Now when you go out to the store, you'll only have to get the matches—the rest is provided for. And do you see how fine it is?—the color of it—the odor!" W. took up his knife—Ed said he would "bet" it was an autograph letter—and this it proved to be, W. retaining stamp and destroying the rest at once. W. first said—"I have had no letters at all today"—then corrected himself: "Yes I have, two— a letter from Bucke—but inconsequential—nothing new whatever there with him."

I referred in rather warm words to Mrs. Gilchrist's article which I had read today. W. reflected: "It is indeed very fine: it certainly ought to go with the other—the two be always and everywhere associated. I think it in many respects the most subtle & far-reaching of all discussions of Leaves of Grass—a wonderful bit of analysis." I asked him if he thought any of her literary power had descended to Herbert. "No—not at all —none of it whatever. Mrs. Gilchrist was a great woman—a greater woman than she is generally known to be—a woman who, I am fond of saying, goes the whole distance of justifying woman—of proving her power, her equality, her consummate possibilities—actualities, in fact. There is a vast gap between such a personality as hers and another's—one like Herbert's—a vast gap. Herbert is not strong—puts no resisting front to the conventionalities of the time—but *she*—oh! she was *all* courage, bravery, power—yet all *womanly*, too—not a jot of the womanly abated for all the force. She was never conventional, unless she chose to be—unless she thought it was as well to be conventional as not." All the time during the rest of my stay he had the soap at his nose. "It is the odor of roses," he explained—it seemed to appeal to him.

He asked me about our Club meeting tomorrow night—Ely's address on Socialism, whether I expected a discussion or not, what would probably be "the drift of things." Then by natural transition he spoke of having read an account of a reception to Wanamaker at the house of the Manufacturers' Club. "It is very easy for those glorious fellows to have their splurge in 250,000 dollar Club houses, but after a while will arise the question—why is it so easy for those fellows to have their 250,000 dollar Club houses and 20,000 dollar dinners?—and then will come the fun. As they said in the play I used to go and hear when I was a young fellow there in New York—'let these fellows go on—let 'em keep on sinning—let 'em keep on believing there is no hell! but by and bye a day!' " Retribution he looked for as surely as for to-morrow's sun. But did he think through revolution? "No—there will be a wrench—a pretty severe wrench, maybe—but not revolution. The vast area—varied interests—the fact that revolution would be weakened by being so spread out—no power at any one point —would defend against violence—at least, concerted violence." But the "wrench" he "certainly" foresaw—and what shape that would take had yet to be determined. "This whole protection of working men—this whole business of building handsome club houses—luxurious displays—for the good of the working man—it will have its day, but will be exposed at

13

last!" He asked me about Fels' views on the tariff, which I thought were rather liberal. I asked Fels once if Free Trade would ruin his business, and he said *not*. Today he told me he even exported a great deal of soap to England.

Friday, April 12, 1889

7.30 P.M. I was down this forenoon, stopping in just long enough to find that W. was improved. Then to town, taking copy in at Ferguson's and receiving proof later in the day. Which proof I now delivered W. It made just a short page. He had written on margin of copy that if more was required to fairly fill the 2 pages he would "eke it out." F. said now that he would have to "eke it out." Asked me again for Francis Larned's name. Said of his health: "I seem relieved—I seem to have shaken off the torments." Whether "for good" or even "for any time" he "dared not say." Word from friends very scarce. "Nothing at all from Washington—in fact, nothing since last Saturday. Bucke writes again, but his letter has no significance whatever." Speaking of Mrs. Gilchrist's article again—"Yes, that is where 'Going Somewhere' came from. I thought you knew it."

Asked me—"You folks are to settle the labor question to-night?" This is Contemporary Club Night. "Yet I suppose ever since time was known, or man, this labor question has been agitated, stirring. Probably now it is more on top—is more palpable—than ever before—more palpable as the prevalence of disease is more palpable, in the first place because there are more people—and in the second, because every one people knows what is happening to every other people." Yet he did not discredit it. "I am in favor of agitation—agitation—agitation and agitation: without the questioner, the agitator, the disturber, to hit away at our complacency, we'd get into a pretty pass indeed." We spoke of Henry George's great tour now through England. I said: "The George men are free traders." W. added: "But a free trader is not necessarily a George man. Did you read the speech delivered by Mills in the West somewhere a few days ago? The *Record* had a good stripe of it—more than a column: I read it all—read it and liked it. I notice that The *Press*, in its own way—in its own great littleness—in its utterly indescribably witless way,—tries to dispose of it by witty paragraphs. But what a display and a failure!" W. had drawn up today a plan for insertion of plates in the new edition—using fully half a dozen. But it was only "a preliminary design"—one he may possibly deflect from.

Advised me: "Give my best love to all friends, known and unknown—I mean rather, *unknowing*, whom you meet to-night." We talked of Dr. Brinton. W. asked: "Is he still in Europe?" Then spoke of his scientific attainments and mental probity, W. denominating this—"the absolute exercise of it" —"extremely rare indeed."

Another moment: "I suppose that under whatever conditions, we would have botherations—the race would have its struggles, trials, growls, doubts, horrors: all it now asked for achieved, it would then solicit more—more and more: the human critter is just that sort of a being—and best so, no doubt." I hurried off to the meeting to-night. He was affectionate and awake.

Saturday, April 13, 1889

10 A.M. W. had been reading the papers. Was mending a little pasteboard box when I entered. Said as to my inquiries: "I am bad again, very bad—somehow start into a new siege: it is my head, my constipation: it hits me severely." As to proof—"I have done nothing with it—you must excuse it: I shall try to-day and to-morrow to do it up as it should be done —'eke it out,' as I have said." Referred to portraits for book. I argued for new portraits as far as possible. "I can see the

force of that," W. assented, "though the world is in no danger of being overburdened with Whitman pictures." At my mention of the ¾ length—"Ah! yes! that I take to be my right bower!" The missing photos not yet found. "I have engaged with Mary to come up and make search today. She is very good at such things—has a good scent." But when Mary came up at the time appointed, he felt bad and advised her, "an hour later: let us wait a while!" To me again—"I certainly had several hundred of those heads: in fact, I remember them, as though they must have been in packages like that in your hands—a hundred in each." It would be a sore point to have them missed now and turn up when too late.

W. had been much stirred by long accounts in morning papers of the Danmark, abandoned at sea, and come upon by the City of Chester—no life on board, sinking—yet had sailed out with 700, passengers and crew. It was among W.'s first questions: "What of it? What do you think of it?" adding: "It is dreadful—dreadful: yet I cannot think them lost: perhaps 5 or 6 hours will tell a fuller tale—explain." "No word from Washington," he said—"but probably nothing had turned up there: if there had been anything, it surely would have been communicated."

Asked me of the Club meeting—how had it gone off? I told him of something somebody had heard from Gilchrist—that the speakers were "all duffers" and would not have been listened to in England. W. highly amused. "What did he mean—sure enough! That is more than I could tell." The last speaker of the evening—some French clergyman, whose name I did not catch—saw no resort for social sin but in the "man of Nazareth"—the labor problem to be solved through such efficacy. But "come to Jesus!" seemed to W. a "decidedly novel" nostrum. "It occurs this way to me: that question of questions is this—to give some men who now have no work, work; to give others adequate return for work done: Now, to give that work and that return, such a specific as the man does not have

16

any pertinency." Besides "the prayer and Jesus business" had always been in our days "overdone." The great prayers were little doers. "The damnable psalming, praying, deaconizing of our day is made too much the liberal cover for all sorts of sins, iniquities." Reference hereabouts to Stonewall Jackson. W. impatiently said: "Jackson? Oh! he was a bad egg,—a bad egg! I know the cuss—know him as few others have had means of knowing him." Continuing: "Take a man who goes off by himself, into the woods, prays,—as Jackson did—as indeed was too often the case with fellows South—and they will bear watching." He instanced again the story of "the Western boy —the poor, sick, wearied, worn out, Western boy," whom Jackson questioned, "how much of an army had the North here and here, and what its purposes"—who (a prisoner) had "refused to divulge" and who "for the very courage for which he should have been honored and commended—would have been by any true soldier, any soldier with the high, heroic, chivalric instincts of the big souls in the soldier class" was doomed "to a walk of 90 miles or so," while lesser men or stronger, "were conveyed in wagons and cared for." W. said to my remark that such was "a damned spot,"—"it was indeed—a damned spot indeed—and all the prayers under heaven could not wipe it out." Adding: "It was not a hastily or eagerly accepted story with me—I did not wish it true: you know me well—know I am not a grabber of conclusions: even way back at the start, you know the phrenologists gave me caution—large caution —what they denominated a great wariness. Well, when I first heard this story, though I knew the young fellow well—he was so affectionate, so noble, so honorable, so reserved—I did not wholly credit it—allowed for possible exaggeration, extreme feeling—investigated it for myself. Everything he had told me was confirmed—everything: I found he had told a straight story—not a break in it. I shall never forgive Stonewall Jackson this. No matter what the magazines, the papers, North here may say in his high honor. I know better—I know

17

his true measure." So it was well not to let "the prayer matter" make up judgment entirely. "You know, all the banditti rob between their prayers! Besides,"—again touching the labor question—"Jesus was himself socialist, communist, whatnot—without property or belongings material."

We are at a standstill in our work again but I am hopeful it may not be for long.

7.30 P.M. W.'s room dark on my entrance, he on bed, and alone in the room. He talked well and at some length with me, though saying—"I am not very well—in fact, none of my days any more seem to be good days." But inquired of the clear beautiful night and the lustrous stars, and appeared eager for every word I said thereof. Said: "I have finished the preface, Horace, and you can take it to-day or to-morrow if you wish." Asked me: "Some time when you are about somewhere in town, I wish you would look into—I think the last volume of Appleton's 'Biographical Dictionary'—I think it is called that: look in the 'W's' and see there what is said of me. Kennedy said in a note to me that there was mention of me there—and with it a portrait." I asked: "Whose work is it—Hunter's?" He was dubious—"in fact, I know nothing whatever about it."

In some way we got into a discussion of portraits. I said at one point: "It is queer, how the passion for steels seems to have gone out." W. explained, "They have gone out because they are not good—because they are not worth staying. Have you seen the steels in Stedman's books? In each volume there are two—and then the others—the wood—these always better than the steels. I think I have been particularly fortunate in my own case—that picture of me inserted there." I expressed myself: "That is because of something in the original," meaning the Linton engraving. W. mistook me and protested "I don't think so—that does not sufficiently—at all explain it: there was a factor present—the potent factor too—beyond or below that altogether—something in manipulation—something in the engraving itself." I at once exclaimed—"That's

18

just exactly what I meant—something in Linton's cut!" He
laughed heartily: "Oh! I thought you meant me—I took that
to myself! Of course that explains it." Then we further discussed the Stedman portraits. Thoreau's picture there among
"very few." W. then went on: "I have a picture somewhere
about here—somewhere among my stuff—a German picture,
of a sailor—which I think the finest bit of work of the kind I
have ever seen—a gem indeed. In such directions I am sure
the French and Germans are at the top. I used to think the
French altogether so, would swear to it—but now I think is
the German. The picture I speak of, for line and effect, complexity, marvellous certainty and power, is the finest I have
ever seen." Then after a slight thoughtful pause: "Though
after all it may not be the wise thing to say any nation or any
class is at the top—only that individuals are farthest forward,
that it is purely an individual matter. I want to see this German picture again and have you get it: you could take it for
your father, who would surely be interested. You have seen the
picture of Scott downstairs? It is a German production—it
was brought me here by Johnston's daughter—my New York
friend, you know: a sweet, dear girl, whom I love much, who
loves me too I think—Kitty her name." Had she brought it
from Germany herself? "Yes indeed—there are several sisters
of them, they were over there together. Only a year or two or
more ago, the brother, Johnston's son (have you met him?
No?) went over and brought them home. That picture below
is a reminiscence of the visit—the girl, Kitty, was very cute—
she knew I had a soft spot for Sir Walter, so she quite patly
brought me that head. And fine the head is, too! It is one of
the best specimens of German art work!" Thence discussion of
tariff on art—its disgraceful narrowness when compared with
generosity of French schools toward American students. W.
was vehement. "Ah! All you say on that point, Horace, is true
—every word of it—every word, however severe. The only
thing one might say in comment would be this—that it is con-

19

sistent. My standpoint is so utterly foreign, I would wipe out not only this but all tariffs,—all bars whatsoever to freedom —everything, the last stone, or wave of any sea, that would serve as bar, impediment, to intercourse, concord of people. And this tariff an act not repealed yet? I suppose not! This is one of the precious bits of work we have to thank our friend Tom Donaldson for: he was the fellow who pushed it. You know, that is one of Tom's lines of business—to lobby bills through Congress—this he did for others—some bodies, persons, interests, backing him up." Then a vehement outcry against "men who stand against foreign musicians, foreign ministers, foreign laborers, foreign anything, just because it is foreign." In Philadelphia a case just a propos of Wannemacher's band chosen to discourse the music at Sunday concerts in Fairmount Park the coming summer—protests thereat from members of a native born band, that though the band chosen is local in one sense, it is still made up of foreign born members etc. Encourage American labor, the cry. W., between laughing at the absurdity of this, and denouncing its bigotry, seemed not at all to lose power by his recumbent position there in bed. In fact stayed on bed all through time of my stay.

As to the missing pictures: "I did not look for them to-day; —we did not have our search—but I expect to have it to-morrow. I suppose, after we have given up the search, had the book printed, bound, all that, they will turn up. That will about follow the usual order." His anxiety in regard to the great missing steamer is manifest. Asked me: "What is the latest in regard to it? have you heard anything? anything at all? There is a dreadful maybe about the story—a mystery, an air of dark probability—which I cannot shake off." But when I expressed faith that the great mass of people had somehow been rescued, he said with a fervent deep voice: "I hope it is as you say—I hope it will be found all right, safe, in the end." Had hoped before this the mystery would be cleared. W.

mentioned William Swinton, and asked: "Do you know him?" Adding after my negative response—"He is a good friend of mine, of Leaves of Grass. Swinton has often said to me that one of the most impressive passages in the book—in Leaves of Grass—is the ten or twelve lines in which I describe the loss of the Arctic: the sonnet, it may be called—and it is hardly a description. I don't quite agree with him—at least, it never impressed me as containing as much as he sees in it. So much in such impressions depends upon, hangs upon, a man's mood— the hour in which he reads it—color, tones, odor, of that hour." We discussed thereupon the part suggestiveness plays in art and literature anyway. W. agreeing to the immensity of its power. Realf's "Indirection" quoted but W. did not remember having at any time read it. Asked me: "Have you ever read much of Harte—Bret Harte? There is a pretty little poem he writes—calls it 'Mignonette,' I think—it is a poemet. In this he describes what odors,—odors of poor, faded, crushed flowers—suggested to him, rather to her"—and perhaps it was by this same power—the mind thrown back upon its memories— "a suggestion, a hint, a line,"—that effect was often produced.

We mentioned Tennyson. W. quoted a sentiment—then said: "I see by the papers indication that Tennyson is at work again, will probably soon have another volume ready. I suppose Tennyson is like Whittier—will work on and on, finally die in harness." I spoke of some of Tennyson's later poems "The Revery," "The Defense of Lucknow"—enthusiastically —said they were "strong" and W. agreed thereto. He then inquired: "Did you read 'Queen Mary'? I think that quite a work—at least, that was my impression at the time." Added: "And I see, too, that Swinburne is publishing again—there was something from him—some poem—in yesterday's Press." He said his capacity for work was about gone. He could do nothing at all any more but "by making a deadly effort." Adding: "Have you read Dombey and Son? Do you remember the fellow there who was always making an effort? It is hard for

21

me to do anything even when I do make an effort." He referred laughingly to Bucke's debate with Charlotte Clifford—and as to Doctor's extreme non-reception of Dickens—"I do not tally with him in that, Oh! I think Dombey and Son a fine, almost a great, book!" Ed here entered. W. asked: "Well, did you find anything?" "One letter, sir." "Let me have it here." Ed giving it to him, the room of course still utterly dark. Ed asked if W. wished a light? And after considerable hesitation, W. said, "Yes, let us have it!" But W. did not get up. As soon as the light was on he did however examine postmark of letter with a child's eagerness.

I referred to item in The Critic that Linton was about to publish volumes of poems. W. said of him warmly: "He is a man of unusual power—of unusual weight—a man of power, weight, even to us—indeed, would be our man: a thoroughly full, workmanlike man, too—and sturdy: sturdy from the toes up. Who is to publish him? in England?" Truly, in England. W. afterwards added: "My quarrel with Linton would be that he is too much of a Socialist, Anarchist, what not—you know I have no soft spot for the Anarchists, the Socialists. Somehow, they seem to take me in (as I do them, of course)—think I am one of them: but it appears to me, that is where they get fooled: because I have divergent views altogether—in fact think our point of view entirely different." He spoke of his faith as "finally resting on the social unit—the unit of a home —say of one, 2 or 3 thousand a year—three thousand at highest—always within that, that as the individual. With it, individual liberty—not land, or anything whatever, in common— but homestead, fee simple, moderate possession, assured every man. That is where the politics of the time is all wrong—the stake of the manufacturer, millionaire, aristocrat, corporation on one hand, their men on the other." He looked forward to vastly other relations between each than existed now. W. has but vague notions of what the Socialistic parties aim for—his discrimination not therefore keen. He said in one breath, "Why do they make such a noise? The world anyhow is about as good as it can be"—then turns about and denounces its sins. I explained to him Anarchism as philosophically considered. His idea of it dim indeed. Asked me then: "Is that then an authoritative explanation?" Then added that he at any rate "felt that what is called individualism deservedly carries the day." As to prohibition—"take whiskey from a man as he is constituted now, and he will take absinthe, hasheesh."

Sunday, April 14, 1889

7.45 P.M. The room dark. I feared something wrong. Not positively wrong, however, though W. had spent a bad day again. He lay on bed—cried—"Oh! is that you, Ed?" When finding it was me he held out his hand in the dark and cordially invited me to take a seat, which I fumbled for and secured. Asked of the weather, of the great night. "It has been a very bad day with me, all through—a very bad day." Said he had been able to do little—had read some, "wrote a note to O'Connor—one to Doctor"—but that was "about all." "Yet," he said, "it seems to have been a marvelous day out in the sun. What have you been doing with yourself?" This evening I seem to have done most of the talking, as is apt to be the case when something I have seen arouses his hunger for detail, of which he is always a sharp questioner. Among other sights on the way was the photographic exhibition at the Academy. He asked of it: "So you think we have won the sceptre back?"— reference herein to his rather shattered faith that Americans in photography led the world. Most of all was he attracted by the sea-pieces of which I spoke. "You say, active—the very movement of the water itself? Oh! it must be *fine, fine*—it must utter for one, new great thoughts!" Greatly interested by the fact of Sunday freedom of Academy. "It is one of the best things I hear." Would know of those who went—how they seemed to regard time, place, pictures. "The advance great" in liberty.

"No more," he said regretfully—"no more about the Danmark. What the deep anxiety of it!" But of the recent Samoan disaster, the papers were full. "Today I read the Press—the great detail there. And the more you learn of it, the worse the disaster seems." How the elements had scattered the schemes of the nations! Remarked having read poems "more of them"—from Swinburne in The Press to-day: "A Word with the Wind," "The Witch Mother," "Neap-tide"—but made no criticism or comment.

I told him I had come for proof and manuscript, and proposed getting it for myself from the table, but after a little hesitation he said, "I will get it for you—I should get up anyhow"—going then first to the chair with my assistance. He leaned very heavily on me—more heavily than I have ever known before—rather by his manner emphasizing my fear that the last month has been pulling hard upon his strength. But of his own trembling self he closed the blinds of the windows and lighted the gas. He had added a goodly paragraph starting with "To-day completing three-score-and ten years" —and ending "Probably that is about all,"—and directed on margin "make the above the first paragraph" etc. It is three-quarters in one sentence, yet accurately counted, demonstrating how clear after all are his mental processes, beyond strain as they are. He said to me: "There it is done. Let Myrick put them into pages before sending proof again." On a sheet accompanying he had diagrammed the two pages to precede the *Backward Glance* preface—the first with title only, the second with copyright announcement. These together he had carefully folded and enclosed in an envelope addressed to Ferguson. "Now we should be able to proceed—all but with the pictures." He had again today not felt well enough to attempt with Mrs. Davis a search for these.

Said he had had no visitors. "Harned—Tom—was here—at least at the door: left me the Tribune." Tom and "little Tommy" here last evening. W. so glad again to see "little Tommy"—"the children always welcome—cheery." I said I thought Tom and Mrs. Harned had the baby with them on an outing today. W. said quickly: "Is that so? and did not bring him in? I feel slighted—I take that as a slight!" But I explained laughing—"The baby was asleep—they thought he might be out of temper if disturbed." W. thereupon: "True— true: I take it back—I am myself again! We must wait for another time!" His references to this child have been singularly frequent, as if its coming bore reference even to his departing and "soon-to-be-utterly-departed" powers, as he puts it. We talked of prohibition excitement in Philadelphia—a special election now approaching. But W. not swerving at all from his usual views.

I examined the Scott portrait downstairs. It seemed to be a photographic reproduction of a steel engraving, but nobly and softly done. But on reverse of little gilt frame was an English imprint. W. said: "I don't remember that—I must look at it again." Really an exquisite print. But no date or name of maker thereon. Nor could W. "guess" at what age it represented Sir Walter. Said he had seen by the papers that Burroughs had been writing something for Wide Awake—"some account of his early life"—"but from John himself, it is now getting a long while again since I have heard. And you hear nothing?" W.'s continued bad condition raises some fears in me. A palpably growing weakness, too. But this may all right itself with the continued fine spring days.

Monday, April 15, 1889

10 A.M. W. stirring up fire. The day fair but rather more chilly. W. had arisen, not at all well, the "torment" of his recent days fully upon him still. We talked little. I had stopped, more to see how he was than for any other purpose. He spoke somewhat disappointedly of continued absence of word from Washington. Referred to a letter from Bucke, "but one without anything particular." I took him down a copy of the

Register, in which I had marked for him a passage in one of Augusta Larned's Venetian articles. Also pointed out to him therein article by Brooke Herford on John Bright. W. said: "Someone has sent me a copy of a Manchester paper containing a full report of the funeral." Said: "I suppose to-day will give us final proof of the preface?" He had hoped things would progress much more quickly than seemed the case, but he was still not despairing but that we would come out in time.

Referred to Walsh's review of "November Boughs" in March Lippincott's. "If I ever saw it," W. said "(and I suppose I did) it did not impress me, for now even the remembrance of it has flown. I don't know what I did with the magazine: it certainly is not about here now. Lippincott's is one of the affairs I bundle up each month and send out to the Blackwoodtown insane asylum. Perhaps this time I sent it to Doctor —come to think of it, it should have gone to the Doctor anyhow!" Had read papers. Absence of news still of Danmark passengers and crew a painful fact to him. His allusions brief but pathetic.

Evening, 7:10. W. sitting composedly at the middle window, his face towards the west. It was decidedly chill out of doors. The western sky a cold bronze and grey. W.'s hands linked, his eye subdued, his whole manner grand and at peace. His head was proudly held and grandly outlined. Ed had told me already downstairs that W. was still as he had been—not at all bettered—yet not complainful. W. is wonderfully candid with himself at all times. Said to me, after his cordial welcome, "I am not having good times any more," then turned the talk by asking, "How is the night out? Chilly, isn't it?" As I have said before, always when W. feels particularly ill, he seems to face the probability of serious issue and is eager to push his work. When better again will say, "let us keep a leisurely pace." Tonight urgent: asked after proof anxiously— seemed disappointed when he found I had only brought him a part of it. "Not the preface?" Well, "waiting in content"—

26

herein his task—"and often a very hard task, too!" I met Clifford in town today—made arrangement by which, if weather is good, he will be over to see W. next Monday, with Hilda along. Had sent his remembrances to W., who said: "Oh the good fellow! the good fellow! thank him for me!"

I told him I had seen good news of Morse. He "must have it at once." Therefore I went over toward the window, stood in front of him, and in the waning light read aloud this from Unity:

Chicago.—The Unity Club of All Souls Church had a peculiarly delightful evening when Sidney Morse talked and worked before it. It was the Kenyon evening in the Marble Faun studies, and the sculptor molded a Miriam so full of beauty, power and poise, that when he proposed to change the features into those of a Hilda, the large audience protested, and it is hoped that it will soon find its way into plaster, that others may enjoy it. Mr. Morse has almost completed a bust of Theodore Parker, heroic size, for this church, and has orders for the heads of Channing and Martineau, also, uniform in size with the Emerson and Parker. It is hoped that these heads of the Four Great Masters will find their way eventually into hundreds of churches, to add dignity, honesty, liberality and ideality to the worship within.

When I reached the point at which Kenyon is mentioned W. asked, "Who's that?" and when I explained, said he had never read the Marble Faun. Was greatly happy over Morse's seeming good condition. Several times as I went along he exclaimed: "Good for Sidney!" "The best news yet!" Afterwards adding more fully: "If those fellows out there—enough of them—throw their panoply over him, I don't know but that's the place for him to stay." Then tenderly dwelt upon Morse's long ambition to get West, and its "seeming fruition at last"—his longing to look at the new heads, the enjoyment he would have if he could sit there in an audience and "see Sidney at work." He did not wonder that "Sidney was liked and is"—for it inhered to the man "to make people affect him."

A little talk of Blake—then a drift into other matters. Tonight another lecture from Davidson. W. asked, "What about this time?" and when I said "Bonaventura," he asked again: "Is that sometimes used geographically? Isn't it a phrase somehow signifying, good luck?" Of the man Bonaventura "he knew nothing." Developed then discussion of common terms of greeting and farewell. W. mentioned *So long!* What did he think as to its origin? He said: "It was very prevalent when I was a boy among the lower orders, so-called, in New York—the laborers on the wharves, stevedores, boatmen, the street boys, particularly the sailors: *So long! So long! So long!* It was prevalent, too—and this would rather detract from it for some—among the prostitutes, the loose women, of the town." Whether strictly English or not—what its derivation, if any,—he had no idea. "It seems to be the equivalent of the French-Italian exclamation, au revoir!—and very tender and beautiful it is, too! *So long!* I like it very much—whether from old uses, what, I do not know—but like it. *So long!* It is full and full!" W. did not doubt but there was a reason in the common fondness for the phrase. I referred to someone's phrase, "do not say goodbye—say good night." I thought it Dickens'. W. spoke of "its great beauty"—and said more fully: "The signification of *au revoir* seems to be, *till we meet again.*" I repeated, "Auf wiedersehen," which W. endeavored to and did pronounce correctly after me, he inquiring then: "In your reading, have you ever come upon a poem from Mrs. Barbauld—it is a poem of her effusion—something with that thought uppermost, the thought like this, (I know these are not her words): we will not say *farewell*, we will only say, good night, and will meet in the morning again. It seems very excellent. There appears to be in the intrinsic man a disposition to turn the back on phrases which signify absolute partings, deaths: he will not yield the whole case—he always feels there is more to be told, more to come, beyond the little he can put his hands, eyes upon!" And then he said again, his face still to

28

the west, his hands still reposefully interlinked, "So long! so long! I like it much! It is a memory! it is also more than a memory!"

Then said as to Davidson: "Give him my best regards—tell him, if you get the chance (for me particularly) that I think things are as good as they can be—all right as they are"—here he paused and exclaimed—"*including the agitation, including the agitation!* especially including the agitation!" He always qualifies his criticisms of the too-eager reformers with a phrase at last that encourages and sustains them, as above. "Indeed, I might think agitation the most important factor of all—the most deeply important: to stir, to question, to suspect, to examine, to denounce!" It is the docta of the universe, he considered. I told the story of Ingersoll's visitor and his everlasting "yes, yes"—and after W. had ceased his laugh over it, he said, "But I guess we have plenty of the 'noes,' too—plenty—under whatever circumstances."

Rosendale today gave me some interesting account of meetings with Ingersoll—depicting his modesty, brilliancy, fullness of information, scholarship. This I repeated to W., who was greatly interested. Then away, with promise to stop in tomorrow forenoon on my way to Philadelphia.

Tuesday, April 16, 1889

10 A.M. Stopped in on my way to town. W. reading the Record. He spoke of feeling better. "There is a lull in the torment—yet not much of a lull, either." But looked and talked as if more at ease than yesterday.

Tidings of Kossuth's bad health in papers today. Had he seen K? "Oh yes! And sure enough, he must be a very old man now." Thereupon reference to Lafayette. I asked if he had any vivid remembrance of his contact with the great Frenchman. He replied: "I don't know that you would call it vivid—yet it is quite clear, has quite well persisted all these years. My father was a great admirer of Lafayette—and Lafayette was indeed a grand man. We went together—I don't know but my brother was with me." I counted up—years six at the time. Hardly the brother. W. said: "That is so—none of my present brothers—but the older, he may have been there." Described Lafayette. "His was a fine appearance—not the appearance of beauty, but of expression. His face was fine as Jefferson's was fine, for what it told, what it held—fine as trees, waters, the deep seas, are fine: the genuine magnificence of elements. They were both of them homely, as facial judgments go—not ugly, to be sure—not even like Lincoln, who came as near being an ugly cuss as could be—but plain, depending wholly on the inner man for their attraction. Jefferson I think anyhow a much larger man than he is usually supposed to have been—not stout, thick—but rather tall, and slender." W. asked me if I had ever seen some "unusually fine" portrait of Lafayette "on exhibition in Philadelphia some years ago." And on learning I had not: "It was the best of him I had ever seen. I saw it somewhere, in one of the tony Chestnut Street galleries. The whole thing was so well done, it hit me as gem-like. It was as fine as the bronze of Jefferson there at Washington—the bronze by David, the French artist. Oh! this was always a deep delight to me. These works had the exquisite aesthetic taste—the faultless power—which so distinguished the old artists—which none or very few of our fellows have at all—which Herbert Gilchrist, for instance, has not—the deep deference to truth which will make a portrait a portrait—absolutely accurate at all hazards, whatever beauty may suffer by it." Touched then somehow upon simplicity of demeanor in great men. Was it not always characteristic? W. said: "Perhaps not always, but often—even mostly." Of Grant then. "I have seen him often in Washington in his little gig—his strong, but light rig—driving along, as if in deep joy of the pastime. I think Grant enjoyed getting away alone—absolutely alone: taking horse, and with it alone covering three or four hours of country. He would sit so—oh! I can see him still, as so often in those days." W. sitting forward, his hands as if with reins—"he would be easy, but not back against the seat." Grant's simplicity always to be valued. "The soldiers used to tell me that at his work, on the field, he delighted in a blouse—would go about camp, easily attired, possessed, calm, unostentatiously, never with arrogant mien or stride. He would wear the stars, the three on the shoulder. I don't know but that was necessary—perhaps an absolute regulation. At any rate it was advisable." I mentioned Appomattox as giving great contrast, Lee and Grant for instance there. W. said "It is a pity no one with a vivid pen—a graphic pen—never takes that up. It is a picture that yet remains to be accomplished." So far but "glimpses, glints." As to Lee, he said: "I am very loth to talk of Lee—my tongue, (I do not know but my pen, too), is slow to touch him, even to mention him: perhaps in part from thought that we must show respect to the dead." But to tell truth, "Lee appears to me as not at all a first-rater, as you put it, not at all typifying our characteristic life—without, in fact, one elemental quality, so to speak." Struck off the difference between Scott and Grant on the side of system and display, and while saying nothing harsh of Scott, paying higher deference to the quiet qualities of his successor. The men of Jefferson-Lafayette type, "get their beauty as the old houses theirs—beauty of color, time, history, association." We spoke of the fine old houses in the Park. He said, "They exceed on general points the best we can do in building; but that has natural reasons for being—deep reasons: time has trailed its exquisite colors across threshold and wall—the trees envelop it—the vines climb up its sides. Only age can impart that."

Twisted his chair about. "Among my letters this morning," he explained, taking up a note from a chair, "was this" adding, "To judge from what is said there, something was reported of us in Sunday's World." The letter was from someone called Edminster. It was fulsome. In one place the writer spoke of himself as suffering with Whitman the penalty of being ahead of his time. W. amused. "I did not read the note carefully—just looked close enough to find out what he said of the World. Tell me, Horace—does it strike you there are any indications of insanity—an insane streak—in this letter?" He evidently had had a strong suspicion. "But I want you to get me a copy of the paper—I want to see what it is all about." He leaned towards me again, took up a copy of The Camden Post, and pointed out an editorial paragraph therein—extract, it said, from The Herald of Saturday. W. said: "Look at that? What does it all mean?"

Took up proof of bastard title from table. "I don't like it," he said. Then reached and put his writing pad on his knee, but stopped again. "No, I shall not. I was going to write out what I think about it, but that is not necessary. It is enough that I don't like it." Would not say how to change it, only change. "I leave it mainly to his taste—to Myrick's: what he may think the best thing, let him do." Had prepared the little note herewith, and now while I sat, he wrote steadily this by way of instruction on foot of same brown sheet:

* As there are now several editions of
L. of G., different texts and dates,
I wish to say that I prefer and recommend
the present one, 422 pages complete, for
further printing, if there should be any.

Put this in small type for a note at bottom
(with a rule over it) on 2d page of the
Backward Glance—I will mark the * on
the proof when I receive it tonight

Thought also: "It is almost time we are having our pictures printed." Of the several new notes going with the pocket edition he was ready I should have manuscript if I liked. Did not now have them together. One sheet we found was in pencil. W.

explained: "It seems to me I had a better copy than that—that I transcribed it carefully. I must look it up."

Papers much occupied with invasion of Lower California by American raiders who try to annex it. W. was dubious. "I consider that least of least things among things in the paper." Gave me the Gutekunst picture of the old Emperor William: "Take it along: left here, it will surely get spotted and you might care to save it." With it the Register in which he had read the Larned extract and the Bright piece entire. Said of the last: "I found it quite interesting; it repaid reading." Alluded still to "the quiet at Washington," not a word. Offered me the 5 cents for paper (World) and when I hesitated: "Oh! take it—I should prefer it so!" Added: "I have another mission for you—a mission to Dave's. You remember I have been gunning after two copies of them. I should like three now—Will you stop in and secure them?"

7 P.M. W. sitting at middle window, much as last evening when I came. This hour of sundown is one of quiet musing for him. We entered at once into an animated talk. I had secured a copy of The World as he had advised, and with it a copy of The Herald (Sunday). In this last found a column of so-called "odd fancies," written up as direct from W. W.'s lips, by that arch-fool Sadakichi Hartmann. They had proved of such a mean stupid, ignorant nature,—bad English, worse thought, unutterably sad taste—that the idea of having them thrown out as W.'s raised my ire. W. realized at once that I was mad,—asked, "What is it about?" I had said when I shook hands with him: "I am glad to get near the *real* Walt Whitman again." He asked, "What do you mean?" I said: "It is the Herald there—Sunday's Herald." Then his query: "What is it about?" I described Hartmann's deliverance. To satisfy W. I went across near and in front of him, stood by the table there in the waning light, and read here and there of the "odd fancies" attributed to him by this man. At first he was inclined to laugh—then to condemn. The passage which most

33

touched us both was that in which S. H. reports W. as saying that "Stedman after all is nothing but a sophisticated dancing master"—and goes on further in that strain. I half-spoke of an intention to write S. in regard to that. W. said: "I wish you would write to him—would be glad to have you do so—that the whole thing appears to me an outrageous astonishing far-rago—from beginning to end a statement of things which, even if they had been believed (as they have not been) could not have been said in that manner by me. You may tell him that. My friends know well enough that I am incapable of so mean, dirty, sneaking, cowardly, a blow." But he laughed again a little (though not as much as at first) at my high wrothiness. "I am used to it—to even worse than that. I have suffered from the like for 30 years—am consequently hardened to it." Yet he was "not only willing but glad" to know I would "send some word of this—of our talk here"—to Stedman. "Not that I wish to make a public denial, though it may amount to that, but that I am agreed Stedman should know my own feelings in the matter." I spoke of my amazement, not so much that Hartmann should construct, but that the Herald should print, such utter and transparent trash—the "odd fancies" of H. rather than of W. W. Yet the Herald had not only printed this, but an-nounced it on the editorial page Saturday, and dwelt upon it Sunday in a special editorial notice, pointing out that here were W.'s opinions of Poe, Emerson, Stedman—and mention-ing others. W. said: "I think there is more than you put into your explanation: I imagine the Herald delights to get in a dab at Stedman if it can—and here was the opportunity." I protested: "but you don't enjoy having them stab Stedman by driving their poniard through you?" And at once, "No indeed —and especially now, after the affair of his big book, in which he has set us up as we were never set up before—generously, affectionately, even nobly. No! No! especially not *now*, if ever —though never—for never, that I know, has anything I have said of S. amounted in the least to a justification of such a comment, criticism, as is put there for me."

I digested to W. the substance of a letter I had written S. some time ago, explaining what I thought of W.'s full but affectionate criticism—a criticism the past year grown more and more affectionate. W.: "I am glad you wrote him that, Horace —and will be glad if you write him again. I remember well the incident of the Scribner essay—I was indignant—Stedman seemed to me there (and this was the one point that troubled me) to unjustifiably dwell upon what people call my filth, sexuality, all that—seemed not only to give it undue weight, prominence, but to twist it, as I thought—twist it. I said all this at the time—don't know but I said it to him—at any rate, said it to his friends, and he must have known of it. But I know Stedman has himself modified all that: especially during the past year or so has he come nearer and nearer. I could not say I was at any time drawn towards him—deeply drawn—but that he was a genuine man (body, mind, generosities, affections)—a patriotic American—Oh! patriotic from the core! —and cute (indeed, remarkable in a sense, intellectually) I have never doubted—never doubted at all. That Apollo expression I have somewhere come upon before. Stedman himself heard something of it—mentioned it in his letter—and I think Hartmann offered it to Kennedy." As to Hartmann: "I can see now that he is a dangerous fellow. He has been here to see me —I have met him more than once—I cannot say I ever really disliked him—but when he attempted that Whitman Club in Boston—you know of it—I put my foot down on him heavily —did this through Baxter and Kennedy, who are the fellows up there now most generously my espousers."

I read him an amusing Emerson paragraph. He laughed: "I not only never said that, but never thought it—never could have said it *that* way if I had thought it. As to H.'s Taine's English Literature "is one of the productions of our age," W. laughed—"Of course—so are we all!" "The whole business," he said again, "is projected from the camel of his imagination: indeed, I should not say that—a worse animal than the poor, quiet, contained camel—a worse far! I can see easily enough from the samples you have given me that the matter is purely and simply fabricated, beginning to end. Even if I had believed such stuff, I never could have slipped into such a statement of it." But the point that most troubled him was the Stedman paragraph. To this again. Referred to S.'s tilt at one time with Holland in which the latter took ground against S.'s references, writing, about W. W. "The point was, that I should not be mentioned within the pages of the magazine. But S. was in high dander, wrote to—sent word to—Holland, that if such a decision was persisted in, he, Stedman, would not only draw the present series to an abrupt close, but would never contribute a damned line more to the magazine; perhaps with more oaths than that, too. This was brave, manly. How could I feel other than kindly towards little Stedman for this—the good, affectionate Stedman. A sturdy defense, and done for me. Of course it appealed to me, awoke my response. Besides I have long known him—never had any but the best feelings towards him. I can easily see how such notions as those of Hartmann's should arise—should get abroad. My friends, a great many of them—friends who, having been kind and near to me have entertained a far more hostile feeling towards S. than ever could have been possible to me; and so, their opinions have been reflected upon me, or taken even as mine." "You know, I took Stedman's clerkship at Washington—knew him while I was there. He came back once to the city, I was introduced to him, I think O'Connor introduced him, and our relations were wholly pleasant." I referred to O'Connor's acceptivity—that he seemed to me much more catholic in his literary judgments than Bucke, for instance. W. said: "You must not wonder at that, Horace—O'Connor is a wonderfully catholic man—of all my friends, he most clearly sees and admits. He is far more catholic than I am, though not more catholic than I want to be. We have had the greatest fights together and he never knew—never can know—but I know, how deep, noble, subtle, has been his influence upon me—his power to soften where I might show unjust asperity." And he pursued: "But

O'Connor is a rare man, and O'Connor, I think, always had hope of Stedman." I spoke of O'Connor's talk with me to that effect. W.: "Yes,—and he feels it profoundly—has in the past year or two written me often, fully, about it."

Discussion of policy of American journalism: that it will sacrifice truth for interest. W.: "It seems to my thinking that the papers abroad, though it may be we only get the best of them, are distinctly superior in this respect—more accurate, scrupulous." Instanced the fine little article by Summers (M. P.) last year describing visit to W. W. The World article was of three columns, and by Hinton—distinctly superior to S. H.'s and of course more truthful—rather descriptive and general than a report of conversation. W. looked and laughed at portrait. Asked what was my impression of this report. I gave a more favorable view than of the other. Had not yet read, only glanced over it. Also brought him proofs. He laid all together. As we sat there in the dark Ed came in for mail, which W. groped for on chair and found, handing to Ed. "Three postals and one letter, isn't that the count?"

W. said again: "We could sum it all up in this way, that I am responsible for nothing—nothing whatever—except what I have written by my own hand—what stands there now in the two books." Spoke of his intention to use the Gutekunst photo-type pictures in the pocket edition. "I find they will do—will stand the cutting. You know the picture? the picture with the hat on?" I kissed him good-night and left him there, the shad-ows now darkened into absolute night.

Wednesday, April 17, 1889

10 A.M. W. in bathroom on my arrival. I sat in his big chair and read till he came back. Ed had to lead him. His lack of strength palpable. But he looked very well—heartily wel-comed me. "Got you seated," he said, in a phrase he so often uses.

Postal from Mrs. O'Connor of 15th. Report *bad*. I asked W.

how he had survived Hartmann's assault. He laughed: "As you see! It is as if a gentle wind had brushed me and I heeded it not!" Then became very circumstantial with regard to Hartmann. Would not repeat my strong words. "No, I try to be more lenient with him. He can't help it! It is in him something basic—something that relates to origins. He lacks what I have often spoken of as not in Conway—integrity. But he is wholly unconscious of it, as indeed is Conway. Hartmann—oh! have you never seen him? He is a biggish young fellow—has a Tartaric face. He is the offspring of a match between a German —the father—and a Japanese woman: has the Tartaric makeup." Here W. paused—then: "and the Asiatic craftiness, too—all of it! I think his father still lives, but the mother is dead. Hartmann has been here often. He has several times been off—in Europe, in Japan—but has always somehow returned. He affects America. The last time he returned, it was mainly to exploit me—at least, I was told this was the cause—Kennedy has written about it. He lived in Phila. for a time—lived with the Brotherton's, the Quakers—and tried to eke out a living writing for the papers. He wrote a good deal for this paper among others"—lifting from his lap the copy of The American I had brought containing article from H. S. Morris. "Of course he often came to see me." But "the crowning shadow" in Hartmann's career Whitman-wise "was spread by his Whitman Club. He was here just before he undertook that thing— in fact, spoke of it, but in a veiled, half perhaps-it-may-be way. I did not sharply negative it then, but I certainly did not approve of it. But shortly he starts up in Boston his Walt Whitman Club: hires a couple of rooms there, puts out a sign —'Walt Whitman Club'—and proceeds with business. It was a curious and astonishing performance. He elects officers, makes himself secretary and treasurer, puts together a most amazing list of Vice Presidents: people who had never been consulted— a long string of them: people who he knew had more or less espoused me—did it with the most eminent assurance. It was at that time I wrote to Kennedy and Baxter, in whom I most confided there, to squelch it. And somehow—quietly—I never knew just how—they did squelch it. It seems Hartmann had started to collect money—got as much as ten dollars from Dave McKay alone. That was a thing we could not suffer—*that* brought us to a point involving responsibility of a sort, so the decisive step was taken—the absolute disclaimer." Hartmann "had heard Kennedy was getting up a Whitman book"—had himself written up thoughts of W. W.—"these here in the Herald no doubt a part of them"—and offered them to K. "I do not suppose he asked pay for them—I do not suppose Kennedy was in any condition to pay for anything above his living at that time. But Kennedy was very cute—very cute, I tell you—for before doing anything at all with the matter H. had given him, he sends it on to me—sends at least paragraphs of it—and inquires after its authenticity. You can realize my quick denial. Most of the stuff was pure and absolute invention—the most barefaced fabrications—the little else was a bungling, incoherent, attempt to repeat what may at one time or another have been thought and spoken." I scoffed at Hartmann's want of literary power. W. said "Oh! he can write: he is not wholly without facility: though this, here in the Herald, is quite the worst thing I have seen from him." Could not account for the publication except by supposing "they need a good deal of matter to fill up the paper: Hartmann has seen Walsh, offers himself cheap—the thing is done." At the time of the Whitman Club affair, "it seemed to me, and I think I so expressed myself to others—to Kennedy among the rest—that not only was a *Club* a factor I could not in itself endorse, but Hartmann, particularly, as the soul of such a club, was emphatically under my distrust." He had always felt a similar distrust of Conway—"he has seemed to me, as I say, to lack *integrity*." I had told Frances Emily White of Conway's Whitman misreports at the Ethical meeting last night, and she had replied, "Oh! Mr. Whitman is an old man and forgets!"

I turned to him with this story and ended with saying, "That is how the Professor explains." W. was vigorous and young enough in his reply, "Oh! damn the professor! What does she know about it? It was not me alone—others know it as well as I do—others heard and were more indignant and confident than I at my worst. No—no—it is no mistake. Conway writes his pieces for the papers, the magazines, bent, first of all, in making them interesting, letting suffer what may. I suppose he has improved of late years, indeed, I have felt myself that he has. I find myself rather respecting his grey hairs, his years, his experience. But as we knew him 30 years ago, he was little to be relied upon." I referred to Morse's exclamation to me once of Conway, "Oh! he's no authority!"—and W.: "That is true of him—that shows that Sidney knew him. He is not a man to be tied to." W. paused, reflected, then went on: "I think that is the best way to put him—to say, *he is not a man to be tied to.* It would be hard to sketch him more vividly than by that." Alluded to Conway's "brilliant flashes of shallowness."

Letter from Ingersoll to me this morning, contributing 25 dollars towards the fund: "Let me know Mr. Whitman's condition. We must all see to it that he is taken care of." I spoke of this to W., and he was much touched. "That is good and noble of him—but him. If you write, boy, say for me: Walt Whitman sends his love and regards: tell him you were here and saw me, that you talked with me about it, that I was touched and grateful."

Returned me the proofs I had brought along last night. Asked me: "Will you leave the American with me?" Desired to read Morris' column there on Browning and Whitman. I inquired if he had read Hinton's World article? "Oh yes! the whole of it." Then after a pause he asked: "How does it appear to you? It seems like three crowded columns of gush. It is no easy task, to work along through all that block of solid matter. Does it not leave you with the feeling—when you are done with it—that it has told you nothing—that it has added nothing to your stock of information?" I asked W. what of the description therein of his visit to Louis Gaylord Clarke's office. He said quickly: "It is a pure invention—it is a pure invention of the good Dick Hinton!" It astonished me to find one after another of these utter fabrications, none, it would seem, in any direction, honest and true. How did he account for it? W.: "It is shocking to be sure, but natural. A fellow tells a story two or three times when he is drunk (though this won't explain Dick Hinton, who don't get drunk)—and the thing gets compacted, solidified, there in his own brain, and thereafter he is willing to swear to it—indeed is astonished, amazed, dumbfounded, to have anybody question it. So far from that story being true, I never took the books around—may have sent some of them away (some, and they came back, mostly)—but to go in the manner there declared was out of the question." He spoke of Hinton as "a newspaper man—one at least to that extent, that he depends for his living upon it—upon such matters as these. He came here with Johnston that Sunday. A few days after he had left I got a letter from Johnston saying that the two of them and several others proposed getting up a Whitman volume of some sort—a volume of the nature of biography—containing memorabilia, what-not—and asking, in effect, for my endorsement. I did not answer the letter at the time—have not answered it yet—and presume the matter is dropped—that Hinton comes out this way in the World instead." But I interposed: "It is hardly abandoned. He speaks of it in this article as still under consideration." And I further protested: "You will have nothing to do with it, will you? What business have you with such a thing?" He answered: "Well—I have not said anything about it. And you are right: if I have nothing to do with it, what my friends or others do I cannot help—but if I approve it, then I am in a sense—in a measure responsible for what they do or say." And he said further: "I have always heretofore kept

41

clear of such things, and I shall hardly be drawn into them now." "I think it was the scheme to have several aid in the volume, but to have it all under the supervision of Hinton." I had got W. the three copies of Bucke's book yesterday.

7.45 P.M. Down with Kemper, who did not go into W.'s room. Took W. proof, over which at last he expressed his pleasure. "I think it will do now." "I got a letter from Doctor today in which he says someone has sent him the World. So I have taken the copy you brought me and forwarded it to O'Connor." At this, he spoke of the "bad, bad news" from Washington; O'C. not then able to read the letter W. had sent him. "The wife says, the last three or four days were the worst. Poor O'Connor!" Spoke of the portrait with Hinton's article. "From the way he speaks, it is to be inferred it is from one of the Cox portraits—but it is too bad to indicate *what* it is; indeed, I don't know but one should call it *horribly* bad, for horribly bad it is!" "I sent the Herald up to Doctor, but did not write him at any length about it, only a few words on a postal."

Returned me The American containing Morris' article "The Revolution against Taste," and simply remarked of it: "It is slight—seems to have no weight—apparently has nothing to tell." With it he had lain Trübner's Record spoken of the other day. Said W.: "It seems to be devoted to the East— to Asia—and to America: big enough subjects, to be sure, rightly handled, but dry enough handled there. I thought you might be interested in looking over it—not in reading, but in seeing what is there—as with me: for I am a most curious fellow, hungry to know about all that's going about all the books, things, policies of governments." Said he: "I have sent off one of the Bucke books. There was a person over there in England pretty hungry to have a copy, so I sent one in this way—not that alone, but sent along with it a copy of November Boughs." Printer had put "Preface" at top of second page of introductory notice of A Backward Glance. W. promptly excised. Objects to use of name altogether in his case. But tolerantly: "Not that I have any abstract exception to take but only exception as applied to my conditions."

The heat in W.'s room great, this evening, yet not probably more than comfortable to W. He tells a good story *apropos*, of two visitors, the first complaining of heat and inducing W. to throw up the sash, the second, entering a few minutes after, complaining of cold, and persuading W. to close it again. "Now," says W. "if people would believe that I understand my own business, we would all get along better!" He always asks me what I think of the temperature of his room, and I always qualify my impression with a "to me." I trust to his own sense for knowing what is best for *him*. But night before last, despite the blazing wood in the stove and the heat of the atmosphere, his right hand was so cold it rather startled me, and I remarked it to him. But although I found the *left*, which I took in my own, similarly conditioned, he said he was not at all conscious of *cold*. Remarked tonight that he had not "for a long time" heard anything from Kennedy that was "notable." And inquired after Morse, too.

Thursday, April 18, 1889

10.30 A.M. W. was writing an addition to foot-note in preface and had written on top of proof sheet—"After correcting please give me five impressions." He wished to send one or two away. Title page he said would do. "I do not say I am enthusiastic about it, but I am willing to let it go and it will look better in the book than here."

"The Danmark," he said, "I see there is no word of it still. Oh! that is a fearful probability!" Said: "I had a note there from Merrill—Bradford Merrill of the Press. Do you know him?" Merrill had sent him a circular—a symposiate circular again—asking—by numbers 1 and 2, what most had contributed to his success in life. W. said: "I guess I shall answer

43

that as I answer all such things, merely by not answering it at all." I asked: "What could you have to say as to that?" And he: "That is so—what?" I asked him if he did not think his enemies had contributed something to his success? He laughed, but made no response. Merrill had written a letter with the circular—wished an answer within a few days.

I wrote Stedman a letter before going to W. Thereupon W. spoke of Hartmann again. I of the transparent falsity of his column. W. said: "There are wise, cute men, who set it down as sufficient disproof of what is called spiritualism that the messages it brings are none of them such as we could not equal and improve upon on earth here." W. said of his health that it was "only so-so"—that he had not got up "in very brilliant condition."

Clifford had enclosed in a letter to me Swinburne's "March" ode (Nineteenth Century) with the preface: "I have not your Swinburne ear" and this delightful play to follow:

To talk true, this tone tries to torture terms that tell trifling totals towards the triumphant tautologies therein tossed together, time, tide, today, tomorrow tumbled thus to turn trumpery tunes to tickle the tutelary tyrant that torments the twitterer. Alliteration (all iteration, and damnable, too). Imagine Walt figuring out the alphabet to its possible variations and agreements so!

W. read with great enjoyment and laughter and to Clifford's closing two lines: "Imagine Walt figuring," &c. "Yes, imagine it!" I stayed only for ten minutes.

7.45 P.M. On nearing house, noted darkness in W.'s room. This always arouses my fears. When in once, found indeed that he was in bed, resting, the night almost fully fallen, his room dark. The weather had grown much warmer through the afternoon. One of his windows was thrown clear up. As I groped my way for a chair, after shaking hands with him, I asked how he had spent the day. "Very bad," he said, "it has been a bad day all through—a bad, bad day." As if emphasizing this, by indicating how little work he had been able to do he said to Eddy, who shortly came in to ask if there was any mail to go: "There is no mail at all, Eddy—I have nothing there." But he added, after Ed had gone out: "I feel much better now—have felt much better ever since I had my dinner." Thence general conversation. His voice was good and strong—his thought clear—and of course his cheer was inevitable. It is rarely, indeed, one could find him with that all gone.

He said to me: "I have had a couple of visitors. Harry Bonsall came in—with him Buckwalter. You know Buckwalter, don't you? Buckwalter, of the public schools. We had quite a good talk—they were here about 20 minutes, I should suppose. Both good fellows, too!" I remarked that Buckwalter was a man of more decision of character than Bonsall. W. responded: "I don't know—it is likely. But I like Buckwalter—he is much of a man." I said: "After one gets through his peculiarity of speech, he is much liked." W.: "I am not at all troubled by that—it passes me by—I am used to it. You see, I have known Buckwalter for a long time: besides, that speech matter is the peculiarity—I may say the inevitability—with New England people: it is almost universal with them; even the wise Emerson had it, in some measure; all of them had it, have it;—I can freely say I accept it—never feel resentful towards its use. It is a sort of extreme grammaticism. Yet I confess that when it is made too prominent—when it is indeed insisted upon—when it is too much poked in one's face—I turn my back on it, it offends me." Added: "But I was glad to have the two come in." Visits from good friends, if not prolonged, threw blessed light across the days of his confinement.

In Standard, out today, Henry George speaks (London letter of 5th) of a drive out with Pearsall Smith. W. was much interested to learn of the affair. He has a way, when he particularly wants to understand what you say, of repeating your explanation after you, to find out if it is rightly caught. He did so now, for this case: "Do I understand you right?—

that George, and our friend Smith, drove out together, there in London, or beyond London, and you think they had a good time and that they like each other?" Then after my assent and a pause, he went on: "Tell me more about it, then—tell me about the drive: what it amounted to, where led, who were along, all that." I replied by saying I would bring the paper down in the morning and let him read it in full. "Ah!" he exclaimed, "that would perhaps be best—I should be glad." Talk somewhat of J. R. Young, Ferguson, others. W. asked somewhat about methods of work at the printing office. Then: "Has Ferguson much work in hand now? Is he kept at it pretty close?"

I casually mentioned having read "Crossing Brooklyn Ferry" last night. W.'s tone (I could not of course see him) seemed to deepen in interest at once. "Ah! and now tell me, what did it suggest to you, what were certain of its prime features: tell me what most deeply affected you—if anything—in the piece." And after a pause, during which neither spoke: "Was there anything pictorial in it—pictorial?" I spoke briefly in reply—of pictorial factors, but others, too: its indirection exquisitely rich, &c. Then of objections often urged that W. was too indirect, too suggestive, presumed too much in powers behind. W. "recognized" that criticism. "That I see—and see its reason." On the other hand, "I suppose no one but the habitue could grasp fully—even measurably—the pictorial significance of the piece: no one who has not been there as I have been, a frequenter of ferry ways, boats, wharves, men, bustling commerces." And he more fully explained: "I have been there in the presence of all its thousand and one changes of color: mine was no casual contact, but the contact of years, love, association—of childhood, boyhood, manhood, maturity—the sailing on the waters, the going out with the pilots in their pilot boats, the tripping it to the sea and back again—Sandy Hook, down to Navesink. Only by such-gathered lights and shades can anyone really know, appreciate, enter into, the fine tones of meaning: that is, by actually living, breathing, bathing, in the life of it!" Only yesterday one of the old boats at New York was burned: the New Brunswick, built in 1866. W. very carefully inquiring after its name. "It was a real old boat, it seems: I do not remember it. Was it a Brooklyn boat?" And when I said, "No—it was a Jersey City boat," he said his interest in it was just the same, even if not so immediate. Spoke of his passion for the waters and his memories of the old days "there in the New York harbor." Further talk of our boats here: the old Delaware now in service again, temporarily. Then of the Kaighn's Point line, which has secured several old boats from New York. Of one of these, the America, I asked W., but he did not know it: "It must have been a North River boat—the name is new to me."

I gave W. the proof as he lay there on the bed. Afterwards, a little while, he moved as if to get up, and laboriously at last was upright. The room still dark. Ed had offered to light the gas while in the room but W. had said, "I don't know of any reason why it should be lighted now." With my help went across to his chair—he himself attending to window—alluded to his "absolute knowledge of the lay-out" of the room—to his weakness, nevertheless—and then said of himself: "I am much shrunken," but no more on that point, nor to my questioning. Then became seated. At the first flow of the light I caught sight of the long-lost package of the Sarrazin sheets under the chair near me and near his rocker. "Ah!" I exclaimed, "here they are at last"—and then directly to him— "I see you have found the Sarrazin sheets!" He swung about, chair and all, as is his way. "How did you know?" I pointed to the package. He laughed. "Yes! there they are"—turning meanwhile to the table. "They turned up today. I made up a couple of envelopes of them for you"—handing them to me. He had endorsed one "Translations (two) of Sarrazin's article" and the other "copies of both) Translations of Sarrazin's article"—both in a splendid bold hand. "There are two sheets in each," he explained—"One Doctor Bucke's and one Kennedy's." One of these was intended for Mr. Coates, of whose friendliness—"and the wife's"—W. spoke with tender feeling.

W. here said: "I must not let my fire go out"—but when he leaned over to examine it he found it was gone out, practically—at least, only a spark left. And although he flung a log on it, and tried to start it up, his efforts were of no avail. Then surrendered it—threw himself back in his chair. The room was really very warm anyhow. He did not look extra well —I could see that his head trouble was active again. I looked half-scornfully at the stove (our new stove of the Fall) and quoted Hinton's contemptuous description of it—"A sheet-iron stove, rusty." W. laughed most heartily—then said: "I don't think much of Hinton's article, anyhow. He has sent me a copy of the paper himself—it arrived today. It may seem ungracious—even unkind or harsh—to say so (for Dick is my friend and means me well) but his piece impresses me most by its emptiness—impresses me as a big tumor or boil, much swelled, inflamed, bulging, but nothing after all. No! No! I don't like either of them: they seem by no means justified."

I opened the roll of proofs and indicated which one Myrick wished him to return. Remarked too that I valued his addition to the footnote. Said he "rather liked it himself." Then conversed of plans of procedure. "We are now about in shape to let the printer take it in hand." And he added: "I am figuring out the affair of the portrait—of an order for the plate-printer to go on. I have about settled upon this—perhaps I may change, but for the present this—to use the three-quarter picture, the McKay picture, as frontispiece, to use the steel in its old place, 'The 70th Year,' the Linton: these in addition to the photos. What do you think?" And he proposed, "Going right ahead with the new small edition of November Boughs," which would give him the chance to print the Hicks portrait with more care, by special arrangement, than had been before. "As it shows up in the book there, it disappoints me." Although he had plenty of the old steels about, already printed, —"I think I shall have that man print me more: I am so struck with the way he does it. I would rather have his steels." And again: "I quite recognize the necessity of having these special printings of the process plates. I had hoped not, but a particular delicacy seems required in handling them." Then of things in general, instructed mechanics, &c.—I quoting the University professor, "Young men—learn to do something well—even if it is only playing a jewsharp." And the old brick-layer who replied to his son's remark: "Oh! this is good enough!"—"No—nothing is good enough till it is good!" W.: "They are both to the point—oh! full of the meat of truth— both stories!"

I told W. I had acquainted Stedman in my letter of the forenoon with our intention to issue a pocket edition on W.'s birthday. W. said: "I am glad you did. I have several times today been impelled to write to Stedman myself—a few lines, anent that affair; for considering his handsome recent treatment of me,—kindness, consideration, generosity—it seems very unhandsome in me to let the matter pass without direct reference. But I have not felt well, and then there is the demon: you know, Socrates had his demon, and that demon made up the whole calendar of life—and my demon today was not altogether persuaded." Perhaps it would be as well to wait and what S. had to say, if anything, in response to my letter. He said: "I know you would like Stedman: he is a quick, all-alive, man—earnest, affectionate, frank." He had often seen in classification, "Stedman and Gilder placed together" but this was "unwarranted" since "Gilder is by no means the man we know Stedman to be—is good, and of course has his abilities —but has not the fine emotional, sympathetic nature that enriches Stedman." Besides, "has not the acumen, the intellectual, the literary, power." "Gilder has written several volumes of poems—I have seen them, but not read them—at least, not read them with any sort of attention."

49

Then he spoke feelingly, in reply to my word—"We ought to be glad that so much has been accomplished the past year, when we think of the anxiety of June that nothing would be done"—"Yes indeed—and I am. It was first of all a great victory to have got November Boughs out. And the big book, bound there as it is, with notes, portraits—I am happy, content, for having secured it. And now this—this on the high way to success! We have indeed had a varied but auspicious experience—things nearly all in shape now. Even this book, this edition, seems to me to have a simple, settled, purpose, all its own—to be made distinctly for a place—bound up as it is, the poems and A Backward Glance together, well-cohering, well-belonging in connection." "I cannot just put my finger on the spot—yet am convinced the significance is real"—"I have allowed myself more egotism in these later words—in what I have written the past year or two—especially in connection with these last books—notes, &c.—than ever before. Yet have accepted the privilege with every consciousness of its dangers, knowing full well that there are a thousand eyes"—I interrupted, "or thousands"—"Yes,—thousands of eyes, ready and eager to see and announce errors, offenses, whatnot."—"But not fearing results—certainly not wishing to have my friends misunderstand me, I have gone on. The final point anyhow being, that I shall satisfy my own second thought of what should be done and what foregone." He referred again to his joy to thus live to "get together an authenticated volume" to which futurity, if for him futurity be, must come: "for authoritative word"—of him, "if word at all." Much interested in the whole drift of talk.

I left and went across the room. The misty evening on the water (I had crossed a couple of hours before) engaged him. We spoke of his possible outing—perhaps a trip up Market Street in Philadelphia and down Chestnut in the city to see changes. "How much must have been done since I last wandered that way." But he expressed no hope of such a trip.

Alluded to Bradford Merrill's statement in letter, that John Burroughs put W. at head of living authors. W. said: "And by the way, John thinks a good deal of Gilder—thinks there is considerable to him. It is a judgment to be weighed." Clifford had seen prefatory note of pocket edition. I met him on the street the other day. He could see no decline of vigor or beauty. Did not know of another now living who could write that way. W. said: "That puts us on our mettle, even in our old age!"

Friday, April 19, 1889

10.35 A.M. Marvellously clear out of doors—and the air mild as summer. W. sitting in his room by the open window, working on proof. Certain wrong insertions of lines. Asked me: "Isn't it a remarkable day out-of-doors?" He thought it had that look. It inspires him to talk of the chair again. Bonsall and Buckwalter had advised Ed to get a proper chair and let them see about payment.

"And nothing of the Danmark," said W.—"not a word! not a word!" If no sailing vessel had picked them up, then was "the whole story in"? "I do not quite understand this Azores business, though I suppose it is intelligible enough if one but knew"—the hope, viz., that the Azores would be the first point touched in case they had been picked up by a sailer. "There is one thing to be said of it—if they have gone down—if the whole crew—all the passengers—have simply been drowned—then is the final word spoken—then, as was the case in the Army when a man was killed outright—then need no sympathy be wasted on that. But if not—ah!" and his face assumed its serious aspect.

He said again: "I got two letters in my mail today—one from Doctor, the other from the Herald. The Herald wants me to send them something for the big racket over there—the constitutional business. Whether I shall do it or not depends entirely on how I feel—Whether I am moved to it or not." Asked me whether anything was yet known of Whittier's poem for the occasion. I gave him The Standard, with marked passages therein relating to George's drive with Pearsall Smith. W. said: "Pearsall is very catholic—opens his arms to everybody —is very enclosing." And W. dropped the paper on his lap and looked over his spectacles humorously at me—"and underneath all, way down, much hid but still existing, I think there is a drift towards the ugly ones, the outcasts, the discredited fellows"—meaning men socially outlawed like George. "I may even say for the Western freedom—cowboys, miners, whatsoever!" He reflected: "Judging from this, Pearsall is still in his home on Grosvenor Road; the last letter I had from him was addressed from a club room—though I suppose that has no significance, as it is much a habit with some of the fellows to write from Clubs, Societies." As we sat there Mrs. Davis brought in a little tin box containing some diminutive spring flowers. W. took and long regarded them: "they look like little spiders," he remarked—and—"Are you going to leave them here with me?" Then put them on the table, and when Mrs. Davis had gone, resumed his talk of the Smiths.

George referred (in his letter) to Smith as a manufacturer. I had not known him in this connection. W. said: "He is in the glass business—at Millville, I think; you must know the firm—Whitall, Tatum & Co. He married a Miss Whitall. It is Quaker stock—they seem to have lots of money. I think the wife must have resigned the care of the money to Pearsall. A few years ago, he had his regular office hours then—3 or 4 hours a day for work." "Mrs. Smith had in her the zest for evangelization. You may have noticed—I have—that in the orthodox Quaker there is a streak which inclines very strongly even to Calvinism. It is a curious exhibit, but it is a solid fact. That streak was in Mrs. Smith. Twenty years or so ago they were both possessed with the spirit of evangelization: went off to Europe together—had plenty of money—pockets full of it,

I guess—and so set out to evangelize the Continent. They went from land to land, had interpreters with them, held meetings, ran the 'Come-to-Jesus!' business to its full. It was a queer freak, but they were in earnest about it. They went to and fro, had even the bluebloods, nabobs, interested." After more detailed description, W. said: "It was just by this thing that Mrs. Smith and I came by our disagreement. She still believes that the world is to be persuaded, driven into salvation. I do not—never did! I always considered how much of a man's self is pre-natal, accounted for by surroundings, parentage, birth, circumstances. She never would allow for that." There had one night been company at the Smiths'—"Mrs. Smith was there in high glow, full of her usual pet theories, and telling them freely. The room was full of people." He had antagonized her there: "I think I drew forth even the resources of humor—quoted Carlyle, trying in twenty volumes to persuade the world that preaching was of no avail. I guess I was very positive, did not leave any one in doubt where I stood. I don't think Mrs. Smith ever has forgiven me to this day." But I asked about Smith's Radicalism, which now seems unquestioned. W. then: "I started to tell you how that came about. After considerable wandering about, the Smiths got back into London, held meetings there. But then there arose an affair— I even think a scandal—women being mixed up in it—into which Pearsall himself was drawn. I never knew exactly about it, only that it nipped the caseization in the bud—settled the whole business at once—and evangelization was done for." He believed "Mrs. Smith still much as she was then. It is one of her virtues, that she is perfectly consistent. But some few years ago—about three—Pearsall himself reacted, turned clean about, became an absolute doubter, not an agnostic—no, not at all an agnostic—but a bitter denier, scorner, flouter, without qualification or giving quarter. I think he has now been softened from that attitude, but for a time he occupied it most decisively. There was some trouble in the family, too—some infelicity: for some years Pearsall and Mrs. Smith had no words—no relations—with each other. You know, my own strong point in the Smith family is not in either of the old people, but, as I suppose I have told you, in the daughter— in Mary Costelloe. Yet Pearsall himself always showed the greatest warmth towards me—was friendly, received me, was joyous in having me enjoy his provender. But I have never felt that his liking for me was on the side of my work—that he really understood that, though he read Leaves of Grass a good deal—but on the human side, the eating, drinking, jovial, good-fellow side. A good deal in Pearsall is explained by the fact that he is a hypochondriac;—you knew he was a hypochondriac? Oh! that illuminates very much of what might otherwise go unexplained!" He alluded to the international copyright scheme. "It originated in part in Pearsall's hunger for a fad, as he calls it: he delights in being at something— in getting near the fellows—in being in action. Even on its own merits I am not sure there is nothing in it."

Here he suddenly asked: "Have you ever thought, Horace —yes, you must have thought—how very much of life consists in solidification—how we settle down to the justice of a thing because it has long been—because it has always been so, per-haps—rather than from any reasons one could give for its intrinsic value?" Perhaps some of our notions on copyright would fall by such a consideration. W. questioned me somewhat upon the subject of Davidson's "Bonaventure" Tuesday night. He had never heard of the man—asked me: "Was there a man of that name?'"—adding that he had always known its "Good Luck!" signification, but never its biographical signification. As to the lore of the mystics, he knew nothing.

Cannot get the loss of the Danmark out of his thought. The passengers and crew "mostly Dane." "I am always interested on the score of the Scandinavian stock: the Danes, the Norwegians; these and the Scotch. Oh! how great is America's debt to them!"

7.50 P.M. W. sitting in chair by the middle window, which was open. There was no light in the room. He and Harned I found engaged in animated and earnest talk about Ticknor's "Spanish Literature." Harned's boy was there, also, coming forward in the dark when he heard my voice and informing me, "I am here, Uncle Horace." W. was advising Harned: "You should by all means read it—it is, if not the greatest book, at least one of the greatest—a perfect, inexhaustible mine. Ticknor—George Ticknor—was a Yankee man, a Bostonese; he had lots of money—went to Spain, spent three or four years there, got rid of many thousands of dollars. He hired several Spanish amanuenses, copyists—worked in that way. It is certainly a great and potent book—and fascinating, too. I remember one of the chapters there, relating to the Inquisition, where he says, there's no use cursing, swearing, about it, it was there. What are you doing now to make Inquisitions impossible? That was the aim of it. Ticknor put the work of a life into the book—twenty years of research, labor, preparation." W. had more than once read it. Harned afterward got up—said the boy was impatient to go. W. solicitously—"Going already?" and then—"are you going to take a walk?" The "Goodbyes!" then hearty and we were left alone.

Turned to me—I could see his head against the uncertain flickering reflections without. "What have you seen new today?" Proof only, the sheet now correct. He said: "It was only a casual error—it was such an error, too, as is anytime likely to be made." Ed had come in in the dark while Harned remained and brought with him a postal. W. had asked, not seeing, "What is it, Ed—mail?—letter, paper, postal?" and when he had got it—"Postal!"—had for the minute relapsed. But now he desired to see what the postal was, wheeled about in his chair, arose, closed the windows, lighted the gas. In doing this last the matches, several of them, one after another, would not ignite. I could hear his provoked "Psha!" in the dark, and at last laughed at him, he joining. "Once in awhile,"

55

he said, "the Yankee sets to and makes a match and a pencil out of nothing; then we have to content ourselves with being swindled." Finally the light was on, however, and he sank back restfully in his chair.

I mentioned having been reading John Burroughs' "Fresh Fields." W. did not fairly catch the title—thought I said Presque Isle. Finally he did set himself right. "Oh! Fresh Fields! that book I know. I cannot say intimately, but I have seen it. I thought you said 'Presque Isle' [which probably explains why, when I first spoke of this book some weeks ago, he expressed a desire to read it]. There is a place of that name, and I knew John was soldering together a new book. I did not know but Presque Isle was his name for it." Returned me the Standard. "I have read all that piece about Pearsall Smith. It was very readable." George had said therein that on their drive he had not broached the subject of tariff to Smith. W. remarked hereupon: "I think Pearsall is open enough on that question: I don't believe he is a protectionist by principle— by abstract conviction—but by connivance, because he thinks it is about the thing to be. That would be my understanding of him." W. said he had written to Mary Costelloe today. I asked: "Did you mention the article?" "Oh yes! I said briefly —in a few words, that I had read it." Said he "liked the paper as a whole"—that "it was full of interesting material." A long address therein by John DeWitt Warner on "Our National Life." I supposed he would, if seeing, read: and sure enough he said of it: "I read all that—every word of it—and it was enjoyable, too!" He liked George's style. The London letter "was fascinating"—"his pen is a good one: he writes very easily and attractively—it is like a good dish, a taste of it makes you want more."

The weather had been extraordinary all day. Seventy-four degrees in the shade between two and three o'clock. It was an anticipation of summer. We spoke of it together—of the possibility of having W. get out. But he put on a very dubious expression—had no confidence that he could have got out even if he had his chair. He has at odd moments spoken both to Eddy and to me about this chair, as if he wished it instantly, but when it comes to the push, he hesitates, and says, "Wait till I tell you." I wonder if he will ever "tell" us? "I feel pretty tired tonight—wearied. I had this afternoon a sort of semi-weekly wash—bath—over there in the bathroom. It leaves me very weak. Except the last hour, I have not all day felt comfortable. It has been a bad day all through—a very bad day." As to getting out: "Feeling as I do today, I should not feel like going out, or if I did feel like going, should not be able to get out." I asked him if he thought the jolt of a carriage would irritate him. "I don't know—perhaps it would." As he was situated now, going at all was out of the question. The mere navigation downstairs would be impossible. "Anyhow," I said, "whether you are going to get out or not, we are going to get the book out!" He looked up at me—I had been standing at his side—a half-smile, a half-serious joy, lighting his face. Then he said with a brave, triumphant air which seems to stick to him whatever the drafts upon his power and endurance: "It looks so, don't it? Sure enough! sure enough!" Which drove us to talk of the book and future plans therefor.

Here W. bethought himself of the postal, which I handed him from the table. His first look—"Oh! it is from Washington—from Nelly!" and continued, "It is dated the 18th, evening—that was yesterday, wasn't it?" Then read the postal aloud, with accustomed deliberation. O'Connor had been well enough yesterday to read Stedman's letter, which they had both liked very much. When W. came to the passage reciting that O'Connor claimed the credit of Stedman's conversion he laughed heartily. The postal closed with a statement of O'Connor's now renewed illness of the moment. W. dwelt upon "the ups and downs" of O'Connor's condition—how really down it was—"no real up." Then he continued: "In my mail today was a letter from Kennedy. I had sent him the Stedman letter—

he was to forward it to O'Connor, O'Connor to Bucke. Kennedy alluded to the letter—rather pooh-pooh'd it!" I feared Bucke would do likewise. W. inquired: "Do you?" But at any rate, his own position was clear. I said that for my part I looked upon Stedman's position as thoroughly firm and genuine. W. acquiesced: "So do I—and I shall not pooh-pooh it. I accept it just as it manifests itself. It must not be forgotten, Stedman has been in a manner converted: he has gradually—only gradually—come to us, but come he has. I think it can fairly be said now, he belongs to us, we belong to him. Stedman is in some measure the conventional literary fellow among conventional literary fellows." But he was more than that, too, and we had no right to confine him as if he was not. "I never regarded him—never regarded Gilder—as outright opposed—I don't think they ever were. In both—especially in Stedman—there was an eligibility, a tendency, a drift, which, now we look back, must have made his course inevitable. I realize—and I think it was you who insisted on it—that Stedman is anyhow a horse of another color: Gilder not nearly so free, does not put himself out, give rein."

I had a copy of Bazaar with me. In it a double-page engraving of General Wolseley, at which (its wonderful effect and delicacy) W. looked lingeringly. He called it "a wonderful fine picture"—said: "I never saw his phiz before," and made comment after comment of a general character without the first hint of an estimate of the man himself. "These fellows nowadays seem to get artists, engravers, printers, of the best class. It is wonderful, marvellous, the effects they achieve." Turned over to fashions in head-dress on first page. "Even these are well done—handsomely done, though"—and here he looked at me and laughed—"I despise 'em!" Inside he turned impatiently from a stiff Madonna picture ("Madonna's threads" —a salon picture by Lucas).

Said by transition to out-of-doors again: "It seems to be perfect summer weather. I had a letter from Doctor today in which he says it is summer there, too. I suppose we will have three or four delightful days, such as today has been—get set up by them—then be brought to a short stop by a frost—the last breath of some snowstorm up in the northwest." He loves to report and to hear report of out-of-doors. Never complaining, never morbid—all that impossible. Even the nurse remarked the other night when Kemper sat in the parlor with us that "the way Mr. Whitman says" the curious and cross things, relieved them of sting. And that is true, and should always be borne in mind. These notes should be read in such remembrance. Imagination, to such as have never met W., may give voice and gentleness to what I day by day quote, and thereby get its picture; otherwise the notes will achieve mistaken results, unjust to me and to W.

I do not regard these as good days at all for W. He describes himself as "far, far down"—and that indeed he seems. But we hope on still, at least for generous respite. His bodily temperature is low. The night so warm, yet he closed his windows and stirred the fire. Harned's youngster had sung out in the dark while here (then the window was open) that he was "awful hot—sweating"—and yet W. even then had not warmth enough—had closed out the air altogether. I wrote Ingersoll this evening—so told W., who expressed his pleasure. Baker came in as I sat in parlor talking with Mrs. Davis. He went up to W. and I left.

Saturday, April 20, 1889

10.45 A.M. W. had been folding up edges of a copy of the Gutekunst picture to discover how it would appear in the pocket-edition. "It will do, I see," he assured me. "I had no doubt of it, but have just been proving it here by a book itself." Ferguson's proof finally correct. Had written so on margin, with directions as to cost and signing "W. W." The Danmark still trying him. "And still no word!" he exclaimed. "I looked all through the Press, in fact, but did not find a word about it. In its usual way it has succeeded in hiding the important matter beyond discovery." But I showed him then quite an article concerning an overdue steamer for this port (the Missouri) which "possibly" had picked up the lost 700. But W. said: "That is hypothetical—purely a speculation—and not likely to have been the case at all."

I asked him of his condition, and he called it "nothing to boast of." But had eaten a more or less hearty breakfast. Signed a portrait Mrs. Burleigh had bought at Gutekunst's— a copy of the sitting picture in Bucke's book. But he was mystified how Gutekunst had got a copy of that portrait for sale. I guess there's no mystery, really, but I am not clear about it myself. My stay very brief. I did not desire to do more than get proof. In talking of pictures he asked of me: "What about the printing of the steel plates?" And in a rough way I described its method. He said he knew nothing whatever about it, nor about lithography. What I said, particularly of the presses used, greatly interested him—at least, I so judged by his manner and his questions.

Evening: 7.45. The unlighted room caught me as I came near the house, aroused my apprehension. W. as I expected on his bed. The afternoon had been very warm and sultry. I went for a long stroll in the Park with Kemper. W. said of his condition, that it was bad—"a sick day—one of the sickest." And when I spoke up: "It seems impossible for you to gain any strength," he affirmed: "It is so—in fact, I am losing instead of gaining." For the present he gives up all idea of getting out. "I could not get down stairs—it would be impossible." To Ed who had entered with me, he said he had no mail at all to go to the Post Office. "But I will let you strike a light if you choose." Which Ed did choose, closing room windows in doing so.

W.'s usual questions, what I had done in town, of course came. I had been to the printer's with proof. He much interested in knowing I had been out for a walk. I spoke of the odor of the fresh damp green grass, already being cut, and he said it was a pleasant reminder to bring into his confining room. Impressed to hear of my father's growing good opinion of German translation of Leaves of Grass. Asked as so often before: "and Grashalme means Leaves or Spears of Grass?"

On a reference to Harper's Bazaar he exclaimed: "And poor Mary Booth—now you are dead and buried!—and what now?" And when I asked: "Did you know her?" "Only slightly —I have met her." Odor of flowers in the room. Out of the neck of his sherry bottle, now filled with water, white and red roses. How had they come? And he said: "I have had a visitor today, and she brought me the flowers. It was Charlotte Fiske Bates. What a fine healthy girl she is, too—and so hopeful! I should say, not at all old—under 30, of a certainty. How cheery, how helpful! She tells me she is now living in New York. She was in Boston for some years. She teaches school." Had she brought him any news of the friends there? "I would hardly call it news, but she sees Stedman, she says, and gives an interesting account of how he sturdily stands up for me." Had she seen the Herald deliverance? "No—it was news to her when I spoke of it."

I said: "I see by the papers that Pearson over there in New York [postmaster] is dying." W. remarked quietly: "He is dead—he died this morning." I had not seen an afternoon paper. "It seems he died with a tumor—a tumor down in the belly; and this tumor, the doctors say, came from over-strain, over-work, too assiduous a regard for the duties of his position there." W. added: "New York certainly has had cause to be congratulated on its postmasters recently—on Pearson, on James—perhaps most on James, the gem of gems among officers. I don't see why, anyhow, such offices do not always go to men simply for moral, business reasons." I said: "These are but secondary, now," and W. responded indignantly: "Secondary? They do not enter at all. It is not a question of fitness but of whether the fellow who is appointed is a good friend of the fellow who appoints him. Even General Grant would appoint men simply on the ground that he liked them! I think Washington and Jefferson—especially Jefferson—looked above all at the necessities of the service, and sought for those necessities the best men to be found. But the period of such ideals is past." I laughingly said: "I see Hartmann has you down for a word about Harrison." He could not but laugh himself: "Yes—and he has never seen me since Harrison was nominated!" Referred to the newly appointed postmaster at New York as "a Republican politician" and had some difficulty in hitting on his name —Van Cott—"or something like that"—doing so, however, at last.

He spoke of his book. "It is now on the eve of its issue—at least of being printed. I am anxious myself to see it. This book is a book I am getting out, not to please the public, but solely with reference to myself." But of course if the public happened to be pleased in his pleasure, all the better!

W. had noted in papers today, announcement of publication of book "Emerson in Concord," by Emerson's son Edward—treating of home life of R.W.E. W. looked forward to a treat in its reading. W. spoke of the multitude of art publications nowadays. "America seems of all places the best market for it —the best popular market. It would make good matter for an important article, to know just how this cheap art product is distributed—whether most North, South, East, West. "Some cute fellow ought to take it up for one of the papers." I had a friend who dealt considerably in cheap jewelry. W. was curious to discover how his product was disposed of. "It all has a great importance as determining the standard of our culture, lives."

Sunday, April 21, 1889

6.30 P.M. W. sat by the window, the Venetian blinds at the downward angle, giving a view of the street. Eminently cordial —spoke up instantly on my entrance: "I have had a call today from Tom and Mrs. Harned"—here he paused, looking at me as if with unusual happiness—"And the baby at last! Herbert at last! Oh! and what a remarkable boy it is, too!—that big, clear, beautiful blue eye—a whole world of him, at least." I was surprised, some little, to find him so enthusiastic. He pleasantly alluded to the usual high opinions of parents, and then of the promise of the boy: "And he is a specimen, too—nobly one; I was much taken, engaged, with him; it seemed to me I found in him the eligibility of any future in the calendar—highest, best—a bright, broad vista!" Expressed fervently his "gladness" that "the glimpse of him" had been "afforded at last." In regard to health, W. expressed a sense of some relief, but not of any great change. His feebleness clings sadly. Ed reports to me a dark discoloration of the urine. This, if continued, may require attention.

I asked him for a copy of "As a Strong Bird" for Mrs. Fels, whom I went to see this evening. W. said: "Of course—and gladly!" adding—"Go in there; you'll find a copy in Ed's room there in the box"—and calling it "Better still" when I found what I wanted on the shelf instead. He took the book—wiped the dust from it on a robe there on the floor—then took a pen and firmly (though somewhat irregularly, for it was nearly dark) endorsed it; sending it, as he put it there, "With my best wishes"—and advising me: "Tell her for me that that is a hard nut to crack—the hardest nut of all." At my mention deprecatively of "The Mystic Trumpeter," he explained: "I do not mean that—that is exceptional—that is more in the popular vein. I mean 'As a Strong Bird'—that is a great task for any one to assume to understand." Perhaps the sweetest nut might have the hardest shell? "I do not know—but the poem is a puzzle, anyway."

I noted that he had taken the photos so far selected and counted them off into fifties, labeling them accordingly. "I found I had plenty of the butterfly pictures. I have put aside there, 305 or over; intended tying them up, but had not the

right string, which Ed will get for me tomorrow. I counted—
discovered I had 150 of the Sarony pictures, which is not
enough by half. I suppose it would be better to have the whole
300 uniform but it is not absolutely necessary." I suggested:
"I would put them in anyhow, such of them as you have." And
he quickly responded: "I intend to—but I have not quite given
up the search yet. I had at least as many of these as of the
butterflies, but now they are either lost or stolen. I should have
had Mary help me look 'em up today, but she went off to the
shore with Warren, her boy, to see some friends." I put in—
"And are just back—came in as I did." And he then: "Oh!
are they? I supposed it was about time. Anyhow, I am sure
there are enough of the pictures—or if not these, others—to
finish." I had spent the day in Germantown. In fact, stopped
in at W.'s on the way home. Book in my hands (a present from
Clifford; Gilman on Profit-sharing). W. inquired of and
looked at it, but was not appealed to by Gilman. But he inquired closely after Clifford's sermon—the substance of which
I explained—an Easter sermon, the like of which doubtless
was nowhere else heard in America today, considering generosity and breadth of purport and spirit.

Weather thereupon—the beauty of the day—my description of fields, of early grass-cutting, of hay, the odor of fresh
growths. W. alluded to the thunder-storm last night. "It is
probably to that we owe the perfection of this day." Then
asked me what of trains going seaward, the boats, the grand
sunset. "Certainly there must have been a great hegira" and
expressed "a great joy" therein—that "the working classes
seem more and more disposed to make Sunday a day of freedom." Then he reflected: "I, too, more and more, as the years
come and go—as I think, experience, see,—am persuaded towards the confirmation of the Sunday to liberty. I believe in
unplugging the day—in inviting freedom—in having the boys
play their ball, people go to the seaside, boating, fishing, frol-
icking, visiting, the whole air one in fact of a grand spontaneity." I quizzed him: "Then the preachers would denounce you

for espousing a Continental Sabbath: that is their great bug-bear." He laughed, but said: "Yes, that—I do favor a Continental Sabbath, if that must name it." But how about the working men? "It would not injure them. Many of them work anyhow—the boatmen, the car men, the railroaders, the hotel men, others; indeed some of them don't mind it at all—in fact, would rather work. There should be some arrangement anyhow which would pay half as much again—or double—for Sunday work. It is so in the departments at Washington. The government is very liberal in its treatment of the clerks—has been known to pay double, treble, day's pay for night work." I spoke of O'Connor's statement to me that he had done much overwork. W. then: "That is very probable; I know O'Connor so well, that easily verifies itself to me. O'Connor was a worker much like poor Pearson there in New York—a man occupying a great position, knowing certain complicated things had to be done, and persuaded that he, he alone, was the man to do it—the only man who could do it." And his casual reference to Pearson enforced some energetic reflection. "Poor fellow! one of the invaluable officers—the right man in the right place (too rarely the case nowadays)—and so to die in harness! So young, too! only 45. It is the bitterest sarcasm possible on the Harrison administration—Harrison the scalawag who was and is, I have no doubt!—That this man, continued by Cleveland, a political enemy,—purely because he was what he was, fit and honest to the core—should have been removed now at this stage of the new administration. But it is of a piece with Harrison— the shit-ass! God damn 'im!—and no more than need have been expected. I never had any faith in him, in his course!" And he further said: "Pearson seems to have been sensitive, too— high strung, proud: and this removal affected his condition. Think of the man, too, appointed in his stead!—a man appointed for political reasons wholly—a good enough fellow perhaps in his way, but after all of the class more concerned for the 2 to 10 thousand-a-year than anything else: a man like thousands of others." Here he paused a moment or so, continuing however: "I was trying to think of someone here in Camden to whom to compare him. I don't know—the Curley's perhaps. I know them—pleasant enough, good natured, with a hand—even a power—in politics, but of intelligence, information, nothing whatsoever—no real ability at all." America was stronger than the curse of this business and would of course survive it, but it was a lamentable experience enough, anyhow.

Monday, April 22, 1889

10.45 A.M. W. reading Press. At once said: "The best news of all is, the Danmark!" Adding: "So after all they are safe— not a person drowned. Oh! what a relief that is to know!" Had indeed been picked up, as the paper predicted, by the Missouri. The day cooler. He remarked it. Did not complain of his condition. Looked better. Said: "In my mail this morning there was a letter from the Doctor." And no word from O'Connor? "Nothing direct—but a letter from Mrs. O'Connor which the Doctor encloses with his. The Doctor's note contains nothing significant. But read for yourself." And as I did so he ran along in comment. "He has the Stedman letter—accepts it." I said: "I am glad—I was afraid he would not." And W.: "I am glad also." Bucke had also received Herald and was quite energetic in decrying the "bogus" Hartmann matter. Said W.: "Yes—Doctor sees through it. Anyone would. Hartmann, his writing, his thinking—the whole mess of him—is a bad egg!" W. added: "That is the long and short of it—as Abe Lincoln said when asked to do something for somebody—'I can't do anything for him—he is already a bad egg!'" How did he account for Herald's acceptance of such stuff? "It is not hard to explain. The Herald is sold to the extent of 60 or 70 or 80 thousand copies—maybe more: it is immaterial; each copy is read by 2 or 3 people. These people are of the mass— not discriminating—not literary—are more or less fond of a

sensation: this constituency must be catered to, catered for—
and there you have it!" But was that excuse? "I do not state
it as excuse—only explanation." But surely Walsh would have
known that was humbuggery? That might be, but W. insisted
still that that was not the question that entered.

Asked me if I thought Brown would understand the sheet of
instructions as to printing he had sent awhile ago? "If he does
not, I should set to work and make him a sketch of it—a more
definite one." I am to see Brown today.

5.50 P.M. W. sitting by open middle window, reading Lippincott's, which had come today. He looked well, as he usually
does after his dinner, and talked vigorously. In front of him
his empty wine-bottle. Why did he not send it up to Harned
to be refilled? He deprecated that—"I am ashamed to do so."

Questioned me about my work at Ferguson's today—spoke
particularly of inside margin for book. I had Brown prepare
a sheet, indicating his procedure. W. inspected, was pleased,
except as saying as to margin as above: "I do not wish to lay
it down as something for him absolutely to follow, but to suggest to him that he should have a care on that point. I have
myself had so much difficulty just there—so much of experience with books which, to be seen, had to be ripped out of the
cover, so"—indicating by a motion of the hands, "and you
have too, without a doubt—that now we have this matter in
our own grip, we may see that it is done right." Ferguson
had given me a copy of The Inland Printer to show to W. for
its typographical beauty. It had been rolled, and stubbornly
resisted being flattened out. W. reflected: "In our printing we
will bye and bye come to make up with reference to the
mails." To fold was "bad enough," to roll was "despicable." I
called his attention to a photo-engraving therein. "I was looking at that," he replied, "it seemed extraordinarily fine: I had
that in my mind to say at the start. And the letter-press, too."
The picture was of a group of tally-hos. W. remarked: "Such
things we don't have at all in this country except as importa-

tions. They are thoroughly English—seem adopted some-what in New York. But only adopted, don't originate." Too much of our life made up so. We don't enough suit our works to our own surroundings and exigencies.

I told W. I had received a letter from Stedman. He was at once greatly interested—urged me to read it—which I sat down and started to do. But there was suddenly started up a great racket out of doors: it was just six o'clock: the factory whistles were blowing in all quarters of the town. W. reached forward to close the window: could not do it. "I am a little deaf," he explained. I went towards him and lowered the sash. "Now," he suggested, "now let us hear it." So I read the letter, as follows, very deliberately:

April 19th 1889
Good Friday

Dear Mr. Traubel,

In response to your kind letter of the 17th, I will only remark that this is the second *private* letter which I have received from you within a year or two, regretting the *public* appearance of alleged interviews with Walt Whitman, which have not been modified with equal publicity.

The special expressions referred to in the two private letters have certainly been most ingeniously cruel, & recall to mind the predicament of the rejected lover.

"To be sure she'd a right to dissemble her love,
  But *why* did she kick me down stairs!"

At a time when a few of us are drawing so very near to our old Bard, in the sunset of life, when the roughnesses of life are over, it is at least a pity that color should still be given, even by vagrant interviewers, to the charge that he *expresses* unkind, if not unfair, judgments of his brother-writers. I suppose we all of us think that many of our clan are donkeys or popinjays in their minds & methods, but we do not feel it an imperative duty to *say* so.

Very truly yrs.
E. C. Stedman

W. was more and more interested, the deeper I got into it: laughed heartily at the couplet, but said it was new to him: and yet was serious enough, regarding the tone of the letter as a whole. When I had completely finished, he exclaimed: "He's mad! He's mad!" I was grieved: had been ever since receiving the letter in the early afternoon, and I could see he was as well. He looked out the window, across at the northern sky, then at me. "I do not think I am prepared to make a public disavowal of it—I have never done so; in all my life, from the very first, I have avoided that." Hartmann's offense was undoubted and heinous. That he felt as deeply as any. "He is Moncure Conway multiplied by five," he said. Yet it was not to Stedman alone that the trouble accrued. "I, too, must suffer it. It is unkind and unjust to me that at a time of such particular friendliness, generosity, in Stedman, I should be put in such a position of vulgar indifference and worse." I said: "It is unfortunate, too, that the worst paragraph, the severest, in the whole column, was that about Stedman." W.: "Yes, that is unhappy. But even about Holmes, it is bad enough. I never said that of him—I never thought of him in that way. I never thought much of him, it is true, but anything I could have thought at any time would have been different from what is put down for me there." As to the paragraph about Harrison, while—"I never have met Hartmann since Harrison has been up, in"— nevertheless—"I do not so much regret that. Because I think very little of Harrison anyway. The only trouble is, this opinion of Harrison is of late growth—more induced or solidified by recent events than any long gone." He did not fully endorse my insistence that the Herald should have penetrated the horrible vulgarity of that column. But he did say: "There is a whole host of writers for the press—there always have been a host of 'em, though never, I think, so wholesale in their methods as now—to whom the truth was of no account, to whom the only things of account were, to create interest and get pay for it! There was a world of this work done in Dryden's time."—

"I have no doubt, as I have told you, that this is the same stuff that Hartmann offered Kennedy, but which K. was too cute to be fooled with—which he sent me on here, inquiring of its authenticity, and which I returned at once with a negative." And in a tone of pathetic regret: "That is the fat of it—that is the whole story," adding as to Stedman: "Time may perhaps mollify him: let us hope it will." He had himself suffered so much from misreports, now for 30 and more years, the list had got to be a long, almost tragic, one. He was pained to have this last happen—but what could be done? I had from the first felt W. would make no public matter of this.

There came a considerable silence. Then he questioned me: "And the Missouri—what of her? Has she come?" Just the few minutes before, in crossing the river I had seen the Missouri being put into her wharf. W. greatly interested: "Is she a fine boat? Good sized? as big as the boats of the American line?—the Ohio, the Pennsylvania?" And then he said: "It is a glorious story all through. The Captain—what is his name? I don't know what will be the future of him—of his exploit, but it occurs to me he will be made immortal." "Many, many years ago, when I was a young fellow, there was a parallel case—a case parallel in some particulars—a grand rescue. It was a thing that affected me greatly at the time—affected me by day, by night, for weeks. Our government was sending some soldiers around the Horn—five or six hundred of them. They started off—were gone several days—probably some hundreds of miles—when a storm—it was said, the worst storm ever known—sprang up. The boat was a good one—among the best ever built—but things went wrong, and the whole business was in imminent peril. There had been a sort of house built on board—on deck—in which several hundred soldiers were housed. An affair to add to accommodations. A big wave—or big wave on big wave—rose, dashed, literally swept the whole house away, soldiers and all—and every man in it was drowned. The situation grew desperate—there were hundreds remaining—even women and children; the government allowed this, the wives of soldiers." W.'s manner, brief, sketchy, was intense: "And now the grandeur of the story. When things were at their worst, another boat appears on the scene—it was called The Three Bells—named so after three brothers Bell, somewhere in Scotland." W. described the Captain—"a homely, stubbly fellow—but brave—circumspect to the utmost": and he had "signalled the sufferers" had "put up—chalked on a board—one message after another, declaring he would stick to 'em; and he did, along on the seas for several days, fast, never fluctuating, now losing a moment's sight of them, then regaining, till the storm was over, the waters calm." Then he had made the rescue, "brought them up to New York." "It was here I met him. The town was full of the story of it." Had he ever written anything about it? "No—it was not necessary: papers, everything, were full of it. And the town would have lionized him, but he objected. One day, on one of the Fulton ferry boats—I was so often on 'em, and knew all the boys who worked 'em—I was up in the pilot house, with Captain Brace, when he suddenly called to me 'By God! there comes Captain' "—here W. stopped—"Oh! the Captain of The Three Bells—what was his name—what was his name? I cannot recall it now—yet it will come, bye and bye, without a doubt. Was it Gibson—Captain Gibson?"—And he asked me: "Is the story at all known to you?" It was not. Then he went on: "Anyhow, Captain Brace turned to me, called: 'By God! there comes Captain Gibson!'—if that was the name. He could not leave the wheelhouse at the time, but he sent word down that if the Captain would not go ashore on the other side, would wait till he, Brace, had seen him, it would be good of him, &c. I was all interest myself and when the boat was over and fast, Captain Brace went down stairs, I down with him. Then we met the man—had a short talk—not more than five minutes in all. It was a happy incident for me—I have always vividly remembered it. The man was thoroughly Scotch—

71

bushy thick hair, round head, stub nose, ruddy color, strong compact body—easy, plain, modest, not a trace in him of self consciousness; altogether the remarkable self-contained man you would have thought necessary to the event." W. said he had been as never before or since, except now, awake and interested in such an act of heroism. And speaking of the emotion everywhere prevalent then as now: "It is the touch of the human: it is the circle of the great unfathomed electric something in nature which makes us one, glorifies us all." My notes show for a week and more past his own dwelling upon the subject. "I suppose the papers will be full of it tomorrow—full of it— part truth, a good part fiction, only that this is an event that baffles the reporter-imagination—that needs no aids, no bolsterings."

Tuesday, April 23, 1889

10.30 A.M. A carriage at the door. W. had a couple of visitors of whose names Ed was uncertain. After a little while went in and found W.'s callers to be Will Carleton, who read here in one of the churches last night, and Curtis of the Ladies' Home Journal. I was amused when W. introduced me as "Horace Tribell." The visitors had already arisen to go. Carleton spoke with W. briefly of the 1887 reception in New York and his absence (enforced) therefrom—a regret coming after by letter, to which W. said: "I think I remember— it came here." He had known C. as "among the absentees." Carleton expressed some hope of seeing W. in New York again but W. was dubious, said: "If I could get out on the pavement only—that would be a great triumph." Adding: "I do not anticipate recuperating." Carleton is rather a handsome fellow —a good body and splendid complexion—sunniness put into flesh. They talked a little about Frank Williams, to whom Curtis referred as evidently in mourning for someone. W. said: "I know Mrs. Williams well, and Frank Williams too, the husband"—adding as to the mourning—"It is not any of the children? I know them all. Frank has large connections." Curtis referred to his own paper, of which W. remembered somewhat when I mentioned that it was the paper Ferguson so largely printed. When they had gone W. turned to me in amused comment on the paper's enormous circulation. "It just shows, a big thing is spread the whole earth over and we know nothing about it."

Rather despondent about his health. "It's nothing extra— not really good at all." And as he looked significantly at his fire in the stove: "It is much colder this morning isn't it?"— seemingly much surprised that I replied in the negative. Had been reading the papers, specifically what is therein about the Danmark incident. Wishes me to see Billstein and get him a few copies of the three-quarter pictures at once. "I want to see them before having the whole edition printed." Added that he meant to have a hundred extra printed anyhow for his private circulation. "To make assurance doubly sure," he said, he would make up a dummy for Brown, so the method of arrangement "could not possibly be mistaken."

As to Disraeli's description of Gladstone—"A sophisticated rhetorician, inebriated with the exuberance of his own verbosity"—W. said: "the damning weakness of that is in its elaborate making-up." Letter from Mr. Coates acknowledging the Sarrazin sheets, "Which," he said, "I am glad to have." W. gratified—said he always "warmed up towards these people."

Evening 6.45 P.M. W. sitting by open window reading Lippincott's. Asked after "new things," and wondered what I had done in town today. Pleased that Billstein would have us half a dozen of the three-quarter plates by Thursday. Of himself said: "I have practically done nothing—seen nobody: not a stranger the whole day." I spoke up: "Not even Will Carleton?" W. smiled: "Oh!—I forgot him. Yes, Will Carleton." I asked him if his days were long—if one day did not often seem two. "I do not know about that; I know today has been a bad day—bad indeed. I have been seriously troubled with the cold in my head—it has given me a fluffy, stuffy, congested feeling" —here he made a funny circle with his arms—"and carried a sense of being that size and shape!" Spoke of the Missouri-Danmark incident. "I did not go into the Press account; it was too long, too full: I took up a shorter, compacter statement— the statement of the Record. Even of that, did not enter into elaborately, studiedly." But the event was "deeply impressive" and "however little" he had read, "no one's thought had been more awake" to its importance.

Referred to Tom Davidson's seeming belief that Dante was "the greatest poet that ever lived." W. considered: "I know that is sometimes believed, sometimes said, but to me the statement is not conclusive." And reinforcing himself with Carlyle, Davidson said again that Dante's was "the serenest"—"the most earnest" book ever written. W. again: "This I do not believe at all." Then acknowledged Dante's high place. "The translations have been many, and, curiously, all good ones— remarkably good ones, too. I know them all—Longfellow's well. But it seems to me that greatest among them—indisputably so—is John Carlyle's, Thomas Carlyle's Doctor brother's." As to Davidson's apparent belief that in order for our modern world to get properly adjusted it would yet have to go back to the Bonaventuras, Dantes, Aristotles, of history, W. said: "The sufficient disproof of that is in the undoubted existence today of as sweet, high, enclosing, natures as ever existed in any past age. It is to be remembered of Bonaventura that he was a picked man—one of myriads, one of unknown millions. In our life today exists as good samples as the best that old times afford. Take the average of men—take measure of the great qualities in what is called the mass of our population, —and you find in fact an elevation never achieved before. And this despite all the acknowledged bad, the evils, the poisonous tendencies. And this, too, as applying not only to worldly situations, conditions, so-called, but what we call gifts, benefits, of mind, the spiritual endowment." This W. considered "remarkable among remarkable considerations." And even among exceptional men, we can match if not excel the past. I mentioned Emerson and Darwin. "Yes—these, and indeed, more than these. In science,—which is the sun of the system— leaders in all branches—first-raters all: not an avenue left unoccupied, not an unwilling heart in all the group: and all of them devoted, unfailing, working on and on irrespective of everything but to find what is the true." I asked W.: "And don't you think that ultimate?" He affirmed fervently: "It is indeed—there is nothing beyond that. No age of any land ever had such a record of such devotion as ours—not one: and you may pick all history for it": as indeed "no age has presented such a spectacle of the elevating of the masses."

Reference to the Danmark again. W. asked me about the reception to the Missouri's Captain in Philadelphia Maritime Exchange at noon today. "He seems to be a veritable Johnny Bull. And my man I told you about yesterday, he was a bonnie Scotchman. These things whack our prejudices." Then of prohibition defeat in Massachusetts yesterday—40,000 against prohibition amendment to Constitution. W. enjoyed it. "I see they have their nose badly knocked out of joint." Asked somewhat after approaching election on same question (16th June) in Philadelphia. "It is a curious mania and will have its day." And then he fragmentarily spoke of old experiences and thoughts, apropos. "Did I ever tell you of D'Avezac, my old French friend there in New York? It was long ago that I knew him—I was a very young fellow—but I can see him now, just as he was, with all the aroma of life upon him—and such a life! D'Avezac was a French Radical—too Radical to stay over there. He was a soldier, with fine human qualities. He was elected to the Assembly from one of the districts of the city. At the time there was such a stir going on—much such a stir as we see about us now. He got up one day in the Legislature and said: "Meester Speakear, I have ze pleasaire to propose"

—W. going on in inimitable style with detail—"and so he went over a series: hereafter lying shall be prohibited, shall be no more; hereafter adultery, being bad, shall be absolutely abolished; hereafter all forms of chicanery, fraud, shall go, be stopped, as decreed by legislative enactment. The Speaker referred to this as 'nonsense,' but D'Avezac, seriously sarcastic, said: "No, it was not nonsense—not more so than other laws proposed and enacted: that these were all good things, we all acknowledged them so, and if the law could cure one, why not all?" I asked W.: "That is historic?" and he responded: "Oh! absolutely so—that and more too. D'Avezac—that is his name, he spells it so"—going over the letters. "I knew him well. He was very popular then in New York—dined, feted, received, addressed—and altogether an inimitable man!" W. spoke of "his bald head," his "significant individuality." Then: "And I have had wonderful good luck anyhow in my life to have met a number of such originals—not men of usual build, of usual ways, but men inherently set apart, a world each for himself. There was Flynn, too, my Irish friend"— spelled his name, also. "And Count Gurowski—I have spoken to you of him. Never more remarkable men, notable, anywhere." And none of them ever written of? "Hardly—the Count perhaps a little—the others not at all." I suggested: "Why don't you note them?" He assented: "That would be a good idea, wouldn't it?—to touch them off with a few lines— a sort of instantaneous photograph. It would make an interesting, a noble list. I don't believe I could find a better thing to do these days than just that. It is interesting, too: all these fellows were of foreign birth. Flynn was something in the noblesse line—had had great monies. I used to have the notion —I have spoken of it to you—that all the great photographs needed to be made in America, but I have come to discover after all that the best are produced across the sea." We had this to remember—at least in a measure—of men, too—of the sea-captain heroics, of the D'Avezac-Flynn-Gurowski logic.

Courage is international. He had himself clipped a bit from an English paper commenting on the heroism of American sailors at Samoa, and pasted it on a card. There it was now on a chair. Human nature fairly vibrated with the honor belonging to such men and such events. And when I spoke of America as "greater than any or all, her own or other that ever were conceived," W. assented with directness and fervor, but said it was a fact too little recognized and too little cherished when seen.

Wednesday, April 24, 1889

10.30 A.M. W. reading paper. The day fine and much warmer. His fire burning brightly. Did not seem conscious of a too-great heat. Reported his condition: "only so-so." Yet looked well, acted well.

Said: "I notice that the Captain of the Missouri is being much feted, celebrated. Last night there was even a poem for him—and a good one, too." He looked up his Press and pointed lines out to me—a plain recitative, with no pretense of art—its human touch taking hold of him. "The Captain sails away for Baltimore today, don't he? I am glad to see he bears himself well—worthily." Then he proceeded: "The caves of ocean bear many a gem—many a poem as good as the good, —perhaps the best—and never seen!"

"And what news have you?" he asked, after a pause, and to my "nothing" he added: "nor have I anything. My mail was small enough: a letter from Bucke—a short one—in which he says his two brothers are still there. But not a word from Washington or anywhere else!" I picked up from the floor a brick-colored pamphlet; "The Church Catholic," by B. F. C. Costelloe M.A. I asked W. if that was our Costelloe, and he said: "Yes—that's the fellow. He's a good Catholic. Take the book along. I don't want it—I have not read it and never shall —I never read such stuff." And again to me: "Don't bring it back again—I don't want to see it again." "I never did read matter of that sort—never cared a paper of pins for it—it seemed to me of no importance whatever." He was sure Mary Costelloe accepted nothing "the like of that." "She is free of it —must be much like us. But the man, the husband, accepts the Church. I have seen him, like him."—"I suppose clergymen— even the most liberal—read very much like that—all sorts of screeds." I stayed there but for a few minutes.

Evening 7.40 W. sitting in his room, the fire burning brightly, the odor of wood-smoke pretty thick. It is hard to comprehend that anybody can without suffering remain in such temperature. Yet neither heat nor smoke were obvious to him. He asked me: "Is it too warm?" and of the smoke: "Oh —is that so? That should be attended to—I know it is not good." He had been reading. Did not, I thought, look very well; but said there had been no change, that he felt reasonably good, that at any rate he was better than yesterday.

He had made up the dummy for Brown. "I was going to propose that you go to Brown yourself and see that he understands it all, but I suppose you intended that anyhow." As I had—my engagement being for tomorrow afternoon. "The corrections," W. said, "are very few indeed—not more than 3 or 4—really a mere pretense, so to say—and none of them urgent." I sometimes get a little anxious lest the book will not get out by the date specified. W. has had such a bad time the past month our work has been often interrupted. The photos for mounting still remain half-collected. A few more days cut out—a bad spell of some kind, disabling him—and we are done for. He remarked this in effect himself this evening. As to "news" today, he said he had none. Everything unwontedly quiet.

I went to the Von Bülow concert at the Academy this afternoon. A great, more or less fashionable audience, but the performance wholly simple and unique: The curtain down, Von B. appearing unattended—appearing with hat (a sailor flat hat) and gloves on—these nervously thrown off on a small round table against the curtain. Two or three times in the course of the 2 hours that followed, Von B. got up, took hat and gloves and left, returning in a few minutes and resuming the programme. The whole subject, Beethoven, and the playing absolutely without note. To me a marvellous and beautiful occasion. I described it to W., perhaps with some enthusiasm. He seemed greatly attracted: questioned me till I had imparted about all the details I had to give. "Was it as informal as that?" he asked at one moment. Afterward: "It must have been a grand performance." Then: "what sort of a personal appearance did he put on?—was he young or old?" W. talked of orchestral concerts, too: of what he knew of them in his youth. "They were not so big—not so elaborate—as ours, but produced, I should say, the same emotionalistic, artistic, results." He felt that "much of the old music was written with reference to small bands, anyway." Still, "I do not sneeze at the big bands—at mass: it is not to be dismissed; the spectacular is not to be sneered away—it has its own effects to secure. Indeed, our modern performances are very great—very great." He added: "I can see how it would be advisable—perhaps indispensable—to have the Wagner music produced through the powerful resources of a great band"—but "the old music was written for small groups and these strings, mostly." "The best orchestral performance—at least one of the best, hitting for me the utmost point of excellence—was by a band of 7 or 8—Gaertner's band there in Philadelphia— a Beethoven night in the foyer of the Academy. This was not in the big audience room—not to a great audience." He discussed the question "only on the side of its necessity." He doubted if it was "necessary to the proper rendering, interpretation, of a great work" that it should be submitted to "aggregated instrumentalities." We talked a little of Beethoven's 7th Symphony—its first movement—its probable greater rendering by a great force of strings than by one instrument such as a piano. W. acknowledged: "There is force in that—great force."

I did not prolong my stay. W. not in good talking mood. In

such cases I never linger. He asked that I come down tomorrow forenoon to get book for Brown.

Thursday, April 25, 1889

10.20 A.M. W. reading his Press. The day much milder. One window thrown wide open. "I supposed it was dusty. And it looks like rain? We ought to be glad to have it come." There are three windows, all opening north, in his room. The west window is rarely opened—not even curtain thrown up—except in warmest weather. Between this and the center window against the wall is a big round table. It is on this table he eats his meals, facing west, and it is the center window by which he sits when not doing anything. The third window (the east) has his big square table nearly against it; and this with a box underneath, and chairs about him, is the repository of his working materials. When working he wheels from his center window, his left side against the square table, his back towards the light. Takes a pad on his knee—always writes that way. The east window he will sometimes raise, and fix the blinds for light, but his main dependence is always on the center window. He never throws the shutters open. The blinds he will put at the down-angle if he wishes to look into the street, and at the horizontal or up, if simply studying the sky, or ruminating. Health he reports "about the same." And then: "No news—except this postal from Nellie." Rather bad reports still from O'Connor—his vomitings and sickness thereto continuing. W. said: "I shall mail the postal to Doctor tonight—this afternoon." And reflecting: "It is a sad report, all around: it shows not only that something is badly out of kilter but that something is absolutely gone—absolutely."

"From unprecedented reasons," he said further along, "the last number of The Critic came Saturday morning." Did not know if he had sent it away or not. Had noted therein this from Gosse: "Even in mere rhapsodies, divested of all real verse form, such as the effusions of Ossian and of Walt Whitman, there is a right way of reading and a wrong." But it had "passed in and out" without impressing him as of any importance. He had prepared me a bundle containing sketch (dummy) of book. "You will go into the press room yourself and see that Brown understands?" The bundle he had endorsed. Is always definite. His sheet of instructions enclosed, wonderfully clear. Corrections only 5, all told. Asked me: "What of Brown? Haven't we two Browns?" When I described Brown, agent for the Photo-Engraving Co., he seemed greatly engaged and amused, whether by his fat or another matter—I do not know.

Evening 7.50 W. reading a volume of Stedman's big work. It proves of absorbing interest to him. But tonight he did not look well and did not feel well. His room almost insufferably hot. The temperature had anyhow grown higher in the afternoon, which, aiding his fire, made his room almost suffocating. I was in and saw Brown this afternoon. He cannot put the book on press till Tuesday next, anyhow. W. somewhat impatient at this, but must, of course, submit. But Brown explains: "I know this is thin paper and that Mr. Whitman is very particular; I have a certain press and a certain man whom I wish to put on the job." Brown is sure the printing can all be done up next week. W. remarked: "I know there is no time to be lost. We must not let Oldach delay us this time. If we fail to get the book out by the date set, it will be ruin!"

Billstein printed me a few copies of the McKay three-quarter length, which I gave to W. He examined them quite critically, as he had before, and said: "I like it—like it well. It is a little spotted—I notice that—but in effect, result, is all right—entirely satisfactory." He discussed the illustrations for the book. "I have counted six, irrespective of the Sarony picture." I went over the list—for the instant could make but five. W. thereupon (tallying with fingers): "There are six—

81

I have the list here somewhere. There's the three-quarter length, the one we have just been looking at; the three-quarter steel; the Linton; the butterfly; the seventieth year." Here he hesitated an instant, as I had done—then suddenly: "Oh! the Gutekunst picture! that makes the sixth. I knew I had that number hard and fast. What do you think? Is that enough?" The Sarony loss was one he felt bitterly, because he had absolutely possessed at one time many more than he could now find or had ever used. As to the steel, it was his first idea to have a new printing, but now said: "I have enough here— have counted off 305." I urged proceeding more declaredly. He promised: "I can let you have the photos tomorrow"— those for mounting—"if you want them." I explained: "They will cost more if you only have 300 instead of a thousand. I got my estimate on a thousand." W. then: "Well, I don't know but I'll have a thousand anway." Might have some mounted even if not for use in the book. Spoke then once more of the Sarony loss. "The 305 and more I certainly had once." Had it been Duckett who used any? "I must not say who— only that they are probably stolen. I have had many things purloined, stolen, from the rooms here—books, pamphlets, papers, clothing, pictures." W. paused and then reflected as if greatly for himself: "I had fully six or seven pairs of gloves —choice gloves given to me—gloves of some value; attractive, too, evidently, to others. I had also half a dozen handkerchiefs, presents, some of them silk; choice, fine, beautiful; they are gone, too. Some of these things were souvenirs, some not. I had a picture—probably so big"—measuring with his arms: "What they called an Italian chromo—a figure piece. It cost 8 or 9 dollars—I paid that for it—it was worth 4 or 5 times that. It too, was spirited away—is gone—utterly gone." And so, summing up: "There then, for instance—you can see where I stand. I know I am a great forgetter, mislayer: I hesitate to explain the missing things this way till all other explanations are exhausted."

I rose and started off. W. said: "You will be down in the morning? My head is in a bad state tonight. I must not worry it with anything at all." Rather pale—and so I left him. Wagner and Taylor have sent in notice of approaching expiration of insurance (May 8th).

Friday, April 26, 1889

10.45 A.M. W. sitting by open window. Evidently better today. Said: "The rain helps me along with much else." Had "nothing further from Washington—in fact, nothing further at all, except a letter for an autograph" and "one of these yesterday, too." Had made up the butterfly picture for me to take, putting on outside of package "photos to be mounted directions inside" (no punctuation) and below "from Walt Whitman 328 Mickle Street Camden N. J." "What is the name of the party?" he asked me: and when I shook my head, not remembering, he said: "I left a place open there to insert it, but it can't be put there if you don't know it." The "directions inside," written in pencil, and pinned to a piece of cardboard and a specimen page of November Boughs was as follows (I observe its punctuation or lack of it):

Attached to
This is the size of the leaf and the page—cut your paper to the size of the leaf—mount the photo on abt the same thickness &c this card—of course the photo has not to exceed the printed page size—if necessary trim it to keep in for that purpose (it may be required a little)—
Of course I shall expect you to make a good handsome little job of it
  W W

He had divided the 305 in six packages of 50 and one of 5—each of them carefully tied up and endorsed (changed simply as to quantity) in effect as on the brown sheet which enclosed them all:

305 copies
(three hundred and five)
Phillips & Taylors
Butterfly Photo
sitting ⅔ᵈ length with hat
outdoor rustic

As will be noted he is not punctilious on the score of commas &c in these little messages, but is always singularly clear and explicit. When he gives me a package, I always examine it minutely, and thoroughly master what he wants done, myself, before delivery. But, as he puts it, "for safety's sake, to give assurance to assurance," he addresses packages, often, and minutely describes contents and purposes, as if they were to be simply delivered—sent by boy, mail, or express—"without a spoken word."

This noon I received from Bucke a postal which read:

Asylum, London—Ont—24 Ap. 89—

Have just written W. urging that he go to Johns Hopkins Hospital to live. See the letter. Let me know how he takes the proposal & what you think of it. Best accounts from fund. The meter bus. looks bigger and bigger.

Your friend R. M. Bucke—

When I entered W.'s room, I found him looking over the Stedman work again. "It is a measureless mine." I did not wait long before questioning if he had received a letter from Bucke today. Did not till later mention my own message. He answered: "Yes—and quite a long letter, too. What do you think he urges me to do?" I did not answer—he paused slightly. "He proposes that I go into the Johns Hopkins Hospital—urges it strongly." Here he reached forward and got a letter from the chair in front of him. "I don't know but you'd better take the letter itself." And he then resumed: "In last Sunday's Tribune which Tom brought in to me was an account of the new hospital to be opened at Johns Hopkins in a couple of weeks. It was that which stimulated, excited, his letter. He advises that I migrate there. They say it is to be one of the finest, if not the very finest, institution of the sort in the world." We talked over the place and the advisable course somewhat, but in a general, non-personal way that struck me as peculiar in both of us. "For the present," W. then said, "I have nothing to think, say about it: if to be considered, considered: if not, not." He questioned me a little about the University hospital appointments, size etc. "Wondered" if O'Connor would be better served and more content somewhere "so surveilled." "Doctor returned me the slip, with reference to my future use of it—it is there in the note." The portions of B's letter relating to this read as follows:

"'I have the Tribune you sent me containing an account of the Johns Hopkins hospital. Walt, if I were in your fix I would think seriously of going there for the next six months or a year (or even longer; but that would depend) as a private patient. They might do you good (they will have the best skill going) and if they did not you would be more comfortable there than anywhere else perhaps in the world. If you would think well of this I would go to Baltimore—make all the arrangements and then take you from Camden to the Hospital. There is no palace in Europe so comfortable for a sick or half sick man as this hospital would be. Think this over seriously (it is worth it) show this letter to Horace and talk it over with him (but H. does not half realize as I do the boon such a change would be to you)." Then in a "P.S.": "I enclose the cutting that you may look over it again if you feel to. The more I think of it the more I think you decidedly ought to go." And still again, in an "N.B."—"I do not suppose the expense would be much more than the present subsidy but if it is we can easily get more money." W. "for the present anyway" had "no inclination to make changes." But would not flout any advice: "only weigh it."

I took the photos through the fearful rain to the Arch Street concern. W. asked: "Did they understand my note?" Asking additionally: "And what is the name of the party—what sort of a fellow do you deal with?" I laughed and joked with him about his hunger for details, and he laughed, too. "I don't know whether too much or not, but I like to know my men—who they are, what they do. You will bring me a card next time?" And again: "Is this the party you went to to inquire about the photographic album for me?" No. "Ah! anyway, this fellow keeps coming don't he?" And after my affirmative: "If I could get a book to suit me, into which I could put the pictures to suit me, I would be happy. I wonder if it could be done?—a book about this size?"—measuring about a foot square. "Not necessarily larger—or larger at all." He had a great mess of pictures around and had often thought to collect them. Thought I could very well order of Billstein the pictures we needed. "The three-quarter length you brought me last night I want 300 or so of, in the small size, then enough to make up 400 in the size he used for the loose copies." He "wondered" about "the 70th year" plate—if he had it or Dave, I saying, the latter, though a little uncertain whether or not returned, now it had been so long. But W.: "I am sure it is on the table there."

Spoke of his condition as "nothing to brag of" though "in no way worse" than yesterday. When Ed came in for mail, he found several letters and packages. To know if E. gets all, W. invariably enumerates what is there, and E. after him, however distant W. may be from the pile at the moment. W. had read the London World paragraph in last Critic paying tribute to Whittier, saying of America "she has given us a goodly number of poets whose words the world will not willingly let die," and naming Bryant, Longfellow, Lowell, Holmes and Whittier but never W. W. But W. would make no comment.

I went in out of the tempestuous rain this afternoon with Kemper and searched the Mercantile Library shelves till I found the Appleton Biographical Dictionary of which W. had inquired some time ago; reading therein the Whitman piece and copying such passages as appeared to me would key the thing to him. He was amused as I had been at some of its biographical errors. "You will leave this with me?" he asked. Did not read while I stayed. As to Hunter's authorship of it: "I suppose that is uncertain?" We talked of the picture: a sitting, hatless picture, chin resting on hand. W. said: "I know it—it was this, wasn't it?"—putting himself into a position that strikingly carried out the picture. "How was it done?— was it artistically of any value?—strongly, easily done?" On the chair near by a Sarony picture—new to me: W. hatted, sitting among accounting bills: I thought fine. He said of it: "I think that is the only copy I have: in looking for other things I found that." In looking about at the Mercantile I had hit upon Lloyd C. Saunders' "Celebrities of the Century" (Cassell, 1887), in which H. Buxton Forman had an exquisite little statement to make of W. W. and his literary position. W. had "forgotten" whether he had seen it or not. The book itself was new to him, he thought. "Probably Dr. Bucke called my attention to it at the time. You know Forman and Doctor were long ago great friends there in England? Forman is very sturdy, too—very willing to avow himself for me." I remarked the "richness" of the notice, and W.: "That is him— he comes naturally by it." He well knew "the shape and extent" of H. B. F.'s friendship, even if this had gone unseen. "I would not attempt to copy any of it" he advised—"it would be a job;—it is not worth while."

Saturday, April 27, 1889

10.45 A.M. On mounting the stairs met W. just coming from the bathroom door. He laughed: "Oh! Horace! and just in time to help me across the ravine, too!" He was not particularly steady, though going part of the way alone. To my remark, "You walk pretty well, after all," he smiled—took hold of bed and table on his way to the chair. "Pretty well? Yes, as you see!"—with a good natured irony. He spoke at once his solicitude at the weather. "I hope it is not going to last over the celebration—to have a wet, sloppy, slumpy day, would have been—would be—bad indeed: would spoil things effectually." But still, "our best hope for Monday, Tuesday and Wednesday, is, that we are having rain—hard rain—now."

I asked him if Baker had stopped in last night? I had met him near the ferry. "I did not see him—he did not stop in on me. I see he is about to graduate." Then asked me what I thought of the prospects of his settlement and where would he settle? And when learning, probably somewhere in the North-west, said: "It seems to me I should recommend it to young doctors—should observe it myself: that for a couple of years after graduating—after leaving the schools: it would be a wise course to stay in one of the big cities—in Philadelphia, for a doctor—stay in the swim of the big, best doctors, practices, publications. It would make up a priceless experience. One of the great elements in the character of the best doctors is unknowingness—to unknow, unload. Indeed, I think this might as well be said of all professional men—of the literary men, of the scientists, even: the quality of reserve, modesty." "It is my invariable test of a doctor, his not too-great certainty. I have had enough experience with them, or near them, to know just what is meant by that." Referred to Washington experiences. "I have known Doctors there—one Doctor in particular—by whom the best things have been done in deference to their modesty. I remember one case in particular there—a case in which all known resources had failed; the doctor had given the thing up—I suggested so and so—he weighed it—said to me: 'While I see nothing for it, neither can I see any objection' and he willingly adopted what I had suggested, and, as it proved, successfully." Huxley had somewhere spoken of

Medicine as "chiefly experimental"—"and," said W.: "I believe it is—four-fifths of it!" "There was a celebrated doctor, surgeon, somewhere, a long time ago, who always insisted, we must not treat this fever, what-not, simply as fever, for itself alone, but treat the whole man—not a bit of him forgotten!" "And that was very wise—very. I had a doctor once who wished to dose me with quinine—he thought it would help my head trouble. I don't know but I took a dose or several doses of it. But finally he saw, as I saw from the first, that while quinine for one section might do, quinine for the whole of me would not do at all." "Always, a man has to be treated for all there is of him—his stomach, lungs, legs, head, arms—his idiocrasies, idiosyncrasies—not a shred of him left uncared for." It was "the great doctor" who comprehended this—"no other was truly a doctor"—yet doctors of such an order were "scarce enough."

He talked of Washington—"its malarious tendencies." Was it a distinctively unhealthy city? "I should not say so—at least, Washington itself is not. But beyond Washington, around it, are boggy, swampy, immensities—flats. Potomac superficies—great exposures at the out-tide. Probably no city in the world can beat Washington in respect to this malarial curse. Yet the town direct might be considered a fortunate place—fortunate in its soil—sandy, dry, not boggy or welly at all. I should say that Washington, if it continues to be for 50 years (and I am not so sure that it will), might loom up as a great town. It was well-planned—it was the creation of engineers who were not stinted on the money side—who had great ideas of what the city should be—who made everything, as they say vulgarly, bang up." Did he expect Washington to continue as the Capital? "Not at all—I have not the slightest notion that it will. I have no doubt myself, but by and by the capital will go west—somewhere along the Mississippi—the Missouri: that is the natural play of tendencies: eventually something like this result is inevitable."

WITH WALT WHITMAN IN CAMDEN

On the table in a bottle is a bunch of violets. "They are our own—come out of our yard." Said he had "no mail—no letter —whatever, this morning." Sat a while with the window open, but as he closed it asked: "It has grown markedly cooler, hasn't it?" Afterward deliberately set to work and stirred up his fire—arranging his wood-coals with utmost care and piling new logs on top, soon having a blazing heat.

Gave me back the Appleton sheet—printed herewith: (note absurd mixtures in detail).

WALT WHITMAN, OR WALTER, poet——

His chief work, "Leaves of Grass" (New York, 1855), is a series of poems dealing with moral, social, and political problems, and more especially with the interests involved in 19th century American life and progress. In it he made a new and abrupt departure as to form, casting his thoughts in a mould the style of which is something between rhythmical prose and verse, altogether discarding rhythm and regular meter, but uttering musical thoughts in an unconventional way which is entirely his own. Expecting the opposition and abuse with which his volume was assailed, he speaks of it as a sortie on common literary use and wont, in both spirit and form, adding that a century may elapse before its triumph or failure can be assured. For thirty years Whitman has been correcting and adding to this work, and he says that he looks upon "Leaves of Grass" "now finished, to the end of its opportunities and powers, as my definitive carte visite to the coming generations of the New World, if I may assume to say so." His experiences during this service (1862–5) are vividly recorded in "Drum Taps" (1865) and "Memoranda During the War" (1867). His admirers, especially in England, have been extravagant in their praise of his works, comparing him with the best of the classic writers, and in this country Ralph Waldo Emerson said on the appearance of "Leaves of Grass": "I greet you at the beginning of a great career." On the other hand, the peculiar form of his writings prevents their popularity, and their substance has been widely regarded as of no value. "Leaves of Grass" has been condemned for indecency on account of its outspokenness, and

90

when a complete edition of the work was published (Boston 1881) the Massachusetts authorities objected to its sale in that state on the ground of immorality.

After detailing thus, it goes on to say: "besides the works already mentioned, Whitman has published 'Passage to India' (1870); 'After All, not to Create Only' (1871)"—and goes on to name others that have become part of the complete work, ending with this absurd memorandum " 'November Boughs' (1885); and 'Sands at Seventy' (1888)."

"A selection of his poems, by William M. Rosetti, was published (London, 1868). Besides the complete edition of 'Leaves of Grass' that has been mentioned, another, edited by Prof. Edward Dowden, had since been issued (Glasgow, Scotland)." From Appleton's Biographical Journal. Refers as authorities to O'Connor and Burroughs but no others.

"I read it all—got along very well with it." Had he any idea it had come from Hunter's hand? "Hardly—it is too full of misinformation. If Hunter wrote it, it must have fallen into the hand of the supervising editor before it got into type; you know, there's always a mess when supervising editors get to work." "The article does not impress me—not at all. Did you see how they did us up in the American supplement to the Encyclopedia Brittanica? That I call very good—that is the best yet."

Thought "the Oklahoma land grab" a "funny affair altogether"—but took no minute interest in it. I returned him Bucke's letter and the Tribune article. We talked somewhat about it. "Nothing has yet come to me, for or against," he said, "I simply let the matter rest and proceed its own way." I asked: "Did you notice, Doctor seems to think I might oppose?" He laughed: "Yes—I noticed: he evidently fears you would say no." And I said then to W. distinctively: "I neither oppose nor favor—I am willing in this thing to defer to those who may know better." W. cried: "Good! good!" And when I said further: "And as to the fund, I shall continue my work for it, whatever turns up, and you should be at ease on that point." His face took on more than its wonted emotion and he assured me: "Thank you, boy! I know! I know!" He is willing to say "if I must, I must"—that is—"if they make me, then there is no appeal," but the question is must he? Ed says W. suggested to him: "I should rather eat my crust on my own dung hill than a good meal on another's." And that W. had explained to him yesterday the substance of Doctor's proposition, then neither assenting nor opposing. He said to me again: "There is no doubt, as you say, but that is a wonderful, complete institution—taking in all the best experience of old and new ages, lands."

He advised me: "I see nothing in Brown's way now—he can go right on any time he chooses; he has plates, paper, instructions—nothing remains to delay him." He found on examination that, as I said last night, Dave has not returned us "the 70th year" plate. Must get it from him and take to Billstein. Matters assume better and better shape. W. is rather sensitive about such reports as Hinton's of the almost squalor of his surroundings. He said to Ed (so Ed reports to me—and it sounds like W.) the other day: "Some people think we live in poverty and dirt here—but it is not so; things are a little dusty" &c—but not more. I find Ed rather solicitous (though easily so) over the prospect of removal. But he is of the opinion that W. will not go. I am not certain myself—rather feel the same thing—but W. hearkens to the propotition rather more than I should have supposed he would. He says that when the conclusion comes, whether yes or no, "it will probably come of a sudden—all in a rush." His fondness for the books about him—the strange disorder of it—"I never was very orderly," he says—may outweigh all other considerations. My own hope is, that whatever is decided upon, may be justified in their results.

We talked of the proposed congressional appropriation to aid in the construction of a flying machine (some fellow with a plausible scheme)—and W. said: "I know many fellows who have a faith in the thing—think future navigation will be aerial." For his own part he was "no prophet," yet could conceive "almost anything possible to man."

7.00 P.M. W. sitting at window. Had a fine talk with him covering full 45 minutes. He seemed very earnest, interested— and far more willing to let himself out than at some times. Of course, much talk of the celebration—its prospects—the rain still persisting. Mention of objections in some quarters to giving prominence to military in display—that America was spiritual and industrial, and these elements should be emphasized. W. reflected: "I am glad someone has had the courage to state that: it well deserves to be said, considered— indeed, should be weighed." But he was not at all sure that there was danger or inappropriateness in the view ordinarily taken and adopted. "America—the United States—came into being through military prowess, forces, aids. Washington himself was really so introduced, sustained, built up. In fact, we might say even more than this: might say the United States came into existence not only with the Revolution of '76 but through our Rebellion of 1861–5. The blood, the fathomless experiences, emotions, of both, joined." And so he would say: "Let them make what they will of their military for the present—not too much, but enough." And then he monologued: "It is always to be remembered that we have been rarely fortunate in our militaries—in Washington, Grant—even in old Zach Taylor—good true, simple Zach Taylor. I hobnobbed much with him in New Orleans. He was a man accustomed to contact with assistants, hired men, slaves—accustomed to command, armies, placemen—yet wholly unspoiled—a wonderful tribute to the essential soundness of American life. And Lafayette, too—count him in: simple as any, a product of the aristocracy of aristocracies, but himself giving shame to all merely personal or class pretenses, whatever their worldly credentials." I suggested: "And never yet an adventurer among the great military men we have had!" W.: "That is so

—profoundly so! Not one! all simple and inoffensive: men knowing America and subserving her. I do not include Scott and Lee—men of that stamp—men for whom I never make place among the high ones—not genuinely great in any sense. But Grant? him, freely and wholly. Washington was more stiff and stately." "But genuine," I suggested. Whereat: "Oh! entirely genuine: I did not mean to question that. I had rather in my mind the memory of his saturnine disposition—reserved, retiring. Washington was an American out and out." Mention of Lincoln. "I should not class Lincoln with the militaries, yet he was the man more than militaire who when they were wrong, quarrelling, doubtful, brought the militaries into right relations again, with each other, with surroundings."

McKay related to me today, the incident of his meeting Arthur Stedman in a New York library. A. S. congratulated him on the big W. W. book. McKay waived the applause, saying the book was wholly W.'s &c. I repeated this to W., who laughed heartily. "That is Dave: with a true publishers' instinct he took a dislike for the book at the start, and the Scotch in him will not yield—not even at the end. Of course I do not let my opinion of Dave be disturbed by such a little item as that." McKay made some inquiries as to terms for books going abroad. I suggested: "I wish it could go in the covers—I should like them to see your covers over there." W. then: "And I too: they would understand it." Clifford had seen the two covers together at my room one day, and at once expressed preference for the cheap one as being more characteristic. W.: "Yes, and it is just such an opinion as I should expect from a man of his strong original tastes." Afterwards: "I do not know that I am inclined to make any exception of foreign publishers—whether to give them the books for less than 4 dollars. I hardly think I shall. Do you know the cost of the stitching? And that stitching—it is the good, isn't it? It might be well to find out, to fortify us." W. amused at things said to me by McKay about Hartmann. And then as to Hartmann's column: "Yes,—and they are such platitudes, too—stupidities. I wrote in one of my letters to Doctor that Stedman was mad. I did not go into the matter at any length—simply explained."

Harry Walsh at Dave's when I entered. McKay afterwards humorously described Walsh's picture of William's immense content in the litter of the Herald office. A place quite after his own heart. Walt said: "I did not know that of Walsh. Is W. S. Walsh such a fellow? He probably likes to get a couple of rooms somewhere and rig them up his own way. I can appreciate that disposition in any man. In that lies one of my cardinal objections to going into institutions to live—to going for instance, to the Baltimore hospital. That there would be much gained by making such a change, I am well aware—the best doctors, surgeons, rooms, nursing, medicines: the brave good Doctors! Apartments hygienically arranged: the best eating. But would there not be loss, too? The question for me is: have I not all these now—or if not all these, at least compensating gifts? Have I not already sufficient to invite content?—sweetest content?" I alluded to my father—his life-long resentment of all propositions to work on wages for others. W. approved by a nod of the head: "I can to the full accept and justify such an attitude in any man: it is the issue of the man's whole being—I may say, even its necessity. But I know how much can be said con to that: I know in my own case—and that is the case we are on—the probability that I am yet to be let down and down and down and down again— even lower, lower, lower, lower—and it might be, for that we should nicely prepare, arrange, adjust ourselves." He had been thinking of the matter much today but to no effect, really. "I do not face it—only let it come when it wills so to do. As I am fond of saying, no man will willingly abdicate his own dung hill. Allowing for all else, what can return to him the price of freedom but freedom? At any rate, boy"—(he said this fervently—his whole manner suffused with a feeling that ran into his simplest word this evening) "at any rate, boy, we will not for the present even consider the proposition to go to the Baltimore hospital. Now, while our book is pending—for the next month or so, while the 70th birthday is coming on—we must not let our way be blocked—ourselves worried, disturbed—by thoughts of removal, change. We must go right on, never tiring. I know everything in this world is a compromise—there is always an opposite word somewhere. Bye and bye this thing—if we do not settle it ourselves—will be settled for us."

Suddenly he broke away from that strain, which more or less disturbs him at best. "I see that Edward Emerson's book is out—the book about his father there at Concord": adding: —"I suppose we will in some way come upon it." I spoke of Emerson's Journal—that in the extracts Cabot gave, W. W. was not mentioned. W. said: "It seems to be a principle with some of the fan-dams of literature to treat me right (as they think) by not treating me at all. They look on me as a passing phase—that soon Walt Whitman will be done, his work done: that silence is therefore wisely imposed." But also said: "I know nothing of Cabot"—and he certainly could not go on record as impugning him. He said what he did in response to my remark that I believed if we had Emerson's Journal entire, Whitman would be found sharing mention with the others. In looking about for a Linton picture to sign and send by me to Mrs. Fels (on whom I had mentioned I was to call this evening), W. took up a copy of the greenpaper (1871) edition Passage to India. "Take this book to your Mother or Aggie," he said, "either one. And do you want another?—this?—for yourself?" Copies in which, across the title page, he had written "Walt Whitman 1889"—and pasted in which was a copy of the steel with this inscription

W. W. from life
one hot July forenoon 1855
Brooklyn N Y

in which I wrote on going, in pencil.

W. much struck with these views, reported of Von Bülow, herewith:

Von Bülow's Views.—Interviewed by a reporter of the Mail and Express as to the relative merits of the various composers, and specially as to his views on Wagner, Dr. Von Bülow said:— "I am not ultra-Wagnerian, and I deprecate the attempt to place his works on a pedestal above many other composers. I knew Richard Wagner well, and helped to advance the Wagnerian school in Germany, but I am sensible and unprejudiced enough to believe there are other composers. I appreciate his greatness and recognize the compliment paid him in America, but I want it distinctly understood that I am not an ultra-Wagnerian.

I believe that Bach is the father of music, Beethoven is his son, and Brahms I consider its spirit. To Brahms I owe my redemption from the ultra-Wagnerian school. The fact is I renewed my musical youth by his acquaintance. He taught me that there are many composers, many musicians, not one, and I owe him much for bringing me out of the sloughs of prejudice where the one-man worship prevails. He is broad and catholic in his musical views. * * * Whom do I consider the master instructor on the piano, now that Liszt is dead? Prof. Henry Ehrlich, of Berlin. He is sixty-four years of age and I consider him the best teacher, musical thinker and writer in Germany. None can approach him. I find the great fault with pianists is that they do not learn to phrase properly. Every pianist should learn to sing and play the violin; then their ears would hear more critically the sound they produce and thereby teach them how to phrase. But the average pianist plays by sight only, and has no ears. He sees the keys, and tries to execute correctly; but the sound he produces, the effect of his work, is not apparent to him. My advice to young pianists—old ones won't take advice—is to cultivate their ears and strive to obtain beauty and expression in what we term phrasing. It is the real beginning to greatness as a performer.

"Oh! how grand that is—a keyword—the keyword—word inclusive of all other words. I don't know but the explication of all highest art—literature. Expression! Expression! Oh! the man who could say that—say it that way,—deserves immortality!"

I left with him a copy of Scribners and copy of Bazaar. "Oh!" he exclaimed, "what a day I'll have tomorrow! I'm laying in a fine store!" And on looking at an English shore piece in the magazine—a marvellous photo-engraving reproduction: "Will they never stop—will they never stop?" Secured the 70th year cut from McKay and took it to Billstein. Told B. to hold it till I inquired of W. if there was any inscription intended for either cut. W. now: "I never thought of it." And after turning it over in a few minutes of silence: "Now I do think of it, I am disposed to let 'em go plain."

Sunday, April 28, 1889

8.10 P.M. W. reading Tribune. Said his health was "half and half." I asked: "Like the weather?" And he answered: "Yes, just that"—for today had been raining and clear by turns. Had made up a copy of the big book to send to Will Carleton at Brooklyn. "No news at all today," he reported, "not a letter." Had read papers—Press, Tribune, &c. "I suppose the Tribune came from Tom," he explained; "he must have stopped at the door but did not come up." Returned me the Bazaar. Had "carefully scanned" both it and Scribners; said of the latter, "it is wonderful, the wealth of its illustrations." It had been "a great joy" to him to inspect—"I went all through with it." Cauffman had spoken to the Cliffords as though the English exhibit at the photographic exhibition was superior. Cauffman—a man of fine and practiced tastes art-ward—paints, photographs, himself. W., as always, greatly taken by the topic. Was greatly interested anyhow in my Germantown trip—in my description of greens—the rain-freshened landscape.

I had referred the Stedman matter to Clifford, asking his judgment. He thought S.'s letter "almost tragic" in tone—

"certainly pathetic"—and wondered if in this case a word or two from W. W. would not be advised. W. listened intently to my rehearsal of Clifford's opinions and reasons, and for the rest of the time of my stay seemed much more troubled and silent than before. I could well see that questions had been raised anew in his mind. His estimate of Clifford's "acumen" high. He made little comment, though questioning and questioning till he felt he had heard all I had to tell him. Several times last week this plan had struck me: that I should have W.'s consent to write to Stedman for my two letters, submit them to W., and if he approved, consent that they be published. Have not said a word of this to W. Clifford seemed to subscribe to that. I said to W.: "Clifford feels as I do that that is the letter of a man who thinks there is at least a probability that you have said such, or similar things, of him." And W. himself: "I can see that myself—Stedman certainly gives out that impression."

Ever since the note from Bucke proposing the removal, W.'s demeanor towards me has been more tender and marked. This has been decidedly palpable—so much so as to strike me peculiarly. What it means—whether stay or departure—I should not dare to attempt stating. Tonight he said nothing directly touching the subject. I had with me an Emerson volume containing "The Poet," and opened it at the closing paragraph, handing it then to W. He remarked: "It is not new to me—I have seen it, read it, of course." But made no comment which either resented or accepted its application to him. He read the matter marked—handled the book, too, as if he liked it. "Paper, print, type,—it is all good for the eye—and then it's a first edition, too, isn't it? 1866?" He did not think that edition "was ever beaten" typographically. I said of "The Poet" quote—"If you last, that describes you; if not, that's not your name!" He laughed greatly, but said not a word.

Dr. Furness preached for Clifford this forenoon. He is

nearly 90. W. dwelt upon it a long time—did not seem able to shake it out of his thought. "A grand old age! a grand old age! It is almost incredible—yet it is! It defies statement, almost—certainly rule and explanation." Asked me then: "How did he appear? Could he be heard?" And added: "It is remarkable how men will stay and stay. Such men must have a wonderful background somewhere—some grand physical base —some sane bottom, eternal, we could say, in its purity of composition." "I remember a very old man down in Washington—I think in the war-time; he came there, was elected chaplain of the Senate or the House. Oh yes! I knew him. And he could be heard. His vigor was a constant wonder to me. It is among the Methodists, you know, that there occur the more remarkable cases of longevity." He did not attempt to explain this, but that it was was undoubted. "Oh! what was his name—his name?"—And after considerable waiting: "It will not come—not a sign of it—yet I knew it well. Nowadays my memory for names seems strangely deserting me—strangely." Nor could he recall it while I stayed, though several times indicating that he had not forgotten his quest. I did not persist much this evening, shortly off and to town again. W. always asks me on departure: "Where are you going now?" and on coming: "And how have you spent the day?—what seen?"— or some such question.

Monday, April 29, 1889

10.45 A.M. W. in bathroom on my arrival. I sat down and waited for him, reading till his coming, and finally he did, Ed hurrying from downstairs to assist him. Sent off Carleton's book this morning. Said: "I have had no mail at all this morning—not even the Critic, though that is usually here Monday morning." Spoke of the Scribner's I had in my hand and with which he said he was finished. Eugene Schuyler's article therein on Tolstoi. He had read that. The group of

Russians with which it was prefaced—Tolstoi, Turgeneff, among them—aroused his thought. "They are a fine looking body of men—seem so solid, so compacted, so actual: Germanic, somewhat, and—you may think it strange, but it's certainly there—a certain dash of American."

Railroad accident occurred already, to pleasure seekers for the affair in New York [Celebration of centenary of ratification of the constitution]. W. expressed pain therefore. Then laughed at report in papers that in deference to Harrison's religious sentiment, his train last night, though boarded before 12, was not started till Monday was on &c. W. said: "That was just like him." Then reflected: "I suppose there will be a lot of people all along who will want to shake hands with the President—would with any president. It strikes me it would be a wise thing to have a big log and saw it into bits, let the people shake that! It is in such a suggestion as that we find the old Greek log story—and good, fitting, applicable, it is too!" I referred to Howard (the correspondent) and his argument once, that it were as well to shake legs as hands, (or something to that effect) so little sensible is this last. W. asked: "Jo Howard? Oh! I know him. Jo must be old now—quite as old as I am I should say. He is a cute, witty fellow—one of a group of fellows—bright, happy, necessary, just the men for the places they occupy. George Alfred Townsend is another I know—'Gath'—and he is good too. Both of them surface—indeed, all surface—of course, but important men, without a doubt." Z. L. White he did not know. "He was a Washington fellow, too. But now he is dead! And Ramsdell is dead, too! Poor Ramsdell! I knew him—he was owner of the Republic there at Washington: is the Republic in existence yet?—and worked hard. Ramsdell was a department man—was ousted by Cleveland." Clouds still go scurrying across the sky, though it has not rained today. W. said: "The weather still seems unsettled. It will be a bitter dose if rain hits the celebration."

McKay asked through me on Saturday for W.'s bottom

price on export copies. I left the question with W. to con. This morning when I referred to it again he replied: "I have not thought it over at all." And now did lapse into quiet for full 3 or 4 minutes—then seemed decided: "Tell Dave that for the foreign trade—for Gardner, if he will take a lot of 25— bound as we have 'em here—taken right out of the lot as it stands—I will sell him the book for $3.80 per copy. I should prefer to have our cover retained, but shall not insist upon it. I should like the fellows over there to see, to have, it. They will understand, embrace—especially the Whitmaniacs, as they are called—though there is another Whitman constituency than that, too. Dave has got taken possession of by a stubborn dislike, has had it from the first, and it will not down. Tell him for me, I think he had better drop it—at least, in some way get rid of it—it is nothing but a kink. It is singular that he is the only one of all who have seen it who now refuses to accept. The printers, binders, book-men par excellence—all agree to its success: only Dave dissents. I put a good deal of faith in the word of my binder: I told you of him—he is a specialist— knows whereof he speaks: he was quite sure of our success— called that a first-rate book. Dave should take his kink and throw it overboard—let it drown—as they do with the super- fluous kitten." The cover anyhow on the commercial side was "a small matter" and "ought not to arouse difficulties with Gardner." I asked: "Would it not be well for Dave to say in writing to Gardner that this cover is peculiarly and only yours?" And he said: "Indeed I do—in fact, he should make it a point to do that."

Although Brown had said to me that he expected to put the book in press Tuesday, W. was dubious about it: "Tomorrow is a holiday." I said, "But Ferguson will be open." W. per- sisted: "no matter—printers are printers. You know printers as well as I do—know that they take all the holidays and more too." "But," I argued, "these presses are fed by girls." This appeared to excite his interest. He questioned: "And who does the heavy work about the presses? Years ago, the ponderous steamers required each a couple of able-bodied men." I explained that in Ferguson's one man did all the necessary heavy work on two or three or perhaps even more presses, "while the girl who feeds keeps on her perch undisturbed."

Talk developed of Emerson and Alcott. I said I did not think Alcott could last. But W. was himself "not so certain" of his "entire" disappearance, of disappearance at all. Described a visit Alcott once made to him. "It was in Brooklyn: he came in about noon—perhaps later, but at any rate near enough to the dinner to be invited and to partake. My Mother had a fine bit of beef there that day—it was especially well prepared—she was a fine cook anyway. When we sat down at table she sliced off a special bit for Alcott—put it on his plate. When the meal was done, we noticed that he had not touched it—that he had eaten vegetables, bread and butter, perhaps even cake—but never a bite of the meat. Nor did he offer any apology for it, either—if I am clear about it, did not remark it at all. Even the absence of apology was quite characteristic of him. Alcott had no belly at all—no body of great amount: was tall, slim—with quite a splendid, beautiful head: but his animality, as they talk of it—especially often when they want to whack at me—was nil. He had no 'bodjal' power at all— 'bodjal': that was said by a girl I know." I objected to the word, that it was an obscure liberty, and W.: "It will not last—I am persuaded it will not: words do often come that way, but that word—bodjal—is too far-fetched." "But although Alcott did not broach his vegetarian doctrine that day, I have heard him say he was a vegetarian. But I don't know that Alcott could have fulfilled his mission except by being just what he was. He felt deeply that he was above all else to uphold the supremacy of the spirit—pure thought, the poetic, the spiritual—we might almost say the high falutin'. Not a universal man—not like the sweet and wise Emerson—but a specialist: a specialist much as we know doctors to be nowadays —as it is said doctors must be—not doctors of the whole man, of the body however affected—but controlling a department only—ear, eye, teeth, brain, what-not—doing that well—oh! grandly superlatively well, to be sure—but only departmentarily after all. Alcott was such a department man. The greatest surprise is, that knowing this, he started out a thorough-going almost overwhelming admirer of me, who am accused of all opposites—and indeed am of a stripe that could be rated different. I always had the impression that Alcott cooled off from this—gradually, surely: I can't quote to prove it, but that has been my notion." Emerson had far other inclination and habits: "He thoroughly enjoyed a good meal—would eat heartily and much, too, I think, in his own way." I repeated the story I had heard of Emerson's criticism of Alcott, that he could not write but could talk &c.—very pithy, when rightly told. W. said: "That I never heard—that is strange to me." Our talk of Alcott had arisen out of my remark that Camden had got its fame through W. W. Yesterday's Press contained an article, with portraits, describing young men to whom Camden owed so much of its development. W. himself remarked having read it. Then my objection as above. W.: "It was true of Concord, anyhow—Emerson there—Alcott, Hawthorne."

7 P.M. W. sitting in his usual place by the window: the night coming on—he simply ruminating. Looked very well, and talked well. Makes no remark of his condition except that he gains no strength. Complained of his mail today, that it had amounted to practically "nothing at all." "I have not received the Critic at all, which is quite unusual. But there was a short letter from Doctor Bucke—only of passing interest, however. Doctor brings up the Baltimore Hospital again—drives the nail farther and farther in." But W. had still no comment himself to make. I asked Mrs. Davis if he had spoken to her of the matter and it seemed that he had. He had explained—then asked her opinion. She had replied that she thought it might be well for all hands to set to here and make him comfortable, and this seemed to impress him, for he evidently made some

acquiescent reply to her. He keeps saying all the time: "It would be difficult for an old fellow like me to conform to rules," &c.—and again—"impossible even."

Asked me as is his wont: "Where bound to? tell me!" Tonight Tom Davidson's last lecture—this on "Savanarola." W. said: "Savanarola? I know little about him—very little—too little. What was his date? He was one of the olders, was he not? long before our century?" And after my reply—"He was a priest then?" I asked him if he had not read George Eliot's "Romola." "Yes, I have read it, in a fashion—probably skipped half of it—it did not take hold of me." I said: "You must have skipped the Savanarola portion, for I do not think you would have forgotten that if you had once read it." W. thereupon: "Probably not—I must have skipped it." And so he questioned me further. I said I understood that Miss Repplier and Morris would be there together. W. smiled—thought I would "probably meet Miss Repplier" and when I looked dubious, said: "It is a good and safe rule, always to take care to be introduced to the fellow you don't expect, or don't want to meet. These do us the most good. It is not a man's friends from whom he gets the most benefit—of course you know that as well as I do—but often the man who despises you, won't have you on any terms, is most rich in benefits." And yet he laughed, confessed it was true, meetings had their own best natural course, anyhow—and as for the denouncers, "certainly they come anyhow, asked, sought or not."

His interest in the New York celebration immense—his allusions frequent. I have not heard him express a single regret in words that he cannot be present, but his whole absorption in it and the tone of his talk indicate that had he his body, the occasion would not be missed. "I see," he said to my more ignorant self—"I see by the Camden papers that the naval affair came off all right—the weather fair—not a rain today at all, was there?" And after a pause and my confession that I had not seen an afternoon paper: "It was from 9 on this morning—and successful, thoroughly. I am glad. The weather seems getting more favorable" (though not clear yet). "Is it a great deal cooler?" The wind out of doors was blowing the fresh green leaves of the trees. W. pointed it out. "I see it must be strong: and here are our windows rattling too" &c. So he dwelt on weather and event, intertwining—regretting even the fugitive clouds, lest they might join and destroy the plans of the celebration. Mrs. Davis came in with violets in a tumbler—beautiful fresh stems: she had them from the backyard; handed them to Walt with a few words from the Lincoln poem—and took from the table the old bunch. W. protested as to the last: "You are going to take them, Mary? But don't throw them away—they are too good still": and put the others to his face an instant, inhaling their fragrance, ere placing before him on the table. Mrs. Davis departed—he looked long and pleasedly at the pure new stalks.

Morris, whom I met today in the city, had spoken quite anxiously of the Hartmann perpetration which it seems the boys in the city had been discussing. W. asked at once: "And what do they make of it? do they see through it?" Was anxious to know how it would be regarded by casual readers. I said Morris had at once realized that it was bogus. "And the others," he asked, "What of them?" But here I could not fill in his information. He adding: "I cannot believe that any-one—anyone with eyes and ears—could be imposed on by it. It is thinnest of thin—not bogus only, but bogus bogus—tepid water watered—what they call on shipboard six-quar-ter's rum. Such sayings as that about Emerson, for instance—ignorant, dull, beyond power to expose—and Taine—and Holmes." Morris had alluded to the Lowell touch, but W. said: "I do not remember that at all. The whole thing is bitter enough—work, throughout, that is self-damning." But had he written Stedman? "No—I have not been moved to"—and after a slight pause—"yet. Yet I confess I am deeply vexed, uneasy, to have had this trouble arise." I spoke of Hartmann's as away the most flagrant offense ever committed against W.

But he for an instant seriously: "I don't know, Horace—I don't know." But when I said, "I know you have been abused and denounced, but abuse is its own condemnation, while here is something more subtly put down as offense in you," he recognized the distinction. Yet nothing seems to move him more toward any public expression on the subject. "I know there is a special bitter twist given that paragraph about Stedman—and it is marked out, as you say, from all the rest, by that particular quality: therein its sadness."—"Nothing —nothing at all—either word or sentiment, mine. Even if they were—if anything so generous could be said of anything so vulgar and low as Hartmann's whole report—even if they did even approximate my sentiments, while that might in a measure condone the offense, it could not wipe it out."

Ed came in—got postal for Will Carleton and several papers for others. W. desired Ed to buy him ten foreign postal cards, wheeling his chair about to the other table in search of the money he had there laid out for them. I asked Morris today who it was among Frank Williams' folks who was dead, describing Curtis' few words last week. It seemed that Mrs. Williams' mother had been subjected to some surgical operation which proved fatal—this in the presence of Frank himself. When I went over this story for Walt he exclaimed: "Poor Frank!—Poor Frank! I know how he must have suffered. I did not know the Mother, but have somehow gathered the impression that she came of uppish stock: how I came by it, I do not know—that they have wealth too,— people of a high place—standards, as it is called,—in Society." And then it was "Poor Frank! Poor Frank!" again, and a word or two more of solicitude. And goodbye and out!

Tuesday, April 30, 1889

10.55 A.M. W. reading his paper. Reported his own condition as "so-so." But was happy that "we have a good day for the show—a good, cool day—and fair skies." "It makes me happy to know that everything passed off well yesterday"— here he paused and his voice was pathetic—"everything except that accident—that was dreadful." Nothing significant yet said, though he had "a hearty laugh" over one of the Chauncey Depew's jokes—"and a very good one, too"—this:

After he had gone from the lawyers' room the irrepressible Chauncey Depew was put on a chair and told a story. He said:
"As ex-president Hayes and I were coming up Wall Street in the crowd a man rose up before me with the most muscular arms I ever saw and protected in those arms was the most beautiful girl I ever saw. As Hayes and I tried to push our way along this fellow said: 'There is no room for the four hundred here.'
" 'What do you mean?' I said. 'Do you know who this gentleman is? He is an Ex-President; an Ex-President of the United States.'
" 'I don't care if he is Ex-President of Heaven,' the fellow replied. 'He shan't squeeze my girl.' " The lawyers howled, and Chauncey had obviously made one of the hits of the Centennial.

Clifford had thought W. W. should have been called on for the poem. W. however was "sure it is best as it is," for, "Walt Whitman himself is glad enough he was not called on."

Baker graduates tomorrow—will probably settle in Duluth. Asks from my sister a letter of introduction to the Strykers. Baker will probably be over, partly to see me, tonight, but as I am compelled to be away, I left a little message with W. Baker will probably go west immediately after the examination. W. spoke affectionately of him—of his service here and the liking for him and the hope and belief in his ultimate success. Complained of his mail: "No Critic yet." Had I seen it? "What was there in it?—anything special?" I quoted a review of Florian's Montaigne: " 'Myselfe am the groundworke of my booke': such were the Whitmanesque words with which old Montaigne concluded the preface to his immortal essays just 309 years ago, and such the reason of their perennial freshness and charm." W. said at first: "I do not recognize the relevancy of the 'Whitmanesque' " but when I repeated the sentence, he said: "Oh! now I begin to see there is reason for it."

Some item in a newspaper had excited W.'s curiosity over Alcott. "Are they to publish his Journals? I have heard somewhere there were volumes of them." Alcott had "always had the idea of a mission," and part of his mission was "to keep these Journals." Wondered in what guise "he would appear in these extensive journals" if at all. I had with me a copy of George Haven Putnam's analysis of Pearsall Smith's scheme of international copyright. W. said: "I have not read it. Pearsall came to me with his scheme—was very anxious to have me endorse it—but I did not—was not disposed to accept it." And he reflected—the number of "endorsements" solicited of him in his time by friends alone was enormous—but he had always kept his own path, espousing none. The one pamphlet recalled another. Reached over to his piled box under the table. "This is the latest—this is from Edward Carpenter. And I think it may interest you—perhaps Clifford, too: send it to Clifford when you are done with it." A leaflet of four pages—"Our Parish and Our Duke: a letter to the Parishioners of Holmesfield, in Derbyshire," starting "Fellow Parishioners," and signed "Edward Carpenter," with "Millthorpe, Holmesfield, March 1889" in the left corner. An examination, with a home illustration, of the land question— the nationalization of the land. W. said: "Yes, Edward is a Socialist." And when I asked: "Has he ever—or anyone—in any way indicated William Morris' feelings toward you?" He answered: "No—I know nothing on that point." Yet Carpenter and Morris often came in contact, probably—even Rhys with him. As to the latter W. said: "I see Ernest is writing letters now to the Boston Transcript—literary letters." W. always read these with "personal as well as general" interest.

Someone had asked W. to write his name in one of the Burroughs books on him and he refused. "I always object," he

109

explained, "to putting my name in a book about myself. I know it may be thought a mere prejudice—a kink—but somehow it hangs on to me—I do not violate it." Then he talked to me a little about the book thus spoken of. "It is a nice little book in shape" (I have one) "nice to handle. And the second edition is better than the first—has an addition of a dozen pages or more." As to the first edition: "It sold, I suppose—at least, was got rid of in some way." A New York fellow (I already forget his name) sent W. a big-enveloped batch of poems in manuscript the other day, accompanying them with an admiring letter. The envelope was inscribed: "Walt Whitman, Poet"—and the letter fulsome. W. little appealed to—has not read. The matter lays as it was, and where, from the first. Advised me: "Keep a sharp lookout for our interests—keep your grip on all that is being done for us. You did not see Dave yesterday? Ah! and Brown—see him. Look at his sheets, if he has started—see that he proceeds as we want him to."

Wednesday, May 1, 1889

10.45 A.M. Was intercepted by the circus parade on Federal Street on my way down. W. had heard the bands, and asked me about it on my coming. He sat in his room, not doing anything. The day lightly clouded, and really cool. In the stove logs lazily burning which he stirred from time to time. No one in the house but Ed and Walt. Ed asked: "How long are you going to stay?" and when I said: "Fifteen or 20 minutes—I'll watch"—went off himself to see the circus. Ed gave me Dr. Baker's address, which had been left for me last night: Minneapolis. Ed said Baker came when W. was stark naked and was having his evening rubbing. B. knocked at the door (it was 9:20)—W. called out: "Who's there?" And after B's signifying and explanation that he had only come to say goodbye, W. said: "Well—goodby, Doctor," but did not invite him in. Would have seen him under any other circumstance. The rubbings help him. He looks well this morning.

Had been reading the accounts of yesterday's celebration. "I found the best report in the Record—it seemed to me the more accurate. Did you see Whittier's portrait there in the Press? It was rather good. I have never seen Whittier in person—never met him." Had he read the poem? "Oh yes! and you? have you? What do you think of it?" Afterwards stating: "It is good—smoothly written—very Whittieresque. I see for one thing, he gets a dig in at slavery: that seems inevitable with him."—"I have carefully examined—looked over—the oration—Chauncey Depew's. It has its merits. The best report of that, too, in the Record. The Press purports to give it all, but"—And then he said—"It is full of sweetness, ease: it is the last dish at the dinner—the dinner given you all sweets, all sugars, and sugar in this last dish brought in cloyingly at the last hour." He missed strong presentation. Had noted markedly and commented on "an evident enthusiasm" at the appearance of Cleveland.

"No word from Washington," he said, "and strangely, too," he added, shaking his head, "I don't know what it means. But here are letters—perhaps you would like to see them: one from Doctor—one from Kennedy." I stood and read. Bucke is making new reading of L. of G. to hit possible errors, but reports none other than those already sent. W.: "Happy" that "the book seems so near complete typographically."

Then he asked: "And what of our affairs in town—what do you know new?" We talked of my interview with McKay yesterday afternoon. I had instructed McKay to this effect; that W. did not insist but would prefer to have his big book go abroad cover and all—that he should write Gardner to that effect—using as argument that W. himself was wholly responsible for it as it stood, not another hand intervening—or planning—that in fact this might as well be the burden of the domestic canvas. McKay assented in the main. W. asked me:

"That is driving the nail in very far, isn't it?" I argued: "Not too far: as you know, from a publisher's standpoint our book is bad anyway: that seems to be what they say: so it has to be justified on the other tack or not at all." There he assented: "I see—and I see the justice of what you say, too—am content to have it so presented then." As to any argument that the book was from old plates: "That is true, but it is old in no other respect: it is new in paper, size, print,—new in portraits—new in cover—November Boughs certainly new— and the ensemble wholly peculiar, its own." "And it is not old anyway, in any circulatory sense—not a Dickens' novel at all, that everybody possesses, has on his shelves: not received, known, in thousands, but in tens only, if even that. Take Chicago: I doubt if there are a hundred books in the whole town. Put on counters there, it would be taken de novo—as a new thing. This is unquestioned. I put the book out experimentally myself—wanted to try it—wanted to see what would be made of it. And everywhere I find myself justified— everywhere—there has not been a single exception. Even the dainty book men—men like Aldrich—take to it. And there is Stedman too—living among books—handling books. And the library men, too! It seems to me almost a unanimous voice." Had he sent a book to Larned yet? "No—but I've a mind to —I feel willing to make Chicago a sort of rallying point for a few books."

I told W. I wished a copy of "As a Strong Bird" to give McKay, who had never had a copy. "Of course—let Dave have one," he said: and when I had secured one from the other room, signed the book. McKay has the remnant (about 300) of the Roberts edition "After all, Not to Create Only" which he proposes to bind up and sell as a first edition. W. said: "I knew he had some of them, though I have not seen a copy of it bound so, as you put it, in solid covers. It is a little thing— very few pages. Dick Spoffard was the fellow who did it— who got it out. He was mad that people would not see what he thought he saw in it and said: 'Give it to me—give it in my hands—and I'll see that it gets out.' And he did. It is more properly a poem to be read at the debuting, adventing, of a big affair—a big exposition; is now included in my big book." And then he said of the big book again: "All the objections I have heard so far I can brush aside as of no importance whatever—none whatever."

I saw Brown yesterday, and he had not yet been able to put our book in press: would however, positively do so Thursday —would then give me a sample sheet. W. said: "I am not so particular about the sample sheet as I am about the whole book—about any full sets." But then: "A day or two— provided it is not longer—does not trouble us—I do not mind that. Though we must be careful of any real delay." And of cover: "I suppose much will hinge upon cost: morocco is rare and costly; it may be beyond our power, as it is: if so, we must find something else that will serve." He had already promised copies—one to Kennedy, who welcomed the thought of it. Had read the Jefferson, Adams, and other letters in Unity—"and with a certain kind of interest, too." But they had not impressed him as of great weight.

7.30 P.M. The room dark, W. on bed. "Ah Horace! Is that you?" Somehow distinguished me even in the shadows. Was he unwell, that he was thus lying down? "Oh no! I am pretty well—I do not count these very bad days." I heard a sheet crumpled in the dark, and knew Ed had brought his mail and given it him there as he lay. Questioned me: "What have you learned new in town today?"—the usual words with which he inaugurates business. But I had learned nothing except that our work proceeded. I had given McKay the little book and had his thanks for it. Then W. asked: "And how is the weather? I suppose they finished up things in New York today—and after all, it was a pretty good day, wasn't it?"

I read all the speeches this afternoon except Depew's and spoke of their dullness. W. asked in regard to Lowell's: "Was he there? I could not just make out whether he was present or whether that was a letter." Lowell had said as reported by the Press:

Literature has been put somewhat low on the list of toasts, doubtless in deference to necessity of arrangement, but perhaps the place assigned to it here may be taken as roughly indicating that which it occupies in the general estimation. And yet I venture to claim for it an influence (whether for good or evil) more durable and more widely operative than that exerted by any other form in which human genius has found expression.

W. was "glad" Lowell had "courageously" said that: "It is true—true: he well-maintained it there—was wise to make free of it." Had read Cleveland's speech, and Harrison's— called the latter a "lot of platitudes"—adding: "What a vast descent from Washington to Harrison! a terrific descent, indeed!" Bishop Potter spoke among other things of "that steadily deteriorating process against whose dangers a great thinker of our generation warned his countrymen just fifty years ago"—the influx of "the lowest orders of people from abroad"—&c. quoting from the Press today. W. exclaimed: "Poor devil! Little does he know America! And yet he has a following. I don't know, either, but that he is consistent with protection America. But protection America—what is it consistent with? I read at least a part of the Bishop's speech but I didn't come to what you quote. It was all distasteful to me— all: couched in a form I cordially dislike—so I stopped. The Bishop stood there yesterday—made his speech there—as the representative of respectable high-falutins—I might say, of anti-democracy. But you must not wonder or feel disappointed, the speeches being commonplace: they were—but the noteworthy thing in this celebration lies just here: that there were such men a century ago, that now there is a fourth generation to celebrate them. That is the prime fact, and we must not lose sight of it." As to Whittier's perfunctory poem:

"It is clear—we can understand it: it is made up as if for Whittier to say: 'here are my beliefs—take them!' "

W. struggled into sitting posture on the bed, groped for his cane and found it, and went across the room, I taking his left arm. He arranged the windows himself and lighted his gas. Then after he had sat down: "And how is it you are here tonight anyhow? Why are you not at the circus? Ed has gone." Then resumed his general talk—referring again to Bishop Potter—"the Cathedral man," he called him. Potter's advocating the grand Cathedral for New York city. "The truth is, Potter is one of the old stock—there's quite a class of them in New York—friends of Kings, Queens, aristocrats: aristocrats themselves—become so in spirit if not inheritedly —people in whom the old feelings have persisted. You probably don't know them as well as I do. It is not the Dutch stock: the Dutch stock was mostly of a truer, stauncher kind." Here he suddenly brought himself to: looked for his crumpled mail—a postal simply—which he had brought from the bed and laid on his table. Put on his glasses, "Oh! it is from Washington!" and turning it over "and the 30th, too— yesterday." Then reading aloud to me: O'Connor had been respited for 48 hours—now the vomiting trouble on again: he therefore weak and in bed. W. exclaimed: "Poor fellow! Poor fellow!" Mrs. O'C. expressed disappointment there had not been better weather for the great celebration. W. commented: "I think it has been very good anyhow, they must have had more rain at Washington." Then reflected: "It is sad news—sad news—looks bad for him." As to O'Connor's eating, W. thought: "He should eat whatever he feels to eat —there is no wiser plan, even for a man in his condition."

Had not received Critic yet. Did he hunger for it enough to want mine? He laughed. "I should not put it that way— probably not. Yet I might see it. Anything coming in here relieves the painful, dreadful, never-ending, monotony of this life. It is with the paper as with my dinner and breakfast: if

115

they are missed—if somebody forgets to bring them—I am strangely out of sorts: yet for the meals themselves I don't care a fig. We live a good deal after all by routine—a dead, dull, yet necessary routine." This was rather a dubious tribute to the Critic, and he laughed at it himself on thought. I told W.: "McKay evidently don't think the pocket edition will be a success!" "In what way?" "He does not think it will sell." W. flashed out: "Perhaps he would like to sell it?" McKay had spoken to me today of some New Yorker who proposed collecting a volume of W. W.'s writings previous to L. of G.—way back in earlier years. W. at first did not comprehend—thought reminiscences were meant. "If he does, they will be like Hartmann's, the projection of the camel of his imagination." But I persisted: "He means reprint." "Oh! does he! I should like to have somebody go over for me—shoot him for me! I should not thank anybody to revive those old cast-offs—I might call them: the lurid miscellanies of early times—sketches, records, what-not. Oh! how those rascals keep at work!" And in comment on publication of Longfellow's early poems and their reputed failure: "There is some compensation in that they failed, anyhow." Wished I might get details more definitely from Dave: who contemplated "such an outrage" &c. Looking over his famous old scrap book today. It lay open on the round table.

Thursday, May 2, 1889

11 A.M. Ed making bed—W. had started to write a letter. Invited me to sit down. But I stayed only briefly. Took him the Critic which he said he was glad to see. Asked me if it was too warm. "I just started my fire—I am always anxious to know." Did not look or feel quite so well as yesterday. I wrote to Bucke this morning on hospital matters, and explained to W. the substance of my note. The New York celebration over. W. happy that it had "well transpired" and added: "I sup-

pose Harrison is at home by this time." He said further: "I think Harrison is the smallest potato in the heap—that he will go down in history so regarded. I think him mainly a gas bag."

Speaking of a building at the foot of Federal Street erected on pilings W. said: "New Orleans affords plenty of examples of that—plenty. I know much about it—was there—have known experts: they sink a heavy log, a number of feet wide—down in the mud—and plant the foundation on that. As long as not exposed to the air, the wood will not corrode—rot, I should say." Spoke of Hollandish ability &c. in this direction. Takes the Pearson matter in New York much to heart. Alluded to entrance of Van Cott to duties as Postmaster in New York. As to Harrison's historic position W. said: "Take due note of my prophecy: it will come true." Then interestedly: "You will go to see Brown today? I rely upon you to keep things moving. Our time is getting short."

7.45 P.M. W. was just preparing a light when I came in. He did not hear me, and I stood off in the shadows watching till he was done. He is quite weak. After fixing windows (he always closes the blinds fast) he sat down on the chair. It was still very dark—and I could hear him breathe heavily. Then he wheeled around and lighted the gas. At once he heard me and saw me: "Ah! Horace! I am just lighting up—have been sitting here for a long time in the twilight. It has all been very fine." And he questioned me: "How is the night—cool? And the moon?" The wind northwest and the moon quite new. W.: "I supposed as much." Had he thrust his head out the window he could have seen the moon easily, for now it sat direct west. "Bryant wrote a fine verse about the waning moon. He was very good in that thing—the best, undoubtedly, of all our men—had a genuine ear which never failed him—and taste. Some would call his taste Wordsworthian, I suppose—but that is not necessary." I knew that Bucke had a high opinion of some of Arnold's early poetry, but W. him-

117

self said: "I know very little of Arnold's poetry, early or late. But Bryant had peculiar powers, felicities: the moon, a strip of cloud, the broad sky, a fine tree, would fascinate him— make him vocal." W. interested to know that my father had gone over to see the Vereshtchagin pictures this afternoon. "What did he report of them?" I thought adversely. W. then: "He will probably go again then. I have been anxious to meet somebody who had gone. And you—will you not go?" Said: "I have had a letter from Bucke—a short letter; but it was of no significance; significant letters are rare anyhow." Wrote to Bucke and sent paper to O'Connor today. No further intelligence from Washington.

"I see," he said again, "that the celebration is well over." "And well," I said, "all except the ball." The ball had ended as an orgy. W. smiled: "Oh! we won't mind that—that was an ebullition of human nature. And you must remember the part the reporters had in it, too: we know well enough how to take them. Events never fail by their telling them." "I have read the Critic," he remarked, handing the paper to me, "and I don't know but you may as well take it with you now." As to the reference therein, quoted the other day, "I saw it—it is all right—though I don't know if I should say it just that way." Left with him copy of the Home Journal, with a column extracted from Myers and headed "The Ecstacy of Tennyson." W. knew the print before he had seen the name of the paper. Expressed his joy to see the article. "It is one thing to lighten up the gloom here."

W. asked for details about my visit to Shillaber with Morse. "I have always had an idea," W. said, "that Shillaber looked like our Mr. Hunter. Was it justified?" On my description W. very readily perceived the differences. At W.'s urging I detailed the house &c. so far as I remembered. I could recall well a reference to Emerson, in which Shillaber talked of Emerson's "idiotic smile." W. was struck with the infelicity of this. "I should accept the word, however—accept it in some

118

such way as saying, 'the sun bathed the world in its idiotic light' or 'the idiotic glory of the sun.' " Morse had spoken of Emerson's smile as among the wonders of his face. W. said: "I should call it that, too. But Emerson's smile was not common—it was rare indeed. But his usual manner carried with it something penetrating and sweet beyond mere description. There is in some men an indefinable something which flows out and over you like a flood of light—as if they possessed it illimitably—their whole being suffused with it. Being—in fact that is precisely the word. Emerson's whole attitude shed forth such an impression. I have always felt something of the same sort in our friend Hunter—his face unvarying in its brightness. Men have that—even have other atmospheres—darker. A lecturer, writer, poet, talker, anybody, carries with him his aura or not—his assurance of success—a quality most real, but wholly indefinable. Emerson was rich with it."—"Carlyle possessed it, too—but in its darker aspects." W. would even "instance" newspapers. "Some of them we like to read—some we despise—all of them have their specific, overlying, all-pervading quality. Take the Phila. Press for instance—its frightful sourness—its disposition to snarl like a small dog, to make complaint, to be small whatever the occasion. It is a color, tone, odor, which hits the reader inevitably." Emerson of all men possessed this aura in its purity: "Never a face more gifted with power to express, fascinate, maintain." W. was very greatly drawn towards the description of Shillaber. I went over the printer anecdote— Shillaber's first offer from a publisher. W. was struck. "That is not only good as an event—a fact—for its benefits to him— but good, excellent, as a story."

W. had asked me among his first questions tonight: "What of Brown—did he get started?" But he had not, and W. was much disappointed, as I had been. I insisted upon some absolute time from Ferguson, and he then promised the sheets would be delivered by Thursday morning of next week without fail. W. expressed a little solicitude lest something interfere with the accomplishment of our task.

Friday, May 3, 1889

10.45 A.M. W. reading his papers. Did not "feel very bad —nor yet very good." Is really now enjoying a respite. "I had no mail this morning except a couple of autograph letters. They come and come—they are inevitable." I had brought him several papers to look over—two copies of Harper's Weekly and a copy of last week's American containing my signed piece—"The Cry of Forgotten Philadelphia." Looked at portrait of Pearson: "Oh! a handsome, noble fellow! and face, too!" And then in comment on the engraving itself: "They are doing wonderful, fine work now—wonderful, effective work!" And sighed of Pearson: "so young, too!"

I met John Curley on the boat last evening after leaving Whitman. Seems he was one of the two Record boys who did the reporting in New York. He assured me the accounts of the ball were not unfair. W. listened to all I thus repeated to him. "I can see—but I don't think it exceptional at all. Balls are more or less free and easy anyhow—they used to be so when I was a young man, anyhow." But these were the Elite of New York? W. answered: "Elite or not—put them at a ball and put some liquor in them and it's all one!" Some of the reporters had lost their coats and hats in the scramble. W. said: "That explains it—that explains it!" Curley had been deeply impressed with the ill appearance of Harrison. W. asked me: "And is it true the Bishop—Bishop Potter—is out in some kind of an explanation of his speech?" There was some such report abroad.

Talk then of night-cars &c. W. asked: "What is the peculiar nature of a night-car?" And when learning asked again: "It involves the abolition of all law, does it?" I rehearsed experiences, in which he was intensely interested. "What a thing it would be for one of the men on those lines to put down his reminiscences. It would make a great book!" I spoke of old conductors I had met. Then of the change in time, from 18 to 12 hours, made in their work of recent years. "They have accomplished that?" asked W., "well it is high time they had. They were driven at a devil of a rate—it was damnable—the whole old constitution of affairs!" Then he said to me reflectively: "There's something I want you to do for me, Horace, some day: I am going to ask you to make particular inquiries. There was a fellow over there on the Market Street lines: I knew him well—loved him—and he me, too, I am sure: Joe Adams was his name. He was a starter there. Occupied quite a humble, working, laboring man's position there—what they call a starter. We used to be on good terms together. He was an asthmatic fellow—had a wife and family: it has struck me—is Joe still alive? You can ask—make inquiries in my name. It has been now full a year and a half since I saw him last—full that—probably two years. I have completely lost track of him. You know, the months pass and pass. I have been in this room now nearly a year—and even before that for some time I was not getting about at all." I asked him for some description. "Oh! he was a sandy-like man—sandy hair—all that goes with that: not tall or strong —asthmatic, as I said—and sickly complected, too. Joe was Quakerish—showed it in his looks and ways. He was born on the outskirts—his parents died when he was quite young; he was taken in by a Quaker family—imbibed their ways, had them to the last." Said he desired "to report" himself to Joe if still alive. "Ask anyone about there. It was right at the top of the hill he kept his station—was there all day. I remember the hill well—it was a great job getting up it—expecially a job of a slippery day." I suggested asking the man there at the stand. W. tried to place the topography clear. "On the hill itself there was a paint shop—you remember that? then beyond, across the first street—Front Street—was a gin-mill.

121

It was here—at the curbstone—stood the starter's caboose." And here his face lighted up: "Yes, you are right—I remember the stand there—the eating stand. They would know. Is the same old Dutchman there?" The old fellow is not Dutch but Italian—has been there from my boyhood. "He had a daughter—she must be 25 now—a very good girl"—after a pause—"of her class. Ask her, she would know about Joe. Ask her in my name—though I don't know if she ever knew me by name. Ask her in the best way you can: make a point of it—you might even do it today. Go to the stand, buy a penny apple or something—strike up a talk—tell her Walt Whitman had sent you—that he has it at heart." Further he instructed: "And should you see Joe—Joe himself—tell him about me: tell him I sent you—tell him I am confined here in my room—have been up here now for eleven months—but am still up—head up!—through them all." Joe was "a man of his own peculiar abilities"—was something of "a character": W.'s affection for him had been "honest and deep."

I gave W. a sentence I had hit on in Emerson today: "Nature never rhymes her children,"—and he repeated it over and over again, as if in huge enjoyment of its import.

7.35 p.m. Found W. sitting alone in his darkened room, his usual window open, and he, as he said, "meditating and not unhappy." Keeps well—sat much as I found him all the time of my stay. These days he is able to do considerable reading. His mind is in far better condition than for a month past. He does not encourage visitors—does not eat much—gains no strength—but is comfortable, for him, and more hopeful. Edwin Stafford in to see him tonight. Harry Wright was over, but coming while I was upstairs, did not ask to see W. Billstein did not have the pictures ready for me today, but promises them absolutely for tomorrow. W. was satisfied. Wants to send some of the three-quarter pictures away.

Dr. Abell spoke to me today rather contemptuously of Harrison in the course of a talk over affairs. W. remarked

(Abell having been a Republican) : "Ah! that is significant—
vastly significant. Let me predict that that will more and
more spread. Harrison will finally be recognized for what he
is—ignorant, superficial. Yet there is something fit that the
ignorance and superficiality of the American people should
elect him as its representative. I wrote Dr. Bucke something
about to this effect: the great celebration is now over—quiet
has come again—the days have calmed down—it was a wonderful pageant: but on the crowded canvas, the most insignificant item was the man we call Harrison—the man who
is our President today. I even assert that Harrison looked
cheap in the pictures." I described to W. a Puck cartoon
representing Harrison putting muzzles on the Press—Reid,
Halstead (attempted) Rice and so on. W.: "Was it good? oh!
I think it must have been good!" Some Republican had
called Harrison "a gassy fizzle." W. was much acquiescent.
"You see, I am not the only one inclined to speak of him in
severe terms. I should without hesitation adopt those words as
my own. 'A gassy fizzle!' Yes, surely! and they'll see it more
and more so as time passes. I commenced to question him the
minute of his inaugural address—that turned me at once.
And things since have but added fuel to the fire—fuel and
fuel—the speeches there in New York with the rest. But the
matter will settle itself—mark my words, will find its level—
the fire will burn itself out!" He shows intense feeling on this
point. "The high future of America" he asks "what has it in
common with this but to have it come and pass away?" And he
insists again: "The people stand up and cheer the office: it is
the office that excites the awe, the acclaim, not the man Harrison in it!"

Reference to a Millet article by Wyatt Eaton in the Century. "Yes," W. said, "I saw it—and read it, too. The pictures were very good—I was much moved by them: one picture there of Millet himself—it was very satisfying." But
W.'s mind never loses its critical force: "But after all, as an

article—taking the literary side of it—it was not of what we call devouring interest. But interesting it was: being about Millet, that could not fail. We might put it in this way: it was an article one would not miss reading because it was about Millet." We discussed the studio—its simplicity contrasted with the great Parisian studios—the nature of the reproduction of the sketches &c. W. asked me: "What do you know about Wyatt Eaton?" adding for himself: "He apparently stands high. I know Watson Gilder used to give him a great importance—I don't know but he does yet. There was the Holland picture: I have spoken to you about it—grand beyond any picture of the sort I have known." Thence much talk of probabilities in connection with the future of American art. I argued that so far no man had done for our art what W. had for our literature, but that one coming with that intent, would find his path smoother in that W. had preceded him. But W. was dubious. "I know that is to be considered, but I am afraid it is not such plain-sailing as appears. There are stubborn facts—these will invite a stubborn contest: and long and long before the battle is won! It will try the mettle of any man who attempts it. American art today is not in a temper to receive it. Our art is a good deal more committed to the schools, the traditions, than our literature ever was: body and soul, both are committed." He spoke of the art of Paris as "natural" to its belongings. "London I may call semi-natural"—but American art—"it is entirely given over to a bondage." This too, "not only to the Greek models—all signified by the ancient art—but the modern, the Parisian as well."

Yet he had looked at the Harpers Weeklies I brought in this morning—at the Salon pictures from Americans therein reproduced and written about by Theodore Stanton—and found them "very worth while" seeing and knowing. And, if I did not want to take them with me now [as I did not], "I'll probably look over them again" for he found that "with such things" if he kept them by him, he will go "over them again and again." Took him a copy of Current Literature—the May issue, which, he said: "I shall have much joy in reading." I asked him if he had read H. S. Morris' poem in The Century? "I saw it there," he replied, "but I can't remember it now at all—even what it was about." This means no lack of memory, but of impression: the Eaton piece, which had appealed to him, was well enough remembered. "The trouble with men of our time—even the men of power—the cutest of them—of what we call the literary classes, is in their disposition to avoid sharp corners—to smooth everything down till every pulse of feeling is taken from it." Men of our day are too much built up "of models of models of models, back illimitably." I contested stoutly that whatever was the case now, our art was bound in the end to have its masters. Just now it is mastered. And I said: "Just as sure as that you came and were inevitable, just so surely will others come." He fervently prayed that America would have open soul for the new inspiration—"I, too," he said to me—"yes, boy—I, too!"

Someone had raised the question in a circle—what so far are America's most distinctive and effective creations? While everyone else spoke of the concrete results, I said, in my turn: "Ralph Waldo Emerson, Walt Whitman, perhaps Abe Lincoln!" W. asked: "Did they take that as something novel and startling?" And then he referred to Lowell's touch the other day in New York. "I was glad for it, too—it was a grand thing for him to say there." I said to W. further: "I do not believe any man in history, having such friends as you have had—received by such men as have received you—ever failed of immortality." W. said: "That sounds grand—seems like a solemn thought—but"—and of course he would say no more as to that. But when I said: "The fight about you is now 30 years old—you are better received, more recognized, today than ever before." W. acknowledged: "That is true—of course—I must see that."

Ed came in with the mail, asking: "Shall I put on the light for you?" But W. negatived: "No—Ed—no: I will do it myself: it can easily be done." And he started to do it as I left. I alluded to going to the city to Mrs. Fels'. W. said: "Ah! our good people who sent me the soap? You must give them my best regards—tell them I use the soap every day— that it is good for me—smells good, feels good, is good—and a remembrancer too!" Although not able to find Joe Adams himself, I had found out today in town that he was yet alive and at work on the line, though no longer a starter. But forgot to tell W. in hurry of other talk. He is anxious to have me see the Vereshtchagin pictures. "You mean to go, don't you?" If he "could get about" that would be a mission, he says, among first missions, this week.

Saturday, May 4, 1889

10 A.M. W. had just finished his breakfast. Had got up feeling very well, and now was engaged with the papers. Seemed in unusually happy mood. Called my attention to several matters, and as I sat down and read he pored over the papers—patiently handled the Press, laid it down, took up the Record. "I see," he said, "that Harrison has been speaking again—welcoming the new British minister." But the speech was, as he thought, "without merit." Returned me the copies of Harpers Weekly with some general word of appreciation. But would "keep" Current Literature, unless I was in a hurry for it—as of course I was not. I spoke to him of Joe Adams—told him what I had heard, but that as he was flitting all along the road I should be compelled to take my chances about meeting him. Said W.: "Well—the main point of your errand is accomplished—you have found that he is alive. That is chiefly what I wanted to know."

"I have a book here," he said suddenly, laying down his paper an instant—"at last—the Sarrazin book—it came this morning. Did you tell me you knew some one who was an expert in French?" And afterward: "Alas! I shall never have back the grand old days, and my friend Obin, here across from me, translating, explicating, as he read! I have told you about him—his help in Washington, in things I could not help myself to—all the French authors, mainly Hugo, our theme. Obin would sit with me, read, about as I am talking now, easily, clearly, deliberately. It was a privilege—a priceless privilege." He added: "I am not certain about O'Connor's ability to read French: he knew the French writers, but how I could not say,—at least do not remember clearly." He had in the meantime handed me the thick volume. It was a soft book —blue paper covers. "And the type?" W. asked, "don't you think that is small pica?" The portion devoted to W. was about 40 pages. W. had cut the prefatory and the Whitman pages. The rest was uncut. He had looked over it. "It is so much Greek," he said, "I can see nothing of it." Among others were essays on Shelley, Wordsworth, Tennyson, Browning—perhaps Byron, too, but of this I forget as I write. W. again: "What a pity I can't read it myself! I should like to see what he says of the other fellows, too: I am quite bitten with his talk of me. The style of that whets an appetite for more." Twelve pages, anyhow, of the Whitman essay were given over to quotes. The book was simply inscribed to W. by the author in a written two or three lines, with no comment attending. W. took the book from me. "And see," he advised, "you notice the typographical beauty of the book? It is really grand—beats anything we do here. I gather a vast satisfaction out of that printing feature alone: the big liberal type, the whole manner and attitude of the volume." I asked him if he did not imagine they would print equally well here if there arose a demand? But he insisted: "I mean what I said—it seems to me we are going backward instead of forward. Look at this book, now"—reaching forward and picking from a pile on the floor a copy of his yellowed, aged, patched, pamphlet Consuelo: "Look at this—wouldn't you call that fine? Do we do anything like that nowadays? It is superb work—superb. I have read this book through and through and through—often and often and often—and not an error, either. Certainly a wonderful production." Graham, New York, Tribune building was its publisher. "I remember the place well," W. said, adding: "And this probably was not considered anything unusual in the way of printing at the time. Probably the printer was some unheard-of man—some not-famous individual." He turned over the title page—read aloud on the obverse—"New England Stereotype Foundry" —saying then: "Printed, maybe, in Boston. Take that Sarrazin book, too—it is cheap, no doubt—probably no big price put on it." Then he explained: "It came just as you see it there—no letter, no word. But I shall write, acknowledging its arrival." Then he said in half-soliloquy as to his French friend again: "No written translation could have the charm of his voice—the charm that always comes of renderings face to face."

Suddenly he turned to his table again. "No word from Washington this morning, but this with the Sarrazin book"— passing over a copy of The Literary News adding: "and somebody has been doing us up big there, I think Mrs. Leypold." After a pause: "Though there are things there which people would say a woman is not likely to write." Full two pages of close matter, really of most favorable quality. A passage there in which it was said W. "occupied" himself at a certain age with "making disciples," excited him to great laughter. He thought if he had ever been guiltless of any one thing, it was of any endeavor to develop "disciples." Said: "I knew Mrs. Leypold's husband—he is dead now. I only surmise, of course, that she wrote that piece." As I left W.'s last words were: "Be sure you get the pictures"—adding slowly, knowing our frequent disappointments—"if they are done!"

7.35 P.M. With W. about an hour tonight. Found him writing a letter, the pad on his knee. "Go on," I said, "you'll want to send it by this evening's mail—finish it—I will wait." But he said: "Never mind—I'll lay it aside now—'tis only for Doctor—and I mean to put the finishing touch on it tomorrow any how." Then as I came near and shook hands with him—he advised: "See this—I'm trying to show Doctor what sort of a book Sarrazin has sent us—puts us in." Had transcribed carefully in ink on a loose slip (the letter proper in pencil) the full title of the book. I leaned forward, found the dubious name Coleridge's instead of Byron's (see A.M. notes) and remarked what had been my doubt. W. said: "That is so— why not Byron? I had been looking for him myself." Then reflectively: "There are several of them here, his contemporaries—Shelley, Coleridge, Wordsworth." But when I said: "I suppose he chose them for purposes of giving different phases," W. assented—"I suppose that is the explanation."

Apropos of the letter to Bucke, I remarked that I thought, from what he said that Bucke had seven or eight hundred of them in his possession. W. appeared startled—looked at me in mock horror. "Can that be? It seems impossible! I am as bad as Carlyle himself. That is doing pretty good for a fellow who prided himself on writing few letters—for one whose early printer predilection for a letter on one sheet only and one side only of that sheet still persists." Then he asked: "Do you suppose Doctor keeps them all?" And when I nodded—he exclaimed—"Good! Good!": I said I hoped he had given us all a good character in 'em, and he laughed. "I did not know that of the Doctor. I can quite understand it of O'Connor. O'Connor is very sensitive to the magnetism of presence, contact, the spiritual forces. I can realize that he would love to take my postals, hold them, keep them in his hands long and long, look at the address in the big spread it makes." I said I thought all his postals to O'Connor were preserved: Mrs. O'Connor had shown me a pile of them on his desk when I was down there.

W. asked: "So that is the case? I'm only sorry they are not more worthy. They are all so short, so empty—so much the result rather of a desire to write than of any feeling of anything particular to say." Yet was not that enough? Presence, without a word, often the sacredest inspiration? I reminded him of his own poem (man and boy &c.). When he said: "That is so—I can see how that—that alone—transcends all speech, all utterance." And he continued: "There's nothing I should like better than to write six or a dozen lines—a little poemlet, poemette, giving in a few words, the picture of the revolution days—the glooms, despairs, sufferings, horrors, suspicions, of that time: the sprinkly trailing of faith through it all, the final victory. Then show how vastly, vastly greater that is than the celebration of it we have been having this past week: the dull speeches, platitudes—Harrison's worst of the worst." And afterwards: "The poor, pitiful Harrison! I should say of him—of all things, he lacks most in background—lacks it utterly. John Burroughs, in one of the pieces in which he is at his best, sets out to show how wholly inefficient beauty is—the world's beauty, so called—without background: that in background is beauty's whole secret, essence, justification. He uses the Spenserian figure of Una riding the lion—makes it a grand figure. There was always a surpassing power to me in this— John so nobly uses it." Then he said: "Poor Harrison! And yet, that office seeking business would knock the devil out of a man. I know it would be a horror to me. I have often wondered if nothing could be done—no scheme be devised—by which to defend our Presidents against this, some scheme by which the offices are given out by others. Have the Civil Service reformers ever tackled the question—planned anything? I can easily see how it must always be the President's function to choose his Cabinet: but for the rest, it seems to me there might be put up a defense of some kind."

Lincoln's, now for the first time printed, defense of the draft (in the current Century) had aroused W.'s interest. "I

read it. That it was not published was not at all wonderful.
People little know how less than a thousandth part—a
thousandth thousandth part—of things written, prepared,
studied, gets into print. All that goes to the making of what is
published is unknown—ever must be unknown. And it is a vast
sea of itself. Oh the tragedy and the pathos of it!" I alluded to
a page I had once written, which had taken me about a week to
write, and for which I got about two dollars. W. laughed—
said it was "like enough" and then proceeded: "And by the
way, there was the article you had in the paper you left with
me—the American: I can tell you I read it with a great deal of
interest too. I should advise you to cultivate that vein. I have
always known you had a quite remarkable seeing power—
power to grasp a fact, a gift to touch easily to the heart of ap-
pearances—I may say, an artistic sense, which you show in
your criticism, handlings of affairs, of things. That you
ought to cultivate. But I should warn you—don't worry about
abstractions—the philosophy of what you see. Keep your
eyes wide open—I need hardly advise you to do that—you do
that anyhow: but I mean, describe what you see,—people,
stands, stores, vehicles, shows, the human curios—and let the
rest tell itself. It will! The French are uniquely gifted in that
way—oh wonderfully—only with this drawback—a tendency
I always dislike, never will accept—a superciliousness which
seems to hold them from mixing with the event, the fact, they
describe. It is a quality our own humorists have had—which is
their weakness: Bret Harte, Mark Twain—the others—who
fairly enough touch off the rude Western life, but always as
though with the insinuation, 'see how far we are removed from
all that—we good gentlemen with our dress suits and parlor
accompaniments!' " W. criticised the want of truth in the
magazine stories now vogued—"the stories of Western, South-
Western, life. 'Hit' they will say for 'it,' for instance. That is
news to me. If it has come into use, it has come lately—for in
my time there was no such exaggerated emphasis. In fact, that

is the prevailing error—an aggravation of the peculiarities of dialects. It spoils some of those very good stories in the magazines—stories excellent in themselves, but too apt to exceed the truth, perhaps to excite our interest, perhaps from defect of ear." He counselled me then: "Watch yourself closely. Make a habit of noting things you see—buildings, people, the crowds you face, stands,—touch off the fakirs along the busy ways—fear nothing except to overstep the truth. It would be a good thing to do if only for exercise, but you will do it for more than that."

I had brought him the long-desired pictures. They proved to be excellently printed with much softness and effect. I could see at once that he was pleased. He asked of it: "Don't you think this should go in as frontispiece?" Adding after my assent: "That is my conviction too. Here was Leaves of Grass in gestation. Nothing could more fitly preface it." And as to the minute reproductions of even the scratches of the photograph—"I can readily see them—but they don't affect me, except for good. You know, a man may be so dressed, combed, he looks too damned nice. We have to look out for that." He signed a couple of the pictures for me "Walt Whitman 1849" saying: "That must have been the time—I should say from 1846 to 1849. What did I sign Dave's?" Put the two dates on Dave's—1850 and 1849. It seems to me that the 70th year picture has been injured by its trip to N. Y. but W. said: "I notice no difference—it seems to me about the same."

The Critic said today, reviewing the Authors at Home volume: "Much is told us by an intimate friend of Walt Whitman's, whose head of silver and heart of gold gleam in these sympathetic pages as never before." When I gave this to W., he would have me repeat it—he saying them after me—"head of silver and heart of gold, eh? That sounds very friendly— very warm. We cannot turn from a good word like that." But when I quoted from Elizabeth Stuart Phelps' Forum paper on "The Christianity of Christ" the phrase "in all uninspired

literature what is finer than the scene between the Bishop and
Valjean" &c.—the word "uninspired" struck W. as unfortu-
nate and he said of it, laughing—"Rats! is the most appro-
priate answer for that."—"I can hear the boys now yelling
'Rats!' in response to it." Then he said: "Well do I remember
Valjean, the Bishop—indeed the whole story." No Critic came
to him today. Said: "I think Kennedy might have the quality
I remarked in O'Connor. Of the Doctor I should not be certain.
I sent Kennedy a postal today—sent off also a foreign postal.
I wished Sarrazin to know at once that the book had come."
Adler speaks in town tomorrow on "The Character of Washington." W. predicted: "I am certain it will be fine. What a
treat it would be, if one could be there. I have no special message to send to the Professor. Only tell him I still sit here day
by day in my big chair, back against the wolf-skin robe, working, thinking, pursuing what I can. Not all bereft of
buoyancy yet. Give him my love and affectionate remembrances." This led him to a little talk of his condition. "It is
better," he said to my assurance, "better beyond a doubt. I
feel ever so much relieved: now if I could only get out!"
Referred to the Joe Adams I had searched for, and W. was
affectionate in his reference. "We struck up quite a friendship. Joe is not a young man anymore—is of middling size, has
a sandy, red beard, is rather pale. He has a family—I think a
daughter of 22 or more—and there is a son, too—a son
named for me—Walt Whitman Adams." W. laughed over the
patriotic conjunction. "Joe is a genuine fellow of the soil—
has about him the flavor of woods, grass, fences, roads. It is
uplifting to get near him."

We discussed somewhat the Millet article in the Century
again. Especially the phrases there quoted from Millet: "One
must be able to make use of the trivial for the expression of
the sublime," and: "The man who finds any phase or effect in
nature not beautiful, the lack is in his own heart." These were
"deeply impressive" to W. He asked me: "And did you find

133

the article interesting—very interesting?" And to the sentence where Eaton says, "Two Americans have reminded me of Millet—George Heller in the general appearance of his figure and Walt Whitman in his large and easy manner." W. remarked: "It may be true, but I do not know how Eaton knows it, I am not conscious of ever having met him. Of course he might have seen me anyhow." As to resemblances, spiritual, artistic or personal W. would say nothing. W. asked me what I made up "as Millet's opinion of Parisian artists?" Returned me Current Literature with remarks of its "wonderful richness of contents."

Sunday, May 5, 1889

1.30 P.M. Found W. just struggling towards his chair. Spoke of his own condition as "quite good today." Explaining: "I have just got up—was lying down for some time there on the bed." And he asked me after settling in his chair: "Isn't the day wonderfully beautiful out of doors? I have been sitting here by the open window." Out beyond, the green trees, birds singing, the plaint of an organ somewhere on the street. W. remarked the dullness of the papers today. "That is so, there is nothing in them. I have just written the Doctor that we seem to be passing through a period in art, literature, science, of absolute dead water. It does indeed seem so." Asked me where I was going this afternoon and when learning of a trip off on P.W.& B. road, exclaimed—"Oh! how I wish it were eligible for you to step in for an hour on O'Connor himself on your walks this afternoon! Poor fellow! Poor fellow!"

This morning I read several passages of "Democratic Vistas" to a group of young people, who seemed much struck therewith. W. said: "Democratic Vistas? I remember—it was a year ago, perhaps two—the Doctor wrote me that he had had a sinking—that Democratic Vistas had sunk in deep water for him—had vastly lessened in his esteem. But then he wrote me that afterwards, when alone, isolated somewhere by some occurrence, he had come back to it, taken in its full scope again—that he had found there, as I had always hoped was the case, close-compacted, the statement of America's future —something like that. Democratic Vistas was a composite piece—the product of different times, really, though coming about directly, as I must have told you before, of Carlyle's 'Shooting Niagara'—which was the emanating integrating force." "I was in Washington at the time—the early years of my stay there—was feeling pretty well—the paralysis not then on. Carlyle aroused me and this resulted." To my question he said: "Yes, Wendell Phillips thought very well of it. And there was another, too, I remember—Mills—John A. Mills—he was in Washington at the time—a Supreme Court lawyer—a man of prominence and parts—of qualities. He was a true democrat—a believer in Democracy—but somehow afraid—not certain of the future. He took Democratic Vistas up very carefully at the time: said in the course of a speech in some public meeting, referring to the book—'He has found it!' I don't know but Mills is living still—I must make a point to find out sometime."

Said he had examined the picture by daylight. "I am thoroughly satisfied with it!" Finished letter to Dr. Bucke. Adler spoke on "The Character of Washington" this forenoon. I was present. W. inquired after it with interest. As I was going he waved his hand—"My best wishes attend you, boy!" Did not stay long. Had only limited time for getting across the river to the train.

Monday, May 6, 1889

10.35 A.M. W. reading the Long Islander. Looked very well. Sat by open middle window. Day deliciously clear and mild. I asked W. if he had read the Critic reference (the Critic laying at his feet), and he said: "Yes and it is quite an

epigram, too—isn't it? 'Head of silver and heart of gold'—
it is new to me. There was something somebody once said of
Diderot, the great French Encyclopedist, that he had a mouth
of gold; that is the nearest I have known to this expression. I
used to take a great interest in Diderot—do still, in fact.
Somewhere I read a description of the French Encyclopedia as
of 200 volumes. I tried hard to get some definite information
on that point, but never succeeded. I asked Doctor Bucke—he
thought it a mistake. Then asked Mr. Hunter—who looked
about some—inquired of book men—men who might be supposed to know—but without result. So I struck the line out: I
had intended using it in my writing—in November Boughs.
The Encyclopedia has always seemed to me a marvel of
marvels—a wonderful moonshine, a wonderful history. And
though I have always approached it, knowing little of its
intimacies, I have always felt persuaded that Diderot was the
great man among its group of writers." W. saw a copy of
Unity in my hand. "What have you got there?" he asked—
and I showed him a paragraph therein pertaining to Morse,
which W. read with pleasant comments. "Sidney has work to
do, surely: but we never hear from him now, do we?"

I had received a letter from Bucke, dated the 4th, which I
showed to W., who in his turn said: "And I got this," handing
me one received by him. In my letter occurred this in reference
to the Hartmann matter:

That Hartmann affair was bad, very bad. I wrote a note to the
Herald for the "Personal Intelligence" Column quoting from a
P. C. of W.'s of 17th April, as follows: "The sayings of S. H.
make H (yourself of course) (an intimate friend of W. W.'s)
frantic angry—they are invented or distorted most horribly. I
take it all phlegmatically" but it seems the H. did not print it.
What do they care who feels bad so the paper sells. But S. H. is
the party to blame damn him.

W. read it through very deliberately. "Yes," he then said, "I
see. But then we must remember the Herald has several vices

in common with the journals everywhere—among them this, that it won't correct its mistakes." Then W. pursued the Hartmann matter: "I confess, this does not stir me as it stirs others. It is painful to have it happen—especially painful to have it happen at a time when Stedman has more and more been proving his goodness to us—has been getting ever warmer and warmer—testifying to all this in the literary way by his mention of us in the big book. But as things go, this matter does not ripple me, even. It seems to be a penalty a man has to pay, even for very little notoriety—the privilege of being lied about. Yet I rest the case finally on the good sense of my friends—their knowledge that, of printed matter anyhow, fully a half—three-quarters perhaps—even a greater propor- tion, is lie—is admitted to be such." I suggested that such a note as Bucke's to the Herald would do more good in the Critic. Which W. admitted—except that he insisted: "I don't see why we need to print it at all: we ought to be able to let such things pass and pass and die, as they will."

W. handed me a ticket for some Woman Suffrage meeting which he had received in mail this morning. "Perhaps," he said smilingly, "this would interest you. I can't use it!" Had been interested in paper account this morning of Ben Butler's charge of cowardice (at New Orleans) against Admiral Porter. Also in account of Camden ministers inducing horse railway company not to run cars on Sunday. "I see," said W., "they have done it—and think they have done a big thing. I, for my part, should say that Sunday of all days they should run the cars. I do not publish myself on the point, but I should argue for absolute freedom—cars, ferry-boats, base-ball, picnics—nothing hindered, prohibited. I do not enter at all into what I call the—'quabble' of prohibition, but believe firmly that man no more now than at any time is eligible to be made good by law—temperate, honest, what not. There is a strong tendency in the human critter anyway to seek oppor- tunities of doing those things which he is prohibited from doing. It is in the child—it is a universal quality. There are certain offenses which the common sense, the universal sense, of all peoples, ages, nations, allow to be policeable: these are easily pointed out—humanity has a clear notion of what they are. But these other functions insisted upon for the law are condemned in the light of history and of man's present constitution." "The great moral forces will ever persist: the preachers about would say it was through them, their palaver: but we all know better than that—are not to be fooled by that."

Bucke had again written as follows about the hospital project:

I had no thought of W. going to Baltimore until after the book was published. At least if he continued tolerably well. I was only "afraid" (rather inclined to think) that you would oppose the move just as most folk oppose their friends going to Hospitals and Asylums from a feeling against it. At such a hospital as this (especially with Osler at the head of it—he being really a friend of W.'s) W. would be infinitely better off than where he is. His surroundings would be unexceptionable and all that modern medicine could do to increase his comfort and improve his condition would be brought into requisition. It is simply monstrous that such a man as W. with friends who are willing to do anything to assist him and with some means and income of his own should live on as he is doing at present. Poor O'Connor is evidently going down down and except for the shock it would give W. I would gladly have him go, for his life must be a burden to him, poor fellow. I am glad to hear that the book is likely to be "on time."

W. remarked of it: "I have had no output whatever on that subject yet—am not inclined in the least to move." I spoke of the absence of sun from this room—my regret that it was so. "You should be on the other side of the street," I said—and he: "Yes—I can see how that might be well." Then I argued for his going out of doors—getting his chair and attempting it, anyhow. Did he think he could not get downstairs? He feels so well just now, he accepts my confidence. I talked with him quite a while—he finally seeming touched into affirmation by my sanguine manner. "How good it would be," he admitted, "to get out into the air—freely to breathe it out of doors once more." And the river! It was a "glory" to him—"the mere suspicion of it." And I argued still again: "When Bonsall and Buckwalter were here, they told Ed to get the chair and they would fix the rest of it." W. moved: "Oh! they said that? and to Ed?" And he went on: "I think we might try it, boy. I have thought to ask you and Ed to go over together: I have the address of a party here—select a chair—you know about what I want. I know very well the chairs they used at the Centennial, but I want one a little different from them in shape: they were short-backed—I want a back up this high" —motioning above his head. "I do not object to plainness—in fact, I want a plain chair, but want comfort—a big back. And the seat must be liberal in size—and it must be strong. Let me see—I kept the address somewhere." Took up his notebook, and examined it page to page. "It don't seem to be here. It was an advertisement out of a paper—I put it aside here, contemplating this move. Now it seems to be gone. Anyhow I'll look and find it, then you and Ed can go." I suggested that we have several sent over and W. could then select for himself. He thought that "a good idea" and was willing we should proceed so. I was highly gratified. He seemed more disposed to attempt it than at any time before. If he can get out, who knows but results would exceed expectation? As to the hospital, he seems absolutely disinclined. I do not argue against, but there is one point which Bucke does not mention even and which to W. seems the most important of all, viz.— that at the best, W.'s going to Baltimore would involve some sacrifice of freedom.

5.45 p.m. W. sitting in chair at open window. Had just finished his dinner. "Summer has come suddenly upon us," he said, "it has been a beautiful, beautiful day throughout." Had had most serious thoughts of getting out. "I have not yet found the chair advertisement because I have not yet looked for it—but I shall look tonight." And he added, "My sister-in-law was here today. The chair that she had thought of up there in Burlington for me has been taken for some other person. It seems they got it from Wanamaker's—that Wanamaker's sent up to Boston for it. My sister thought she would anyhow go down and see what it looked like, so she could tell me of it, but when she got there, the lady reported that the chair was gone—that someone had probably come in the early morning and taken it off with them." But he was sure we could get suited our own way. "I shall want a plain chair—no cushions—not a cushioned chair: wicker-bottom, something like this—and solid." And liberal in size, I suggested—whereat —"Yes—that undoubtedly. But that will come about easily. Most of the users of these chairs are old plugs like me—broad at the beam—who won't be squeezed down at their time of life. See," he said leaning over, taking up a postal and handing it to me, "that is for O'Connor—I speak on it of the chair"—as he did: reporting the day as beautiful and that he was "cogitating" the project of purchasing a chair and getting out. "The back of such a chair will be a very essential part— we will need to have that high, so my head can rest on it, so—" throwing his head into grand repose on the wolfskin. "And after all," I said finally, "there's nobody but you who can properly select such a thing and have it suit." And he replied: "That is so—it all comes back to me at last."

Signed a copy of the butterfly photograph for me. Said: "And I will have you bring me three more of them before you take the bundle to Oldach." I brought him a sheet of the first fold book. Brown had got started and finished to p. 128 today. But with an unfortunate error on the title page—Myrick, in changing date of signature from Italic to plain Roman had made "May 13" instead of "May 31." This was lamentable, and W.'s eye struck it the instant he looked at the sheet. "A bad mistake," he said, "an error right off." And pointed it out.

But did not worry at all over it—only tried to get comfort out of the experience. "They will have to print a single sheet," he said—and then with a smile—"and that will make it easier for me to sign, and you will only have to bring over the 300 single sheets." "It is not a serious twist, but I am sorry he made it. If the worst comes to the worst—if we should fall short on paper"—this was a special lot which we could not add to—"then we could change it ourselves." I suggested writing to Brown at once about it, but W. suggested: "If you get over to the city in the forenoon, would anything be gained by writing now? Better be patient—let it wait."

I had brought him over the several copies of the Butterfly picture. Was in to see McCollin today. Pictures are all mounted, well done. W. at once expressed his own liking for them. "Are they all like this?" he asked, adding: "If they are, I shall be thoroughly satisfied." And he looked at it long and critically, for five minutes saying scarcely a word. Then: "Have you found any dubiety about that?"—pointing to the moth—"Do people generally look at it with dubiety? I have found there is often a doubt what it is: yet to me there don't seem as if there should be: which, I suppose, is because I am so familiar with it—know it so well—myself." I left bill. The price had been put at four dollars per hundred. "I expect to have a good many more to mount," he explained.

Speaking of the horse railroad anti-Sunday affair again: "I do not believe the Methodists did it: they may think they did, but they didn't. I see Armstrong is their counsel and that he is in favor of Sunday cars. That is very significant, too, because he is a Presbyterian." I interposed, "Baptist." W. then: "Well—Baptist: it is the same thing for my purposes. The church people themselves would be in favor of it if they knew anything, which generally they do not. In cities where Sunday is free—the cars run—they avail themselves of all opportunities."

We talked this evening somewhat about the fund, W. ex-

141

pressing in tone and word a tender gratefulness. In the early summer of 1888, O'Connor had sent twenty-five dollars, which was used. Later on he sent twenty-five more, which was sent back to him. W. found it hard to see through this till he thoroughly understood there had been two payments. "I requested that the money be sent back to him. Oh! I did not understand—did not know he paid twice. The dear noble O'Connor! the poor fellow!" And he asked: "and Bob Ingersoll—how did he come in? Tell me about that, too?" I had before but he would listen again. I said further: "I have no prejudices against going abroad for money, but as our boys here had growled that we had before gone abroad before giving them a chance to help you, I thought I would give them the chance now." W. considered that "an idea," provided it was kept within the spirit I stated. "I should not myself connive at anything which looked like shooing them off. I have always had it clearly understood—wished it understood by everybody—that I fully realized what the men and women —friends—abroad—had done for me. Not only were they wonderful and saving in their generosity at a time when I needed it—if ever I did need—in 1876: paying the full price for the book—the Centennial edition—that year—ten dollars—which, God knows, was enough of itself: but some of them even four, five times that sum. Not this only, but helping later on. I could not forget this—should not wish it obscured. It was a great service. They literally put their hook overboard, rescued me, a drowning man. I never could disregard that. I consider the Smiths as good friends, if not Americans —Mary Smith, Mary Costelloe—as any of 'em." I admitted to him I had no prejudices in the matter—should necessity impose it I should still go abroad. And W. made it clear he thought it "a good plan" to do as I had done. "Gilder's phrase was, 'it galls me.' Tom Donaldson told me that Irving said to him—Henry Irving, the actor—that if anything of this kind was projected, he wished to be counted in. And Tom said he spoke as though it was a thing he had at heart. Yet I can see the wisdom of your plan." And he asked me about Gilder: "Was it his own expression that you should 'nudge' him if he did not pay up?"

Alluded to the current slang—one phrase of it: "He's not built that way." W. said: "I think that very good—very good, should think it would last, I should be willing to use it myself. Years ago in New York there was an expression similar"—here he stopped a minute—"but that was indelicate. The phrase was, 'He does not hang that way.' You can see its import. Of course that could not find adoption, especially in literature. It was vulgar, had its brief day, is gone." I did not stay long, though W. was in very good mood. My sister afterwards went down, taking him some flowers, and from me Lounsbery's "Cooper." She saw and talked with him some little while. He spoke about getting out, what kind of a chair was advisable—spoke also a great deal about Tom and the family. The weather continues beautiful beyond words. I go to Germantown in forenoon, tomorrow. W. gave me copies of the three-quarter portrait for Mrs. Baldwin and J. H. Clifford, signing them "Walt Whitman in 1849."

Tuesday, May 7, 1889

8.05 P.M. W. reading Lounsbery's "Cooper." Room mostly closed—rather warm. The day had been fine again. W. himself asked: "It has been another warm day, hasn't it?"—adding as to his own condition that it had only been so-so, "though not of course in any sense what is to be called bad." I had been out in Germantown the main part of the day, working with Clifford over Johnson's Parker manuscript. I spoke to Mrs. Baldwin about a translator for the Sarrazin essay. She said Agnes Gay could read French as some of us English, but that she would not do anything for W. W., who she thought ought to be razed from the face of the earth. W. was excessively amused when I told him this. "Walt Whitman echoes that sentiment," he said, between laughing. Miss Gay had further appealed to Mrs. Baldwin to desist on one occasion when reading aloud from W. W.—urging that her high ideal of Mrs. B. would be disturbed if she continued. W. again laughing: "Tell Mrs. Baldwin Walt Whitman would advise her to take the advice and stop."

Had he found the advertisement for the chair? "Yes—I found it. I was in hopes you would come in today. You won't go till afternoon tomorrow? Well—then, anyhow." And he reached forward to his loaded chair. "I made this out for you to be guided by," he said, handing me a card on which he had pasted a sheet containing these instructions:

"Wanted:

"A strong first-rate out-door chair for an old 200 lb. invalid —to be pushed or pulled along the sidewalks and on the ferry boats—roomy chair, back high—ratan or reed seating and back (no cushions or stuffing)

"Go to Wanamaker's first and interview the charge of the chair &c. Department and show him this card—

"Then to Luburg's 145 North 8th Street"

The above just as he punctuated it—and down in the corner his address, part written and part printed. "Put that in your pocket," he said, "and tomorrow at the proper time use it."

I was in at Ferguson's today—instructed the correction for title page. Brown somewhat put out, but it was their error unmistakably and they saw it. W. had been today examining more carefully the sheet I gave him, and criticized it in a way precisely like mine to Brown when I first saw the specimen. "I don't think much of the printing, so far as I have seen it—it has a blotchy appearance—it is by no means what I had hoped it would be. But I suppose the sheet I had was but an isolated sheet and not to be taken as a sample. If the whole book had this same appearance, I should not be at all satisfied. But Brown must know—must know full as well as we do and better." I am prepared for some disappointment. His skepticism is justified. Yet he could say later on: "I think that if

144

ever any man should be satisfied in having had his own way
pretty much through life, that man is me, Walt Whitman."
And whatever the abatements "the solid fact" of his freedom
in that particular remained.

Harned came in and was heartily greeted. W. inquired after
Tom, after the family. "How is Anna?" he asked, "I got a
sort of suspicion, from words said here and there, that she was
not very well." Afterwards Harned said he had witnessed a
base-ball match this afternoon. W. then asked: "Tell me,
Tom—I want to ask you a question: in base-ball, is it the rule
that the fellow who pitches the ball aims to pitch it in such a
way the batter cannot hit it? Gives it a twist—what not—so it
slides off, or won't be struck fairly?" And on Tom's affirmative—"Eh? that's the modern rule then, is it? I thought
something of the kind—I read the papers about it—it seemed
to indicate that there." Then he denounced the custom roundly.
"The wolf, the snake, the cur, the sneak, all seem entered into
the modern sportsman—though I ought not to say that, for
the snake is snake because he is born so, and man the snake for
other reasons, it may be said." And again he went over the
catalogue—"I should call it everything that is damnable."
Harned greatly amused at W.'s feeling in the matter. W.
again: "I have made it a point to put that same question to
several fellows lately. There certainly seems no doubt but
that your version is right, for that is the version everyone
gives me."

Harned here said that his mission tonight was another than
base-ball. Then described a plan of citizens of Camden
(Buckwalter and Harry Bonsall and T. B. H. heading), to
give W. a testimonial on his birthday. They wished to keep
open house at 328, have refreshments there, let the public
come, and have W. receive them in such a way as he cared. We
all discussed the question, running into great detail. At first
W. was reluctant. "You must remember, Tom—must have it
understood—I am all banged up, unable to get out, to move
around." Adding: "I am starting now to get a chair. Whether

I shall get out will be a problem." Tom argued the wish of Camden people now to show their appreciation of his presence here. W. laughed a little: "I am sure I appreciate all that—appreciate Camden people—but I don't think, Tom, that the globe either begins or ends or is enclosed with Camden." And yet: "I must not be whimmy—must not give myself away to a kink." And to Tom's further urgings: "Well—you must remember the story of the French physician who took a quart bottle to his patient and was told " 'But, Doctor, I only hold a pint!' Remember Tom, I only hold a pint!" "If I could get out, this thing would better adjust itself—but my getting out is wholly uncertain." As to keeping open house: "I can see no objection to that. It seems to me it is all best left to your own taste and tact. I know, Tom, you are able to set that into order without my help." He was not unmindful of the good-feeling intended—"only, I am an invalid—all knocked up—careful of my ways" &c. I suggested the appointment of certain hours—say, 2 to 4 or 5 in the afternoon—a reception season, so as positively to relieve W. of strain. "Yes," he said "that sounds good—that seems feasible." Harned had come in to consult with W. about it. The point would be to raise a purse, exclusively from Camden contributions: to issue cards, for home and abroad—in other cities,—explaining the design —and having the day so well attested. W. was "well-pleased to have it so"—said again: "Tell Buckwalter 'Barkis is willin' ' " —but of course everything "must submit to the exigencies of my condition."

Showed Tom a copy of the three-quarter picture, which he had put in his big corrections-volume. "Is it good?" he inquired. Tom asked: "Is that the picture Gilchrist don't like?" And W. laughed—"So I have understood. But never mind, never mind!" Harned hit it off with a Shakespearian quip. Then asked W. if he had seen anything of Gilchrist lately. W. shook his head. "No—Herbert gets over very scarcely. It is a long time now." Showed Harned a sheet of the new book—a cut sheet given me by Brown today—and W. said to me: "This already looks better than the sheet you brought yesterday." Then again: "Time is short—but I anticipate no difficulties with Oldach—it seems plain sailing." As to photos mounted— he came nearer my own fears. "This card will never get out straight. I wish he had followed my own hints on this point— chosen a board more like that I sent him. But the picture as it is has so many virtues. I accept it."

Has had acknowledgment of book from Carleton. Tom asked him if he wanted anything further in his bottles there. W. said frankly enough: "Yes, I do, Tom—that bottle there." Tom started to denominate what he had, and W. put in: "Nothing but sherry, Tom—nothing but sherry. Whiskey I could not stand, though I should like to!" Inquired after the boy—"that fine boy"—the baby. Talking of getting to the ferry, W. said: "I don't know about that—don't know if I can stand it: it will be a great trip at first and for me!" And as Harned was going out the door, W. called again—"Remember, Tom—I only hold a pint!" Harned asks me to get up a card which he proposes to have engraved.

As to anything the public thought adverse to his career, W. said tonight: "I should not retort in the words of Vanderbilt—not so severely as that—but can say there is nothing in the world I care so little about—that so little worries me— as what the public may think, say." W. said to Tom of Bucke: "There was a letter came today. Doctor was off Saturday and Sunday to Sarnia. You know about Pardee there—he is very sick—almost dead—dying. This dying is a long process, often —but dying he is."

Wednesday, May 8, 1889

10.45 A.M. W. not looking very well—nor feeling so, as he said. And he quickly revealed the reason. "Bad news from O'Connor," he remarked, "almost the worst news. Here is a postal from Nellie this morning." Handing it to me from the table. O'Connor yesterday unconscious. Mrs. O'Connor said if William ever recovered consciousness he would no doubt enjoy W.'s postals, but seemed dubious. "Whether this is almost the end"—W. reflected—"whether the story is now nearly closed, it baffles us to know." Sometimes it was asked him, would he not rather have O'Connor dead than suffering so? "But I refuse to look at it that way. Yet the case is very dark almost hopeless." W. very serious, with less than his usual color.

Talked for some time over book matters—stamping, cover, &c. W. said he had no "arbitrary notion" as to how it should be stamped, but was "disposed to have the lettering adopted in the title page reproduced—indicating, along with Leaves of Grass, that A Backward Glance is included." Finally settled that I should advise with Oldach about it. We ought to have copies here by his birthday: if people then come in numbers, some may be sold. W. said: "I can see—and we may easily have copies by that time." "I have a pretty good idea now just where I am to place the portraits. There is nothing in the way of procedure. Do you think you will get the folded sets today?" Brown had promised to have the sheets ready for delivery by tomorrow forenoon.

I said to W.: "People who see the three-quarter picture think it incredible that that is you at 30." W. replied: "But it is me. I must confess, I am more and more satisfied with that picture—what it indicates. All my intimate friends who have known me for many years—know well enough that that appearance of age came on early. Some have said to me that I look younger now than I did in my youth. The grey was there just as you see it as early as 30. The steel is combed, I know—looks different: but the steel is all smoothed off—that is to be remembered. Of all the pictures I know, that new one most fills and satisfies me—and whatever people may say and think, I am content with it just as it stands."

148

Mr. Ingram came in and stayed about fifteen minutes during my stay. W. was very cordial with him—forgot we had met and introduced us again. Asked after himself and people. In reply to questions said: "I am here, you see—not worse, anyhow, than when you saw me last." Ingram said his daughter had given him flowers to bring to W., and here he had come without them. W. said in mockery: "Oh! you base fellow!" But, Ingram smilingly told W. he had left them with a prisoner down at Moyamensing, at which W.: "Oh! that was the way of it! Well—I can say in the language of Mrs. Harris, now I know, that I forgivages you!" Ingram asked for news. W.: "There is not much news. I had a postal from Washington this morning of rather dark import—telling me my dear friend William O'Connor is quite low—has lain in a fit—or was so yesterday." As to Johnston—"No word lately—though yes— a letter from Kitty Johnston. Nothing new in it—yet I have answered it—sent a reply." Rush, confined in Moyamensing, had sent his love to W., who said to Ingram: "Thanks! Thanks!" Rush had spoken to Ingram of the World piece and I now asked W. if he had a copy. W. responded: "I have had a copy, but have forwarded it to Dr. Bucke." But W. advised Ingram: "It don't amount to much—it is not profound." And in response to Ingram's question, "Who wrote it?"— said: "Yes, he was the Harpers' Ferry fellow. Dick is a little Englishman—I have known him about forty years or so. He meant that article well enough. The World wanted an article of three columns, for which they would give good pay, and Dick, wishing the money, made the article just so long. That is my surmise only—of course—but I am willing to bet on it. Dick was there at Harpers' Ferry—has always been a great abolition, underground man. Was out in Kansas at the time that tried men's souls there. Dick has always been of newspaper proclivities—writing for papers, magazines. But that article reminded me of a saying of Falstaff's: Falstaff speaks somewhere of a drop of rum (he don't call it rum—he calls it

149

sack)—a drop of rum to a quart of sugar and water. That was about the mixture of Dick's article."

Ingram described the country—its glorious spring-time dress—fruits, grasses, &c. Was enthusiastic. Said jokingly, if heaven was as good as that he'd like to go there. W. bantered with him: "You will get a good apron—a nice clean white apron—and be given a harp or what-not—and so take your place." But Ingram protested, whereat W. said: "Oh! they won't have you there if you don't do as they want you to!" Then murmured—"But this world is good enough: what could be grander than to get off in the country somewhere these days," &c. Ingram inquired after Dr. Bucke. W.: "I do not think so—don't think he is likely to be on here very soon." Ingram had to catch a train at one o'clock, so did not prolong his stay.

W. gave me back the "Cooper." "I have read it all—the whole book—and liked it too: was extremely interested." Had a pamphlet there by Elizabeth Porter Gould—"John Adams as a Schoolmaster"—which he handed to me. "Would you like to have it, or take it to your father? That is the great John Adams. The little pamphlet is very good, too—not abstract, the philosophy of the matter—but direct—without pretense— reported only—like a newspaper article." Miss Gould had written on it with purple ink—"Walt Whitman—With the good wishes of the author."

Asked me about our going to town. I made arrangements with Ed to meet me this afternoon at ferry. W. said: "You have my card?—make use of it!" How did he account for it that Herbert Gilchrist seemed to dislike all the more characteristic portraits of W. W.? W. said: "It might be thought in some sense a mystery, though it is hardly that. In many respects Herbert is a complete reaction from his Mother. Mrs. Gilchrist, with all her supreme cultivation, was gifted in a rare degree with a necessary don't-care-a-damn-ativeness. In fact, this was so marked in her that it was often thought she was inviting destruction." He spoke of Percy Gilchrist: "He takes no stock in me—in fact, I doubt if he likes me. I have never seen him. But I have seen the daughter—the daughter who died—Beatrice. And she threatened to be the most Whitmaniac of all, and the biggest woman, too—which is saying a good deal, for they were very big women. She came to this country—was along with her Mother—was going to make a doctor of herself—studied for two years in the female college here. Oh!—she was a noble girl!—noble—noble! But I think I know Herbert as few others do: I am sure I may say in some respects as no other can. I am sure these qualities—good solid qualities—are not all gone from him: they are obscured now—dormant—but may be reawakened some day. I do not despair for him at all."

Reference to Paris Exposition. W. said: "I like the make up of that man, the President there in France, Carnot—like his whole bearing. He is quiet, self-possessed, certain, yet makes himself felt wherever he goes. He seems to be a little man too, but one of whose littleness you soon become un-conscious in the emphasis of other qualities. Like the elder Booth, who was a little man, yet never obscured. The minute Booth would step on the stage, you would forget his physical proportions. He was much smaller than Edwin. It was singular of him, too, that though so little—though so often on the stage with a crowd of people—he was never lost in the crowd. The actors used to ask him where they should stand and he would say—use your own judgment about that—stand any-where, so you are not in my way—I will reach you." I referred to O'Connor's description of Booth—that his mere entrance on the stage deluged the house with electricity. Said W.: "That is so, too—I know it for myself. It was a subtle something back of voice, manner, eye: perhaps there is no better way of saying it than in just that way—that he had background—a something defying analysis, but deepest deep of fact and cir-cumstance." I likened that to a parlor group, all stiff till

151

released by the entrance of some person of magnetic presence who seems instantly to take down all bars. W. assented: "That is just it. But we must never attempt to make an outline of it—it is a quality we cannot chain."

W. keeps a vigilant eye ever upon the local papers. He said to Harned last evening: "You must be very busy. I see you down for a great number of cases." And to me again: "Is it Björnson at the next meeting of the Club?" I said: "Boyesen." "Oh! Boyesen! I am quite apt to get the names mixed." Again going back to "magnetism"—"and Alboni's voice! What a joy, a grandeur, an illimitable inspiration! Yet who could tell by what it all came?"

5.35 P.M. I met Ed as per appointment at the ferry about two o'clock. Thence we went to Philadelphia in search of a chair. At Wanamaker's we hit upon a chair which Ed fell in love with. The result at Luburg's not so good. On the way back Ed stopped at Post office, but Bonsall was not there. Furlong, however, spoke to Ed about an informal meeting in W. W.'s interest to be held tomorrow to plan for the birthday event. When we arrived home, found W. eating his dinner. We talked with him of affairs, he in the meantime eating on. As to any chair for self-wheeling, W. remarked: "That would not do at all. If I live, I shall probably get weaker, much weaker. I am preparing for that now." And afterwards: "It seems to me from the description you fellows give, as though you had struck the right thing." He questioned us a great deal about what we had seen. Asked Ed: "How could you handle the chair?" And asked me: "What about the price?" And laughed heartily when I told him the salesman who waited on us was numbered 1827. Altogether was gratified with the result of our quest. "I want no cushions," he repeated. And again: "You fellows went off on a speculation, didn't you?" The day had been so fine again. "Oh! if a fellow could only get out into the free air!" How had the river appeared?—and so on. Yet was cheerful—looked better, too, than in the forenoon. Had consulted with Oldach as to stamping and cover. For cover Oldach gave me an estimate, 68 cents for morocco, 46 cents for imitation. W. said: "We want no imitation. The price anyhow is far within what I had expected it to be. It quite sets me up!" Oldach thought the stamped facsimile of title page would have to be reduced. It was for that I had to consult W., who said he would give me definite answer to-morrow. "I should say we ought to go right on," W. remarked, "I think Oldach should be told our decision at once."

When I went to Brown today and told him that W. had said the printing would not be satisfactory if it was through-out like the sheet sent to Camden, Brown got enraged and said: "Well—we are doing the work our best way, and if you don't like it you don't need to take it. I don't want people to come here and criticise it when the work is nearly done," &c. All in a tone which I resented and which Ferguson himself afterwards told me was entirely uncalled for and unjustifiable. W. himself was aroused, but only said, calmly: "I do not say it positively—do not set it down at all—yet feel that such a remark is uncalled for if not absolutely impertinent. We are supposed to see, and to tell what we see, in a business trans-action involving what that does to us." Then however: "But I am inclined to take the happier view—to believe that the book as a whole is to be far better than the sample of it we saw—that we hit upon one of the first sheets." At any rate "we can but wait" and "tomorrow or next day will solve our doubts." Brown thought he would finish our sheets by tomorrow evening.

W. had been dwelling much upon O'Connor. "But there is no further word." He feared some fatal termination any time. Worked today at arranging the pictures for book. As he feels now, will after all not use the 1849 picture for frontis-piece—in its stead the butterfly. W. sat there and we meas-ured chair &c. He joked of his helplessness and the doubt whether after all he could get out when he did secure the chair. "It is questionable anyhow whether I'll ever be able to do more than go around the block." I ordered insurance renewed for three months. W. wishes to pay bills. "I will give you checks when you want them." Things are pushing on.

Thursday, May 9, 1889

10:45 A.M. Mrs. Mapes just came out of the room as I went up stairs. W. not doing anything at the moment. Ed had gone to Bonsall this morning. Bonsall said we had best leave matters as to the chair till Saturday. But our fears lest the one chair we wished would go before that date constrained protest. W. at first said: "Let it be done their way." But afterwards: "I think the chair you describe is just the chair I want—should not like to lose it. What do you think?" And then again: "You go to Harry yourself and explain—take Ed with you. Then Ed can go right across the river and have it sent." W. spoke of the day, of the desire to get out. I argued: "I hate to miss all these fine days"—but he smiled—"Oh! well—there are plenty more to come!" He speaks to everyone of the possibility of getting out at last. Pointed to flowers in a glass on the table. "Little Anna Harned was down—brought me these—wisteria. Oh! how tender and beautiful!—I have never known any of them more so!" Outside the door, on the floor, was a pitcher of lilacs. I had seen them on entering. Now went out and brought them in. "Are they condemned?" I asked. He said pleasantly, "Oh! no indeed! I put them out there last night—I thought them too heavy for a sleeping room—now I will have them back on the table there. They were brought me yesterday by Mrs. Allen—you don't know her? They have an unusually strong odor—that is distinctly the case with some of them. I cannot imagine any odor more delicious than this in sunlight, in an open room: but at night—the room closed—they seem out of place."

Said: "No word from Washington this morning—nor from Bucke—indeed, no word from anybody." Spoke of Brown and the book. "If you don't get the sheets today [I do not expect

154

to] I shall be greatly disappointed. Brown promised them Tuesday of last week. He never acted in this way before." W. gave me a check for $12.30 for McCollin and money to pay insurance policy. As to cover, he said: "I shall trust to Oldach's taste. But the most important thing now is the sheet. We can do little without that." We talked about stamping, and where. "This—to put it on the page with the flap—is the polite way: but the question is—is it the right way for us?" As to what should be the nature of the flap—"I am unable to make up my mind. You may get two models, one each way: then I can quickly tell which one I prefer."

I received a letter from Gilder this morning, enclosing one from Bush. I read these to W., who was visibly touched. " 'Lachine Falls'—yes—I know the place—have been near it." And then of "the unknown friends" who everywhere in his old age "seem to be given voice to greet" him. He said to me: "You should write—or Gilder—you more properly." I called his attention to Gilder's note again. "He has already advised Bush to write to me." W. hereupon: "Oh yes! then wait." Someone spoke to Clifford the other day as if adverse words on W. W. were written in Edward Emerson's book. W. curious. "It would be well to see the book in a library first—wouldn't it?" he asked, when I suggested I might buy a copy. Yet he looked forward to seeing it himself.

After leaving W. I went down to Bonsall—talked with him —and he gave me an order on Wanamaker for chair—only, asked that I go over with or instead of Ed and explain. Asked me to attend a meeting at 4:30 this afternoon at which preliminaries for the celebration are to be arranged. They seem to have some idea of getting W. to a hall, but that would be impossible. Still nothing is formulated. Possibly there won't be a dinner. I suggested a wholesale purchase of W.'s anniversary book to be issued that day. Bonsall did not think it a bad idea.

Early Evening: 5.45 W. sitting—had just finished his

155

dinner. "Here I am," he said, offering me a damp hand. "I have been washing my hands and eyes—to ease them. It has been a hot day, hasn't it?" And when I asked him: "But do you suffer from it?" he shook his head. "No—I can't say that at all." I said to W.: "I could not get back in time for the meeting this afternoon." W.: "What meeting was that?" I explained. "Oh! and for me!" and here he relapsed. "Horace," he said after a pause, "you must warn them all not to make too much of a racket—make them see I only hold a pint." As to meeting in a hall—"It is as you say, boy, out of the question —entirely out of the question. I don't get credit for half the decrepitude I realize myself. Nobody believes I am badly off —yet I am a fearfully banged up cuss. Of course I am always glad to see my friends. It is to my interest to put my best foot forward. So they come and go, believing I am only half as sick as I pretend, if sick at all." "Even the house here, I cannot see any reason for decorating it. I know you understand —I think Bonsall does, too—and there is Tom. But Buckwalter—oh! I think he is inclined to be a little flamboyant—to like to make a big stir—to be party to a big stir—to see himself in it, for one reason, and then for another out of an inherent good-feeling in the matter for itself. But I am wholly opposed to anything in the way of a splurge. I think some of my friends imagine that my condition bites—that I feel the bite of poverty, inattention, poor quarters, neglect, hatred. I know you do not—I know you see the case exactly as it is. But many—even of the good fellows—go off the handle, thinking I sit and brood over it. But it is a great mistake—I don't care a damn for it, whether or no. I have quite enough fame in quarters where I should desire it." "Yet I hold up pretty well—they are deceived, many of them, who come here. Though badly gone in body, my talking, thinking powers remain, perhaps as good as ever they were. When the fellows come and warm me up I get almost voluble: from that comes the mistake."

I explained to W. my plan in connection with the books: that the friends desiring come and receive a copy: that so W. would be helped, the visitor have a souvenir, and an event more consistent with W.'s feelings be sustained. He appeared to take to it at once. "It is certainly an admirable idea—the best yet. If they came in and bought 50 or 100 of these books, it would settle the question of expense. It would be a sort of Burns matter over again. You know: the poor fellow was far down that time—all for being off for Madeira—creditors everywhere—he in despair. Then came forward the friends— a hundred or so—took the books at a handsome price—I don't say such a price as ours—and Burns was saved. Instead of running off to Madeira, cocked his head"—W. simulated it— "and told his creditors to go to hell. Then this would do another thing—it would answer Dave's question, what are you going to do with the books after you get them?" I asked him if he thought Dave was exerting himself to sell the big book. "No—I do not—not at all." So in face of the additional good reasons for having the books out on his birthday, W. re-marked: "We'll certainly have them. I'll have a hundred made up in the first lot. What was the price he gave you—Oldach? —68¢? And that includes a gilt edge?" And he said again as to imitation: "I don't want it—would not have it. I expected the price to be much higher than that, anyhow. The morocco must be green." We had some discussion as to the proper place for stamping. "I cannot see the objection to having the flap on the bottom of the book instead of the top. Is there a law for it?" I asked if there was a law for paging books from left to right? "But," returned W., "that is made as it is by the un-broken consent of centuries and centuries of experience. I am not disinclined to consider things which have by long usage been established and recognized. Just now I don't see why my objection in the case of the book is not legitimate. Yet there may be something which of necessity disproves me." I explained my talk with Oldach today. Oldach will make W. the two models he desires, has already ordered stamps, does not like idea of stamping on bottom, or of putting flap there. "There is no better way," he said, "than to make all lettering free flowing in a generous open space." McKay had initially got a line to put about the script "Walt Whitman," but had subsequently cut it out, W. thereat much pleased.

I had got sheets unexpectedly from Ferguson today. Gave me six sets, one of them cut. W. handled them in all ways—scanned, felt, ruminated. "So these are the sheets?" I still dissented from the printing. It did not strike me as being at all adequate. W.: "Well—never mind: it might have been worse, if that is any comfort. It certainly is not a thing to be proud of. Yet we ought not to growl that things are not perfect—that we cannot have everything as we want it is no wonder. Considering our plans—arbitrariness—we do well to get along as well as we do. I thought to send a copy to France—to the American book department there—but I can't, for one thing, find out who is the man in charge—do you know?" I said I thought we could easily secure that. But W.: "Well, we will let the matter simmer for a couple of days—then see what it suggests." Then after a pause: "But Ferguson ought to be ashamed of himself—ashamed; it comes hard to send such printing over there when they are always sending us such beautiful work—the rarest, finest." I said: "Ferguson would probably not get mad to hear that, but Brown would." W.: "Well, we won't say it to make anybody mad—only say it out of justice, because it ought to be said. Oh! You may tell it to Ferguson that way—tell him we had aimed to send a copy abroad, to France, but were ashamed to do so. If he is a true printer—and he is—he can have no deeper damnation to contemplate than that." "Considering that we were willing to pay for it done well—it is a great pity we were not gratified. We did not stint them in any particular." But "we will submit, knowing we came out pretty well on the whole. Besides, handsomely bound, as it will be, the defects in printing will not be so striking." Thought we had best push things. Would get up one set of sheets with portraits for me at once, so Oldach could proceed. "Come tomorrow, about noon," he said jokingly, "and the victim will be ready." We discussed the flap again. He seemed to understand my point—but still said: "I don't think I shall be able to tell until I see them in the flesh." He endorsed a set of the sheets for me, with the legend above, "Horace L. Traubel from his friend the author."

Then referred to the reception matter again: "I have no doubt you and Tom and Harry will be able to keep things within bounds, in taste. It would never do to have any display performance—would not fit me, the occasion, most of all my present condition." I had great difficulty in getting the chair. At Wanamaker's they would not charge it to Bonsall. Finally, they telephoned Tom at my suggestion and he had it put on his account there. Promised to deliver it in the morning. There is but one delivery to Camden per day. W. discussed it. "The getting downstairs—I think that will be the difficult point— if I can get over that I have some hopes of getting over others." I had told Captain Lindell, when he asked after Walt today at the ferry, that he should not be surprised to have W. appear in person there within a few days. W. said: "Yes— and to see Ed will be one of my first points if I get down there at all." His thirst to see the river is great—spoke of it again. Very carefully took up and folded the several brown sheets in which the printed matter had come. "I'll keep it— it will do to put up the great morocco book. I'll have to make them up handsome—a nice, fine little bundle for Mary Costelloe first of all—for others abroad there, too." Mrs. Davis came in for W.'s tray. She said Captain Adams was in to see her and W. asked: "Is he here now?" And then: "Did he leave you any money?" Mrs. Davis hereupon explaining to me that Adams years ago had failed, owing her $1800—and had ever since little by little been paying the debt off. Mrs. D. told W. Adams had brought money—also: "He sent me some from

Matanzas, but I never got it." W. did not just hear, and got out his "Good! Good!" much to our hearty laughter and eventually his own when he found some other person had got the money.

The Sarrazin book, lightly pasted in covers, has been coming apart—so W. has tied it up with a piece of red tape. I asked him if I should write to Dr. Gould about translating it—but he said: "Let us have it here—rest—for the present." Paid for photographs today and ordered them sent to Oldach. Insurance paper not yet ready, though I called for it. Account from Billstein only a little over seven dollars. W. thought it "cheaper." Billstein also will send pictures to Oldach. Now nothing remains but for us to take over such portraits as we have in Camden. W. said: "I have not all the packages fully endorsed, but will finish them at once. I intend getting them together in such shape that even a very dumb man could understand what we wanted." Asking after Tom's baby, I spoke of walking it, and his pleasure therein. W. reflected: "The wonderful new babies! Oh! how fully I have entered into them! It used to be my delight to get the youngsters, the very young ones, take them in my arms, walk them— often sing to them—hours and hours and hours. I don't know who got the most joy out of it—it seems to me the baby's could never have equalled mine: the wonderful alluring babies!"

I sold a book for W.—a complete Whitman—to Fred L. May. W. asked: "Who is he? Do I know him?" And finally did remember a copy of Specimen Days May had purchased of him last summer. A meeting of some sort was held this after-noon, but Harned not home when I called in the evening so could not get particulars. Fear plans are such that W. would not approve. Harned had intended seeing W. on his way to Philadelphia. I think they have provided for a banquet. But W. insists to me: "What good is a banquet? In the first place I don't like the idea of it for itself: then it would be impossible for me to attend: then if I did attend I could not eat."

Friday, May 10, 1889

10.45 A.M. We were all sorrowed this morning to light upon this item in the paper: "W. D. O'Connor, assistant general superintendent of the Life Saving Service, died in Washington yesterday." When I went into W.'s room, I found him getting up model for binder. "You come a little too soon," he said, "I had not expected you till later." But kept on working, I not disturbing him. He spoke instantly, however, of O'Connor—appeared calm and collected, but solemn. "William is dead," he remarked, "you saw?" And then: "It was in the papers. But I had two letters here about it—one from Nellie, one from James L. Sill." He handed them to me, and took up the thread of his work again as I read. We said little after I finished, but W.'s whole look and tone were pathetic. "Poor Nellie! Poor Nellie!"

I retired downstairs—talked somewhat with Mrs. Davis— then sat with Ed in the parlor till about half an hour had passed. Going upstairs then, I found that W. had finished his work and was regarding a sheet of instructions he had written to go with the model. Here is a copy of it:

Walt Whitman's 'Leaves of
Grass' for the Binders

to be bound pocketbook form green
real morocco, gilt edged
all round
trim off the edges as closely
as they will admit—use
your own taste and judg-
ment—I like a little
more white margin at
bottom both in print pages
& pictures
six altogether
put the pictures as in

sample herewith—see to
this carefully—face them
carefully as requested.
(I hope the stitching will
be first-rate & strong—
the big book you bound
for me seems to be first-
rate
duplicate sample of pictures
herewith numbered
No. 1—the frontispiece
2   to face page 29
3   "   " 132
4   "   " 214
5   "   " 296
6   "   " 383

Punctuation altogether and form mainly as above. He had
also tied up the different heads carefully and put most specific
descriptions on the package. "We are fortunate with the
binders," he said, "they seem to have a wonderfully accurate
man at that work. So far we have not had a mistake with him.
The pictures have always got into their right places." I tied
up package. "I think we are now all done—for our part,"
W. reflected. "Tell Oldach we are now in his hands—that
we wait now for the two models—that we ought not to have any
delay with them."

Then of O'Connor again. "They will bury him in Washington, I suppose," W. said, "I can see now how well it is that
things are as they are. Poor O'Connor! Poor William! Poor me!
And yet," W. said again, "yet I can understand him. I knew
him so well, I can comprehend how true it is, what Sill writes
me there, that O'Connor himself dreaded anything like a long,
persistent, lingering illness." Then he turned upon himself:
"I am myself not so well today as I was yesterday and the
day before. I quite anticipated a change—and I knew before
I got up that I was not in prime condition. What it is, I don't

know—probably the heat—the unpropitious heat." "Or the bad news?" I asked. And he: "Not that—I should not say that—for I have been anticipating that for a long time— the last day or two felt it was here—its shadow upon me. Though I know well enough that I am depressed by it—that it has borne in on my mentality, emotionality, to a deep, almost sorrowful degree." Yet it was no "shock." "I wrote postals to Doctor, John Burroughs, Kennedy, this morning, telling them of it: Eddy has mailed them." He had taken up the papers, shortly hit upon the terse three lines—had then ceased reading. The pictures of past days, the memory of old experiences, the Washington days, "eloquent with friend-ship"—these he only briefly touched today. His manner pathetic—in perfect command. Looked beautiful—complexion with some paleness intermixed, eye distant, at some of our brief touching references, tears out of their unusual depth.

W. said: "Boy—I have seen Tom. The fellows seem after all to set out to have a big time on the birthday. What shall we do with it?" I had seen Harned this morning. At the meeting yesterday, it was decided to have a banquet, 200 seats at $5.00, surplus to go to a W. W. purse. To be held in Morgan's Hall. Harned laughingly referred to W.'s "whimsicality." Had seen W. last night after my opposite talk and practically had his assent that he would attend. They plan for a big affair—toasts &c. Nothing except bare outlines so far. Harned advised with me about letters to men outside of Camden. May cable Tennyson. W. says: "We must submit, I suppose." And of the purse: "That would be nice! After the expense we have gone to the past year to get our book out, this would help reimburse." And I said: "We'll have the book there—they'll probably sell anyhow." He laughed: "That would be fishing with two hooks, wouldn't it?" Will not promise speech. Chair had not come up to the time I left. I picked up some writing paper from floor. W. said: "I never look for anything but what a lot of white paper turns up." This paper was ruled. "Oh! I use ruled paper, but I don't write on the lines!"

5.40 P.M. W. had just finished his meal. A terrible storm was raging out of doors—wind driving the dust about in a complete fog. I had just crossed the river, which was aroused to fury, the dust horrible, the boat tipped clean to her side, many passengers (women) terror-stricken in the extreme and crying. W. sat at his closed window regarding it. I had delivered the package to Oldach. The chair not having come at one, I went to Wanamaker's about it. They assured me it was on its way, as was the case, for now it stood there at W.'s in the parlor. Also delivered W.'s message to Ferguson, who expressed concern and regret. McKay had a letter from the West from someone who solicited all the portraits of W. W. &c.—which is laughable, when one considers the array of these that exist. I promised to get Dave copies of the Linton and the 70th year portraits. W. said he would look them up.

W. spoke of the storm. "I noticed it as I sat here—the dust flew up in a perfect cloud—I got my mouth full of it. Shut the windows forthwith—that is as forthwith as I could, which wasn't very forthwith." Ed had come in as I had, covered with dust. Now a quiet rain had set in. The green trees swayed to and fro. "It has already cooled things off," W. remarked, "how fine the breeze!" Had he yet tried the chair? "No—it is still down in the parlor. Mary asked when it came if she should bring it up and I advised against it. I have been hoping Ed would come in, so we could make a short trial trip around the block this afternoon. But the rascal, he's gone off somewhere. I sent him up to Tom's about 12 o'clock with the bottles, for what Tom calls the rum and the sherry; he has not appeared since." W. laughed heartily: "If Eddy was not such a sober fellow—if I didn't know he was strictly upright, I'd be inclined to believe he'd run off with the drink."

On the table a paper addressed to John Burroughs. W. said: "This big racket they are getting up—would you call it a bar testimonial?" I laughed outright—he said it in such a way I thought he was hitting at its drink features. "What's the matter?" he asked in astonishment. And when I said, "I thought you spoke satirically," he caught the idea and laughed heartily himself. "I see," he said, "but I did not mean that. I saw here so many names of members of the bar, I thought it might go by such a name. There is a pretty good statement of it in both the papers tonight. The Post, The Courier: and it is all right—I take no exception to it." I told him Dave had already given me $5.00 for his ticket and W. said: "Good for Dave! But Dave is a good fellow anyhow!" Would he speak? "I not only did not promise to speak, but did not promise to be there. How can I promise anything? It is not yet even proven that I can get out at all. Then see how I feel. I am sure I have been miserable all today, though now I am a little better. Such a day as this would wholly disappoint the affair." "I suppose the unusual and sudden warmth has something to do with it, but then so also has my general sensitiveness." But who could explain the blues? W. said: "Poor O'Connor! He had 'em! Would get 'em in the most violent way—was subject to such attacks. Poor O'Connor! But it was constitutional with him. Thank God! my own tendencies—inherent belongings—have been of another character—I can say of an opposite character—reaching into buoyancy, joy, confidence: a result of most beneficent progenation!"

I read W. a little piece on O'Connor I had written today. It was quite short, would not fill a column in The Critic. I asked W. if I should send it to the Critic? and he said, "Yes indeed—yes indeed: it ought surely to go there." Several times as I read, I could see his eyes watering—and as I finished, he exclaimed fervently, still looking out across into the northern sky: "Good! Good! The grand fellow"—adding reflectively after a pause—"O'Connor was a chosen knight— a picked man. Like the Arthurian heroes, true as steel, chivalric to the bone, high in hope and intention. What the knights were to chivalry, O'Connor was in literary action.

He had an ideal so high—a human, literary, social, moral, religious, aspiration so pure—a passion for right, justice, the race, so intense—a disdain for mere literary craft and skill so overwhelming—he seemed out of place in the modern world, its so-often mean ambitions. A cat in a strange garret indeed. The grand O'Connor! Who can take his place today? Who can take his place for me?"

W. when sending to Harned for his drink, had defined his desires on a little card, and closed with this: "My dear friend William O'Connor is dead." I spoke of having Stedman here at the dinner, if possible. W. gladdened. "That would be very good indeed, if it could be accomplished. Did I tell you about Kennedy—the letter I had from him the other day? You remember what I said about the Hartmann column—that he had offered it to Kennedy—oh! it was months ago—indeed, more than a year, for it was before I was sick—that Kennedy had written me about it—that I had at once replied, disavowing, saying they were not only not my thoughts but the very opposite of my thoughts. This was about the time of the Walt Whitman Club business that I put my foot down on. Kennedy wrote me the other day—I think only 3 or 4 days ago: this week, anyway—asking if I would consent that he should show my letter to Stedman—send him a copy of it. I have a bad habit nowadays of losing my letters—dropping them everywhere—so to make it certain that this should not be passed unreplied-to, I wrote that same day, that afternoon, making a special point of it—of course saying 'Yes.' Perhaps Stedman has the letter by this time." I said I intended writing to Stedman, telling him of the Herald refusal to publish the contradiction. W.: "That would be well, too! The good Stedman, who for years now has been so generous and kind to us! —and here, in the very latest moment, giving us extraordinary evidence of his feeling on the big book!"

On his table a flower. "What is it?" I asked. He smiled: "That's the question. None of us know. I had a couple of visitors from Boston today—Oh! what were their names? Let me see?" But they would not be seen. "Anyhow—they were young fellows—only came in a minute—left this flower. This is a poor place for it—there is nothing propitious in a warm room—it needs the free air. I am going to have it set down in the garden, where it can no doubt be made to thrive." I suggested that we bring the chair upstairs for him to see. At first, he thought not, but finally consented to have it brought in for inspection. I went down for Warren to help me up with it. When it was once in the room W. was greatly struck. Started to rise instantly. "It looks like a glorious opportunity!" he exclaimed, "Guess I'll just step into it at once and have the question settled." And when once in: "It seems just made for me—or I for it! A perfect fit! And so easy too!"—and he sat there composedly. "Move it, Horace," he said, "let us see how she goes." And when I saw that the mere motion seemed to rejoice him, I said jokingly, "If the worst comes, Ed can wheel you up and down the room," he replying, "That is so— but that would be a poor apology indeed for the real thing!" I called Ed in, and he came, moving it about, manipulating it easily. "And would it tip over?" W. asked. Ed advised W. to try, and try he did, but it would not tip. "If it was to tip over, it would knock my neck badly out of joint. But then," he said with a laugh, "I shall not go to any trouble to knock my neck out of joint just yet!" Warren kissed him good-by and went out—and Ed left after him. W. said: "I guess I'll stay in it a while. With my usual instinct to keep comfortable when I am so, I'll stay in this good position!" And so there he sat, still in the middle of the floor, cane dangling from his hand, when I left. "Over there on the box," he said, "is my red handkerchief: will you hand it to me?" And he put it about his neck. "I have been accustoming myself to this, and so it may be better to be on guard." And W. urged me again: "Yes—send the article to the Critic. Don't expand it—let it go just as it is. I do not see how it could be condensed."

Saturday, May 11, 1889

10.50 A.M. W. was not very well—certainly did not look very well—this morning. He said to me: "I had the chair taken downstairs." Then, looking out on the clouded sky: "I don't know whether we'll get our trial trip today or not. I have just been taking a bath, and it has tired me out—tired me a good deal more than I could have expected." He said again: "There is no further word from Washington—but a letter here from Doctor: read it," handing it to me. Bucke spoke there of wishing W. could get the spring air. W. said to me: "I wrote him a day or two ago—'By the time you get this I shall probably be getting out in my chair'—to that effect anyhow." He had laid the two pictures out for Dave. "They are the ones you wanted?" Also reminded me—as I had asked him—of the big book for May, which he endorsed with May's name. I received from Oldach a design for stamps, which W. approved at once. It adheres to title page main lines. W. said: "I am quite curious still to read Edward Emerson's book." "And I to buy it," I put in. W. laughed: "Are you still determined to buy it—have it?" And when I said, "Yes—I must have it"—he pursued the matter: "Well, why not buy it today, then?" And I promised him I would. I spoke to W. of Dave's remarkable opinion—explaining how his edition of Emerson differs from others: that "Emerson went to Europe, saw Carlyle, got a small case of swelled head" and came home and revised his book to their misfortune. W. was serious over that: "Oh no—Dave—oh no Dave—it is not that: you have gone far wrong there if ever!"

Asked me if I had mailed the paper to Burroughs. Then indicated the Post editorial and local items treating of the proposed celebration. "Take that along with you—if you don't mind, send it to Bucke when you are done with it." Curiously, another of Bucke's letters went astray before W. got it—this time to Red Bank. W. thought: "That is very remarkable. How could they make such a mistake? If ever the Doctor is guiltless, it is in addressing his letters." Warren brought in a big bowl of ice cream, which W. took with a laugh. "It is a cartload, Warrie—a cartload." Then: "Give me the blue coat there"—it lay over the chair. "I was just going to ask Horace to help me on with it." And after it was on, as he sat heavily back in his chair: "Thank you boy—thank you boy!" Took up the ice cream and ate it eagerly. "This," he said to me, "is one of my weaknesses: a weakness of long standing."

A reference back to my O'Connor article: "I intended writing something myself—not with any particular paper in view—only to relieve my fullness." And again: "The good Stedman—I never think of that scamp but to feel for him." As to the Herald: "The devil is in 'em—they must have something that will make a stir. Hartmann was evidently not discouraged because Kennedy would have nothing of him. The Herald must have paid him liberally." Remarked: "I see from my post at the window that it is so—that the bustle is being discarded. I for one do not regret it. It always seemed to me a hideous deformity."

Evening. 7.45 W. had just been walking to the door to fix something in the hallway. "Come in! Come in!—and sit down!" he called to me. He took his own chair by the window. We talked for more than half an hour. W. seemed very bright. Said at once: "I have been out at last! The experiment has proved a success!"—"I was out, I guess, more than an hour and a half. I sat half an hour in the front here, under the trees. We made quite an extensive detour, though we did not start out with that idea. I expected to go around the block, then stop. But when we got down the street, I had Ed go on, so that by going four or five blocks, we got to the river." But not the ferry? "Oh no! This was down—that way"— pointing to the southwest—"I would not have dared Federal Street, or the ferry, today. It would have been like rushing into the thick of the fight at once." How did he feel because of it? "Better—much better!" Not wearied? "No—quite the contrary—it exhilarated me." He was tremendously elevated. Talked for a long time of it. "I see it is a thing I must more and more encourage. I see I must get out all I can—day after day." He did not think he could have got out in this way last summer? "No—it would have been impossible—I have evoluted to this point quietly, naturally—by some unexpected good turn of fortune." And he added: "It was towards evening—I had already had my dinner. Oh! the day was grand! And cool, didn't you think? I mean pleasantly cool? I kept on the sunny side of the street, thinking to get as much sun as possible—certain it would do me good." "And the chair," he said in his fervent way, "it was a wonderful true support—a revelation of ease and comfort. It went along with perfect gentleness, and Ed said he could handle it without any trouble." On the table before him lay his hat, just as he had put it down when he came in. "Horace, boy!" he said again, "it was a great triumph, wasn't it? Who would have believed it of me last summer—that we would remain to conquer this? I consider it a victory—it would be a victory if I never got out again." And again: "We went quietly on our way—no one disturbed us—no questions were asked." And he thought the getting out "solved many questions." I did not ask, but wondered if he meant it solved the hospital question. For one thing, as he remarked himself, it made his attendance at the dinner more probable. He talked of the felicity of the experiment—"the green trees—to get out into the free air —to catch once more the sight of the river, the big city beyond, the boats on the stream." It has been a long time since I have realized such a quiet joy in him. "And we're going again and again," he said repeatedly, "and we'll send the good news to all our friends."

W. asked me: "Horace, what about the O'Connor article— the one for the Critic?" And, when knowing I had sent it off: "I am glad—glad." I asked him about the idea of writing a page for the American dealing in a more strictly biographic way with O'Connor. He said: "That is an idea and a good one—making it biographical. But if you write remember the idea I started last evening—that William was a chosen knight —was selected of the select—as truly and grandly chivalric, in his own field of action, as any knight of feudalism, any lord or gentlemen of the past. And not only so, but more humanly chivalric than any—more democratic: a man profound and sweeping in his knowledge of the great literatures, especially of the Elizabethan, whose nobler fellows he in some respects resembled. Who like O'Connor ever knew Elizabethan literature to the heart. If you write, I should approve of your saying that—I should say it myself—of saying it for me."

I asked him if he did not think it an idea to issue some circular in relation to the big book and for us to issue that and sell the books ourselves. He replied: "It is an idea and I shall act on it. By and by, when the pocket edition is out of the way, I shall get up a circular—a nice one." I put in: "And I'll send them out for you"—he affirming—"yes—I should have hoped that. It should certainly effect something." He did not think Dave was making exertion to sell the book. I took the pictures to McKay this afternoon. W. said: "Tom has not been here today, but came in last evening—weren't you here?—brought me the cognac." I took the design back to Oldach's today and advised that they proceed at once with models. Will let me know probable time required. W. said: "I hope Oldach will not delay us. But we know his terrible perversity and I am not altogether sure of him." May paid me for the book. I brought W. that money, with the Insurance renewal and change therefrom. I had left with him several Vereshtchagin pamphlets this morning—from Tom: a Catalogue, and two of V's essays on art. W. said of them now: "They were very satisfying to me—I read them with an intense interest. The catalogue especially—with the illustrations, was graphic and powerful." He would greatly like to meet the man. "He seems like a handsome, forcible man."

I brought W. the Edward Emerson book, which I had bought today. Stated to him the substance of the only reference to him in the book—this on p. 228:

When Leaves of Grass appeared at a later period than that of which I speak, the healthy vigor and freedom of this work of a young mechanic seemed to promise so much that Mr. Emerson overlooked the occasional coarseness which offended him, and wrote a letter of commendation to the author, a sentence of which was, to his annoyance, printed in gold letters on the covers of the next edition. But the first work led him to expect better in future, and in this he was disappointed. He used to say, this "Catalogue-style of poetry is easy and leads nowhere," or words to that effect.

over which he reflected and finally said: "Well it makes no difference." "I shall," he then added, "take a great interest in the book. I am very glad you brought it down."

McKay reports Hunter back in town. I spoke of Hunter's picture. W. thereupon: "He must make a great one—that piercing eye—the big fine head of him all through!" As I got up to leave, W.—asking me where I was going, added: "It seems to be a fine night—and cooler—much cooler—more gratifying." And out to the north the stars shone clearly. "You are off again across the water? My good wishes with you!"

Sunday, May 12, 1889

7 P.M. W. sitting in front of his house in the big chair surrounded by children. He was attempting to take a splinter from the finger of one of these. I went quietly up, took a seat on the step in their midst, did not say a word. Finally, he did see me, and extended his hand with great heartiness.

We were there a full half hour together. The children continued more or less with him most of that time. He had his arm about the waist of a little boy, who seemed content with his position for a long time. The children would come and go. W. greeted them—called them by name. "Here's little Leoni," he said to me of one of them, "the nicest little girl in all the street!" And as she ran off, her light red curls floating on the wind: "See that hair—its transparency—can you beat that?" And he would take part in the interests of the youngsters. Says to one "and is this the little one who don't like Eddy?" adding to the tiny body remonstratingly—"You must not dislike Ed—he's one of the best fellows alive!" He would ask their names, joke with them. "Danny," an old-clean-shaven ferryman, now weak enough in the legs himself came up. W. said: "Ah! Danny! is that you? Give my love to all the ferry boys—all of 'em! And how are you yourself, Danny?" And Danny said: "I heard you were out—I am glad to see it. We all want to live a long time if we can, don't we? I know I do!" And went off muttering something to himself. Mr. Button the architect, living next door, was another to accost him. "I had never expected to see you out again Mr. Whitman." W.: "And this is the second time, too!" "So I heard—so they told me." And then W.: "It is a great victory—a great comfort. And how is the Madam? Tell me that?" Asking again: "And so she holds her own? That is good, anyhow!"

The chair was up by the step. W. said to me descriptively: "I have been out a long time. We took quite a stroll. I saw Ed Lindell today: went down towards his house. Ed pulled the bell, and Lindell himself came to the door. He appeared much surprised, but glad—very glad! Of course I had to receive him sitting as I was. I wanted Ed to know Lindell, the other Ed. Lindell—you know it—is a great fiddler. Maggie came in, or out, too—she too is a great fiddler. They will be good for our Eddy therefore to know. I think Lindell is one of the best—perhaps the best—fellow, on instrumentation in Cam-

173

den. That would make him important to Ed. You know what I mean by instrumentation? A sort of apportionment of tone—what part the clarinet, trombone, flute, fiddle—any other instrument—is to take—can sustain in the harmony. Ed is great on that. If I were a young man, still with hot blood, I know I should fight him—know we'd have many a tussle, for Ed does not believe in expression—thinks it humbug—while to me expression is everything." Lindell also impeached the importance of the human voice, its musical quality &c. "But then he don't know—I doubt if he has ever heard a voice that justifies what we call the vocal powers: the great, overwhelming, touching, human voice—its throbbing, flowing, pulsing, qualities. Alboni—or that strange, awkward, obesely, ridiculous figure, the Italian who recently died—oh yes! Brignoli. Such voices—do they not justify all—explain all?" And the voice—"It is the extreme height of heights: what instrument can reach it?" Then he went on about his trip. "We did not go to the ferry, but southwards again. I tried to get a position somewhere down there on Second Street that would put us right on the river, but it could not be found—I could see the glisten on the water—see beyond—but could not get down absolutely to the bank. We must take everything by degrees. I started out late again—the spirit did not move me till towards evening." As to trips: "We must develop into them—into long distances: must not attempt too much at once. I have thought—what do you think?—that early morning would be a good—perhaps the best—time. How does that strike you? I don't know—it may not do at all, may be just the thing. I had an idea of stopping up at Tom's today, but hesitated, finally did not go: was afraid of the champagne—I know too well the temptation of that champagne. Some other time we'll attempt it." Spoke of the remarkable good the thing seemed to do him already. "It were a great victory if there never come another trip on it—though we hope for more and more. Some years ago the Critic fellows wrote me for an

174

article or articles. I replied that I was sick—that I was not disposed to write. They wrote back that they must have something—must have something over my name. So I wrote a little piece, starting with some statement like this—that after books, writing, medicine, home, everything else, had failed, then take to the open air, get out under the sky, on the green fields, under the trees—into nature itself. I have thought that of myself today—failing in everything else, came this—came the chair—came the trips out into the sweet sun: and already what a blessing this has been!" And he had met as yet "no reporter on the road—thank God!"

Said he had had several visitors today. "Grace Johnson was here—she was here while Mrs. Harned was here. And there was Tom, too—and a young man he brought along with him. I was glad he came—oh! what was his name?" I knew— Callingham. W. then: "That's it, I guess." "And quite a Whitman man," I said, and W. laughed. "Poor fellow! I wonder, does he know what he invites upon himself?" W.'s color was exceedingly fine—perhaps with more suggestion of delicacy than of old, but strong still, and true.

Said of the Emerson book: "You can have it tonight, if you want to take it along. How grand it is as a book—as samplifying—the book art itself! It is one of the most striking samples of bookmaking I know—simply beautiful—as good as anything they send us from abroad: the paper, type, inking—rich and grand—a joy merely to look at." He thought he would not "include the binding" in this "specification"— "that does not strike me so fully, satisfyingly. Horace, you ought to take the book over and show it to Ferguson—to him of all men. It so impressed me, I have felt like sending word up to the boys who did the printing—the printers—sending some word by Kennedy indicating that I had seen and applauded it. Houghton surpassed himself in this." Dave had evidently imitated the cover of some of Houghton's recent books in his production of the "First Series." "But Dave's

books come nowhere near this." Then W. proceeded thoughtfully, as he looked in a fixed way at me: "But, Horace," he
said, "this book quite revises, recasts, my idea of Edward
Emerson. Biographically it has no value at all—it is not
skillfully constructed, strongly stated—it really adds little or
nothing to the stock of what we know of Emerson. But it is
interesting, nevertheless—anything about Emerson, even repetition, is interesting. The notes there, for instance—the extracts from Emerson's Journals—and here and there little
incidents—appeal to me; they will to you. But of Edward,
as I said, I catch quite another conviction—yet one I should
have realized before, from the first—which I should have
acknowledged to myself long ago." I knew then he touched
upon the explanation of the Whitman foot-note. "It is a lie!"
he said vehemently, as he looked straight at me, "it is the
concoction—I know unconscious of Edward, of Ellen. The
two put their heads together—produced it. Ellen hates me like
the devil—always did. This note—this was never Emerson!"
And then W. quoted contemptuously—"or words to that
effect"! "But," he then said, in his same kind way—"it is of
no value. Would you like to take the book back tonight? I
am through with it—read it through today." He spoke again:
"Edward is a stoutish, good-looking fellow—I remember him
as such. This book puts a whole new face on all actions with
me—his words—invitations—there at Concord. Yet he seemed
to feel generously at the time."

He had been reading the Tribune today. "Tom brought it
in. They have quite a piece there about the 31st affair. They
enter largely into it—tell even who is to be there: have about
every big name in American life except the President! And
the President! Oh! the president! No—he is not my man.
There are several elements which we reckon indispensable to
the make of a big manly man: these are surrendered to bad
substitutes in Harrison. Think of it—Harrison, on the one
hand is deacon of a church—on the other an advocate of ex-

treme protection." Anticipates that Mrs. O'Connor will "be alone" probably some day shortly. "Did you know that O'Connor lived over the river in Philadelphia? He was editor of the Saturday Evening Post—or Morning Post—that's the name." He advised me to "collect and use" the details of O'Connor's life. "The most noteworthy person I know of to inform you is now in California. I mean Eldridge—Charles Eldridge—but he is so far off. Yet it ought to be done: I even want to do it myself. I wrote to Mrs. O'Connor today—sent the letter off tonight. I suppose William was buried today or will be tomorrow! The grand O'Connor!"

I reminded W. that it seemed getting chillier and he said: "Yes, I shall go in." And called Ed. "I feel greatly better for getting out—slept last night like a top—awoke with all sorts of new ambitions!" W. leaned very heavily on me when he went in. "I shall stay here a while," he said, edging off towards the parlor, where he went ponderously into the chair. "This seems natural—seems just like old times—is just as if we were made for each other—this chair and me!" We discussed the pocket edition, W. eager for it: "I am anxious to have a few of the five-dollar edition. In the first place, because a few five dollars' would be very helpful to me just now—then I have been determining to send copies to those people—the group—a few—who have been very kind to me—whose kindness I feel bound to recognize." Then off and away, leaving W. there in the room, his hat on still and talking to Ed in brief snatches.

Dined today at 5 at Harned's. Discussed the dinner. Circular herewith had been issued. I fought the principle of exclusion against women, and Bonsall and T. B. H. decided that the objection was well assumed and promised to see the plan to that extent revised. I argued its gross inconsistency—that it neither comported with the modern spirit at large nor with W.'s, to put up bars against anybody on such an occasion.

Monday, May 13, 1889

7.05 P.M. W. lying in bed. "Ah!" he said, "I have just come in—just laid down—we have had some long trips out." The empty chair had been at the doorway entrance. He said further: "I have not felt nearly so well today—yet I have been out twice. But this catarrhal affection bothers me a good deal—troubles my head." I went in to see Oldach about books, but could as yet get no definite word from him. He has not received the stamps as yet. W.'s inquiries anxious. I spoke to W. about the participation of women in the banquet. He said: "I suppose it would be replied to that—as it is replied when suffrage for women is suggested—that the women will not take it themselves, do not want it. But I see what you mean. You raise a previous question—that whether they want it or not is theirs to decide—ours only to see that we don't stand in the way of it!" He always preferred the "free" way, and if they consulted with him &c.: going on to explain pleasantly. He asked: "Have you one of the circulars? It is singular—Tom was just in, too—but said nothing about that." W. wondered "how it was written" whether as "conservatively" as should be.

We spoke again somewhat about the Emerson book. W. said: "The note was undoubtedly lugged in—inexcusably lugged in—an attempt to force an utterance of disdain from me. Emerson was a good father—his children were loyal to him —they served, advised. The main wonder of it all is—the wonder that yet remains to be written—how in heaven's and hell's name—how in the name of all the angels, all the saints,— in air, on earth—below the earth—Emerson, surrounded as he was by those influences, by adverse, benumbing literary currents, persons—remained, and undoubtedly did remain to the last, unscathed, unhurt, untouched." Then W. reflected: "I, of course, knew nothing of Emerson's first wife, but the second I knew—met—and to me she was a hideous unlikely woman. How Emerson could ever have got spliced to her beats

178

my explanation. Yet it can be explained, no doubt—for undoubtedly she is a good woman, with her own virtues, which I
should be the very last to in the least question. But Ellen?
Oh! that hag! She is a hag! That guardian, watcher—afraid
the great old man would make a mistake, commit some error!
She is repulsive to me beyond utterance. I know the position
she held with respect to her father—the position generally
accorded her outside of Concord—but I doubt if she has any
standing there." And he said again: "No—no—neither of
them—neither mother nor daughter—was our woman at all."

W. alluded to matters of another nature. "There on the
chair," he said, "you will find a couple of letters—they are
done up with a rubber. One is from Burroughs, the other from
Doctor. They do not contain anything we would call news—
yet for all that you will want to see them. John had not yet
had my postal about O'Connor—but writes of him—had read
of it in the paper. Doctor evidently had not heard of it at
all." Burroughs' reference was the following:

Yesterday on my way up to Olive [or Clive: Burroughs is not
clear here] to see my wife's father, who is near the end of his life's
journey, I read in the Tribune of the death of Wm. O'Connor. It
was news I had been expecting for some time, yet it was a stunning
blow for all that. I know how keenly you must feel it, and you
have my deepest sympathy. No words come to my pen adequate to
express the sense of the loss we have all suffered in the death of
that chivalrous and eloquent soul. How strange that his life has
all passed, that I shall see or hear him no more.

And it is sad to me to think that he has left behind him no work
or book that at all expresses the measure of his great power. What
a gift of speech that man had! If you can tell me anything about
his last days, I shall be very glad to hear it. Also where he is
buried. [And then the letter went on] I am pretty well, and have
been immersed in farm work for the past six weeks. We have
rented our house to a New York man for five months. Julian and
I live in the old house with a man who works for me, and Ursula
boards in Po'keepsie.

I hope this great heat for the past few days has not prostrated you. Tell Harry Trauble to write to me.

The wave of orchard bloom has just passed over us and the world has been very lovely. Drop me a line, my dear friend, if you are able to do so.

With the old love.

John Burroughs

The letter was written at West Park, May 11, and started off "Dear Walt"—as usual. W. had felt that I "ought not to lose its suggestiveness." W. said: "The grand O'Connor! And not a word of him in the Critic! The truth is, the New Yorkers know very little about him—would not have him on any terms if they did: he was not for them. I don't know if William ever met Stoddard at all—if he did, it was not intimately. But Stedman he did meet—had a great affection for him, too— as we all have, in fact—and naturally, too, because something in Stedman himself enforces it upon us." We spoke of O'Connor's letters on W. W. I argued that, "daring and radical as they were, they were so sweeping, so inclusive, so affording welcome to all writers of all ages, that they accomplished much more for W. W. than any one-sided espousal could." W. responded warmly: "That is so—I can see it— perhaps see it even more than you could—more than anybody could. The great letters I rank as integral to Leaves of Grass— necessary to the volume—I realize it more and more. I have urged it upon Bucke, for instance, that he keep his book as it is now, intact—excising nothing—if writing more—if deeming some further word necessary sometime, not inserting or destroying, but adding—inserting as a sort of appendix; touching the book in no other way. And all this chiefly with an eye to the preservation of O'Connor's letters. Oh! William's sweep, as you say, was tremendous—astounding: he found a place for all—even for poor Poe in the days when I myself would question and doubt." O'Connor's letters were "ever-fresh— perennial—natural to new airs, seasons, as to old." So little in

180

them of formal literary art—yet literature in its true sense, crowded richly and grandly. "How little the average literary art values freedom, instinct, expression. Writers write for exercise—determine that they should write—therefore do. Would never think of writing as the trees put forth their green—as men fall in love—perforce—because there is no other thing to do. But O'Connor! This crowd could not touch his heels!"

Alluding to Harrison and his lack of heroic qualities, W. said merrily: "To make much of him is the old story of fitting a square plug to a round hole." "Harrison has too clearly signified that he is not our man to let any doubt at all remain on that point." Bucke's letter contains the following paragraph,—evidently the portion W. particularly wished me to see: "If (having a chair) you were living in a cottage with a lawn, trees, &c., &c., and living on the ground floor (as might all be arranged well enough) there is no reason why you should not spend a good part of your time during the summer in your chair on the grass, under the trees, among the flowers. You are not tied to one house (and that about the worst house and the worst situated that could be found for you) and there is no reason at all why you should not go where you would have the surroundings you need. Why not get Horace to look about for a good cottage for you?" This evening he said nothing in comment. As usual, holds in reserve till he has heard from me.

Tuesday, May 14, 1889

7.15 P.M. W. I found sitting in the parlor, in his big arm chair, facing the open window. It rained out of doors. The night, however, was pleasant, the storm light. W. said: "We had our trip long ago—if we had not I should have been 'left'—this rain would have trapped us. We have had quite a jaunt down along the river. We found a good point, there at the foot of Cooper's Street—Ed wheeled me in—then we settled ourselves. Yes, I was out of the chair—for a few minutes." Ed says W. composedly sat on a log for a little time. "The river was there—the great city opposite. Being fixed as we were, there seemed an impassable gulf, but it was very enjoyable." He said again: "The chair has certainly been a great success. It provides us an open way." "I saw Harry Bonsall on the way—stopped at his place a few minutes—the Post office. He did not enter into the subject of the dinner." He had observed how the Pennsylvania Railroad was extending its wharves out into the river. "It seems to be accomplished by a complot: railroad officials, politicians, perhaps even judges—anyhow they make their point and the public may whistle." As to his health: "I am not extra well: this cold in the head—this catarrhal trouble keeps up a buzzing and fluffing and stuffing; it is very irksome, continuous. But as one can't have the whole man, having to pay some penalty for being here still, I suppose I should regard this lightly, as indeed I do." He tries in every way to test his strength. Often, he will come downstairs alone—seizing a moment when nobody is about, so as to avoid their offers of assistance. A dangerous procedure. All this has come about since the arrival of the chair. It seems like renaissance.

I spoke to W. about Bucke's new proposition. "Yes," he responded, "I have taken note of it. Doctor thinks I am not occupying here the quarters he could wish for me—thinks I am not well enough fed, housed. Perhaps I am not. But I think I must reply to the Doctor by repeating a story I read long long ago. A man wandering in a graveyard found this inscription on a tombstone: it said, 'I was well—I wished to be better—I consulted a Doctor—I am here,' or something to that effect." W. told this with huge enjoyment. And then stated it in another way: "I was well—I thought to improve on what was unimprovable—I called in artificial aids—with result that you see!" And W. reflected once more: "And that

I must carefully apply to myself now—take it, use it, as sufficient present answer to the Doctor." He did not say this with any disrespect. He listens to all Bucke's counsels physical with great attention.

W. said: "I had a letter from Kennedy today." Tried to find it in his pocket but it was not there. "I thought I had it with me. Kennedy puts a question to me there. He says that in one of his last letters—perhaps the very last—from O'Connor, William said that he wished no memoir of himself written after he was dead—no memoir, either short or long, or for any place. Kennedy wants to know from me—asks me quite fixedly—how far I think that request should be regarded, if regarded at all. What do you think about it, Horace? I cannot see that Kennedy is in any way bound to observe it"— and undoubtedly Kennedy was not. "What Kennedy designs doing he does not specifically state: I judge he will get up some satisfactory memorial paper about O'Connor, of what cut I don't know—probably something very definite in the way of data." Who would print much on that subject? "I don't know —don't know even that Sloane has written or will write anything. It all seems now in the air. But there are hosts of magazines, papers, of countless kinds and sizes, over America, and one of these might be glad to have just that particular article."

I had received my article back from the Critic today, with this statement—(which I now read to W.): "We have a letter or two of O'Connor's, which will give our readers some account of him—pretty much all we can allow ourselves." W. said to me: "Read it again, Horace—I don't entirely take in the significance of it." And after I had done so, he was quiet for several minutes, remarking then that he did "not exactly like the tone of it" and urging me—"Anyhow—let me give you a piece of advice; send it off to the American— I should not hesitate a minute." And he asked, "Who is the note from—do you think—Jennie or Joe?" And when I said,

"I suppose from Joe, by the writing, though it is not signed," he added: "I suppose from Joe—I suppose most of that work—the disposition of such matters is left to him." Then further: "And how would it do, Horace, to cut out from the little article, the Walt Whitman portion—some of the reference to me?" I objected and stated why they were pertinent as they are, whereat he acquiesced. "So you think they are necessary to its integrity? I can see—I can see!" Thence talked freely of "the New York literary crowd"—adding "with not a really first class mind among them! The literary school over there keeps its own counsel. A man like O'Connor is a monstrosity, a pestilent fellow, to it—he is by all means to be avoided. How would they understand him? There is anyhow something despicably little about that whole atmosphere—something so small, petty, picayune, about it. It is true, they have just such like classes in London and in Paris—but these have at least this to excuse them—that is they have intellect, power—indeed, in the case of the Frenchmen, especially, the typical Parisian writer—a force and brilliancy that amounts almost to genius." "But one would despair in New York with having to search for a first-rate—or first-class mind. The staple of their material is of the Willie Winter, Dick Stoddard, order—even smaller than these, if it were possible to have anything smaller than Willie Winter." He spoke generously here of Stedman, as if to make an exception to his large criticism: then—"I read the Critic. The Lounger is DeKay, isn't he? I have thought so—it seems to me somebody told me so." But "DeKay is flat enough, Lord knows! He has written volumes of verse—'Nimrod' was one of them. They have been sent to me. And how handsomely produced! I think DeKay is Watson Gilder's wife's brother. It has been my impression always, though perhaps from no actual knowledge at all, that DeKay is rich—comes of big family connections. His books have been sumptuously produced—oh! beautifully: and yet must have been produced at his

184

expense. I cannot imagine a state of affairs in which any publisher would be willing to risk five cents on DeKay's poems." As to Gilder as poet, W. said: "Oh! he might count for more. And then as things are now, his position itself gives some currency to a book sent out in his name." But W. felt: "These fellows make family, cabalistic affairs of their literary actions—cabals, cliques."

Referred to Critic notice of Linton's two volumes of verse. W. described Linton thus: "He is a man of varied parts, as they say—polished, informed—as full of knowledge of tradition, of human history, as any man alive—yet radical as a boy—even a socialist—all around I should judge a William Morris sort of a man." W. is very solicitous to know "How does the work in the bank go?" indicating a position I newly assumed on Monday. "I should think you would be exactly suited in it: it will give you time to do your writing—jaunt it about some—all that—a semi-freedom, at least!"

Wednesday, May 15, 1889

8 P.M. I found W. sitting out of doors, in his chair against the side of the step. On the steps themselves, Ed, Warren and Harry. W.'s greeting tonight was—"Howdy? Howdy?" He said he had been "tripping it" again. "We have had two trips today—one about noon—one a while ago. I feel better and better—always more like going." "We went along to the Cooper Street wharf. I have not yet got to the ferry—not that I especially avoided it, but that the spirit has not yet moved me to go. But I shall go. The day will come." I have got models from Oldach today. W. saw the bundle in my hand, asked about it, so I tore it open in the semidarkness. He felt the one book (one was case only) carefully—looked it all around—said that "from what I can judge, seeing it this way, I am likely to be pleased." But "I shall hold them over tomorrow—study them by daylight." Oldach said book would

be 70 cents, which appeared to satisfy W. As we talked there (W. with his hat on) Lindell's daughter Maggie came up, introduced a young man she called her brother, and handed W. some flowers just picked from her garden. W. greeted her heartily, held her hand—said: "Thank you girl—it is good of you." And turning to the young man—"Have I met him before? I don't think so—no." Adding: "Well—I'm glad to meet him now, anyhow!" She spoke about his "getting" out, and W. joked of Ed—"I'm afraid he'll go off with me some day and leave me somewhere—never bring me back." Then added: "But somebody will, surely—surely!" Then turned to Ed with the flowers: "I'll ask you Ed, to take these to Mrs. Davis for the present—have her put them in water—then in the morning I'll have them in my room—enjoy them." Adding: "and while you're in, Ed, go upstairs in my room—you'll find there on the chair a little package of letters, fastened with a rubber—letters I wish to give Horace: bring them along." Then, after a few words more, Maggie departed. W. cordially calm, and to her counsel to "call to see us" responding: "I shall, some day—and before long!"

He had asked me when I came: "What have you in the other bundle? Books, too?" And when I explained not, but Whitman dinner circulars which I had promised to send off for the committee, he said: "Have you one for me? I have not seen it." So I went inside to open the bundle and secure one. When I got forward from the kitchen again Ed had helped W. into the parlor. W. had questioned me on my first coming: "Is it too cool out here for me?"—and now seemed to conclude that it was. I gave him the circular, which he stuffed into his side pocket. "Shall I send one to the Doctor or to others?" I expostulated—that we would write to Bucke, as the folks wished a letter from him to be read at the dinner. "Well—I shall do as you advise about that—only I wished to see a copy myself." He said of Burroughs: "John is not a diner-out—would not go to such an affair for the meal—but he

186

loves like the rest of you to get about—to go anywhere so as to
meet the fellows—to come into touch and speech with the boys.
I should not wonder but he would come." And Ingersoll—
would W. feel "insulted" in his presence? He replied earnestly:
"No indeed—honored, rather: I should take that as a crowning
event." But Ingersoll "shocked" people—and was not he
(W. W.) shocked? He laughed. "That is funny to ask.
Shocked? I consider Bob one of the constellations of our time—
of our country—America—a bright, magnificent constellation.
Besides, all the constellations—not alone of this but of any
time—shock the average intelligence for a while. In one respect that helps to prove it a constellation. Think of Voltaire,
Paine, Hicks, not to say anything of modern men whom we
could mention." I referred to my intention of writing to
Stedman this week. I wish greatly to have him come over,
attend and speak at the dinner, and see W. W. counselled me:
"If you write to Stedman, of course, you may say what you
choose about the Hartmann matter. But say for me—that is,
if you will—say for me, that I, too, was vexed and mad at the
incident, but decided, after thinking it over carefully from all
sides—oh! almost intensely, and for days—to take no public
notice of it whatever. As you say, if we could have Stedman
here, it would be a great point gained—if we could have had
him at the time, the difficulty could easily have been obviated."
"I am sure," he said again, "if Stedman could have been here
with us, he would have appreciated our position. We have
never in our career so far—I mean I have never in my career,
made public explanations, retractions, what not. I know Stedman is hot-headed—but not more so than I am. Not more so
than you are. And we were all mightily wroth, God knows!
But perhaps my Kennedy letters may mend matters some—
he probably has the copy by this time—I suppose Kennedy has
sent it." And he went on further: "I have been dipping into
the Stedman books today again—reading Channing—William
Henry Channing"—I interrupted—"You mean William

Ellery, don't you?"—and he: "Is it that? I mean the great Channing, anyhow. He is there in the book quite copiously— I may say, satisfactorily, too. Stedman shows wonderful taste in his combinations. He selects from the best—I wonder often if not the best—the very best—of every man he touches. I am sure if we may judge by his treatment of us—his rare judgment there—if he has gone all around with like discrimination —we are all fortunate in our judge. For I don't believe we were ever set forth so wisely and handsomely before anywhere."

W. said about the letters Ed had brought down for me: "I thought you would like to read them at your leisure; take them along. Put a string about them—include with them the letters I gave you the other day—then return to me. You can finally have them to keep, if you wish. I thought it might be well to have Nellie O'Connor see them. When the heft of this affair is over—and the after-quiet has come—she would like to read. At any rate, I'll keep them by me—if sending to her, will ask for their return eventually so you can keep them together." Then: "Kennedy writes again—writes of the O'Connor article—wants particulars. He will probably be doing something in the matter." In the package were two letters from Bucke, a letter and a postal from Kennedy, and a letter from Barnhill (Cambridge)—the Henry George preacher, I think—who asks of W. some expression of opinion "on the subject which is now cleaving literary Boston in twain," viz—the question raised by Howells whether literature "the old world literature" is not "saturated in the aristocratic spirit and lacks that enthusiasm for democracy which the coming literature must have?" These are Barnhill's words. W. made no comment on this tonight except that he had received it and that it was in the package.

He asked me: "How about the Club last night? Was it a success?" And he asked me if Boyesen "handled the English well"—if he "was much of a fellow in port and manner" &c.

188

I tried to say something about Agnes Repplier's brilliant nothingness in shape of reply to Boyesen, but he did not care to listen and I did not press it. He has little patience with "talk for the sake of talk—talk that foregoes truth, so it can startle or surprise an interest." Harned in to see me tonight and brought me a box of invitations to send off to Club members and special persons.

Thursday, May 16, 1889

8.10 P.M. I went down to W.'s with Forrest West, who had casually called, and was on his way to the city with me. W. sat in the parlor—his hat on—a robe across his knees—his cane in his hand—exceedingly easy and bright. "I have been out twice today," he said, "and threatened to go a third time—though this was not effected. We did not go to the river today—we went out—not towards the country—about the City Hall—in that direction." He said he felt "better and better" except for "this persistent cold in the head, which hangs on whether we will or no!"

Said he had "considered" the book "well"—and sure enough, expecting me, he had it there on the chair, a letter tucked under the strings of the package. "It is a brave book," he said, "everything about it is honest—satisfied me—everything that Oldach did was square and true." But the printing —"that vexes me—that is by no means up to the mark— neither registered well nor inked well. I should say, the ink not only very bad, but very sparingly used, too. After the beautiful Emerson book—after Sarrazin—it is almost enough to shock a fellow to come across this. And look at our great English Bible upstairs! The same paper—the same margin— but with a distinctness and marvellous delicacy throughout. Oh no! Ferguson has not done us up well this time." But the book "as a whole" would "justify itself." If it failed at one point it did not fail at all points. "We must congratulate ourselves that there has been no disaster—not complain for a shock coming here and there." And he added: "I had expected a lighter green in the cover. He can still get it so, if he has not put in his supply—but if he has, this will do." His letter was very clear and simple, and goes over this ground. Here it is:

328 Mickle Street
Camden May 16 '89

Dear Sir

This sample of your binding (old-fashion'd pocket-book style with ordinary tongue or tuck-flap, all holding snug, but not too tight or stiff) is satisfactory & suits me best. The dark green morocco, if you have it already, will do—but if you have to get it get *a lighter green*. Bind the whole ed'n alike, no variety. Make a short paper pocket (see last page as written on in sample)—In trimming the plates, &c. (if yet to be done) trim them, especially No: 1, and No: 4, a little *more* white paper at bottom, & *less* at top, the trimming in this sample seems to me to be the very reverse. The plates are all put in right in this sample—the stamp on cover is right—& altogether the job looks satisfactory.

I particularly want 50 copies (or 100) in a week.

Walt Whitman

And on the envelope, addressed to "Mr. Oldach Binder, Phila:" he added

Please send this up to the binders (men or women) who are working on my book—& I herewith send them my best respects.

W. W.

I returned him his batch of letters from Mrs. O'Connor. Could not get him the first fold from Oldach today. W. wishes to sign them—are promised for tomorrow. "I see," he said, "there was to be a meeting about that dinner this afternoon. Was anything done? Did you hear?" And when I said: "I am not sure—but I believe a hundred tickets were guaranteed." W. laughed. "Well, that is good, anyhow—that has some ring to it!" I am writing letters right and left for the Committee and sending circulars about among literary characters.

Allen Thorndike Rice died today. W. said: "Yes—I saw it in this afternoon's paper!"—how vigilant he still is!—"and it was quite depressing. How many of these deaths are happening now! I did not know Rice personally, but he was very friendly towards me. I remember when James Redpath—I think, last wrote to me, he spoke of Rice—of Rice's desire to have something from me: then of Rice's personality: spoke of him as a steam engine—all force, vehemence, power, exhilaration, push, life, vim. And now Rice is gone—gone forever—and never even a warning of it! Does it not advise us of our littleness? No matter what the man—no matter what his place, his duties, his public importance—he is hewed down—cut off—with as little ceremony, as remorselessly, as the little fellows—as even we are!" And "now Rice is gone," W. speculated, "what will be the policy of the Review? Will it get into strange hands—new policies?" I started off shortly with W.'s messages. "Don't forget, boy," he said to me, "We want our books—some of 'em—in a week if we can get 'em!" And again: "I hear from Bucke almost every day—though not every day to any great effect."

Friday, May 17, 1889

7:40 P.M. Went down with Tom Harned. W. sitting in front of the house, his chair drawn next the step. A couple of boys, quite small ones, lounging there with him. These slid away in a little while after we had sat down. W. greeted us heartily, two or three flowers in one hand, his glasses in the other, the inevitable cane blocked up between the knees. People came up and shook hands with him, now one, now another. The city editor of the Post was carefully greeted. Once a little girl of the neighborhood who shyly shook hands, W. asking: "How is Ruth? How is little sister Ruth?" Then he suddenly turned to us. "Now that I have two able-bodied men with me, I shall take advantage of it"—rising slowly from his chair, I did not know for what. "I want to go next door," he explained, "take my arm, Horace"—then going toilsomely on, step by step. We did not go up on the steps at Mrs. Button's, only stood there and had a little boy who was near ring the bell. W. said to me, "My friend, John Forney, used to say that one of the best parts about having a good thing was in being able to share it with the neighbors." And he added: "Colonel Forney was a good fellow!" I espied Ed coming down the street. "And here comes another good fellow!" I exclaimed. W. looked—his eyes did not reveal Ed at first, but when he was near W. broke into a laugh. "Why, it is Ed—the rascal!—and a good fellow, too!" The door here opened, and W. handed up and in the flowers he had in his hand. A little girl took them. "Give them to Mrs. Button: tell her they are from Walt Whitman—that he left them at the door himself." Then we started back again. It was a duty he had not wished to delegate. "Mrs. Button is sick—is an invalid," he said explanatorily. Finally he got down in the chair again. He had seemed to me to walk a little better than when indoors. I asked: "Do you find yourself getting stronger in the legs?" But he shook his head. "No, not at all, not stronger in the legs: my strength does not come back to me." Tom dwelt upon the good fortune of his getting out. W. responded: "It *is* a great joy—a great joy simply to get out of my cell." But somehow, *power* would not return. "But to get into freedom—even this freedom, to get sun and air—is greatly a gain on the old condition." Then he said laughingly to Tom, "Why, Tom, we have just now come back from a drive: we drove down to the foot of Cooper Street—to the wharf there!" But he spoke of his head. "Getting out seems rather to aggravate than to benefit that. Yet even with that it is worth while. I have not been to the ferry yet: I am waiting till I have gathered strength for it. I find no sudden return— but perhaps it will come bye and bye. The great thing with me is the *spirit:* as the old man said, my *spirit* is *tremenjuous*

—*tremenjuous,* thanks to myself in part, thanks in part to an occasional sip of sherry!" Tom laughed at this: said to W., "I don't think the sherry you take would ever add much to your spirit!" But W. expostulated, "Never mind about that, Tom: I don't always take it—I wait for the right time to come—then take a swig of it: I can swear that it goes to the right spot, too!" Then he went on: "Anyhow, I am on the go. Ed is very faithful to me—sticks by me honestly—we go out often. This morning we went out even before my breakfast—took a trip around the block." Tom asked him if he had his breakfast served upstairs, and he replied, "I have had it so, so far."

W. talked with Harned somewhat about Rice. He acquiesced seriously in Tom's lamentation. "Yes, it was a great loss—Rice seemed to be a fellow big in promise. He was said to be irrepressible—an immense worker—and rich, too—well using his riches—full of determination to have certain things done and to do them himself. The great feature about Rice was his promise—Oh! his promise! And he appeared to be a handsome and quite a young man too. Rice was very generous towards me: I had a letter from him once which was very warm, if not enthusiastic: it must be about here still—I do not think I have given it away, though I know I am apt to." And W. continued after some questions: "No—I do not think you have seen it—it dates several years ago. I had at his solicitation written him a piece for the magazine, for which he paid me a hundred dollars—and a good hundred it was—for I needed it much at the time. About ten days after the article had appeared, Rice wrote me a letter warmly commenting upon it!" He thought Rice had "improved vastly the tone of the Review."

I had secured the first sheets for W. from Oldach today. He would have it that they be safely placed up in his room. Commented on the book again—its printing—"greatly a disappointment to me—bad—bad: a sickly green—as I told you last night, bad ink and not enough of it at that!" "If our printing was in accord with the cover, how handsomely we would appear!" Promised to sign a hundred of the sheets for me by Monday morning. Harned going over this evening to hear Herbert Gilchrist's closing lecture of the course. I turned to W.: "Aren't you sorry you can't go?" He laughed in his quiet way: "Oh no! Not at all—I should not be disposed to go if I had means of going. Of late years especially, I have noticed that I never get in a hall and am there to stay, but soon there comes upon me a terrible inclination to get up and scamper out. This is my invariable feeling. Meetings I do not seem to take to naturally, even under the best circumstances. Wilson Barrett there several years ago—I remember well— I sat that out—it was 'Clito'—and somehow I persevered through. And there was the other Barrett, too—the play from Boker—'Francesca Da Rimini' he calls it—I mainly held up under that: in fact, liked it—thought even Lawrence did well—though not as well as Marie Wainright: She pleased me greatly." Asked if we had heard from Ingersoll. We talked of slang. W. of the "naturalness" and "fittingness" of some of it. "The boys in the army were first-rate slangists—invented lots of words—'switching-off'—'skedaddle'—lots of others. And genuine creations, too—words that will last." Tom had subscribed for the Century Dictionary. From which had arisen this theme. W. said: "I have almost been disposed to write to Gilder or one of the fellows myself, cautioning them not to omit my word 'Presidentiad.' Oh! that is eminently a word to be cherished—adopted. Its allusion, the four years of the Presidency: its origin that of the Olympiad—but as I flatter myself, bravely appropriate, where not another one word, signifying the same thing, exists!"

Saturday, May 18, 1889

7.50 p.m. W. sitting quietly in his chair: saw me approaching, held out his hand cordially. On the step next him was a bunch of daisies and several papers. He did not look well, was rather pale and wearied. Hat on—the red handkerchief about his neck. During the first few minutes of his talk with me, he seemed confused, his mind not keen. But he afterwards woke up and was then himself again. But this advised me that something was the matter with him, and I asked about it. He then said: "It is my head—I have not been at all well today, though not giving up entirely. This is my first outing—this, now, in the evening; though," and he said this rather triumphantly, "I have signed the one hundred sheets—every one of them!" And he added: "They are ready for you when you want them." In a few minutes Tom stepped up and they engaged in bright talk. W. spoke of his head again: "It keeps up an awful buzzing, sawing—keeps me deaf full half the time—oppresses, threatens, discomposes: so that my comfort is short at least!"

I spoke of the O'Connor notice in the current Critic—its lameness—its milk-and-water reference to O'Connor's great Whitman letters as "certain articles on the genius of Walt Whitman." Had W. ever known those letters so tamely referred to before? He thought not, but—"It is no more than we have a right to expect. But there is a notice in the Transcript of the 16th—I have a copy of it upstairs. Kennedy sent it on—sent a postal with it: says it was written by a fellow named Heard. Do you know him, or about him? I know nothing at all—it is an entirely new name to me. I was going to send the paper at once to Bucke, but it struck me Nellie might like to see it, so I put paper and postal together for you to examine and then will send the paper to her, she to forward it to Doctor." When I proposed mailing it, he protested: "I think I shall do it this time—because I'll take advantage of the occasion to write to Nellie explaining that—explaining other things too." He thought I would have to wait for morning for it—"for I don't think Ed could find it in the confusion upstairs, though, if you want it now, I'll go up myself and get it."

Harned cabled Tennyson today about the dinner, soliciting some word, but expressed doubt of much if any reply. W. said: "No—Tennyson is old—he is lazy too—and, I understand, delegates a good deal of his work to his wife and daughter." Tom expressed determination to rescue the dinner from *local* color merely. W.: "I would not, Tom, at least not too much. But limit the speeches—don't let any fellow go on as long as he wants to: except of course, the big guns, who must take their own time." Tom said: "Clifford, for instance"; and Walt responded: "Yes, Clifford—Clifford should speak— we want a speech from him—and he must not be restricted, for Clifford will know just what to say." I wrote a number of letters this evening to Gilder, Stedman, Whittier, Garland, Bucke, Cary (the Century), Mark Twain, John Fiske, Larned (Chicago News) and Bush (Canada). Yesterday I wrote to West (New Ideal), Morse and Kennedy. The day before to Gannett, Salter, Blake, Carnegie, Adler. W. spoke of Cary: "Yes—and he likes me well, I think." And as to substance of my letter to Stedman, which I gave him, he said: "That is good: and if he comes!" Advised me in several cases of people he thought might like to come or to be advised of it. As to Lowell: "I would not write to him: it would seem out of place— he would not appreciate it." Then suddenly: "What is this I read in the paper today about the dinner—that the rule excluding women had been rescinded?" And when I explained, with my arguments with Bonsall and Harned against it, W. exclaimed: "Good! Good! Why—some of my best—in fact, my very best friends have been women." Then: "I should like my friend Col. Cockerill, of the World, invited—Col. J. Cockerill, I think it is. And there is Frank Williams, too— and the wife: Oh! the wife has been very good to me! And have you sent word to Sanborn? Sanborn should be notified: Frank has done nobly by me! Address him at Concord—a letter so will find him. You have not forgotten Julius Chambers?—nor Elizabeth Porter Gould—there at Chelsea?"

And so ran over a list: Mrs. Spaulding, Mrs. Fairchild, Walsh, and others. If he thought of others still, would "note them down" for me. The short notice cuts off many possibilities of correspondence.

W. evidently had suffered from heat today. Asked us, "Isn't it very warm?" It did not seem greatly so to me. His condition no doubt aggravated it. Harned described the lecture of Gilchrist last evening—one sentence thereof touching "the unknown" art of England &c. W. greatly laughing thereat. "I think I should report upon such an expression by telling a story—the story of the old man who was writing a history of Ireland—came to one chapter—chapter seven, say—headed it 'Snakes in Ireland' and put into the chapter but two lines— that the whole measure of it—'There are no snakes in Ireland!' That would seem severe perhaps—but taken with a little allowance, would be strictly true." But he asked: "So he spoke of the Rossettis? I suppose of Dante? That must have come in." I reminded W. of our long promise to Morse to send him a copy of the big book and he assented to the duty of sending one shortly: "Sidney ought surely to have one" he allowed. Tom described a George meeting he got into after Gilchrist's lecture last evening. W. greatly interested. For some time we discussed the matter. "The raw material of the earth," said W.—"that, I suppose *can* be no one man's— isn't that true? Hasn't it always been true? And yet, what a man puts upon it—the direct result of his own personal labor—isn't that his—and always?" Roughly stated, this was the single tax theory exactly. Yet W. has never read a description of it with care—confesses—as he asked again tonight "What *is* the single tax?" Then Tom gave a warm description of what he took to be the theory. W. said: "Edward Carpenter's piece to the Duke—wasn't that the same thing?"

It was very funny to listen to his joking banter with Tom that followed. T. invited him to lunch tomorrow at *one* or dinner at 5. W. said "I think it best that I should make no engagement, but if I can, come!"—and he laughed heartily at the prospect of it. And he would have to take something to drink too—"Indeed, that would be a great point of the visit." But Bucke's prohibition? "Oh! that must not count—the little drop, now and then, I take, would hurt no one." Tom spoke of claret, but W. was dubious: "I don't care for claret," but Madeira, "that might do," though after all, "sherry and champagne—these are my favorites—these I shall never surrender! Indeed, Tom, nothing but a bottle of champagne will satisfy me!" He went into paroxysms of laughter over a story I told him of a late car the other night on which a young fellow invited the car out to take a drink (20 persons responding)—taking off the driver with him—and anxious even for the conductor, standing on the step of the saloon and calling after him as the car rolled off. Tom said: "They were all drunk!" and W.: "Yes—that's so: but it was so funny! I should like to have been there!" And to me: "That's a good story to keep. The young fellow must have been a drunkard!"

Harned spoke to W. of Donaldson's treatment of us in the fund matter. W. told a story of Jim Scovel: "He would quote somebody who said 'money'? Oh! watch the money!—for money is sacred!'" And to Tom: "Whatever we do Tom—we must look after the checks!" I got him his model copy of the pocket edition L. of G. from Ferguson's today—the copy sent to guide the printers. Secured from Ferguson also his bill: $9.00 for composition, &c., $27.00 for printing. Ferguson is very sensitive about the bad result of Brown's printing. Then of the dinner again: "I have so many good friends abroad, too!—and the biggest too! But we will get along with the second or third raters!"

Sunday, May 19, 1889

10.30 A.M. Mrs. Davis was in the room, talking to Walt. He was trying to find her a certain newspaper. I took him Tribune from Harned, whom I had met on the street. I said to W.: "I just left Tom down at the corner with his high hat on." W. queried: "Going to church, I suppose?" I nodded assent. "I thought so," he proceeded, "One belongs with the other, high hat and church—each equally detestable." Then after a moment's pause, as if to confess a doubt of his own position: "That is from a severe point of view. I remember when I was a young man one of my placards for remembrance—for every-day contemplation—was this: to not take a severe view of things— to guard lest I settle into the mood of the book-bookies, scholars, critics—growling at the *universe* in general and all its particulars. I think I have mainly succeeded in holding myself in check, if check were needed." Gave me copy of Hobby Horse guild periodical, picking it from floor and saying: "Take it along with you. I think it is edited by Horne, who is friendly to me—thoughtful of me and sends it on every issue." And he now referred again, as so often before, to its "superb ink and press-work and paper."

Mrs. Davis came in again, holding a couple of tiny chickens extended in her hand. He smoothed and fondled them—talked pleasantly and low—"Oh! What mites! And black ones, too! O you dearies! Are you glad you have come?" And so on. Suddenly he turned and scanned the table, then back again to the chickens, still there in Mrs. Davis' hand. "I have nothing here for you, darlings—nothing at all—nothing but *Leaves* of *Grass*—and *Leaves* of *Grass*. When you come to want them at all you will want the genuine, which, unfortunately, we have not about us here." And as he still handled them: "How serene! just as if they had a right to be here!—which is the most beautiful feature about it all."

I called W.'s attention to the card printed after Hannah Stevenson's death, embodying her noble life—vista, &c.— reading thus:

Hannah Elizabeth Stevenson's Expense-book Motto.
To postpone my own pleasure to others' convenience,

My own convenience to others' comfort,
My own comfort to others' want,
And my own want to others' extreme need.

At the first mention of her name he repeated it: "Hannah Stevenson? Surely I know her. It seems to me she must have sent me money during the war." And as he read the rules: "Grand! Noble! Sublime! Supreme! Oh! What a personality, to have projected that! That is projected right out of her rich and saving inwardness." In his usual vein he kept on soliciting details. I told him all I had heard and remembered of her from Clifford, who had known her friendship years ago and intimately—a mother-help and more. Then W. resumed: "Ah yes! now the name assumes a positiveness. *Miss*, wasn't she? I am certain of it. I must have it in memoranda there in my note books"—pointing to the table. "There was another woman in Boston, too—have you heard of her too? She sent money from time to time—Miss Wigglesworth or Rigglesworth. It all comes back to me. You know, much money was sent to me in those years of hospital experience. Many rich ladies in the land devoted time and money to the cause—bled themselves copiously, bravely. Hannah Stevenson was one of them, I'm sure."

The day has been clouded but it does not yet storm (noontime). I advised that, as the day looked ominous, he ought to have a ride without waiting for the afternoon. He assented: "That is true, and I'll get Ed to rig up before long. I rather like a day such as this—half-clouded, quiet, subdued. Take note of my prediction, too—that the weather will remain just about as it is the rest of the day, unchanging." [And it did: I was off in the woods most of the rest of the day, and barring a few slight showers, it did not rain at all.] W. looked very well this morning, his color splendid. But he continues the complaint of head trouble.

"There are the autographs," he said, pointing to a bundle on the table, "103 of them. If you want more I can set to work and get them ready for you today." But there was no occasion. I put the package in the hallway, so I could get it in calling before he arises tomorrow. Had not yet sent a set of sheets of the pocket-edition to Bucke—was afraid they would make a bad impression—thought the parts would "best hang together" when in the handsome cover. His circumspection is remarkable. I wrote letters to Howells, Sanborn, Aldrich, this forenoon. I asked W. quizzically about Holmes. He shook his head. "No—I should not write to Holmes—he is not one of our men —we all must realize that. I have met him—he was pleasant enough then. Holmes is not without decided, splendid, sparks of high talent—he has great smartness, brilliancy. But Holmes is most famous as an epigrammatist, rather than poet, though he has written fine things, I know—a number of fine things. But Holmes belongs to another world than ours—comes by right into another heritage—an important agency, too, as I always realize and acknowledge."

He pointed out the fine roses on the table. "They are from Grace Johnson—she was on here the other day—came to see some school friend, I think—there in Philadelphia. I don't suppose she went right back home, for a day or two after she saw me, these roses came—so she must have still been about." Then he went on: "I have many serious, delicious experiences —none more touching, exquisite, than with the flowers! Oh! the transcendent flowers!—see these, how they hold up their proud sweet heads!" He pointed to the bunch of daisies I had remarked on the step last night: he had just clipped the stems, and now the flowers stood in front of him on the table. "A youngster—I suppose about ten—came up to me last night— it was already quite dark—in front of the house. He was a chubby, big, I should judge ruddy-faced boy of his years. He came up to me—never said a word—held the flowers straight out this way—and I took them. 'Are they for me? Thank you! Thank you! Thank you, boy!' I said, and so off he went." "And not even then a word?" I asked. W. responded: "No—

not a word—not a whisper!" And then he exclaimed fervently: "The wonderful, inexplicable children!"

On the chair was the Transcript containing the O'Connor notice of which he had spoken to me. "It is very good indeed," he said, "considering it for itself, as an unpretentious newspaper notice." He had written on the margin of the paper, plainly with ink—"Kennedy thinks this was written by Hurd." Was he sure about *Hurd*—I had known the name *Heard*. But he persisted: "H-U-R-D is right—I am sure of it." But he looked in vain for Kennedy's postal. "I was sure I had laid it carefully for you here—but, as usual, my best care would not save it."

Monday, May 20, 1889

I found W. sitting in the parlor, at the window, hatted and cloaked, with the lap-robe duly in its place, and Ed across the room at the other window fiddling away at a great rate. I had written to Burroughs this forenoon and told W. so—who said: "How good it would be to have John come, and who knows but he will? The fellows like once and awhile to tear themselves away—go off somewhere—get into new scenes—shake off the monotony of their usual life. Even John, it seems to me, likes it. And Kennedy would, too. I should not be surprised to have Sloane down here—not at all!" I had told Burroughs it would be more acceptable to W. now than in September, the time of the other trip. "Yes, indeed," said W., "I was in a bad way then—bad—bad." And he added warmly: "And if John would only come—only come! And Stedman, too: how much *I* would make of that!" And he advised me also: "We would enjoy John Hay too." And after a pause: "I have thought of another, Horace—our ex-President: Can't you send a circular to Grover Cleveland? I am told he has read Leaves of Grass—read it to some purpose." As to the circular, he said in reply to my direct question: "Yes, I like it: It is in perfect good taste

—was it Tom's or Harry's?—or did they put their heads together to produce it?" He thought it "quite well-done—well said." I told him Clifford had absolutely promised to speak, and he took the information up with evident pleasure. "That is truly good to hear—that assures us *one* good thing—whatever else goes wrong." And he asked: "Will Tom take matters in hand? Some one should—he should—so that the longwinded fellows don't get possession of things." I said: "Some fellow who will speak about 'the Camden poet.'" His laughter was great: he is always moved by references to him so couched (and they frequently *are* so couched).

Said he had been out "enough to keep up" his "reputation" —and that was all today—"out in front of the door a little while ago—for a few minutes only." He had received and read the Critic. "I sent it off to Mrs. O'Connor. The notice is indeed, as you say, weak enough to be namby-pamby: it is only barely saved from that." But he was not surprised. "Joe Gilder gets on with the New York clique—and the New York clique believe first of all in *finesse*, finish, polish—afterwards in naturalness, elementalism. Joe knows Dick Stoddard too well—I think Stoddard and he are close friends. At any rate Joe is affected by the tendencies that to Stoddard are all in all." Then W. proceeded into considerable quiet statement of his own conception of the function of books in our civilization. "What we want above all—what we finally must and will insist upon —in future—actual men and women—living, breathing, hoping, aspiring books—books that so grow out of personality, magnificence of undivided endowment, as themselves to become such persons, stand justly in their names." I should read Kennedy's piece "there towards the close of Bucke's book" for "it says this—or says part of this—well, nobly well—I don't know but better than ever it was stated elsewhere. At least, I am convinced that Kennedy so far grasps the pith of the lesson. It is a meaning I always invoke—a meaning, I hope palpably in all my work—to be drawn therefrom and acknowledged, one at least of several sacred (oh! how sacred!) commands, if I dare assume to have commanded at all." "The world has had its fill of dandies, ladies and gentlemen, dressiness, smartness, skill, respectability, formalism—in literature: it still waits for the natural man to come—to come nobly, unhesitatingly—in quiet, in composure—and so to take his place and to stay!" W. spoke this in his strange deliberate way, but with the fullness of tone that so impresses one when he is in unusual earnest. "Read it again," he pursued—"read it again, Horace—it is worth while knowing well. I for myself, more and more appreciate its satisfactoriness."

I told him I was to read from "Democratic Vistas" before a circle tonight. He said: "Good luck to you! Tell them how the piece came about—that it was directly stimulated by Carlyle's 'Shooting Niagara' among other things,—by the state of our national, social, affairs at the time. Probably during or just before the war. Before the war was itself war—things seemed more portentous and bloody before the war than during it." Took sheets to Oldach today and he promised to "push" the books. But W. was incredulous. That "push" aroused his suspicion. He had "no idea Oldach *could* push things even if he wished to." He laughed, but was hopeful with it. Has promised to give me a list of addresses of his friends abroad who might wish to be remembered for the dinner. Johnston has written Harned that he has been unable to meet Ingersoll or to get a reply to his notes. I shall write to Ingersoll myself. W. expressed pleasure with the idea that Frank Williams would be present and possibly speak. Harned got a few orders for tickets.

Tuesday, May 21, 1889

8. P.M. W. was in his room, lying on the bed. Mrs. Davis was on the big book-box nearby talking with him. There was no light in the room. Mrs. Davis at once arose to go, and W.

protested, but she insisted, and so we were left alone. W. said
to me without ceremony: "I did not get out today." Was it
because he was ill? "Not particularly, though that in part—
just thought to lie down awhile." Yet Ed told me W. had
been quite disturbed the whole day through, and had spent a
restless night. Asked me what news I had. I spoke to him of a
letter I had today from Aldrich. "That," said W., "would
seem to show that Aldrich is moving forward into the ranks:
don't it seem so to you? The whole statement is important and
significant." He did not think Aldrich had ever so put himself
on record before. I referred to something Harrison Morris had
told me today with respect to Lincoln Eyre's high opinion of
W. W.'s character and work, as prophetic of the future
America. W. was very curious to know all about Eyre. Then
said: "The point is in this—not that he says what you say he
does but how he comes to say it—the nature of his argument."

Shortly he essayed to get up, and I helped him. When I
protested he replied: "Oh! I have been here a long while!
It is time for me to sit up." I helped him across the room—but
he insisted himself upon fixing the windows and lighting the
gas, though it was a slow process. I could discover in his increased unsteadiness an evidence of the bad day: it is an
invariable index. Suddenly he said as he stood up: "I should
like that somebody write to Baxter about the dinner," and was
pleased when I told him I had already done so. Baxter had a
poem in the current American ("Sympathy") upon the mention of which W. was full of curious inquiry. "Are you sure of
the name?" and was it "written first in the American, do you
think?" &c., &c. "I have put your names together," he here
announced, "such of them as were suggested to me. There may
be more, but these seemed particularly near and necessary."
This was a sheet indicating those he had particularly wished
notified of the dinner. He makes quite a point of Cleveland—
alluded to him again. "I haven't put Rhys there, but he should
have been named." Had laid out a sheet from the Christian

Register and marked in ink on the margin—"Agnes Traubel." "It is for Agnes," he now said, handing it to me, "she will like it—it is about something which always interests the girls— about Paris—the women of Paris. How well the women are doing nowadays! This Augusta Larned is a very bright woman, and there is Margaret Sullivan, too—the correspond-ent of the Paris Exposition, doing splendid work." "Parisian Street Life" was the piece by Miss Larned which he had marked for my sister. He had himself "read it with a great interest."

Spoke of having put up for me several things. "Kennedy writes me about Howells: have you heard of it? He thinks Walter Scott a humbug—prefers Tolstoi—there seems to be some discussion up about it. No—Kennedy does not endorse him—is on the contrary indignant. You have heard about it then?" And afterwards, a little pause between: "Kennedy sent me a copy of the Transcript—it is there in the package. It appears Stepniak—you know much about him?—is a reader of *Leaves* of *Grass*—enters quite largely into it. There is someone who writes to the Transcript to that effect. I shall have you read the paper and either send to Doctor Bucke yourself or give to me to send." He would indeed like to read "Underground Russia," which I named as among my books. He had "never read any of Stepniak's books." Stepniak, ac-cording to this correspondent (Harriot Stanton Blatch: Lon-don, May 9), had said to her: "Ah, here's another of my favorites" (holding up a volume of 'Leaves of Grass';) "An author who is not sufficiently appreciated in his own land." As to Tolstoi, I suggested that W. send him a book, and he said: "I will—I will send him a copy of our pocket edition: do you think you can find out how to address him?" I have wondered if Tolstoi had ever encountered W. W.'s book.

W. called my attention to the fact that Stoddard "has been essaying again"—and commented: "It is in Lippincott's— this time it is about Fitz-Greene Halleck—it is quite inter-esting in a light way—gossipy—contains nothing new that would be called of account." Morris had spoken to me of Stoddard as "sour." W. laughed. "It is sufficiently descriptive —it don't need addition." I said Mrs. Baldwin wittily describes Miss Repplier as Miss Replyer. W. was greatly moved. "Oh!" he said between his laughs, "that is very good: it reminds me of Mrs. Johnston—Col. Johnston's wife—who always spoke of Gosse—poor Gosse!—as *Goose*." He hunted up the magazine among his papers and handed it to me. "I should take it if I were you—it will not weigh you down but it is worth looking over."

I told him I had not yet had word from Stedman. W.: "Don't go on expecting too much—Stedman may yet be mad." I replied: "He may have been mad and may be mad, but he won't stay mad." He asked: "You think so?" Then went on: "I told you what Kennedy wrote about the Hartmann squibs —that he referred to my old letters and asked whether it would be advisable to send a copy of it to Stedman. I suppose he must have received that letter by this time. I told Kennedy —or intended telling him—that while making no *public* utterance on the matter, I might even ask that the letter he referred to should be sent to Stedman. About the piece itself I care little. Any man whose head comes above the horizon must accept—be prepared for such liabilities. But in the exact way that turned—hitting such a moment of union between us—I find plenty of cause for my vexation and anger." He had been reading Stedman's "Poets of America" today, and looking over the Cyclopedia—also reading Arnold's prose. Speaking of women in attendance at the dinner: "True enough we must not bar them out—but the thing that troubles me is, that they probably won't come anyhow."

Asked about reading of the Vistas last night. I had read, among other things, "Blood-Money," and had explained its exclusion from L. of G. on sectional grounds. W. at first said: "I don't know that there is any particular reason for their being where they are, except that they got there once and have been kept there. Probably they might just as well be included in Leaves of Grass; perhaps by and by will be." But afterwards he more or less acquiesced in my explanation. "There is a partisanism in the poem which makes it to some extent non-exact—nonrepresentative. In those days I fell in mostly with abolitionists—rabid abolitionists—noble, big fellows, many of them, but all consumed by the notion, which I never would admit, that slavery—slavery alone—was evil, and the universe contained no other. There will always be this objection to including those poems with the others." Had he written many poems in that early period? "No—not many—but some: there are two or three of them in Specimen Days, as you know."

He spoke of radical claimants to exclusive endorsement of him. "These fellows are too eager: I do not end with them: while it is true I speak for Anarchists, socialists, George men, whatever you choose, I include as well Kings, Emperors, aristocracies, financial men—not only am one with the masses, but with all men—with the mass that holds the masses. Even the churches find in me a friend: for while it is true I am radical—that Leaves of Grass takes the ground from under the churches as churches—for the fact back of all churches, all everything, I speak one enclosing word." Is anxious for the book. "I would give much to have some of them this week."

Wednesday, May 22, 1889

8 P.M. Found W. sitting in the parlor with Mrs. Davis, who retired on my entrance. W. said he had not been well today. "This is one of my bad days—a cold-in-the-head day. I have not been out at all. I attribute the bad turn to the weather." His window was closed: he had his hat on. My sister Agnes had sent him down a bunch of flowers. "Good girl! good girl!" he exclaimed as he buried his nose in them, "Oh! how wonderful sweet! The grand genuine syringa—which has all the virtue that odor can give the cultivated plants, and yet has a strength—an integrity—which is often wanting in them—a briariness!" And then: "And here are roses too! Oh! it is a

good gift!" After awhile, a little boy entered the room. W. greeted him with a kiss, and when he essayed to go, exclaimed: "Why! I thought you and your mother had come to pay us a visit! You will go out to Mrs. Davis, anyhow—won't you?—and get me a mug for the flowers." I explained the fine floral decorations in Clifford's church Sunday—first overwhelming the pulpit in their profusion, then after the services, despoiling it for the sake of the sick who are so in bonds, kept away. W.: "That is a very fine thing to hear; so they kill two birds with one stone, do they?"

Wondered about the book—if we were likely to hit upon copies this week. "If I could get one or two copies by Saturday night, I should count it a great triumph." I reminded him of his own frequent admonitions to me "not to be too certain of events till events are events," and he laughed heartily, saying: "I do well remember it—and yet I hope to have the book!" I spoke of the Stepniak piece, that in respect to W. "It was just enough to make you want more." And he responded: "It is—but it is possible more was said." I asked if he thought it authentic? "Yes—I have every reason to think it so, it has that sound. Besides, I have all sorts of indications pointing the way this does—intimations that the radical fellows pretty generally abroad there, applaud me—conceive that I am one of them—belong their way—as, in a sense, I have no doubt, I do. I unquestionably aim to cut the ground from under the feet of institutions, formalisms, notions, precedents—yet must cut it away by including all these!" And then: "I think I shall at once send Stepniak a copy of the pocket edition when once it is in our hands. If you wish to write to him, you might do so in care of Mrs. Costelloe, who would forward it. How do you pronounce his name?" And after my answer: "Oh! the obvious way—the way it is spelled. Well, I don't know!" I proposed writing to Kennan for Tolstoi's address and W. was agreed. Did he think a copy of L. of G. would pass through Russia without excision?—or obstacle? "I know it is questionable," he said, "I know I am on the prohibited list; but I

209

should be disposed to risk it." And then spoke of the "artificial" strain at which such principles as are in vogue in Russia entail. "In fact, till very recently, it was a method which held sway in most European countries—Germany, France, Italy; though perhaps with modification in Germany, which is very hard to talk about anyhow, as Germany was so many-headed, and one place was cloudy while the other was clear."

Reference here to prohibition. "If drink, why not clothing, what we eat?" Then he asked, "Has not Prohibition had a black eye? or won't it have, after they vote in Pennsylvania next month?" As to drink at the dinner: "I should say they must have *something*: a dinner with no drink whatever seems strange to me—I have grown to imagine something—something only—necessary and significant." I had letters from Adler, Howells, Blake, Garland, today. I read W. Howells' note, which appeared to surprise him. "That certainly is very sweeping," he said, "Aldrich and Howells certainly appear to be moving on." He thought the letter "worth a great deal," and thought too—"Howells gives out signs of great growth, it has been so for some time." Frank Williams said to me yesterday that he supposed Stedman was still "disgruntled." W. asked, "How did they get to know about the affair of the interview?—the Hartmann escapade?" I told him Garland had written that he would if possible attend. W.'s whole manner changed—"Oh! I wish it might be so! It is too good to hope!"

I met Watts, Brinton's one-time partner, today. He said Brinton would probably be home next Monday from Europe. I had not expected him till the fall. I said: "If the Doctor comes on, I want him to speak at the dinner." But Watts objected: "I don't think he will speak—but you may ask him!" When I asked for the why of it, Watts explained that Brinton had once delegated him to buy books from Whitman for him and that W. had charged him double prices, protesting, when objection was raised, that "Brinton could afford it." W. was annoyed by this story. "I do not remember anything at all about it—no such incident now comes back—but I have no doubt that with the facts all in, this would be found easily explainable. I don't like anybody to go from me with the sense of having been wronged—in fact, I don't believe they do —there must be some mistake in this. I have editions and editions of the books. The Centennial edition has always been five dollars a volume—even now with the few copies I have left I keep the price at five dollars. Then there is the McKay book —that is two dollars: I always charge that. Ah! I do not think it can be accused of me that I have been ungenerous with respect to my books: on the contrary I have given away freely enough." And then: "Anyhow, I want Brinton to speak if he comes: I personally, should like him to be there." I read W. extracts from Adler's letter of regret sent me. Much touched—his "Yes indeed!" was frequent.

Thursday, May 23, 1889

7.10 P.M. W. sat in his chair, Ed and Warren with him, in front of the house. He was explaining to them—indicating the electric light swung across the street at the corner: "All the lights in New Orleans were hung that way. The effect was fine, and the utility, too, for it threw the light four ways." W. inquired after "the news." I referred to a letter from George W. Childs. W.: "Ah! and I had a letter, too!—a letter all full of sweet things and friendship!" He opened his big coat and finally found and handed me the letter. "Childs sent you the money for a card?" he inquired. And then: "He sent you the Longfellow letter? He did me, too—and good it was, indeed—fine. I liked it very much. I had half a notion to send it down to Harry Bonsall and have him print it—it seemed all so well done, said." Childs had enclosed in our letters a little slip, containing the following letter:

Cambridge, March 13, 1877

My dear Mr. Childs:

You do not know yet, what it is to be seventy years old. I will tell you, so that you may not be taken by surprise, when your turn comes.

It is like climbing the Alps. You reach a snow-crowned summit, and see behind you the deep valley stretching miles and miles away, and before you other summits higher and whiter, which you may have strength to climb, or may not. Then you sit down and meditate, and wonder which it will be.

That is the whole story, amplify it as you may. All that one can say is, that life is opportunity.

With seventy good wishes to the dwellers in Walnut Street, corner of Twenty-second.

Yours, very truly

Henry W. Longfellow

I also had letter thus from John Burroughs, and sat there on the step and read to W.:

West Park N Y.
May 22^d

My dear Harry Trauble

I wish I could promise definitely that I will be with you on the 31$''$ but my coming is very doubtful. I am of no account on such occasions & have little taste for them. Of course I will take a ticket, & if I do not come will write a letter. The truth is my affairs here demand my constant presence. From now till July is the critical time with my young vineyards & I am in the field every day at work. One of my men has left me & I cannot yet find another. If I come it will not be to speak but to see & listen. I am rejoiced that Walt seems better. Is it not possible to get him away from Camden the coming season? I fear he will not be able to survive the heat. I hope you will write to Gilder. I think he would attend.

Very cordially yours
J. Burroughs

W. was touched and pleased. "The dear John!" But then he asked, "What inducement could there be for anybody to take the trouble to come on? I do not see it!" And when I contradicted him, he laughed. "I see you have your own way of

212

excusing yourself!" Then he said: "My advice to the boys would be, let it be a local affair if it must." But I asked— "Isn't it consistent to have John here, for instance—the only one left out of your early group, except yourself—and able, as no other, to stand for and speak for something that we, with our best intentions, must fall short of expressing or even conceiving?" He said to this, warmly: "Ah! boy! That is a way of putting it as it has not been put before. I can see there is something in it—much, even." Then he cried: "Poor O'Connor! or poor me without him!" But as yet there had been no word from Stedman. W. said: "I don't know, Horace: I fear Stedman is, as they say, 'in suspenders.' I think he regards me with a good deal of suspicion. The devil has been in reports about him and me: he has got hold of them—is troubled by them." And he further explained, half-reminiscently or as if making up his opinion as he went along: "Stedman has been so demonstrative of his affection—always so nobly demonstrative—and genuine, thoroughly, as I know; as you know—and I have been so little responsive it might appear—that I scarcely wonder he is a little doubtful. And yet I don't know —perhaps it is not that: there is something probably more or other. I remember the time of his paper: I heard it very often discussed—on several occasions was myself appealed to with respect to it—rather pooh-poohed it at the moment. But I am confident that, whatever the critical mood or things said, my affection for Stedman has been honest, genuine, a steady stream, especially during the past year or so." I reminded him of Burroughs' liking for Stedman. "Yes—I know about it— remember it. And so did O'Connor like him—and these facts had great weight with me."

In the midst of our talk I interrupted to urge W. to go in doors. It was getting very chill. He at once gathered his cloak about him (the long blue coat). "I have been thinking myself it was about time to go in." Then Ed and I helped him into the parlor. We finished our talk there. "Often we do get too late

213

out of our dangers." Then resumed discussion of the dinner. "I am surprised you have not heard from Kennedy," he said, "for in his hot way—his nervous haste—he is constantly projecting himself—if he means to do a thing, throws out hints of it—couriers—days ahead." Bucke had written promising a letter for the dinner. W. was "pleased, but not surprised, to hear of Doctor's willingness." Then: "And how about Brinton: have you heard more about him yet? It would be a great victory to have him come." I suggested: "If willing, he could tell how he, as a scientific man, comes upon the meaning of Leaves of Grass." W.: "That is so—and if he came, would be well so! How will you arrange for the toasts, anyhow? You will have—or ought to have—concerted work so far, that the speakers don't tread on each others' toes." So far Gilchrist, Clifford, Frank Williams and Harned are sure. W. said: "That sounds friendly and good—I am in the hands of friends when these have me! I have no doubt you and Tom know me well enough to know what I like, and to have things done simply and honestly." At one point, when I said "No" to something, and assured him—"you are not to have things all your own way in this matter"—he said: "So I perceive—I see you are using your own notions." I had written to Cleveland this forenoon. I explained to W. that I had mentioned to Cleveland, W.'s desire for his presence. He said: "That was right—I do not object." And: "Have you written to Sheppard yet? I am not so particular about him, but would like to have him know." And there was O'Reilly, too, to whom I had written. "He is a great fellow: I wish he could be with us,—and friendly, nobly so, to me, too!" We discussed the foreign fellows. I wondered if Castelar had ever hit upon L. of G. W. did not know: "I have never heard anything, pro or con; but now, when we get out our little book—our pocket edition—I think I shall send a copy to him—indeed feel quite positively that it will be done." And he reflected: "A great and lofty soul he is, too—one of our supreme men." "I suppose," he inquired, "a letter addressed to him in Spain would reach him just as surely as a letter addressed to Tennyson in England?" He had himself received letters addressed in all sorts of curious ways. Spoke hereupon of the postal union: "A great beneficence it is, too!" —and of the English system of letter delivery: "It seems much more complete than ours—more complete than ours *could* be, probably. That was Trollope's great work, you know—you have read of it?" At this, Trollope's Autobiography was mentioned. W.: "I have read it—and it is a very interesting— almost curious—book." He did not rank Trollope high, but thought him "manly and a person of considerable talent."

He said of his "outing" today: "We took a jaunt of about an hour. Ed is very good to me—takes me everywhere I wish —humors me—treats me nice as a child." But he has not been well—"My head troubles me a great deal. These are bad days for me; but perhaps when this spell of unusual cold is over, I too, will recover myself." My sister's flowers were still on the table and he took them up affectionately—holding them to his nose for a long time. "It was good of Aggie to think of an old fellow pinned down here. Tell her so." Mrs. Davis came in the room. W. explained to her that he had "sent for peppermint sticks—one intended for Warren, one for Harry, one for Mrs. Mapes, one for Ed, one for you. But, as usual, the devil got mixed with the mission, and they brought me these—they call them drops—instead of sticks." He took the bag from his pocket. "See—drops: I guess I'll take one"—as he did—then handing the bag to Mrs. Davis. "These are too strong—they are not nearly as good as the twisted sticks"—violently wrench- ing his hands—"the sticks twisted so—these have a taste of medicine."

Friday, May 24, 1889

8 P.M. The day much warmer, W. sitting in his chair out of doors. Ed on the steps. Down the street the electric light

gleaming strongly. W. referred to it. "Ah!" he said, "does it seem to you as if that light justified itself? It hardly throws as much here as I had expected of it. What is the reason?" And yet—"It is a beautiful, efficient light. Perhaps my objections are whimsical." I tried to prove him the strength of the light and he answered: "You no doubt see just what you say you see—but not seeing it myself, I cannot acquiesce." But of electric lights for principle—"I am heartily in favor. Undoubtedly, it is the light of lights. I should not feel disposed to object to it. I remember well when gas was first introduced: the dandies of the time protested that it was too strong a light —that it glared, hurt their eyes. But the dandies succumbed, as they always must." We discussed the dinner somewhat. W. asked: "Is Tom home? I have just sent up to him a man who wanted tickets—two of them: Ingham: you know him? the old man: he wants 'em for somebody else, I think." Harned had just been at my house, discussing affairs with me.

I received today a note from Ingersoll, which I now read to W., who listened and was greatly pleased. "That sounds encouraging and warm. Herbert [Gilchrist] was in to see me today—stayed, I guess, fifteen or twenty minutes—gave me in outline, by hints, his speech, which I thoroughly endorsed and consented to. Herbert is going to speak of the English boys—for them—their good deeds for me—all that—and nothing could please me better. I want it always understood that I feel a never-ending gratefulness for those abroad who helped me, that time of my sorest need. It ought not to be forgotten that they upheld me bravely when I was most sadly pressed—sick, weak, poor, maligned, misunderstood. Then they came forward, took my book, took me—and saved me. I know there is a feeling in this country as though this had been accompanied with insult, ill-feeling; but that is a mistake— gravely a mistake. Gilder says or said—it 'galled' him. But why should it?—him or anyone? Taken rightly it seems to me it could be complimental—a tribute to the literary guild—a test of the great fellowship—a proof of it—of our world-

union. I know they won't have it so, but we must not be too
sure of the insult. Of course for me, from my person, the great
moral, emotional, testimony the story bears is never to be
slighted or in any way questioned." Therefore, to have some
word of it at the dinner was "eminently proper," and he was
"glad Herbert" had "undertaken to say it." He was eager too,
to have "the Colonel" come, though "even if he does not, we'll
have a very good time anyhow." I proposed that he give
copies of the Birthday Book to the main speakers, and he
instantly took hold on the idea. "Yes—that would mean
Clifford, Tom, Herbert, Frank Williams, perhaps the Colonel
—who else?" He was not surprised that I had not yet heard
from Stedman: "I do not think you will hear. I fear Stedman
is angered—that he distrusts us—will stay quiet. I had a letter
from Kennedy today in which he said that he had after all not
forwarded that letter,—he said he thought it would make
matters worse instead of better. I don't know what kink could
suddenly have struck him—been revealed to him. As I recall
the letter, it is entirely in the right vein. When Kennedy asked
about it, I even parenthesised—told him I would not only consent but even advise that it be given to Stedman." He said at
this point. "I had a proof-slip from Joe Gilder today of a little
paragraph about the dinner which he is to print in the Critic.
I should describe it as in style much like the O'Connor article—
lamentably weak, almost puerile—fearful, timid, afraid to go
on record decisively. Gilder is too much affected by the New
York cabal—right in the hands of it. It is the last lingering
malignancy, striving still to object, to make a fight; like Lee's
troops—or Lee—keeping up the war—persisting in his forays,
battles, raids—hating to give up to the last, but at last having to." I referred W. to a letter from William C. Gannett today. Writing from Hinsdale, Illinois on May 20th he says:
"May he live as long as loving and being loved can make life
beautiful to him! In Mr. Morse's studio I last week saw a
noble picture of him with his arms around the children." W.
was curious about his reference to the picture. "I wonder what

original Sidney used for that, or was it a picture from memory? There was a New York picture which is suggested by that description. The New York photographer who took the whole dozen photos that time has a picture of me with some children. I was sitting one day—and Jennie Gilder came in. She had with her two children—beautiful children—her sister's, I think. For the sake of them I consented to have us done together. I have seen nothing of the picture from that day to this."

A letter from Canada today, also. W. was much touched by it as I struggled through its reading there in the dark.

London—Ont—22.May 1889

My dear Horace

I enclose the letter asked for and along with it $5. for a ticket— The letter is addressed and the order made payable to T. B. H.

If there is anything more I can do let me know—I would give *anything* to be with you at the dinner but am too much of a slave at present—there may come a better time however—Have not heard from W. J. Gurd for two weeks. I suppose the gas meter is coming into being.

R. M. Bucke

"How fine—how genuine that sounds! Almost as if the man himself were here talking!" W. suddenly said: "Isn't it wonderful, Horace, how the best of us like to be flattered? I am quite surprised at myself more than often."

He regretted the probable absence of women from the banquet. "There is Mrs. Harned now—and you tell me she wants to go? It seems to me—now I face it in a serious way, as I should—that here it is in a nut-shell—here in the denial to include her. It is a real hardship—entirely out of place too, inconsistent with my best-held convictions, as expressed from the start, which would include women equally with men and on as satisfying terms. But then, what can *I* do? This is a case in which I can but submit." I had said to W. that the best way to have the question settled was for half a dozen men—by concerted understanding—to take their wives. W. thereupon:

218

"That is a very good notion—indeed I am convinced that that would be the best way to go about it." He took the matter up thus very seriously.

Saturday, May 25, 1889

7:45 P.M. Harned stood in front of the house, talking with W., who occupied his chair and spoke as though in unusually good condition. His voice was strong and his manner animated. They had been discussing the dinner. W. had been turning his speech upon the joy of the old days with Harned, and "those famous dinners." We jokingly reminded him of Bucke's "feeling" that those dinners had much to do with W.'s present condition. W. exclaimed: "Oh! the doctor be damned! On the contrary, those dinners helped me—did me a vast deal of good, the best proof of which is in this, that the next day I always felt better than before—at the worst as good." It was true. "I ate hearty dinners there—good, square, tempting dinners—but how could they harm? They did not. In fact, if I had the means of doing so here I should break a bottle of champagne every day. It does me no harm." He had some hope of getting up to Harned's tomorrow, the day being clear. "I will if I can: and I want to get in, too." Tom said something about bringing the champagne down, but W. laughed at the idea. "No—don't bring it down—I want to go for it myself, I've been craving for it for a month." (After Harned had gone he asked me: "I wonder how I will get in if I reach Tom's? by the side way? But we'll find a way—take the front way, boldly, if no other offers.") They discussed the question whether there should be any drink at all at the dinner. As to lemonade, W. exclaimed: "It is a damnable drink, I wouldn't have it—nor anything—only some punch." He seriously raised the problem how he was to get in the hall. "I think I should like to be taken in, Tom, just as you suggested—if that can well be arranged." That was, to carry chair and him together, up the broad stairs at the hall. It seems easily

219

feasible. "And as to the dinner—I don't know how much of it I shall see. Of course I must be there, at least through part of it. When my friends gather from all parts in my honor, it would be a cruel, an inexcusable, slight, for me to stay away for anything short of necessity. And [replying to Tom] I shall say something, too, no doubt. What I shall say, or *how*, or how much, that remains undeveloped—is nebulous enough still. I guess the moment itself will finally decide that." He afterwards declared to me, when we were alone, that even the coming in any shape "might be clouded over" if there happened Friday "one of my miserable sick spells." I told him that I had in all my letters, when speaking of his presence at all, spoken of it as contingent. He said: "That was right—that was as I could have wished you to do: I should not have liked a promise to go forth when all I can give is a promise *not* to promise." Tom told him Charles Emory Smith would positively attend the dinner. I looked lugubriously at W., who laughed heartily. "I see, boy," he said in a chiding sort of way: "But though Charles Emory is himself a hell of a fellow, and his paper about as bad as they make 'em—even Charles Emory is welcome—our arms will open even for him." Then he continued, still on these engrossing affairs: "Do you know," looking at Tom, then at me, as if addressing both, "I like Herbert's speech a good deal: he was here again today—I met him around the corner, against the Methodist Church: as we went along he gave me the substance of it. It says many things I particularly shall enjoy having said, by him and there." Later in our talk, after Harned had gone, W. referred to Gilchrist again. "Herbert has a good deal more of the democratic in him than he is given credit for—than even he knows himself—a dash even of the Anarchist—enough of it to establish him, to brace him. No one can know this as I do—you could not know it, neither could any other, nor Herbert himself, who little suspects its proportions. I have had talks about it with his mother, with Talcott Williams—controversies—at least, if not controversies, strong statements in self defense. I mean controverting in the customary understanding of that word."

Mention was made by me of Gilder's notice in the Critic that I had just read. W. said: "It is easily explained—Jo is still in the toils. That paragraph is even weaker than we care to say—written by someone determined not to be mistaken as one of us—who wants it very plainly understood that Walt Whitman's poetry is not the be-all and end-all of American art." He suddenly reached for his breast pocket and brought forth a rubber-fastened packet for me. "There are several things—Kennedy's postal for one thing—then the checks—one for Ferguson, one for the plate printer." Ferguson's bill was for $36.10 and Billstein's for $7.65. He said: "And I want you to tell Ferguson again that I am not at all satisfied with the printing—that here, at the point where we set most hope, where we were willing to give most to effect our end, there has been a serious set-back. I know it is not his fault—that it is Brown's. If this printing is to be taken seriously, then I am afraid Ferguson has done his last printing for us. If he were sitting here now, I should tell him all this just as I am telling it to you now,—candidly, composedly, but frankly. Yet his printing of the big book was very good—satisfactory—I was looking at it again today." Kennedy's postal was that spoken of last evening (as follows) and touched also upon my invitation for him to write a letter for the dinner.

Walt Whitman
Camden, New Jersey
Dear W. W.—

No I haven't sent St. the card. I had rather not on second thought. It would only make matters worse. I fear I can't get to Camden on the 31. But am going to send a note for Traubel, for the dinner speech dept. Wish you would tell him so for me, please. I much fear that the excitement will be too much for you. Look out!

Affec. as ever
W. S. K.

W. asked me: "Did you know we drank the health of the Queen here last night? Well, we did! There were seven or eight of us—we were there together—in the back room—I at the head—took that big wine bottle from my table—drank good luck to the good Queen's 70th year. Yes indeed, we did it with a vim." The Childs letter he had sent to the Post, along with the Longfellow note. "It was very genuine." I spoke of it as "stronger than Longfellow's usual style." W. said: "That was what I was about to say—Longfellow is usually more interlineated, literary, but I think I feel in this a genuine heartbeat." W. said, in the room, (to which we after a while assisted him)—"I sent a copy of the Post to Mary Costelloe." Spoke of Pearsall Smith: "Did I put him on your list? He ought to be there." Referred also to Roden Noel as another. I promised to write him. Last night I sent off notes to Rhys, Carpenter, Pearsall Smith, Dowden, Rolleston, Symonds, Sarrazin, Schmidt, Rossetti, Forman. W. expressed himself as "glad to know it."

We spoke of my good luck in seeing O'Connor, and striking a day which found him in condition to see us. I described to W. again, as I had before, O'Connor's emotional greeting of me—the second handshaking when we were alone. W. spoke pathetically: "I can see him doing it—it is so thoroughly like him. So like the man I always knew. Oh! it was all the opportunity—the opportunity: you grasped it, and were victors. That was what I thought so fine in Longfellow's letter—life, he says, is opportunity—and it is, profoundly and profoundly again! Edward Emerson uses something like that for the motto of his book—a line from his father."

I want to tell you something, Gentlemen. Eternity is very long. Opportunity is a very little portion of it, but worth the whole of it. If God gave me my choice of the whole planet or my little farm, I should certainly take my farm.

Mr. Emerson's Journal for 1852

After W. had gone over it, he said: "How wonderfully that rings in one's sense! It is hard to catch at first glance—needs to be chewed on—but finally enforces its intense meanings!" And then he concluded: "So it was opportunity that so happily gave you that first and only glimpse of O'Connor. I am sure you will never forget it. O'Connor is not a man whom anybody can forget."

Mrs. Davis came up while we were out front, Ed with her. "Ah!" exclaimed W., "here are the truants!" They had been off on a boat together. Last night an English seaman was here—a friend with whose family Warren stopped in Liverpool—a splendid ruddy man. He had joined them in drinking to the queen. The vessel is down the river—English, with a crew of Hindus. The folks had gone off to bring W. one of them, so now he asked: "Where is the Hindu?" But they explained, his father would not let him come for fear he would be spirited away for a museum! W. laughed: "I am not a good subject to spirit anybody away just now!" W. explained to me: "There's a young fellow down there in the boat—not a Hindu, I suppose an Englishman—who knows something about Walt Whitman and his works and wants to know more. So I sent down by Mrs. Davis a copy of Leaves of Grass—an old copy, an old edition—I had about here. Perhaps he will come to see me." Much to W.'s interest, Mrs. Davis described the garb and habits of these Hindus, as she had seen them. W. always fully alive for such details. When I got up to go: "You should get a copy or two of the Post as you go along. That Longfellow note is worth keeping—worth studying: for, little as it is in word—extent—it is great in meaning."

Sunday, May 26, 1889

1 P.M. I went to Harned's to take dinner. W. had already arrived. The chair stood in the hallway, next Anna's wheeler and the baby's coach: suggestively stood there, it seemed to

me, and W. afterwards remarked, this constituted his first visit to Harned's—in fact, his first visit anywhere, since the 3ᵈ of June, 1888. He stayed till 3 o'clock—talked vigorously all the time—seemed, as he sat there in the parlor, the past revived. His familiar figure struck and appealed to us all. Ed stayed. At dinner he was very bright and strong. Corning came in for a short space. W. was immensely taken with the baby. "Generally," he said, "in the first year or two—the babies fear me: but they get bravely over that." And once when the baby smiled upon him: "How instinctive they are! How they divine us—expose us! And yet I think even more so later on, after the first year or so is over." And when the baby was excused for some of its noise: "Oh! let it go on! A baby is not a baby who is denied that privilege!"

At the table he looked tenderly at what he called "the dear drink!" He had a glass of Madeira on first arriving—at the table took champagne. "I have been patiently waiting a whole year for this!" He said later on that he probably had taken more than he should—"but then a fellow must once and a while be allowed to step across the line: especially a fellow as slow-paced as I am, whose whole life has been evenly run." And when someone spoke of his being led away: "No—no—don't let anybody run you away with that idea: nobody ever led Walt Whitman away but Walt Whitman himself. That is the whole story, if story there be."

Had he been invited to write anything for the Herald Decoration Day number? "No—the Herald does not so readily come to me any more. You know my bright particular friend there, Julius Chambers, is now on the World. And it is just as well I have not been asked to write for the World." Had he any objection to the World? "No—none at all—on the contrary, I believe it a great paper: only, I am not nowadays moved to work up anything myself." He again talked of the testimonial—why could the dinner not be local, if necessary? He said: "I don't think Jerseymen take enough pride in their state. I came here years ago—fifteen or sixteen years ago—poor, weak, sick: circumstances kept me here—bound me—here I am still. I don't know but it was the best thing that could have happened. Thrown here, into reserve and quiet, I have been helped, restored, maintained: I could not have stood New York or Brooklyn—the rush, the drive, the excitement, there. But West Jersey—why should we not be proud of it? I like its soil, its people—I should enjoy having someone take it up— pay it tribute—at the dinner." Subsequently he said: "I should like someone to say something for me—to start off with telling of my paralysis,—that I was in Washington, worn out, endangered—this in 1873—that I was ordered away by my Doctor—and a good one he was, too (Dr. Drinkard)!—that I came here, and for some time was worse, but finally picked myself together again." And so he went on, mentioning that "this personal history has an importance for such an occasion —should not be slighted."

Corning said to W. at the dinner that he would make a good subject for Rembrandt—that no other could paint him. W. said for his own part: "I am persuaded that my painter has not yet arrived. I know I have been very successfully taken— taken in all sorts of habits and hours—but somehow there is an elusive quality which so far no one has caught." He said again: "There is Eakins' picture—Doctor thinks it perfect." I expressed some surprise. "Oh! it is true!" W. asserted, "Doctor worships it, and I too recognize its greatness—its value—that up to the present it hits high water mark. But even Eakins' picture don't go to the right spot—even it is inadequate." As to Herbert Gilchrist's picture, W. was rather cruel. "It is all right—all right as it is—Herbert thinks that if that's not what I am that's what I ought to be, and anyhow, having the dude in nature, why shouldn't we have the dude in art?" W. alluded to the fleeting quality in Lincoln's face that had never been caught: "I know of no satisfactory picture of Lincoln. All sorts of pictures exist—many of them good in themselves, good as pictures—yet all of them wanting in the last, the essential touch. Yet the skillful fellows were there—often pointed their cameras at him. Frank Carpenter was much about Washington those times: and Alexander Gardner"—turning to me—"the man who made the picture of me I gave you"—and then continued—"but no one seemed equal to coping with the subject. Lincoln was a gigantic figure on our stage. He was ugly as the devil to start with—yet beneath all that ugliness—under it—the base or background of him—Lincoln in essence—was an exquisite fine, great, high nature—a nature too great for words, too intense for cold speech." He had himself seen Lincoln under "strange and fascinating conditions." "I saw him quite fifty different times, under various circumstances. I knew John Hay well—John (who was an intimate of O'Connor), liked him, admired him, loved him." W. was asked, why did he then not write of him in the Tribune? "Just because he did love him—because we always hesitate to write about those we love, for reasons that would restrain me from writing of him." Then he described Lincoln's homely ways, and instanced cases of them. "I remember one day so plainly—it was a reception day—there were crowds of strangers present, waiting their turn for a word, for words, with Lincoln. But Lincoln was engaged with an old friend—a minister—a clergyman—who had come on from Illinois, was now talking to him. He was an old man—a splendidly preserved fellow—not large, but with a good eye, in spite of his age, and certain step, too—and bye and bye he had come upon the time to go, and Lincoln went along with him towards the door—as if loth to drop him—as if for old time's sweet sake he would continue the talk. "Oh!"—here W. bent sideways—"I can see him turned this way, now—the ear bent down to catch the last word—the almost ungainly figure—the whole sad, strong, rugged, homely face lighted up." Here W. paused: "It was such incidents as these—I saw many of them—that revealed to me the real Lincoln. The old man at the last

226

moment, wanting to stay, yet knowing there was an impatient crowd still there—and Lincoln lingering still. Can you think of a better picture—or more realistic?" Art had never caught this from Lincoln. Had he ever seen satisfying portraits of Emerson? "No—none wholly satisfying—but there are pictures of Emerson that will do." At one point in the talk W. alluded to "my dear daddy" in a tone that was half-pathetic, half-joking.

There was talk of an incident in the paper the past few days: Gladstone knocked down in London by a carriage—himself ran after the cabby and had him arrested. I said I had a sneaking sympathy for the cabby. After a hearty laugh W. said: "So have I—I couldn't help but have. I generally do side with the roughs anyhow. The nearest I ever came to getting into a conflict with the authorities was in interfering that way in behalf of the roughs, so-called. Yet we must accept Gladstone, too—we know what newspaper reports are anyway and must be chary of accepting them. My sympathies all go out towards the outcast." I asked him again about his toast to the Queen. "Yes, we drank it—and heartily, too. Why not? My friend Ben Tucker, who was always a brave defender of mine, got mad as fire because I wrote the piece about the Emperor. Even O'Connor was furiously disturbed. And yet I meant it. A great many years ago, at Pfaff's, I got into a regular row by defending the Queen—and there were Englishmen present, too. But in my philosophy—in the bottom-meanings of Leaves of Grass—there is plenty of room for all. And I, for my part, not only include anarchists, socialists, whatnot, but Queens, aristocrats." I spoke of the dearth of Presbyterian ministers (just lamented by the Assembly) and someone asked: "Even Presbyterian ministers?" And W. affirmed: "Yes, even them. What right have I to say no? Isn't there a scripture phrase which sets forth—'Why should you, Joseph or Samuel, resent this man a few days with you when the Lord has tolerated him for years and years?'—something like that. Besides, we must recollect, man is such a scamp, such a wickedee,—so essentially an ignoramm—that it is hard often to stand him—yet it is but right that the scamp should be represented. We must conclude that as long as there are Presbyterians, Presbyterians ought to be. It seems to me this is the spirit in which our fellows should approach the question."

I wrote today to Lyman Abbott, Julius Chambers, and Jeannette Gilder. Happening to touch his cane, W. said: "You know all about that cane, don't you? You know who gave it to me?" Then spoke tenderly of Peter Doyle. "I wonder where he is now? He must have got another lay. How faithful he was in those sick times—coming every day in his spare hours to my room—doing chores—going for medicine, making bed, something like that—and never growling!" He listened intently while Anna played a fine air (and played it finely) on the piano. "I always knew," he said, "that she came naturally by what I call touch." He left Harned's, flowers in hand, with cheery words on his lips.

6. P.M. Met Clifford at Broad St. Station at 5.15. He had a box of flowers from Mrs. Baldwin, which together we took to Camden and to W. W. was in very good condition. The dinner had not at all discomposed him. He talked quite freely and well. Greatly enjoyed the flowers. We took these and arranged them on a plate and in a cup. He took them up: "Oh! syringa!"—and again—"And what a rose is that, too!" —and then on the plate where there was the monotony of white flowers, he carelessly placed a soft red rose, which transfused it at once into a glory. "That relieves the monotony!"

A newspaper nearby he picked up and handed to Clifford. "The Long Islander," he explained—"I started it, I suppose fifty years ago—set it going—as a mere boy!" Clifford looked for W.'s name as founder but of course did not find it. Then referred to the old twit on the Tribune which had always printed on its editorial page, "Founded by Horace Greeley" and to which a wag added—"And foundered by Whitelaw

Reid." W. said rather laughingly: "It would be a severe thing to say of the Presidency, that it began with Washington and ended with Harrison!" Singular, his natural and sincere pleasure in the flowers. No profuse thanks in receiving them, but a natural flow of quiet appreciation. Picks them up—smells them—frequently. Cherishes them for days and days—the best uttered thanks likely to come days afterward.

I had the following letter from Gilder today:

House 55 Clinton Place
25 May, 1889

Dear Mr. Traubel,

I'm trying to arrange to be at the dinner on the 31".

Can you tell me about the trains? What train gets in just before the dinner & can I get off to Bordentown the same night?

Sincerely
R. W. Gilder

Spoke to W. about it. He asked: "What? Is it Dick's? Dick Gilder's?" And then: "What does he say?" Handed letter to him, which he read. The prospect of Gilder's coming raised his hopes. He said mockingly in response to some word of Clifford: "They have been going their own way about this dinner—they little consult me." I remarked the stationery Gilder used. "Yes—it is fine—fine—but they have plenty! I remember Rice years ago—he had asked something of me—had letter—replied—had letter again. He appeared to have a thorough contempt for my stationery, for by and by there came along a big bundle of paper, envelopes, whatnot—a bundle big as this"—indicating several feet square—"full of the best material. I believe I have some of it yet. Rice must have been interested in some paper manufacturing establishment—or perhaps bought it wholesale—probably this."

I received a four-page note from Mark Twain, full of generalities, with practically no word about W. W. Have not yet referred to it in W.'s presence. W. spoke: "I am always so glad to see the fellows: it grows so monotonous here, I crave to be relieved." We looked at one of the Washington portraits. I showed Clifford the book, a stitched unbound copy. W. had come directly home from Harned's. The day raw and uncertain. W. advised Clifford in regard to his speech to trust to the exigency: "Do not greatly prepare: it will come all right when the time and occasion for it comes."

Monday, May 27, 1889

7.45 P.M. Found W. sitting in his room reading one of Scott's novels—went there with Harned. W. looked very well. Had he any ill effects from yesterday? "No—none at all: my only trouble was, that I insisted on eating supper after I got home: this was superfluous." Harned said he had only come up for a minute or so. I explained to W.: "He wants to get home and go to work on that speech." W. laughed: "How is that, Tom, and a lawyer, too: I thought you fellows could get up anytime, with a few headings, and fill in your speech?" Tom interjected that this was a special literary occasion. "Oh! the literary fellows be damned," exclaimed W. and then: "Well— if all you fellows are to deliver speeches, so much the better for me—then I will not have to deliver any!" But he said further: "Of course I must say a word, but I find that the moment will take care of itself—all I shall say may be said— must be said—in three or four lines, and these unpremeditated. I should announce that all I have to say I have said in my books, which anybody may buy for himself;" And then with a laugh—"which would be having an eye to business, too— wouldn't it?"

W. said: "I had a peculiar visit last night after you had gone. Three Hindu fellows came in—the fellows I spoke to you about: they could scarcely speak a word of English. They brought me this bamboo cane, here on the floor." I picked it up and handed it to Tom to inspect. "And I have used it a good deal today—it is very nice—strong; Warren is going to have a ferrule put on it for me. They brought me also that gay handkerchief you see there on the chair—pull it out." It was a gay dotted red and blue silk affair, over which W. laughed goodhumoredly. My sister Agnes had sent him down some roses, which we arranged in a glass on the table, where Mrs. Baldwin's still were. Anna also had given him a bouquet yesterday. He is joyous over his good treatment "by the girls, old and young." Asked me about Mrs. Baldwin again: "Is she a good reader of Leaves of Grass? Does she absorb it?"

I asked him if he could guess who had sent 10 dollars on to me today? He looked at us comically—then admitted, "I give it up: how could I know?" And when I said to him then that no less a man than Whittier had shown this interest, he said in mock concern: "Poor fellow! I thought he would be saved such a fate." I showed him the note which he read with zest.

Amesbury Mass—
May 24th 1889—

I have received thy kind letter and the invitation to the proposed observance of W. Whitman' seventieth birthday. At my age and in my state of health I can only enclose a slight token of goodwill, with the wish that he may have occasion to thank God for renewed health and many more birthdays, and for the consolation which must come from the recollection of generous services rendered to the sick and suffering Union soldiers in the hospitals of Washington during the Civil War.

At the point where Whittier uses the expression "to thank God"—W. paused and said: "You see—there are fellows who are so afraid Ingersoll will be present (at least in spirit) that they are determined for themselves to show that they recognize the powers that be." Mr. Curtis, of the Ladies' Home Journal, had said in Harned's presence at the committee meeting this afternoon that he could have sold more tickets had it not been known that Ingersoll might appear, T. B. H. retorting that anyhow people who would object to Ingersoll in such a way had no call to attend a Whitman dinner. W., when told, said: "I should have said something stronger—much stronger—than that." Tom quizzed him quickly: "What is that something stronger?" But W. only laughed, and said: "I shall not say it—not tell you: it can best be imagined!" At which, all hands "imagining" and probably hitting the same key-word, there was a common laugh.

Of Burroughs' article in The Critic on "Literary Fame," W. remarked: "I think it must be pretty good: I read it—but not carefully. I suppose they wrote to him for a piece—put a light offer upon it—and John said, 'Take this then—it is all I have?' I think it would be allowable to make that explanation. I did not read the dinner item there in the paper, though I saw it was there. I had it here on a step: I told you. I sent the paper off to Mrs. O'Connor: she is generally greatly interested in such items. And yet I have not had a word from her—not a word—not even about the funeral."

W. said at one moment: "Bucke's voice is one of his virtues: it is always strong, firm, definite." Tom said the question had been asked if there was any probability of W. W.'s brother attending. W. said: "I don't know—I had not thought of it: in fact, if I had it would not have made a particle of difference: he would not have come, he don't like—don't take to—such affairs. Besides, though we are very brotherly and affectionate and all that together, neither he nor any member of my family knows or cares anything about my literary work, fame —none of them: it might just as well not be. The goblet is full and overflowing anyhow, Tom—there is no use adding to it."

I informed W. that Clifford intended making some reference in his speech to the Whitman note in Edward Emerson's book. W. remarked: "I wish I had known when he was here Sunday: I could have put him up to some things and that note is a shameful lie: it is exposed on the face. They wished to clear Emerson's skirts of me—did so in this way—or tried to!" By and by he half-laughingly spoke of Edward as "that miserable skunk!" Then: "Emerson is now dead—there is no direct evidence. See how Edward uses the word 'mechanic'— calls me a 'mechanic'—yet I am not a mechanic. What or who could be nobler than a noble mechanic? I wish I had Clifford

here to talk to about this. There is one thing true of Emerson
which has never been put on record: he had a real personal affection for me—liked me—liked to be with me—sought me
out. I do not say this boastingly, but only as a fact communicated by others as well as through my own senses." He went
over the Sanborn story again. "I know it was generally said at
the time of that last visit to Concord that Emerson was under a
cloud: it was debated with us what to do in the matter, whether
to go or stay. We decided finally that nothing should be done
—that we should not go. The question had come up in that
shape—I put in the deciding vote." Then he had anyhow met
Emerson at Sanborn's—was invited to the meal subsequently.
"I remember the day we went so well—and the after-ride. A
young Jewess up there, with a noble white team, came to
Emerson's—took me up there. I was always quite well aware
that Ellen—the daughter—and Mrs. Emerson were inimical
to me, but at that point I knew nothing about Edward's
position"; and he went on with fragmentary reflections:
"There is no doubt but Emerson was much set upon by the
formalists—the Unitarians—the Unitarian literary men—the
fellows of the Lowell stripe—of the stripe you have met—who
put good grammar before all else—who make all emphasis at
that one point. These are the fellows who will not have such a
critter as I am and such blasphemous utterances as Leaves of
Grass. Think of Whittier—how surprising that note, reserved
as it is! I have it on very good authority that when Whittier
first fell upon Leaves of Grass and came upon what are called
the obscene passages, he threw the book into the fire." And he
said still further: "And Emerson was always himself—had a
great self—just the self we find in the books: there in him, as
in most men—perhaps all men—there was another self, too—a
sort of contradiction of that self—which had ductility, malle-
ability—he had an eligibility to be impressed by the literary
clowns." I agreed: "But if Emerson ever changed in his feelings towards you there can be no written record of it—not even
in his journal—else Edward would not have been forced to

resort to 'words to the effect.' " W. responded: "I acknowledge, that is very significant. But there is more even than that to be said. I have told you the story of Lord Houghton? And George Childs knows something about it, too. Emerson came down from Concord—stayed with him—came over here then to see me. O'Connor could have told Clifford a good deal on this point, too."

Tuesday, May 28, 1889

7.45 P.M. Harned in to see me about the affair. Going afterward up to his house, we met Gilchrist—with whom we subsequently went to Walt's. Found W. just going indoors, feebly, helped by Harry and Mrs. Davis. "How old he looks!" remarked Gilchrist. W. very cordial for us all. I went right in and sat next him at his side. He took his own seat in the big chair at the window. He looked very well—talked, I thought, strongly. Said to me, the minute while we were alone: "I am all well but the head: that somehow won't become adjusted." Said he had "just come in"—in fact "am just back from a trip."

Harned asked if he had not received foreign letters today. He said: "Yes, two." And upon H.'s further curiosity: "One of them was a request for an autograph" the other—"a genuine letter from Edward Carpenter." Tom inquired if it might be made available Friday. W. said: "No—I think not: it was a letter full of good feeling—containing a remembrance of my birthday, the 31st—a handsome remembrance, of money." And he added afterwards: "It was a letter that went straight to my heart," pausing and continuing waggishly—"you know the heart is often reached through the pocket!" Talked with Harned particularly about Carpenter, describing him. "Have you never seen him?" for Carpenter was "one of the finest samples of the young Englishman I have almost ever seen!" Asked Gilchrist if he had inserted Carpenter's name with the others in the speech they had already conferred about. Gilchrist objected that that would not be in keeping—that he named Tennyson, &c., as "big fellows" whereas Carpenter was "not a big fellow"—which W. recognized, only still persisting that "in the true sense Edward is one of the biggest fellows!" Gilchrist admitting—"He is to us but not to the world." W. further described Carpenter as a "socialist"—as "having money—making good use of it" and said—"I have one excellent, fine likeness of him which you ought to see."

W. spoke to me of the pictures of his parents in the parlor. "Oh! this of my father is much the best. Did you know about Henry Inman? This was not by him, but by his son—a regular painter—who went to Rome, studied, was grounded in what they call the principles of art." For his mother's picture "no pretensions can be set up."

We conferred with W. as to the wise hour for his coming on Friday. He thought about 6: "and I shall stay, say about fifteen or twenty minutes or half an hour." That fifteen or twenty minutes raised protest, to which he listened carefully but made no response. He was willing to say his "few words." I told him it was now quite certain that Gilder would come, to which: "I am glad—he is a very good fellow!" I had heard indirectly today that Stedman was off in New England. W. remarked: "That possibly accounts for his not answering you —we'll believe it does." I had quite a long and fine letter from Kennedy today, but with unfortunate controversial words about Christianity at one point. W. said: "You must exercise a wise discrimination: it is not necessary to use everything that is sent: it would be well not to adopt such an utterance for that place." I sent Whittier his two tickets today. W. asked: "And what of the books, Horace: are we to have them?" Talk various. Gilchrist had his toast ready—proposed reading it, and did so, before starting summoning Mrs. Davis. W.'s own window remained unclosed, but he rose in the midst of Gilchrist's reading to lower the sash. Gilchrist sat at the other side of the room—facing us all. Read deliberately and earnestly—W. a quiet listener, hearing every word. At the outset

235

Gilchrist used the word "banquet," and paused to say that he hoped we would all call the affair a banquet instead of a dinner. W. laughed unrestrainedly, and by and by remarked: "I should call it 'hash': but go on, Herbert: I have no influence with this administration!" Adding after awhile that "anyone who knows anything about cookery knows that soup is best when it is two or three days old." At the close he judged: "It is very deep-cut, very radical—but I do not hesitate to say I like it." He thought also: "It will all be toned down with the thought that I am old—that it is my 70th year!" But Herbert Gilchrist did not think so. W.: "But anyhow, the lines are sharp, decided—and well so: at a dinner, a man must be sharp, quick: when people have been eating and drinking, they don't want anything dull or flat, to go to sleep over." Stoddart (Lippincott's magazine) had sent to Bonsall for a ticket for Julian Hawthorne. W. remarked: "I think I have met Hawthorne: a handsome fellow, isn't he? and dark? I do not remember much about our meeting, except that he was warm, rather inclined to be enthusiastic."

Referred to the Edward Emerson matter again as "the meanest, sneakingest act I have encountered for a long time" —but "wondered" a little if it was "a good thing to bring up at the dinner?" Received today a poem from Elizabeth Porter Gould which is hardly of a calibre to read. I spoke of it to W. who said: "Well—exercise your taste—you need not use everything that is sent." Wrote to Habberton, Frothingham, Walsh, Cockerill. W. keeps in prime condition (for him). Our hopes are great. He sat with his hat on as we waited. Postal from Clifford, asking for extracts from the Emerson letter on W. W.

Wednesday, May 29, 1889

7.50 P.M. W. sitting indoors, in parlor, Mrs. Davis with him. He talked with great hope and cheer, though expressing a weariness from his visitors today and his excursion. "I have been out—just got back." he explained. "We had a good ride—some about the streets—then down to Cooper Street wharves. That river is a never-ending fascination to me. But if the weather continues as it is now, I must take another hour for my outings—a noon hour or thereabouts. It was quite chill on the way tonight."

When I entered I had found W. signing an express receipt. The books were just being delivered. Oldach had not disappointed. W. had sent the box upstairs. I had half a dozen, which I had carried over, to insure against express delay. W. examined them—was well pleased. "Everything seems just as it should be—and there is the pocket, too, just as I wished it! I like the 'lay' of the book much!" He would send a copy off to Bucke tomorrow. "I shall probably, indeed, send a dozen off at once. Stedman must have one, and Aldrich too: Aldrich has been kind too: I told you about the twenty-five dollars he sent me?" He will also prepare copies for the toasters of Friday, "but will wait till the last minute for that, to find out just who they are." As to my own copies, he advised: "Take one now—take it along with you": and then jokingly: "It will arm you—more than arm you, load you: for it is not only a weapon but a weapon primed!" And still again he said: "You can have it ready-handed for the encounter with the enemy." He desires that copies be sent to the hall Friday. "There may be some coming there to whom it would be a temptation." But —"I leave that with you, to be arranged as you think best." I read him extracts from a letter received from Salter today. He said: "Why that is fine, sure enough!" And finally: "When you write him, send along my love: such word as that deserves something!" He inquired after Hamlin Garland, who had promised either to come or send a letter. "I should like him to be here: New England should have a representative." As for his own say, he has written something which is now in the hands of his printer. He will have it produced in slips, probably to be variously distributed. Referred to Clifford's speech again: "I take a great interest in that. I only regret that I have not had a talk with him in the matter (alluding to the Emerson note). There are things I could wish said which probably will not be, people not having the way to know." He spoke again: "There should be something uttered counter to Edward: that was a damnable invention and superfluity. I have long thought of making some statement myself—of finding a way of putting myself on record in this matter—in justification to myself, in justice to Emerson, too. I think no one appreciates as I do the pressure that constantly drove in upon Emerson's high and exquisite nature—it was great—it was, heavy as I know, inevitable. Think of his wife, alone: think of Emerson,—the great, the free, the pure—united in marriage to a conventional woman: yes, a conventional woman and worse, a fanatically conventional woman: that alone is hard to conceive, sad to know." I suggested: "Why can't you sometime dictate your story to me? Then it could be carefully preserved and finally used." He acquiesced as I hardly expected in this: "Why yes —that would do—and wonderfully, too: perhaps some time we may get at it. I have much knowledge—direct and indirect —that would illuminate this whole curious mystery, so-regarded. How much I have suffered from people in their haste—simply their haste! They do not understand 'Leaves of Grass': they do not understand me: something puzzles, baffles, perhaps outrages them: instantly they are in arms and fly at us!" He realized that he but suffered this in common with others who were pathfounders, but "beyond all that might ordinarily be said on that point, the opposition to me seems to have had a property peculiarly, bitterly, its own."

He is now very positive about attendance on Friday. "I shall come, without a doubt, unless the body should assume conditions irretrievably bad. If it should storm, I shall require a closed carriage—but still I will be there: nothing in the ordinary way can now move my determination." And he said further: "I want Ed to go up to the dinner—then come back for me when it is time." He then asked: "And there is something you can tell me, Horace: has any toast been arranged for the brother-poets?—brother-writers? I think that should be—in fact, regard that as a necessary part of the speaking, on no account to be slighted or forgotten." I explained that I had solicited Gilder to answer for American Literature, which in a letter received today he had declined formally but tacitly consented informally to do.

55 Clinton Place
28th May 1889

My dear Mr. Traubel,

Yours just received. I expect to be present—& if desired will be glad to speak—but I am sorry to have to decline to speak to a formal toast.

Sincerely
R. W. Gilder

Where is the dinner by the way?

W.: "I like that." I added: "I have to write to Gilder tonight, to send him some direction. Suppose I make some suggestion from you?" Whereat: "That is a good idea: I am perfectly willing—indeed would request that you do so. Emerson, Bryant, Whittier, Cooper—others of course to be mentioned, but these particularly for me: Emerson (always Emerson)—and Bryant: oh! there is something here that appeals to be said— that always abides!—and Whittier—and certainly Cooper— Cooper, the strong, true, brave, Cooper!" I explained a discussion the other day. Some one had said that Whitman and Whittier were naturally antagonistic. I objected that this was a mistake: that they agreed—only that Whitman accepted all of Whittier and went beyond. W.: "That is very good: I am sure I accept that myself!" And then he repeated his counsel: "This must not be forgotten, Horace: if I may dare suggest anything, let it be for the brother-writers: the occasion certainly could not be complete without that." I spoke again of

239

the passage to be cut from Kennedy's letter and he responded: "I should approve of its being done: without entering into any argument—any reason—I should approve of it." And then he asked: "Can't you let me see Kennedy's letter, anyhow?" And so I promised to submit it to him.

At last there had come a note from Stedman, and a truly noble and affectionate epistle. It comes from "'Kelp Rock,' New Castle, N. H." and is dated the 27th. It justifies my faith—gladdens us both. Walt sat there and regarded me happily as I read it. And passages were to be read again. "Ah! at last!" he exclaimed—"and the good fellow, too—and noble!" And though we lose much by not having him Friday—"we have him, too—for there he is in the note!" Gilchrist had been over again. "Herbert seems greatly to enjoy the affair. You know, Herbert is not only artist, but has a literary bent as well —or ambition: bids for literary place. Of course, you know about his book: and by the way, Dr. Knortz has my book: he asked to keep it a little while longer, and I consented—but that little while was a long while ago." "I am free to say, too—I rather like Herbert's speech: it is perhaps too warm, too extreme—but excusing that, it comes up well to the mark. Besides, I wanted all that said, and said positively." He half-suspected, "it will make Gilder mad." As to his own share in that speech—"There was none of it direct, only by inspiration." The Hotspur speech "may be thought strong"—yet it "seemed in place." "I am very notionate, particular, about quotations: I never lug them in: if they don't come naturally by their place—fit to the last angle—then I reject them." He thought we "must keep the affair as much as possible in the family," not inviting men merely out of their liking for occasions or a dinner. He said he did not understand Herbert's disparaging remarks on Julian Hawthorne last night. "They are a mystery to me—their origin." Had I remembrance of the Lowell-Hawthorne interviewing case? "I do not know it well enough to tell. I know that it was accused of Hawthorne at the time, that he went to Lowell in a private capacity and sold his talk to a newspaper." "Lowell was towering mad—wrote a letter about it: there was hot debate—men argued on both sides like priests over a doctrine. So far as I have known Hawthorne, or been impressed by him—it is favorably."

Thursday, May 30, 1889

11 A.M. Just a year since the day we went down to W.'s with Kennedy and W. opened with us the bottle of Egg Harbor champagne! W. this noon, on my entrance, sat looking over a copy of the pocket edition. "I have just taken it up," he explained—"Everything seems to be right but the printing: even that is not as bad as it might be, though bad enough, to be sure. When we think of the elegant prints that come from abroad—of the English Bible—the Guild periodical—others —this makes you sick. I have tried to believe it was the paper, but can't convince myself that it is to be put off that way: it is the printer—the printer alone—who is to blame. Look at this margin! It is miserably registered." But the book as a whole impressed him. He asked me what I thought of the McKay portrait, over which he hung for a long time. "I am going to send a copy off to Dr. Bucke at once. It may be then that he will get it by the end of the week—by Saturday night. The book will, in form, be wholly new to Doctor—wholly—and that new portrait will be something for him to look at." I helped him bundle the book up. He addressed it in a large hand, and put a ten-cent stamp on it. Was that not more than was necessary? "Probably—but I always put it on that way: and look at the stamp—don't you think it a beauty? I think it the finest stamp Uncle Sam has ever issued."

W. tried to find me Edward Carpenter's letter, but it was not about, though the registered, blue-streaked envelope was at hand. W. laughingly said: "It was curious—the two letters came in the same mail—both had these same marks of registry

—I opened Carpenter's first, and there was the money—then took up the other, expecting something substantial there, too —and lo! there was nothing but an autograph man again— the redoubtable!" Then he added: "Edward's was a very simple letter all through—very direct, very touching." And he promised: "If I receive letters that could be used for your purposes, I'll save them for you—give them to you." "Here is one now," he went on smilingly, handing me a big envelope— "here is someone writing a poem about me—a fellow way off in the West—Milwaukee—take it away—and be sure you don't bring it back again"—though adding with half compunction— "I should not like him to hear me say that—for he meant it honestly." I told him I had Elizabeth Porter Gould's poem with me: should I read it? He shook his head. Nor would he read it himself? "Neither: keep it in your pocket!" I read him Horace Howard Furness' letter, in which he was much interested. "It is Shakespearean all through"—and had me re-read the quotation. "And very kind and warm for me—perfumed." He spoke regretfully of Furness' enforced absence: "Although badly afflicted—deaf, almost utterly—he likes to get with the boys and have a jolly good time." Read him then a letter I had from Jennie Gilder this forenoon, which pleased him as being "more radical, positive, than Jo's usual manner." A third note I had this morning was from Cockrill, of the World. This, too, touched W. But most enjoyably of all did he listen to my reading of Kennedy's letter. He was intent—insisted on a second reading of good phrases, and at the end, when I called it "the best letter so far received," he nodded assent and said: "It is!—it is!—far! I do not see how it could be better." As to the excised phrase on Christianity, he laughed lightly: "It is right not to read that there: it would not be wise to open up a discussion on anything at such a moment. As men were involved in the arrangement who are very sensitive on that point, it would hardly do to raise the wind at that precise time. But you must print the letter—it must go along in the pam-

328 Mickle Street
Camden May 16 '89

Dear Sir

This sample of your binding (old fashion'd pocket book style with ordinary tongue or tuck flap, all holding snug, but not too tight or stiff) is satisfactory & suits me best. The dark green morocco, if you have it already will do — but if you have to get it get a lighter green. Bind the whole ed'n alike, no variety. Make a stout paper pocket — (see last page. as written on in sample) — In trimming the plates &c. (if yet to be done) especially No: 1 and No: 4) trim them & leaving a little more white paper at bottom, & less at top, x the trimming in the sample seems to me to exactly very reverse. The plates are all put in right in this sample — the stamp on cover is right — & altogether the job looks satisfactory I particularly want 50 copies (or 100) in a week.

Walt Whitman

A letter from Walt Whitman to Oldach (binder)

CWP is located (July 24 '90) at 3819 Lancaster av: real estate office Phila

This Memorandum Book was a present
from my dear young friend, what has been
Clayton Wesley Peirson of him
bro't to me by him Evng of March 22, 188

May 31
1889
Write this ab't 11 a m in my big ratan chin Mickle street Camden. Have just had a
wash & bath — a newspaper reporter, (News
has call'd but I am tired & head-sore & thick
& I cut the interview short. It is cloudy & loo-
like rain. The "public dinner" is to come off
at & after 5 p m. To-day finishes the 70th yea-
of my life. Have had a bad year past, near
all the time imprison'd in this room. But
here I am yet with my head above water.
Big time-marks (al's some gloomy enough)
the late ones. My dear friend
William O'Connor is dead & burned. My big
book "complete works" is printed: the best
ed'n "Leaves of Grass" (pocket-book binding
with "Sands" and "Backward Glance" included, 422 pages, $4 to
I shall try to get around & show myself &
speak a short word, to my dear friends at th-
^to-night^ dinner. The event itself, & what is done &
said, will show what it all amounts to.
The old memorandum book being now
fill'd. I henceforth write in this.

sent pocket-bk ed'ns L of G to
Sarrazin, France   Frank Williams rec'd
Dowden, Ireland. 2 copies rec'd   Herbert Gilchrist rec'd
Lou rec'd   Sylvester Baxter rec'd
Judge ——— rec'd   Mrs. Stafford (Glendale)
Clifford rec'd   Dr Bucke (three)
Hor.... 2 copies   N S Kennedy
R W Gilder rec'd   Phillips Stewart
John Burroughs rec'd   Mr Bancroft (Washn)
T B Harned rec'd

(*above*) Walt Whitman with the niece and nephew of Jeanette
Gilder (Photograph by G. C. Cox) (*below*) Horace Traubel's
ticket for Walt Whitman testimonial banquet

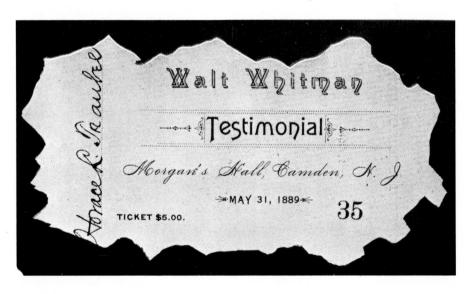

Gabriel Sarrazin

Hamlin Garland

Trial make-up page (unused) for frontispiece to "CAMDEN'S COMPLIMENT TO WALT WHITMAN"

I must get in one large (probably solid brevier will do it) dollar copy

cap1 Autobiographic Note

tel from an old "memoranda copy"

I was born May 31, 1819, in my father's farm-house, at ... Hills, L. I., New York State. My parents' folks mostly farmers and sailors—on my father's side, of English—on my mother's, (Van Velsor's,) from Holland immigration.) *run in next*

There was, first and last, a large family of children: (I was the second.)

We moved to Brooklyn while I was still a little one in ... and there in it, I grew up out of "the frock"—then, as child and boy, went to the public schools—then to work in a printing office.

When only sixteen or seventeen years old, and for two years afterward, I went to teaching country schools down in Queens and Suffolk counties, Long Island, and "boarded round." Then, returning to New York, worked as printer and writer, (with an occasional shy at ...

1848–'9.—About this time went off on a leisurely journey and working expedition (my brother Jeff with me,) through all the Middle States, and down the Ohio and Mississippi rivers. Lived a while in New Orleans, and worked there, after a time, plodded back northward, up the Mississippi, the Missouri, &c., and around in, and by way of, the great lakes, Michigan, Huron and Erie, to Niagara falls and lower Canada—finally returning through Central New York, and down the Hudson.

(Have lived quite a good deal in the Southern states.)

1851–'54.—Occupied in house-building in Brooklyn. (For a bit of the first part of that time in printing a daily and weekly paper.)

1855.—Lost my dear father, this year, by death... Commenced putting *Leaves of Grass* to press, for good—after many MS. doings and undoings—(I had great trouble in leaving out the stock "poetical" touches—but succeeded at last.)

1862.—In December of this year went down to the field of War in Virginia. My brother George, reported badly wounded, in the Fredericksburgh fight. (For 1863 and '64, see *Specimen Days*

1865 to '71.—Had a place as clerk (till '74) in the Attorney General's Office, Washington.

(New York and Brooklyn seem more like *home*, as I was born near, and brought up in them, and lived, man and boy, for 30 years. But I lived some years in Washington, *and partly lived up* and have visited most of the Western and Eastern cities.)

(a sudden climax and prostration from paralysis)

187... took a two months' trip through the New England States ... the Connecticut ... Rhode ... Vermont ... Burlington ... with this short Lake Champlain ...

1873.—This year lost, by death, my dear, dear mother—and just before, my sister Martha—(the two best and sweetest women I have ever seen or known, or ever expect to see.) Same year, Quit work at Washington, and moved to Camden, New Jersey—where I ... write these lines.

have lived since, and now (September, 1889)

take in / run in

(Had been simmering inside for several years; broke out owing those times temporarily and then went over. But now a serious attack beyond cure. Dr Drinkard my Washington physician (and a first rate one) said it was the result of too extreme bodily and emotional strain continued at Washington and "down in front" in 1863 ¼ and '5. I doubt if a heartier stronger healthier physique ever lived from 1840 to '70 My greatest call (Quaker,) to go around and do what I could among the suffering and and wounded was that I seem'd to be so strong and well, I considered myself invulnerable.) *run in next*

three (advertisements) at bottom of page
set close — make as close as possible
wave line

3 By mail (or Express) address Walt Whitman
Camden New Jersey. Send P. O. or draft, pay
able to W W's order.

Complete Poems & Prose (1855 to 1888) of
Walt Whitman. Portraits from Life. Au
tograph. 900 pages, octavo, plain binding.
Price $6 — (when sent by mail 40 cents more)

Leaves of Grass (small ed'n), includes "Sands at Seventy" and
"Backward Glance". Six portraits from life,
Autograph. Full gilt; morocco b'd'g, pocket book
style. Price $5.

Several Portraits from Life — photo'd or eng'd —
autographs — all well envelop'd. Price $3.

Whitman's revised autobiographic note (*on facing page*),
and (*above*) his copy for advertisements: both to be used in
"CAMDEN'S COMPLIMENT TO WALT WHITMAN"

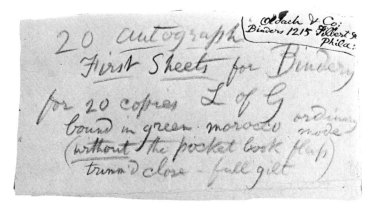

Directions by Walt Whitman to Oldach (binder),
on wrapper of package

Manuscript page in
Richard Bucke's copy
of LEAVES OF GRASS,
pocket-book edition

Walt Whitman, April 15, 1887. Portrait by George C. Cox, called by W. W.: "the laughing philosopher"

Death's Valley

(to accompany a picture – by request.)

(Art End)

                                                            well I know 'tis   That Valle
Aye it is ~~grim to~~ ~~compart~~ ghastly to descend in
Preachers musicians poets painters ~~have always~~
Philosophy ex~~ploited~~ ~~from~~ the battle-field, ~~the~~ ~~from~~
        ships at sea, the myriad beds of death,
All all the past con~~jucted~~ have ~~and has entered~~
        the ancien~~test~~ humanity we know,
Syria's India's Egypt's Greece's ~~and~~ Rome's,
Till ~~the~~ now for us, under our very eyes, spreadi
Grim the same to day, ~~out~~
Here, there, tis limned ~~entrance~~ yours and mine,

fearful

Age

Yet you and I am all

All
yet all the past, have enter'd ... and you
and I all ... this valley, we know,
And here 'tis limned

to accompany a picture — by request

musicians,
Preachers, and poets, painters, have render'd
it
Philosophs ... — from battle-fields, from ships
The myriad beds of peace, have forwarded
the very ancient
Syria, India Egypt Greece and Rome,
And there under our very eyes to-day
it ... the same

A partial draft and trial lines for "Death's Valley."
Although accepted and paid for, the poem was not printed
until after Whitman's death in 1892.

To celebrate   Sweet peaceful welcome death"
And of the struggle and contortions, and the hard tied
                                                   Knot,
                          many
For I have seen the wounded soldiers die
After long via suffering wasting — and have
          their living
been the life pass off with a smiles;
And I have watch'd the death hours of
          the old — and seen the infant die,
The rich with all his nurses and his doctors,
And the poor in his meagreness and poverty,
                        long
And I myself joy many, O death my every breath,
And the thought near and nearness and the silent
          thought of thee,

                      well, well recalling
And out of these and of thee contemplation
          of thee and thee
I make a scene, a song, brief not for thee
Nor death
To celebrate the struggle, and contention, or the hard tied Knot
But of the blessed light, and just perfect
          better air with meadows, rippling tides,
          and flowers trees and flowers and grass
And the low hum of living, and in the midst
          thy thee dim, God's right hand
Then holiest minister of Heaven only thou, envoy,
          usherer guide at last of all
Sweet, peaceful, come long, welcome Death,

Not gloom's ravines
Nor fear of thee, nor bleak, nor empty,
          dark — for I do not fear thee,)

                  pride   dissoluter
Rich, florid, happy, better, living,
          Loosener of the stricture-knot
                  call'd life,

Richard Maurice Bucke among his books

TINTYPE BY DOUGAN

Harrison S. Morris and Horace Traubel, Sept. 1, 1890

Mary Whitall Smith, 1884

Alice (Alys) Smith

Robert Pearsall Smith

Edward Wilkins

Geoffrey Buckwalter

phlet." He repeated it over and over again, that here was truly "a good word at last." Said: "I have my own speech prepared: it will only be a couple of lines." Here he paused: "I should say, to be more accurate, six lines or so: it is not a speech nor yet is it a poem. I want myself rendered right if at all. By some curious mischance, newspapers have the faculty of sending to you, fellows who put down what you do not say, but carefully avoid giving a word of what you do. It is to protect myself against that accident that I pre-arrange this. Men seem to have very little conscience on this." So many came to him, "yet so few worthily." "I think the best fellow of all is a young man—a tall young man—named Jeffers (Jefferis)— Upton Jeffers: he comes the most near to having a conscience of any of the crowd of boys that chance in. I knew a printer there in the Courier office who told me a little about 'Jeff'— they call him 'Jeff'—and a piece that touched me up." And W. proceeded: "It was not this exact thing, but something like this: that the printer had put a small D when there should have been a big one, and promptly 'Jeff' was back in the composing room. The form was made up—locked—and what difference did it make anyhow?—and so on and on. But 'Jeff' insisted that Whitman wished it so, had particularly wished it so, and so it should be. That is the nature of the incident, rather than the incident itself—but thoroughly excellent—a manifestation of conscience one is hardly prepared for in a newspaper man." As to Hartmann, to whom I antipodally alluded: "He is away from home—helpless—a poor enough creature—yet I have a soft spot for him—a liking for him— after all—poor boy!" W. asked me how I had written Stedman, that I had received such a noble reply. I gave him the substance of my letter. "That is good—I have no doubt that was what brought him back to us—the spirit of it, probably. And noble fellow he is, too! Well—we are all glad: and that is a birthday gift worth while!" He was strangely demonstrative towards me—as, indeed, last night, too—so much more so than usual. I gave him a list of names of those for whom to prepare books. "And we'll give them tomorrow," he said, "we'll have the boys receive them tomorrow—and from your hand, if you will!" There was Gilchrist, Tom, Clifford, Williams, and Gilder.

W.: "There is a thick letter down stairs from Dr. Bucke—enclosing Mrs. O'Connor's letters to him. I want you to see it: aside from its general interest it has something in about you. When you go, take it along with you. I gave it to Mary to read." W. suggested: "I think you ought to read Kennedy's letter, at least—if not others." I said I never attempted such a thing in a big hall. "Well—then now is the time to begin—read it just as you did here, only raising the pitch." "It ought to be read by somebody who knows us—who knows Kennedy."

I opened the box of books for W., and found therein 97 copies, making, with those I had brought over, and the model, 104 in all. W. joked about his pocket edition, as he had before: "The folks would always protest to me, what good are big pockets, anyhow? no one uses them? And then they would say, no gentleman carries a big book in his pocket! But I always said, I do! that is the puzzle! It seems to me that two things are indispensable in tailoring—to give a man the best buttons and provide him with plenty and strong and big pockets. I always lay this down as the law to anyone who works for me."

8.15 P.M. Found W. sitting in front of the house, the old man Curtz on the step nearby. W. said: "Ah! Horace—I was just about to go in!" So he called Ed, who responded, and between us he went laboriously into the parlor, Curtz along with us.

W. said: "I have been having your mail come to me—a couple of letters addressed here to my care—besides something of my own." He handed me a bundle of letters, four of them. One of them from Harrisburg, containing another bit of doggerel. Had he read it? "No—it got dark—I let it go." Another letter from Garland. "He is coming—he tells about it there:

I am glad." The letters addressed to me were from Baxter and Sanborn. I also had a short note from Habberton this evening from Fortress Monroe, promising a note for the dinner. I read all these to W. who was much touched. He remarked of Baxter: "I count him one of my very best friends—one of the securest: his letter is fine, and very warm—perhaps too warm —not warmer, however, than was to have been expected." I read him Curtis' letter, which came to Cattell today. "Well— that is about the most positive thing that George was ever got to say, I do believe." Sanborn pleased him: I read parts of it over to him a second time. As to a telegram from J. H. Gilman, Rochester: "I don't know who he is—do you?" And he re- marked in a general way: "There seems now to be a drift our way, the tide all set in for us—all for us: it makes us almost fear something, as if a disaster must be on the wind!" Spoke of his own response: "It will not be a speech or a poem—only a word or two to show I feel all that is being done for me, and shall cherish it." The old man Curtz started off on one of his long dreary monologues. W. listened patiently for a great while. I was in a hurry to get off. Suddenly I went towards W.: "Did you wish to go up stairs?" He caught the touch at a glance: "Yes—I must go." And so I helped him up and to- wards the door of the parlor. "I will have to say goodnight," he said to Curtz, and as we passed out into the hallway, Curtz following: "Get the labels done for me—as I said, the end of next week will do." Curtz had noticed his hasty withdrawal. "I always welcome opposing views," he protested, as if to mollify W.—who said, "Oh! I know—that is all right: only I have had a long day and must go." So Curtz, after a few more words, W. hesitating in the hallway—departed. Then W. smiled and switched off. "Let us go in to the back room here," he said, and there found Mrs. Davis and Mrs. Mapes sitting together, with whom he stayed a while. So he balked Curtz of his debate on the woman question. On his neck the gay handkerchief the Hindus had brought him: the inevitable grey hat on his head:

his color good, though eye rather lustreless. "I am just back from a ride, and a good one," he explained. And said moreover: "I sent no books off today except the Doctor's—even that not till night." And he asked: "Is everything well? Buckwalter was in with what seemed a whole roll of what he called replies. It must be quite a batch. Will you get through with them all?" Spoke to Mrs. Davis: "This ceiling seems to be getting very black," adding, with a laugh, "but 'taint my funeral: if you will have it so, then have it so!" I left, having the long letters from Baxter and Sanborn to transcribe. I recall this as from him: "The most significant thing about these modern pictures of Jesus is the absence of the aureola."

Friday, May 31, 1889

This the memorable day for which so much has been prepared. I stopped in a few minutes with W. after eight, and found him breakfasting. Said he was very well, had "got up well," and thought the day would be a success. No mail of consequence—"But a note here from the West, which might interest you but wouldn't do to publish." The writer, Henry Latchford, writing in a wittily-facetious vein, which I could well understand would not appeal to him. He started it "My dear comrade," and signed himself as having "the ardor of a regular—or irregular—dyed-in-the wool, born Irishman" and "attached friend." Enclosed were clips from the Chicago Journal, discussing Whitman, Dowden, and O'Connor as espousing Whitman &c. W. advised: "Take it along—see what you can make of it." I had received letters from Morse and Burroughs, but did not pause now to read them to W. Then to town.

Clifford came in at the bank at four, and together we came to Camden, stopping in at W.'s before going to the hall. W. sat there in a black coat, looking nobly well, a touch of unaccustomed color brought out by this same coat. He urged me to

read Burroughs' letter to him, which I did. It had been to me a
rarely beautiful consecration of the day. I had read, re-read:
then read it to Clifford, who had been deeply touched. Now it
was for W. Several times my voice almost betrayed me, and
W.'s usually so-calm face now was free to the emotion beneath
—the eloquent tears not hidden or confessing a shame. I shall
never forget this brief glimpse of him—the few minutes so
full of heart-thought. When I had done, W. called the letter
"the noblest thing John has done in years—perhaps has ever
done"—and "it is all heart-throb—the throwing-off of himself, his being, into the moment." And there was the letter,
evidently just as it had come, interlineations, excisions and all.
W.: "How could anything be finer, stronger, nobler? It is not
to be conceived." Surely this is the highest word so far drawn
out by the occasion.

As if to break the force of his emotion (it is his way: I have
often noted it) he suddenly reached to the table and picked up
a covered stone mug, holding it triumphantly and boyishly
towards Clifford: "See," he said—"this is one of my presents
—this is from Warrie, the sailor boy," &c. We did not linger
except for such half words. "I have a telegram from Aldrich,"
he said, "but it contains nothing significant—not as significant
as your letter: and a whole host of telegrams, in fact—from
girls, most of them,"—one of which he kept face down: "This
is from a St. Louis lady—and there is one from brother Jeff."

At the Hall there was already quite an assembly. One by
one the strangers came in—among them the handsome Julian
Hawthorne, and Gilder, whose refined good face was apt to
strike into one's affection.

The public prints go full into the externals of this celebration. I have no heart for that for myself. All for me was read
in meanings of the spirit and such a glory as seemed reflected
this day upon us all! A poet honored! and our poet: and dear
to me beyond all, a man into whose friendliness I had unac-
countably been intimately admitted and for which I had

247

labored and pledged my sacrifice. How joyful then the scene! How my heart leaped into every action of others that went to the finer significance of the occasion. After the moderate meal —the happy encounter of unsuspected friends—the great heart-glee, with which W.'s near fellows witnessed the concrete success of the hour. Came, bye and bye, the whispered intelligence: "Whitman is coming." The entrance—Ed faithfully wheeling the chair—the whole audience rising in murmur of pleasure and sympathy—W.'s waving his grey hat, first this way and that. Then the progress forward to the head of the hall, the center of the short table, facing us all! It was a graphic touch, W.'s simplicity deeply impressive. He looked a little weary on first arriving. He sat there with Gilder at his right—Sam Grey (who presided) at his left. Next to Gilder was Gilchrist—next Grey, in order, Hamlin Garland, Julian Hawthorne, Judge Garrison and Clifford. Before W. had been long present, Gilder motioned to me, and on my coming, asked if there was not something in the way of drink accessible for W., upon which I sent Ed up to Harned's for a bottle of champagne, which was duly brought and all in time disposed of and enjoyed by W. At another time in the midst of things W. himself motioned to me across the hall and put into my hands copies of his own speech "for the boys—the reporter boys," as he said. And he suggested: "You'd better take charge of these boys, there's no one here knows so well what to tell 'em as you do." The speeches came in order mostly as announced— Grey, Harned, Gilchrist, Williams, Clifford, Garrison, Armstrong substituted for Abbott, Gilder, Hawthorne. Gilchrist appeared to be terribly agitated, which detracted sadly from his naturalness and force. Harned spoke ringingly and to the point, with excellent simple directness. Grey's introductions were commonplace. He knew nothing of Whitman's history or work—confessed afterwards to Harned that he had never read a line of Whitman—and therefore was dull, if not stupid, in his attempted felicity. Frank Williams was plain,

248

straightforward, unostentatious; Gilder delicate, happy, with a touch of sweet humor which was inevitably enticing; Hawthorne pungent, compact, wise, discreet, in value with the occasion. Out of all this, how deliberate the process of my content! In Garrison I found no proper touch with the hour or the man celebrated—a discussion badly composed of natural and other law—while Armstrong was simply clap-trappy, telling in a style laboring to be pathetic and personal, things of W. of a very dubious authenticity; one of them, of his denominating it somebody's "misfortune" that he could not comprehend L. of G. [W. afterwards doubted this in a very decided manner.] The orphic word of the day—the word that of its own merit would preserve a place—was Clifford's—and this he had not only finely proportioned and shaded but rendered with exquisite feeling and spirit. Having the most portentious theme: "Prophet and Bard"—he had of necessity to avoid the curious and persiflage—any shred of which would belittle the appointment. I best measured the importance of his contribution by trying to picture the celebration with it left out or the theme treated by another and a slighter hand. I had Frank Williams at one side at the table, a Press reporter on the other. This Press man informed me confidentially that he was here, not to get details, but to report the spirit of the occasion. W. was taken with this when I repeated it. His own bearing was throughout of its wonted exquisite simplicity. Frequently he called me to him by a look or a gesture, with some gently-suggested commission. Through the speeches he was greatly interested. At one moment he arose—it got too warm for him—and Gilder helped him off with his big blue gown. At the mention of Carpenter in Gilchrist's speech, W. murmured: 'Good! good!'—I knew for what, since Carpenter, as will be seen the other day in these notes, was not at first included though urged by W. But the public knew nothing of this. When his big coat was off, the short black jacket gave him to others, as to me, the aspect of change. Frank Williams said he had never seen W. in such a guise before. A number of times he vociferously applauded by beating his champagne bottle on the table. Ingersoll's telegram was brought to me in the hall and subsequently read aloud by Clifford. W. remarked with a laugh that when the Colonel was as old as he, he would not be so vehement; also, that "that was not written by a reader of L. of G.,"—which was too severe, since I have record of many things as severe from W. himself. But the air of the moment was of good nature and that he wished to see preserved. "Though I guess I was always that old," he said, playfully after making his first trial at Ingersoll. But the meeting enjoyed Ingersoll's telegram. I also received a telegram from Julius Chambers while in the room. W.'s interruption of Gilder—"Do you think so?" and "I am a New Yorker": —of Clifford's reference to Edward Emerson with a "That is so—good!":—and at the great applause to Hawthorne: "That is for your father, Julian"—were naive and exquisite. How many saw the negro cook there in the hallway rush up to him to embrace and shake hands? He had nursed her husband in the hospital at Washington. So the whole evening was in full spirit for him—everything entered into. By and by there came for me the final summons from him. He wanted Ed, whom I signalled—soon was on his feet, Gilder, with me, adjusting the blue gown to him again. "Auld Lang Syne" was proposed and sung, W. joining in it as he stood and we fixed his coat. W. said as he was leaving: "Do not fear; I shall keep everything —letters, all—for you." Then the departure—the rush to shake hands with him—the difficulty of steering his chair through the crowd: he took the flower on his lap, Ed took his gift of brush and comb from Johnston. He said to me quietly: "Come—we will never get out of this," and he was urged gently but persistently along. Out now into the hallway, again into the good strength of brawny policemen, down the stairs, out to the exit—kissing me then goodbye. "And now how do you feel?" He smiled at me: "Oh! gloriously well and sassy!"

And was off for the night. After his going there was no use trying to detain the meeting. When I got back in the room, three quarters of the people had gone, and Buckwalter was trying ineffectually to read the letters. Once more a great event had come and gone. Whose so solemn as mine the thought and emotion of the moment?

Saturday, June 1, 1889

7.45 P.M. W., as frequently happens, sitting at his doorstep. I approached with Ed and he was very hearty in welcoming me. Said he was in very good condition. "I have just been out—been up around the City Hall. It was a good trip." Quick allusion to the banquet. "Everything seemed to pass off wonderfully well—everything; they tell me even the dinner—the eating—itself, which I didn't share in, was extra good. I was satisfied with it all—with all the speeches—it seemed to me everything was well timed." He had come directly home. "And I slept well—not a bit disturbed by the excitement." In fact: "When I got into the hall—up the fine broad stairway—had my seat there at the table—a good bottle of champagne, a glass of cold water, and lots of roses—then I knew I was safe —all right. And then, the spirit of cordiality that streamed through the room—flooded it—that was enough to satisfy even a fellow less contented than I am by nature. There was no difficulty in getting there. When I got into the hallway, the big policemen there asked if I was going up; I said, yes, I had come to go up, but thought, if I got up at all, it must be bodily, by their aid. So they set to and transported me without the least effort on my part—chair and all. And so down again. But you were there and saw that. I thought there was one other who had hold of the chair in going: who was it?" Really no others but Tom and I. I remarked: "Clifford's speech was the gem of the evening." And W. looked at me earnestly: "I think so myself: it must have been." But he also said: "Tom

251

did handsomely: Hamlin Garland was over today—he was enthusiastic over Tom's way and what he said." But W. insisted: "There seemed an almost surplus warmth—but that probably belonged to the hour, the fellows, the good eat and drink. We seem to invite good, positive, apt things, at dinner." He had sent some papers away. "I have chosen the Press report as the best among those I saw—but Bonsall's was very good—very full: and he had the letters, which is an advantage. I sent Doctor a paper—sent him also one of the dinner cards. I wished more of these, but only got two—one of which I still have." W. asked me if I had had enough slips for the "boys." "I had 25 printed—looked for one today to send to Doctor, but could not find a copy. It is the usual fate of my things upstairs." He had heard all very well: "They gave me a good position—all the speakers were near and audible. I heard Clifford's whack at Edward Emerson," and while it was not for him to prompt such a statement there, "I thoroughly entered into and justified it! This speech of Clifford's surely would make noble literature."

While we sat there talking, Gilchrist came up with Tom, and stayed some fifteen minutes. They had come for a copy of the Post, which they could not secure at the stores. W. had a number and supplied Gilchrist with one. Gilchrist is to write his English letter tomorrow—is getting his material together. He spoke to W. of "Ingersoll's unfortunate phrase—'granitic pudding-heads of the world.' " It was a bad figure: pudding was soft, &c. But W. laughed and explained that the expression was "all right"—"a current saying"—adding: "I have heard William O'Connor use it—and with tremendous vehemence and enjoyment." Gilchrist had seen a column report of the dinner in the New York Tribune, and W. was eager to have the paper shown to him. "Let me have it, if only for a day, or half-a-day. I'll return it to you if you want." He thought, as we thought, that the reporters this time had done unusually well. Was greatly amused with some little things I had to tell him of the group that clustered about me. These "boys"—as he calls them—always appeal to him. All the Philadelphia papers were liberally supplied with reports of the banquet.

Spoke of O'Connor's pamphlet on Donnelly, and offered it to Tom to read. If Tom came down tomorrow he could "take it along"—and as Tom was already up the street, he sung out: "It is a lawyer's book, Tom—you will want to see it!" We then discussed the matter somewhat. "The whole controversy," he said, "is, as I often put it, like the conflict of theologians over the question whether the sacramental bread and wine were the actual body of Christ or not: a question that little by little has lost pertinency and importance. I used to argue so with William—oh! many's the strong sweet talks we've had over it!—of what value is it to us, here in this year 1888 or 1889, in the United States, ourselves afflicted with grave questions—of what use for us to argue and fight this battle. But William would not have it so—it was to him a living, breathing question—and indeed, looking at it in his way, with his nature, it could have assumed no other shape." He had not seen the glorious tribute in one place to Emerson. "I have but glanced at the book: yet I must go through with it systematically."

Spoke of the ill-carriage of the mails now and then. "I am convinced the trouble is not here—that the trouble is in Philadelphia—the worst city in some respects—big city—on the continent." A Jerseyman, buried in some obscure corner of the state, wrote to McKay for a full account of the dinner. W. said: "Send him the Post—I can spare him a copy: or the Press, maybe?—which?"

I took him copies of N. Y. Home Journal—one with minor references to him, another with a three-column piece by James Huneker. "I know Huneker—oh! yes!—and the wife, too—they lived years ago in Philadelphia—West Philadelphia. Huneker was a musician—a good writer, too—wrote well: it seems to me they went over to New York afterwards—proba-

bly live there now." "There is something almost startling—
or mysterious—that now, here, almost at my last day, there
come all sorts of tributes from all sorts of men, all converging
to the one point of applause. What does it mean!—What?"
He was "almost afraid of it"—it assumed "such an unusual
force."

Shortly I helped him indoors. "I shall go for a few minutes
into the parlor, then up to my den." And as Ed led him
slowly forward: "I am putting a great dependence on Ed's
circumspection: he attends me closely—knows just how to
handle—to secure me. I always assume that nothing can happen to him." I joked with W. about the black coat he wore
last night—the unusual color it gave him. "But I thought the
blue gown hid all that?" I asked: "Didn't you have Gilder
help you off with that?" "Sure enough—now I remember: it
got so warm I was forced to throw it off." And then he told a
story laughingly: "Well—it was allowable, wasn't it? It gave
'em something to talk about. I remember dimly a story of
Alcibiades. It appears he had a wonderful dog—with hair,
fur, that was exquisite beyond words—and that one day he
outraged the whole community by cutting off its tail—its
beautiful tail. When remonstrated with—Why did you do
this? What possessed you to commit such a folly?—he
laughed at them and said, 'Well it is just this: the public is
bound to talk about Alcibiades—whatever he does or don't do,
is bound to gossip about him—therefore, I thought I would
give them something to talk about which, not bad in itself,
saves them from touching matters that might do them or me
harm!' It was in such a way he retorted: and I adopt the story,
as fitting my coat!"

He remarked: "Bonsall printed the letters so well—the reports in the papers were generally so good, I am tempted to
ask, what is the use of a pamphlet? But I suppose there is a
use." And of Burroughs' letter he said—"It was noble—the
noblest word ever written by John: the very throb of his
heart." Gilder had spoken to Harned of Bucke as a "crank."

W. said to me—"That is very weak of Dick to say: 'crank' is no word—it means nothing—has no value. Doctor has nothing in his make-up to validate such a statement, anyhow: he is himself—has his individuality—a marked one—but who would object to that?" He thought, too, "Herbert did very well, didn't he? I was myself satisfied enough." Gilchrist had spoken to W. of Gilder's change and growing warmth—that Gilder had at one time "considerable gall"—which now had worked itself off, &c.; but W. had not the disposition to repeat the criticism. Gilder's high estimate of Cleveland was much to W.'s liking, while his rather disparaging picture of Rice W. did not endorse. Read W. Morse's letter, which he thought "very fine—very like Sidney."

No more letters. "Chambers—Julius—has not sent me his letter yet; yet if he said he would send it, it will doubtless come." "You boys have had your way now—and I must say you did it gloriously: not a block in the way: everything smooth for me at last—and the long years behind!" Mrs. Davis sat in the parlor part of the time with us.

Sunday, June 2, 1889

10.15 A.M. W. was writing postals at this time. Looked exceedingly well. I had brought him a copy of Stepniak's "Underground Russia," of which he said, as he casually turned over the leaves,—"I have heard so often of this book—been spoken to so often about it—it is time I had it in my hands." Referred to its probable simplicity. "I remember Tolstoi's 'Sebastopol' vividly: a remarkable, powerful volume, in which I grew more and more interested as I went along." Also took him the June issue of Current Literature.

He had reserved a little budget for me—telegrams from his brother Jeff, Adler, Fanny Taylor, Aldrich; letter from Dick Hinton; letter from George Hall, Curate of Normandy— (Lincolnshire, England); the letter from Edward Carpenter, spoken of the other day, which is as follows:

Millthorpe
nr Chesterfield
18 May/89

Dear Walt—

I now send you on with loving remembrances & good wishes our little contribution to the record of your birthday—a draft for $194^{95} (£ 40) from Bessie & Isabella Ford, William, Ethel & Arthur Thompson, & myself. I hope it will reach you safely—you might send a line in reply. The draft is payable at the Tradesman's National Bank, Phila.

Glad that you notch another birthday among us—tho' I fear the time is often wearisome to you. The spring comes again with the cuckoo & the corncrake calling all day long, & the grass growing thick about our feet already (very early this year) and the trees all in leaf—the old vigor somewhere down, the perennial source which even in extreme age I guess people sometimes feel within them. I trust you have still good friends near you, and do not feel cut off from those that are remote. Ernest Rhys has just sent me some lines or verses of greeting to you—but perhaps he will send them on himself. I heard from Bucke a fortnight ago telling me he had been with you. I have just been weeding strawberries & come in to write you these few lines.

All goes well with me. I am brown, & hardy—& tho' I live mostly alone I have more friends almost than a man ought to have. Some kind of promise keeps floating to us always, luring us on. With much love to you, dear Walt,

as always
Edwd Carpenter

ans'd
May 28

and contained the following inscription by W. on the envelope: early forenoon May 28 '89.—Seems to me one of the leading best missives I ever had—goes to my heart—from Edw'd Carpenter England

He had laid a couple of books out for me to do up for him, and he said laughingly after I was done with it: "It is as good as I could do it myself." One package contained two copies of the pocket edition for Edward Dowden: the other

256

one, one copy for Sarrazin. "I never hear but that the books find their way in perfect order—and they go abroad for the same postage as I pay for them here: it is wonderful indeed, the cheapness with which we are served—the too-cheapness of it, indeed. I was never in favor of reducing the postage from 3 to 2 cents—and now somebody even proposes to make it one —I do not believe in it. We have such a vast extent of country; and then the postals are a great convenience. The postal service is a wonder—yet is not at all complete. There is too much politics in it. I am in favor of having men like James Postmaster Generals and serve as Postmasters as long as they live. There is no other way of achieving effective service."

We spoke of getting out a circular with respect to his book. He quite accepts the idea. He spoke affectionately of his Lachine Falls friend [H. D. Bush]: "We ought to give him a book or something, as a token of our remembrance and appreciation—something personal, that he would like to have." Spoke of the frightful disaster at Johnstown—the flood there. It had greatly aroused his concern. "It is beyond all precedent—almost incredible."

While we were together, there came a light knock at the door, and Buckwalter entered. Thence talk once more of the dinner. Buckwalter spoke of getting more menu cards printed. We had just been lamenting their dearth, and this was therefore a great satisfaction to learn. W. dwelt upon the "spontaneity" of the banquet—"what I call the individuality of the occasion." As he expressed it again: "Things seemed to proceed so naturally—so easily—no shock or jar"—the policemen "hoisting us bodily"—chair and him—into the hall; "That itself a touch to be taken note of." He added: "I think one of us—one of you, or I—should write about this. What we should want would not be anyone's reflections, sentimentalisms—nothing ornate—but just simply a recital of facts: the hall, persons, what happened." Here a funny and vehement allusion to Ossian—spoke of himself as "one of the few persons yet living in whom there persists an admiration for

Ossian." Ossian's MacPherson—"introducer, what-not"—was "a bad egg." "It is one of my books there on the floor." MacPherson in many respects obstructive to the clear meaning of the poet by attempted exposition. "As some one has said, though, that was not Ossian's, but the work of that God-damned scoundrel MacPherson!" This was to admonish us, to write our honest description and let reflection thereon take care of itself.

I left when Buckwalter started off. W. told me he had found the missing slips of his speech. "They were of course just where I put them myself." Would get books ready for Clifford and for me by afternoon if I called. Looked extremely well and said he felt well. "I have not felt so chipper for a year."

2.15 P.M. He was reading the papers. Said: "Tom was in —brought me the Tribune—got William's book." He had said to Harned, speaking of the dinner: "The people were very glowing: they lauded me to the seventh heaven—and to the roof of that!" He had put up my book with Clifford's and had written our names therein, with this addition—"from his friend the author (on W. W.'s finishing the 70th year of his life May 31 1889)" not an abundance of punctuation or care for it. Thrust under the string of the package was an envelope and within it a note. W. said: "You will get 5 minutes when you reach the boat; go into the cabin and read it."

Then his thought turned back again to the other night. "I haven't, as I said, in a year felt so chipper as I did the other night. I have been reading Tom's speech again: it is full of heart-ardor—direct, plain: I don't know but that—excepting Clifford's—it is the best of the night; it is so wonderfully charged with good quality—fire. Oh! the whole event was delicious—the transition so easy." I referred to his evidently weary look on entering the hall. "Yes—but if I looked weary I had no active sense of it. Ed took me easily down to the hall —everything there was genial and friendly—I slept well afterwards—have been well ever since." He picked up John-ston's comb—as he had done in the forenoon. "I have discarded my old comb and brush—though I rarely use a brush. This is wonderfully adapted for use, in spite of its richness. Silver, isn't it? I was almost afraid of it at first, but it seems to take hold of me now. Johnston is a big-hearted, true, enthusiastic, ardent friend. Oh! as time passes, you will get acquainted with the whole family!" I asked W. if my observation of W.'s ap-plause at Herbert's mention of Carpenter's name in the meet-ing was not true? And he said: "Yes—you have hit it. Herbert objected to naming him there: Herbert does not think him a big fellow."

On the point of his own serenity he spoke at some length. He had not felt in any way unmoved. "I never get nervous: I have heard about it in others: it never affects me. I remember, my friends always remarked it, that in crises, I never was disturbed or gave out any consciousness of danger—as, in-deed, I did not feel it. It has always been so: it is a part of my ancestral quality persisting and saving. Yet, Horace, this does not mean—must not be supposed to prove—that I am not susceptible—on the contrary, I am very susceptible—few more so: alive to all acts, persons, influences." Very amusingly last evening Mrs. Davis had come on the step and said, it was a bad sign; she had seen the new moon over the left shoulder. W. had repeated the word with his own—"And so did I—and they used to take it that way, Mary!"

Monday, June 3, 1889

8 P.M. W. sitting in his parlor, hatted, and seemingly in very good condition. He sat by the window, I next him—and there we talked over affairs for well upon an hour. "I was out for some time today, up to half an hour ago," he said, "and it was a very happy time, too." I had seen McKay today, who was not averse to undertaking the book, but wished 200 copies

guaranteed. He would pay a royalty of ten percent on all copies beyond what are required to make cost of production good. W. remarked: "I have been wondering today, how it would do to have the book bound in cloth—whether it would really cost materially more, whether it would not have decided advantages. It will be mostly a Camden clientele, anyhow, with, perhaps, a good palpable fringe from across the river in Philadelphia." "As time passes, the importance of the occasion more and more impresses me. For Camden, at least, it was altogether unmatched—something out of the usual run; —it put Camden in her best possible spiritual attitude." Alluded also to his birthday book. "It is a great triumph—a palpable victory—that we could produce the book against the difficulties that beset us—produce it absolutely, too, our own way, whimmy as that may have been." "But," he added, "after all, the big book is the book, in my estimation: has a quality not imparted by any other edition. I suppose a book to be what it ought to be, should be loaded. My effort has always been to pack, condense, solidify—to get my material into the smallest space compatible with decency: but some of the fellows recoil from that—they make it an accusation. But whatever may be said by others about the big book, to me it best of all exploits, exhibits, presents me—the whole book,—and particularly Leaves of Grass, which after all is the main thing."

Referred humorously again to the champagne that was brought him at the banquet. "It was an extra good brand, sure—and I never shared it with a soul—drank perhaps four-fifths of it before I left. I had a letter from Jim Scovel today about the affair—and he speaks of the drink matter—apparently thinks it a great deprivation. Jim is enthusiastic over Tom's speech which he thought the best of the evening. Jim sent me a piece from one of the Sunday papers written by him, and in it he quotes—and quite accurately—from Goethe." Scovel had also written to Harned, much to the same effect. W. as yet has had no note from Julius Chambers. "But there were a couple of letters came in today, marked again 'missent.' It is curious that this should be done with the plainest addresses." McKay still urges W. to send out editors' copies of the big book, but he is, as he says, "reluctant to do so;" for "ours is a quiet book—must go its own way: the edition is very small. When the big publishers—Harpers, the Century folks —issue a book, they use as many as my whole edition for editors' copies alone." Judge Garrison writes Tom for half-a-dozen copies of November Boughs, and the same number of L. of G. W. will fill the order. Speaks of the "extreme kindliness of the Garrison family—women and men."

Talked again of the dreadful catastrophe at Johnstown. W. remarked at one point: "I cannot make head or tail of it— even now cannot altogether make it out, though your explanation does a good deal towards clearing it up." He wished to get "the lay" of the town. He spoke very solicitously—very tenderly—and it shocked him to know the disaster was at its violent phase "just about through the hours last Friday when we sat so happily and unknowingly there together in the hall."

Dave suggested that W. have a new picture taken for the pamphlet. W. did not demur—neither did he consent. But he did say: "I have more and more been driven to the idea of having one of the Cox pictures processed: the one I call 'the Laughing Philosopher': it seems to me so excellent—so to stand out from all the others—that something ought really be done with it—something more than has been done. The pictures are in the hands of William Carey—and are subject to copyright: I suppose we would have to get their permission to use it, but I have no doubt they would give consent." Thought he would even let me proceed as early as tomorrow. Gilchrist has not yet been over with Saturday's Tribune, a copy of which I found out at Clifford's on Sunday. Report of the dinner therein much above the average. W. said: "Whatever the Tribune says would be likely to do us more good than the Herald." The flowers with "70" in them, still lay on the top of the stove where he put them Friday on his return. I said they smelled rather rank now, at which: "It is true: but smell this for charm, freshness"—putting forth his hand, in which was a twig of woodbine Mrs. Davis had just brought in to him. I gave him some ideas as to shape for the book. He listened and responded: "That all sounds well—very well. I can see how that is urged and justified."

Tuesday, June 4, 1889

8 P.M. W. sitting out of doors, talking, as I approached, with Mrs. George Whitman, with whom he seemed to advise about some sewing. I sent to Garland today for his undelivered speech of last Friday, which I design to print in the little book. W. expressed his gladness that I had done so. W. spoke of his own speech as "the least of the lot—without any significance or importance whatever. But I could not have gone there and said nothing—been quiet altogether. Out of respect to all the others I was bound to show myself, to say a word." He had, he said, "messages both from Kennedy and Bucke today. Both of them speak about the posthumous O'Connor book—like it, of course. Kennedy says he has seen something about it in the Transcript. He had "not yet seen the paper I sent him—I think Sunday." W. is very much interested in the pamphlet pertaining to the birthday. He asked amusingly tonight: "Well, how does 'Camden's Compliment' come on?"—adding: "Would it not be an idea to issue it, say in ten days or so? Though I suppose it can't quite be done in that time."

Had laid out "the Laughing Philosopher" picture for me to take. "It is upstairs, at the foot of the bed: you will find it there—and with it Current Literature, which I have read through from beginning to end." Said he had read Huneker's piece in the Home Journal. "It is very warm—very. These things are getting to be invariable now. I get letters almost daily—many of them—and all to the same effect. They are like a whole fleet of ships, bearing down upon you. It recalls a Greek proverb which warns you, when all is grown so kind, to beware lest something is on the wind!" But as to being spoiled: "I am not in much danger of that. A man who has had my career is safe against the like. Now, in these late days, as I look back upon the past, I can see that, in a sense, my misfortunes have been my fortunes—that it must have been altogether right for me to have travelled a rough, hard road—so to be tested, at last secured!"

He was very anxious to make sure of the printing of Tom's speech in full. "You have a good copy of it?" he asked; and then suggested that I bring it down and let him read it, which I promised to do. W. said: "We did not go to the river today, but out towards the hospital—and had a good time." It had been a good trip, and he felt better for it. Since the banquet he had felt unusually well—"as if I had by that occasion been given a new lease." I paid Ferguson's bill today, and now gave W. the receipt. He spoke again, therefore, of the pocket edition—its satisfactoriness. "The printing was a bad job, I know, but then I have not lost sleep or meal in worrying over it. It is, however, disappointing, especially when we consider that we gave him carte blanche—stinted him in no way. Think, too, of the books we get from all quarters—particularly abroad: but in America, too—the handsome Emerson book for instance—brilliantly printed, almost; and then the magazines, too—especially the Century: perfect, nearly, in its registering, inking, impression."

Referred to a story Scovel had told him once "with great unction"—"It was always so funny to me—to think of a thief —Jim would tell it characteristically, rebuking others as bad, in a band of thieves—'Money?—Money?—Why, money is sacred, boys'—something like that. It was irresistible.' I put in: "And more so, coming from Jim himself!" Whereat W. responded with a great laugh: "Sure enough,—Jim himself!"

Wednesday, June 5, 1889

8 P.M. Went down to W.'s with Harned, finding W. sitting in parlor at the window. Had but a little time before returned from his outing. Talked directly of the Johnstown affair. "It seems to hang over us all like a cloud," he said—"a dark, dark, dark cloud." And then he asked: "Do you think this Cambria matter interferes at all with the passage of the mails? We all live in Cambria County now. I had a letter from Bucke today. He speaks of having received the pocket edition—but never says a word about the dinner—evidently had not got my papers yet. His letter was written Monday." But in "such a time as the present, any delay is excusable." He asked again: "I wonder if the American people are not the most enterprising on the globe, in history—any land, any age? They seem to be in readiness at all times for all emergencies: places of peril they transform instantly to safeties: certainly a wonderful peculiar gift, in which, in whatever else falling short, they undoubtedly excel, stand at the head."

He was "sure" I would get "responses from abroad"—and he said moreover: "I see that the Transcript copies Whittier's letter—all the papers do or will: his name will carry it along." He had at last "received a letter from Julius Chambers. In clearing up the table I found also a telegram from Irving. I had forgotten about that when I gave you the batch the other day. I shall save and put together for you all I find." I told W. I hoped we would have the poem from Rhys referred to in Carpenter's letter: had already marked out a place for it in the book. I saw McKay today and substantially arranged with him to proceed. I proposed myself to write up the banquet— some sketch of its appearance and events. W. was "pleased," and knew I "would do it well." I told him I would print the telegrams together as a "budget," including his brother Jeff's, and he assented: "Yes that will do, if you think it worth while to print them at all: I can see no objection as they are none of them private: let them come in a bunch: and you will put Bob's first, won't you?" he asked, and when I nodded in assent: "That's right—that is where it belongs." Which would seem to indicate after all that Bob's telegram hit home, in spite of W.'s mild protest the night it came.

Harned repeated to W. passages of a facetious note received from Gilder today, and W. was much amused. "It seems to show that Dick has humor," he said, and then recounted, with us, some of the hits in the little speech at the banquet. Harned again repeated Gilder's reference to Bucke as "that Canadian crank," and W. was as prompt as before to resent it. "Bucke is no crank at all—he is simply individualistic. If to be individualistic is to be a crank, then he is one—not otherwise." As to Gilder's "evidently warm feelings towards me" W. said: "They smack much more of approach than I ever believed possible in Gilder. I am sufficiently amazed—was the night of the speech." And when Tom spoke of Gilder as "genuine," W. responded warmly: "Oh yes! he is certainly entitled to that." Harned shortly strolled out and towards home—left us talking together. Lincoln Eyre sent through me to W. a copy of his lecture on "Fashionable Society," which ends with a warmly commended quotation from W. W. In it I stuck a newspaper paragraph stating that W. W. had said at the recent dinner that he had quit writing poetry, whereas there were some would like to ask, when had he ever commenced? W. laughed, and reflected: "In the first place, this fellow invented the saying to get off the wit—if wit it is—and I guess it is." I talked over with W. plans for the book, and he was greatly interested. But so far as I had formulated anything, he presented no criticism. I was in to see Brown today about the reproduction, but in the hurry of other talk tonight, forgot to say a word to W. about it—nor did he ask.

While we sat there, there came a ring at the bell, and after Mrs. Davis had gone from the kitchen to the door, the entrance of a short, black-bearded man, whom at first W. did not recognize, but who proved to be Browning, once the N. Y. Herald, now the World permanent man in Phila. Browning had a telegram from Chambers instructing him to get from W. if possible "a threnody on the Johnstown dead"—so at least Browning rendered the telegram—stumbling over the word "threnody" and being rather amusingly extricated by W. Browning explained that he wanted it "to send off by the afternoon mail tomorrow"—that was, before five—and asked W. what time he should send over for it? W. had said at the outset: "As they say at Washington, I will give the matter my thoughtful consideration," but would give no promise. Now he said, "You need not send: leave me your card here. I have a young man here with me who can deliver it to you—provided I have anything to send." Browning then said: "Well—I will wire Chambers tonight that you would probably give him something." W. still however, in his quiet imperturbability: "I can give no promise—except to consider it." W. had held a curious little colloquy with Browning. "Are all the fellows gone from the Herald to the World?" he asked at one moment—and again: "What is it that gets you away?—bigger pay?—or do they treat you better?" But Browning would say nothing, only that he was absorbed, which amused W. Browning indicated to W. that the price of the piece was noted in the telegram. W. sent interested queries after some of the men—asked about Foley, Cook, Major Williams. "Who have they got in Julius Chambers' place on the Herald?" And "John Habberton is there still, I know." Gave Browning a rather specific account of his own experience with the Herald last year: "For four or five months there I was very sick—the doctors thought I was going to peg out—and indeed, I thought so myself. Not that I thought much about it—only, that was my impression, gathered of long doubt and dubiosity. There came at the end of one month there, a check for my usual amount—the usual stipend. I had done nothing for it—nothing to deserve it—so sent it back. But in a day or two, they sent it back! Then I wrote quite a full letter to Bennet explaining the case." Nowadays, however, he did little writing of any character, neither for the Herald nor other periodicals.

I afterwards met Browning on the boat and had a short but interesting talk with him. He had some hope of getting the piece. It is uncertain. Spoke of his interesting intercourse with "the old man" in the past. Secured copies of North American of Saturday. Account of the dinner on front page, and leading editorial about W. W. Left paper with him. Kennedy wrote to Bonsall for Howells' letter, and Bonsall replied that all that matter was to be printed.

Thursday, June 6, 1889

8 P.M. W. sitting in parlor, and alone. I asked him at once about the World matter. He responded: "Yes, I got it off— I suppose it will be in tomorrow's issue." Was it a poem, or prose? "A poem—or supposed to be—written for that—although till I see it in print I shall not know myself what to call it or whether I am satisfied. I don't know what it was—whether the money, or my own condition, that inspired me. They offered me 25 dollars for it: no doubt there was some spur in knowing that. At any rate, it was done. When I got up this morning I did not feel at all well, but by and by, later on, improved. And in the time between twelve and two—in about an hour and a half—say to half past one—I accomplished the poem. Eddy took it over." He said he had been doubtful enough himself "whether anything would come" to him on the subject—but "somehow" it had. I told him I had met Browning last night on the boat and he said: "I am glad; he is a quiet,—what they call an old fashioned,—fellow, but very good—I always liked him."

I received Garland's speech today, and with it a short note in which, among other things, he wished W.'s attention called

267

to certain passages. I read all to W., that public piece as well as this private one. I tried to go over it in the waning light there at the window—but it would not do. W. then hastily took a match from his pocket and struck it, I igniting the gas. He drew his curtain down. "Now," he said, "now we can have Hamlin's deliverance!" Listened intently, face bent towards the ground, hands clasped, hat on—easy, fine, well. He called it "all aflush with applause" but was still "glad" it had come. But "it seems genuinely written—Hamlin meant it—every word of it." And he said again, what he has said so often, and what he said to Browning yesterday: "I must have been unusually well the day of the dinner, else how could I have stood it, to be so lorded over it by everybody?" But his gratefulness for Garland's friendship did not end off in such a strain as that. "I know it is very warm—but in itself, it is fine—a good bit of literature, taking it that way—and a-throb, too—it has pulse: an all-important point." It seemed to him "quite an accession" to the matter of our pamphlet.

Said he had been "out towards the city hall" again. "The air is freer there than here—purer—more tempting: in fact I don't know but the best in Camden without exception. Had I the way, I should take my house and lump it down there: or if an opportunity came to exchange it—who knows?" I now spoke with him touching the picture left with Brown. Said he would write to William Carey, asking permission to use the negative. "I shall have it made the biggest that will give it entrance to the book. I prefer to deal with Carey, too—he has charge, and knows me well—is so friendly and true." I could definitely inform Brown that we would have it done. Very noncommittal about the Lincoln Eyre matter—more ready to ask about Eyre and the delivery of the lecture than to lay down an opinion. But he said: "I have looked through it—have read the last part there, connected with the lines from Leaves of Grass." This question I raised to him:—should we not quote a few words from the Lachine Falls man in our pamphlet?—

would it not indicate that we had appreciatively heard him down here? W. caught eagerly at the idea: "Yes indeed: it is a striking idea—and to all of us would explain itself. How nobly his few words—some of them culled here and there, would well go along!"

Said he had heard from Bucke. "He has received the pocket edition—is very warm in speaking of it—calls it a perfect book—says nothing, however, about the printing: probably the copy I sent him was not the worst: anyhow, he did not remark it. Now did he say anything about the portraits. He has received the papers about the dinner—and so has Kennedy: I heard from him, too—though not newsily—just now." He dwells pathetically on the Johnstown incident. As to reported thieves there, he is dubious. "There may be some scalawags there—there are such everywhere; but they are not many. It would be impossible to go anywhere and not find representatives, but they never figure to any great extent: make a noise, perhaps—and confuse us—but that is all." And he reflected: "The cloud is dark and dark. Now they fear pestilence: I wonder? I wonder? They will burn bodies—which is well— the best thing. That seems one of our future questions, anyhow: whether that is not always the best disposal of the dead." I think W. has so lived in this the past week that to write of it must have come easy to him. Clifford had made some suggestion of the sort to me Sunday, and when I repeated it to W., he was pleased and interested and said so. Clifford had intimated that W. was the only man living who could rightly hit the emotion of the moment in presence of such a disaster.

Directed me to his bed, upstairs, on which he had laid out for me a packet of letters and papers. After leaving I found the copies of Home Journal I had left with him, letter from Julius Chambers, Bucke's letter of June fourth about the book, letter from Alma Johnston. On envelope of the Chambers letter he had pasted Transcript publication of the Whittier letter.

Friday, June 7, 1889

7.45 P.M. Had a long and delightful talk, running on to within a few minutes of nine. The night half-clouded—the moon struggling to make a way through the mists—the air rather chill. W. sat with us out of doors most of the time, then went slowly and painfully in, yet is wonderfully well. I had secured a copy of the World from Browning today. Found W. himself had Ed buy eleven copies. Said to me: "I have several copies left. Do you want one? I sent one to Dr. Bucke—the others abroad—no others domestic." I expressed my high value put on the poem, and spoke of its "power." This appeared to strike him. "You really think you see power in it? That is significant. I am waiting to hear what the fellows think of it. Power? Power? That is very significant! And yet it was but dashed off—dashed off!" Then he was very definite in his expression of pleasure on its appearance. "It came up with splendid accuracy—not a mistake of any moment—a few commas, probably two, out of place, or absent—but that was all—which is doing wonderfully well, when you consider it is only a casual piece, sent away in greatest haste—in the night —and set up by strange printers unused to your manuscript —appearing in an early morning's paper. The very fact that the thing can be at all effected is in itself wonderful." "I was very careful myself, how I wrote it: put there on the back of the sheet an admonition, follow copy—and they have followed it very handsomely. Indeed, I have had excellent fortune with these fellows anyhow. In the Herald days, though they presented on to fifty of my pieces, never but once or twice— probably twice—did any serious baulks occur—and they were baulks, to be sure! But aside from those everything was happy and to have been felicitated upon." The trouble often was more deliberate than was supposed. "The printers themselves get it into their heads that a thing should be thus or so, and they make it thus or so—and the author must suffer."

He referred now again to Garland's speech—it was "very fine—as one coming to think over it must see." I told him that he had not put the telegrams he supposed in the budget he gave me last evening. He was surprised: "I was certain they were there. Irving's was quite short, but signed with the full name. It of course belongs with the rest." And at the mention of Irving's name he said additionally: "And by the way, Tom Donaldson has not yet sent me the Irving draft. What do you think is the reason for it?" Donaldson has had the draft some time—is suspiciously slow in forwarding it. Spoke to Harned a month and more ago about it. W. said: "He spoke of it the other night. After the banquet he came along down the street with us. Didn't you hear him talk of it, Eddy?" But Eddy had been busy with the chair, and while he had heard the word "check" or "draft," had not attended the conversation. W. then went on: "Anyhow—I shall make no bones about it—I shall write or speak to Tom Donaldson about it. It is evidently drawn to my order—intended for me—I ought to have it." He had heard rather questionable stories of Tom, "but I give them no credence—never did: I put the matter down to that frailty of so many good fellows—procrastination, carelessness, delayedness." As to the Weir Mitchell matter, that he could not understand, any better than we could. "I remember years ago it was quite well known that abroad men collected money for me which they pocketed. They no doubt thought I was old, about to peg out, needed nothing, could not use it anyhow, so simply retained it."

Talked about the great fire at Seattle (loss running into millions). "See-at-tle," he said it was pronounced. "There was someone over here today who spoke to me—told me about it— someone who had been there. It is a town of about thirty thousand people—with much more of thrift and enterprise and life than Camden; though it must be remembered of Camden that its adjacency to Philadelphia—to the big city—where are theatres, amusements, excitement, pushings, enough—re-

271

moves this from its own necessities. But these Western towns are a wonder anyway. Seattle is for instance to other smaller places what Philadelphia is to Camden—and more, because it has peculiar institutions of its own." I said, "In reading of the terrific loss there—ten millions or more—my first wonder was, that a town that seemed almost a new growth should have that much to lose." W. responded: "Yes—and that is the wonder of every thoughtful man. But to anyone who has been west, much is explained, elucidated, takes a natural place." He recited his experience at Denver. "It had something in its air that fascinated me—held me. I could never entirely shake off the desire to stop there—stay there—become part of that new country." Described his visit to a smelting works there—"it was towards the end of my stay,—but a revelation to me." Described the complicated and delicate workmanship as "marvellous"—and said: "A good deal of the wealth of these places consists in actual metal—the precious metal—coins. Indeed, the wealth of this whole western country rests in just such possession, and I think Seattle must have held much in the raw, as we sometimes call it." He remarked "the prevalence of greyhounds" there in Denver. "They are utilized in antelope hunting—are very fleet—do not run but bound—before the poor beast knows, is inevitably upon him—at his neck—and then the game is up." And here he laughed at another thought revived in him. "I never forget the plenty of big-backed men there at Denver: it seemed to me, wherever I went, it was to see one after another of these remarkable fellows—stature almost giant-like: looked at from the rear, the broadest, brawniest backs under the sun. We see no such grand men—at least, in any frequency—here: and yet at Denver they seemed commonplace."

Said he had sent the books ordered by Garrison today. Promised, also to prepare books for Harned, Gilchrist and Frank Williams. Sent a copy over to Dave today, and is anxious, or willing, to have Dave sell them. "I will give him a very liberal discount—say a third, at least." Asked me to talk to this effect to Dave—also to ask of him payment for the rest of the big books purchased in the winter. Referred to Johnston as "a wide-awake American—a Pennsylvanian, I think: quick, active, confident, enthusiastic, worldly, but generous—Oh! generous to the bone! He is the sort of a man you can always count on."

As we sat there a voluble man stopped with W. It was interesting to note how quietly W. fenced with him till the quiet, sweet reticence drove the man away. The man drawled out remarks about the reception. "They're beginnin' to take ahold on your poetry I see." W.: "Ah! So it seems!" And then the man: "But as they're always sayin, the prophet has to wait a long while for his dues." W. again: "Ah! so they say!" And the stranger: "But it comes at last." Thereupon W.: "I reckon—I reckon." The man further: "Some of us is glad you bore up so well under it!" And W.: "It don't matter much either way—we don't let ourselves suffer, however the wind blows." The man then abruptly remarked the inefficiency of W.'s legs, which remark W. scarcely touched at all—then of the Johnstown and Seattle disasters, the weather &c. Finally, W.'s answers so short, the man said, "Goodnight" and off he strolled. Ed at once asked us: "Has that man ever been confined—been in an asylum?" W. quickly: "How did you know —did anybody tell you?" But Ed's cute sense, sharpened by experience in Dr. Bucke's establishment, had caught the revelation. W. then described him as "having misfortunes in business—lost money—had a tannery or something down the street here"—and "being worldly, suffering deeply from it, went out of his mind—was confined for some years." He was much engaged with Ed's penetration in the matter.

Said again: "Horace—I don't know but after all the Ledger is the best of the Philadelphia papers. Whether it's from old habit, or prejudice, I don't know: but it seems to me, the Ledger summary of news, day by day, is the best, the finest, to be found anywhere in America. Warrie in there has been getting the Ledger lately. I feel I must return to my first love. The summary is brief, yet always definite and satisfactory. The New York Tribune undertakes something of the kind, but condenses too much—condenses so much as to be vague, indistinct: and so the Press here tries its hand, but weakly enough, after all." He "wondered if Jo Gilder" would "render" an account of the dinner.

Saturday, June 8, 1889

8 P.M. W. sitting out of doors, a red-dressed little child on his lap, Tom on the step next him. He appeared in quite a lively humor, though saying: "This has been one of my bad days and I have done nothing." Had not written to Carey or in the books or worked in any way. "But I was out—got my trip with Ed—just came back a little while ago." Read him a letter received from Morse today—dated the 7th—in which he was deeply interested—saying when it was done: "Well—that is one of the very best letters from Sidney in a long time." Everybody speaks to him of the strength of the World poem. He is pleased thereby. But when the Ledger today, as proved, used the closing stanzas, leaving out the pictorial earlier lines, he said: "Well, that's the way they do it—they prefer—but to me they are the lines for which I care least except as they go along with the others." He rides less in his chair now to the river—more out in the open, where the boys play ball, the game much engaging him. The little girl on his lap played with his big hand, his beard—finally, murmuring something, slid down and played around the chair. The father afterwards came for her.

W. said as to the pamphlet: "When you get your matter all in shape, I want you to bring it down and let me see it." He had laid aside some letters, &c., for me—had found the Irving telegram, and one from Mrs. Spaulding, Boston, and put them with a copy of his speech he had pasted on a card and a couple of letters from Bucke. Also along with them a curious letter from Cuneo, Italy, and a letter from Dr. A——t of London, Ontario. "Some of these," he said, "will be of use,— some not: you will have to discriminate." He had sent Ed up stairs for them—was very specific—"a package the size of an envelope, tied up in a red string."

By some mention of Garland and his advocacy of the single tax theory we developed quite a warm talk of social questions. W.'s part in it was warm and large, but taken without any understanding of the peculiar base of the theory. He said: "I would not put a straw in the way of the Anarchists, Socialists, Communists, Henry George men," but he did not see that "while such a theory as George's might be very wise and necessary in a country like Russia—or in crowded England, owned by a few titled frauds," he could not see its pertinency here. His objection mainly was that some had cited it as a panacea. "But is that not the attitude of every special re-former? Look at Wendell Phillips—great and grand as he was: with him light and darkness were all for the one ill and that alone—all: he was one-eyed, saw nothing, absolutely nothing, but that single blot of slavery. And if Phillips of old, others today." "But my contention is for the whole man— the whole corpus—not one member—not a leg, an arm, a belly alone, but the entire corpus, nothing left out of the account. I know it will be argued that the present is the time of speciali-zation, but that don't answer it." I presented objection at points—for instance, suggested that it was no answer to the George theory that it would not bring about perfection. But he persisted: "It is an answer for me: I want to lift the whole man—to elevate the whole man. I know it is argued for this that it will bring about great changes in the social system— even perfect adjustment, some would contend. But I don't believe it—don't believe it at all."

"In Europe, the fact of landholding means one man out of a hundred, in this country 60–70ths of the population any-how." He pointed to the great west. "The great question of questions" (he had a question himself after all, and laughed when I pointed it out to him!) "is, to have small holdings in fee simple, the whole population of America participating and enjoying"—which was in fact just what in essence the George theory at least aims to accomplish. "But go over the great west: millions and millions and millions and millions and millions beyond, and millions beyond that, of acres of untilled, unoccupied land." Was not that field and solution in one? He quoted Tennyson's line again—"the poor in a lump is bad"—and—and—"Look about at the great body of people in all the cities—in Camden here, for instance—in New York, in Philadelphia: don't you see they are a bad mess?" To legal objection to the George theory urged by Harned, W. gave no attention whatever. Would not the argument against specialization have thrashed [?] the anti-slavery logic? But he said: "No—not at all: the idea of slavery—of the holding of one man by another, in personal subjection—under dictatorial investments—was palpably bad—damnable—not only condemned by civilization,—by development—but condemned in the first breath of our American genius—of that force and faith at the base of American institutions." And he said further: "We all believe every man born should have a fair chance, move about as he chooses, possess and retain what justly belongs to him: it is the entrance step to all the rest." But suppose the land question involved a point at which a man was not guaranteed possession of what was rightfully his and therefore suffered the slave's condition? Here he stumbled, but with a laugh turned to me and said: "No—no—Horace! I am not to be entrapped into a retreat by any subtle question such as that, or to be drawn into fine-spun argument. I am a great contender for the world as it is—the ill along with the good. Indeed, I am more and more persuaded that the ill, too, has its part to subserve—its important part—that if ill did not exist, it would be a hopeless world and we would all go to the bad"—a singular

276

paradox! "Look at the elements—think of this Conemaugh *
disaster—horrible, cruel, almost cowardly—the elements evilly
at work, with terrible effect: and stormy disasters anywhere—
are they not all part of the scheme? And is the scheme in-
validated because these exist—or the social scheme, that Vanderbilt, Jay Gould, possessing their hundred millions, exist?
No—no—no!" "I must confess that the come-outers—the
Anarchists, Socialists, Georgeists, Communists, Bob Ingersolls,
do not take hold of me clean down to the heart and gizzard."
But the minute after, when I contended: "You may be a great
contender for things as they are, but you yourself have been
a rebel against such things ever since you were born, and
have been condemned by your own argument," he laughed
heartily and said: "That is so, too: all my sympathies are
with the radicals, the come-outers, I know."

Sunday, June 9, 1889

7.45 P.M. W. had already retreated in-doors. His chair was
in front of the house, but occupied by Eddy. W. inside at the
parlor window. Had had a bad day—felt weak and ill—worse
than yesterday, by far. When he first got up, he said in reply
to Ed's question: "I don't know how I feel." Finally the bad
took hold. It has been very warm and close the whole day. He
had secured a ride, but one that was not as warm and comfortable as usual. Said he, anent his condition: "Tom was in today
for a short visit—very short; and he brought along a bottle of
champagne, which set me up wonderfully. I think this brand
Tom has is the best that ever was known—I know no other
like it. What," he went on, "do you know of the history of
champagne? Who invented it? When? Is it a modern drink?
Sitting here today, I have wondered. Then I have been asking,
what of the California Champagne?"

Was very insistent with his question, what is the news? I

* Conemaugh Valley, the place of disaster that gave rise to W.'s poem.

asked him about the Cuneo correspondent—if he had enclosed a draft?—and what he knew about him. But he responded: "That's a question I wished to put to you—how did the letter impress you?" And he said further: "I should judge he was a proofreader, or whatnot." Upon my expression of opinion that I supposed from the tone of the letter he had enclosed a draft, W. smiled—"Assurance, you think? You think he is cool? Probably that is the right view to take." He thought it a "curious" puzzle, how to take such a distant, and so cool as to seem innocent, letter. Said to me: "You are going to let me see your bundle of manuscript when you have it all ready? You can bring it down and leave it over night." He wrote to Tom Donaldson today about the money. The other day when Ed proposed taking a letter for it, W. declared—"why take a letter?—tell him"; insisting upon the view he took with me, that "we must make no bones about it, but, the money being for us, must demand it."

Called my attention to fact that the Courier of Friday printed his poem in full. Everybody remarks its "power." I said this to W., whereupon he affirmed: "It is a pleasant, gratifying thing to hear. The next question is, is it true?" Speaks of "having material for another poem," but makes no allusion to its subject-matter, and I do not question him. The other day when he got up expecting to write the Johnstown poem, he told Ed he did not wish to see anyone at all should there be callers. He jokes a good deal about the fee attached to the poem. "It was before my eyes all the time I was writing." Tom left him the Tribune today as usual, and this he read with interest. Says he has been reading Stepniak —that it is a book to seize upon one. But the weather and events had interfered with anything like consecutive reading. Had not yet written to William Carey. I urged, let me write. Upon which he said—"I don't know but I shall"—giving me very specific directions how to address Carey.

278

Monday, June 10, 1889

5.45 P.M. Stopped in to see W. on my way home. He remarked my early coming. "You drop in en passant?" he said, and added his well known "good!"—this time not in its formal, but its pleased, tone. He had just finished his dinner. Remarked that he intended going out as soon as Ed came back. (Ed was already back—in the parlor—and had not reported to him.) "I sent him up to Squire Curtz's for some slips," he explained, adding, "Slips I want much, too." It had been very warm today—he had felt it, too, but not severely— sat there even now fanning himself. His color and eye seemed greatly bettered since last night when I saw him. He had remarked to Ed immediately on waking that he was conscious of improvement. He laughingly and directly declared to me: "You see!—the champagne set me up, in spite of all the doctors! Even yesterday, for a couple of hours around the time I took it, I was respited, eased—felt almost jubilantly released—though there in the evening—in the evening—even while you were there—the trouble came back as bad as ever." He yesterday gave Tom Harned a copy of the pocket edition. Inscribed it as he had the other. Spoke of his letter to Donaldson. "I wrote him yesterday—yes indeed—and told him that if the draft was sent for me, drawn to my order, I should have it. I do not understand: it is exceedingly mysterious why Tom has held it, now nearly if not quite a year." But "crookedness" he would not believe. "Once Tom explains, it will appear natural enough, I suppose." But he was emphatic that "the time has come" for him to get, as he explained it, his own.

Our rather loose-charactered Item (Phila.) republished W.'s Johnstown poem Friday last. A young fellow called my attention to it on the boat. I related this to W. Everybody remarks its strength. W. said again tonight: "That is a splendid thing to hear: nothing could more touch me up." I half-queried: "And you'll have another volume written yet before you're done!" He took the matter up: "So you think it is demonstrated there's life in the old dog yet? Who knows but there's still to be an annex to the [referring to Sands at Seventy] annex! I have sometimes thought of it myself." He pointed to the table. "There's a piece now, made up for the Herald." The letter lay open, the envelope addressed to Bennett. He charged ten dollars for the matter. "That," he said, explaining, "is what I am waiting for the slips for: it is only a poemet—a little conceit—suggested by the Exposition. And that is not all—a couple of days ago I sent a little piece over to Gilder, for the Century: perhaps he will use it—perhaps not; either way, I shall be satisfied. While the whim is on I shall keep it up—write as inspired to write. So after all the Annex to the Annex may not prove only a joke or a dream!" He urged me to keep a sharp eye on the Herald. "I should not say tomorrow, particularly, but for the next 3 or 4 days." He suggested in his note to the Herald people that they put the piece in the personal column, as of old. Another of his expressions to me was this: "I do seem to have taken up my pen again. Maybe they'll say I would have been wiser had I let it alone!"

Said he had no letter "from any of the fellows"—and remarked "the strange quiet." In Clifford's speech occurs a reference to Morse's bust of W. It recurred to me, why not use a reproduction of this for frontispiece? Referring it to McKay today, he readily assented. So now I explained to W., who was greatly pleased. But he quite concernedly spoke of its "dangers," saying that Frank Harned's experiment at photographing it had been "totally a fizzle." My plan is to have my father oversee a good photographing of it—then to let it be photoengraved. "I am quite taken with the idea," W. said again, "only—if it is not well done I shall put my foot down on it—shall not allow it to be used. The other version—

Frank's—was weak, lame, defective, futile: it would do well enough as a recovered bust, pick-axed out of old ruins, old Greek ruins—would have an interest as representing some forgotten great man, perhaps. But for Sidney's head?—Oh! for that it would never pass." He repeated as so often before his own high estimate of the head. "Somehow, sometime, it ought to be justly rendered, made current. There is something in it to me finer, truer, than anything so far done by anybody in any way whatever. If only that can be caught!" As to the pamphlet at large, that we could "proceed with" our "own way, of course." "I shall not interfere, whatever course you take with that—the letter-press—speeches—what-not." But he said again: "I have been wondering today whether it was yet too late—I don't think it is: too late to make Dave revise his condition about the 200 copies. It seems to me Dave is greedy in this: I am certain a hundred copies should do—guaranteed." We debated the question for some time, and finally he said: "I suppose after all it is best to let it go as it is—as it has been arranged for. There may be some sale for it: it is difficult to know." Would it be put in the stores?

I spoke to Dave today about settlement for the big books, and he promised to pay the current month. I told him also that after talking the matter over from all sides, I was sure W. would not give out review copies of the complete works and pocket editions; that if sales were somewhat embarrassed thereby, W. was willing to lose all that was so sacrificed. W. now both nodded and stated his approval. "Yes—I should have said it that way myself—should probably have submitted that as a finality, to close with. If these books were issued as books mainly ought to be—in plain, cheap, acceptable but genuine form, I could spread it abroad, furnish many; but printed as they have been, for a special purpose, it must be handled as I have concluded to handle it—yes, even if at a pinch to have most of 'em kept on our hands here a long while. Our purpose in getting out these editions was not to make a popular book but to put together, to verify, what was written—to preserve its integrity, send it out under our seal—advise that others in future should follow us closely—heed our solemn admonition." And he concluded with a terse sentence: "I think we have succeeded in that—therefore we have succeeded!"

Tuesday, June 11, 1889

8 P.M. W. sitting in parlor, hat on, and Mrs. Davis there talking with him. Had but just returned from his "jaunt" with Ed. "It was baseball today." He takes a great interest in the boys out on the common. Sits watching them for long stretches. Talked freely tonight. Said he had had "but a middling day." Yet not at all "severe." Mail he reported scarce. "There's always something—if nothing else, the autograph fellow—but even he's quiet just now." I had a letter from Brinton today, written at Vienna. In it sent inquiry after his "venerable friend" W. W. I read the note to W., who is always interested in Brinton, liking him greatly.

"I sent off several books today," he explained, "several: one went to Dick Gilder—the other I sent to John Burroughs. And by the way, I have John's new book—it is upstairs—he sent it: 'Indoor Studies.' You can take it and read it any time you choose—of course you'll want to!" Mention of Jo Gilder's colorless description of the dinner in the Critic. W. said: "It is quite characteristic of him: I think Jennie Gilder has other irons in the fire—leaves all that part of the work to Jo—and it has always been Jennie who was my friend there—good friend—if any." Sent off the Herald piece today. "It went at last. I sent it, uncertain what would be its fate. There have been changes on the Herald—Joseph knows not his friends longer. I don't know how they feel towards me now, nor who is high-cockalorum there: it used to be Julius, but Julius is now gone. It is true Jack Habberton is there still, but Jack has not that place—Jack is a sort of general utility man." And he added: "Walsh, as I understand it, has particular charge of the Sunday edition." The World W. hesitates to approach: it has an unfamiliar atmosphere. "Now," he said, "is your time to watch the Herald: to see what they do with me."

Questioned: "What is new? What progress with the little book?" I have made arrangements to have the bust photographed. He listened intent, with a gently counselling word now and then. Referring again to Burroughs, W. advised me: "You should see John in his house: it is a beautiful place." And as to a projected trip down the Hudson from Albany that had miscarried with me: "That is the right way to go: it is a good plan, to take the boat at Albany—then simply loaf and look the long trip through: for it is a long trip: you would probably get the boat in the morning, and reach New York about this time. And the beauty of it all! It is a glimpse never to be forgotten, even if only known once— never! For grand, rugged, life-throbbing effect, it's the best on earth—the best! Earth could have no better!"

He touched upon O'Connor's book on Donnelly. Harned has his copy still. W. remarked: "I am in no hurry to read it— in no hurry for my copy—I can very easily wait. What place this Bacon-Shakespeare matter will take in the future I would not dare to say—whether a great or a little. One point is, in the Shakespeare advocates themselves—men who are wrong in pretty nearly everything they touch—men like Willie Winter, Dick Stoddard, Richard Grant White—that crowd. It brings back to me John's saying—John Burroughs' saying. You know John is not given to saying witty—especially sarcastic things." Here W. paused an instant—then: "I told you of it long ago—you remember? perhaps at the time. It occurred when Swinburne made his somewhat savage attack on me: John thought Swinburne's antagonism—turn-

283

about—set things to rights again—said he had often wondered if he had not been too hasty in endorsing, espousing, me, a man accepted by such a fellow—such fellows—as Swinburne." And to a chance mention of Oscar Wilde's name— "Wilde was very friendly to me—was and is, I think—both Oscar and his mother—Lady Wilde—and thanks be most to the mother, that greater, more important, individual. Oscar was here—came to see me—and he impressed me as a strong, able fellow, too." And as to O. W.'s espousal of W. W.: "He never was a flarer, but he has been a steady light."

Wednesday, June 12, 1889

8 P.M. It rained mildly, and I therefore found W. indoors. But he sat there at the parlor window with hat on, and appeared more quiet and silent than usual. He had not got out of doors at all—was really in rather indifferent physical condition—in his own words, "only so-so" and "not up to much."

I had with me a stenographic copy of notes of the testimonial, furnished by the man Harned had placed there. I asked W.: "Do you wish us to use your remarks on Ingersoll's telegram? They are all here in this document." He responding: "Yes—why not? I should think they might be used." I had had a discussion with T. B. H. at home, arguing he would not—for I felt sure he did not wish that to stand as his mature utterance. Now, therefore, I said: "Well—let me read it—and you listen, whether he has caught you accurately." So I read, he intent upon my word and my face, as I saw in several times looking up. Then he remarked, what I always expected he would say: "Yes, that is what I said—the words of it—but now I hear it again, I should not advise that they be used. Why use it? Why use it? It is not called for." And after dreamily looking out the window, his hands folded as usual:

"It has a harsh, rasping tone, as it comes there, that I do not like—that is not what went with the words—not at all. Besides" —and here he laughed—" 'pudding-heads' is not so bad—it is a good old phrase—I have used it often myself—often— perhaps never printed it, but used it—and O'Connor, too." And after another pause, during which I said nothing: "No —no—we will not use that thing—I do not think I want it to go on permanent record as mine—as maturely uttered, en- dorsed." I was confirmed—as I was sure I would be, and I was glad of it for one reason, if for no other. Some who were present that evening had seized upon W.'s retort to the telegram as "a mighty good rebuke of Bob!" W. told me tonight, when I spoke to him of these phrases caught, had "never in any way intended it for such."

I read W. others out of the speeches in the notes—Gilder's and Hawthorne's—and his comment was exceedingly brief, though his interest was keen. He did say however: "It starts out to be a memorable pamphlet, don't it? When the fellows are all in, we'll see—what we see!" He rarely has more to say than that in dealing with matters of the sort. The only other remark he made concerned Gilder—that G.'s presence, "coming from such an environment" as he did, was "significant beyond statement." W. asked me: "And how about the title for the book?—have you hit one yet?—how does mine strike you?— 'Camden's Compliment'?" We talked it over a little and he promised to "rake about" for a headline that "while having the local tinge, tone" would not have exclusively that.

His poem did not appear in today's Herald. He said he was "not surprised." Photographs of the bust were taken to- day—two of them. I have seen negatives, but impressions will not be ready till tomorrow. Ed carried the bust there from Harned's, and my father superintended the job. W. "Glad it is done." My stay but brief. Ed reported W. as "quite bad" today. W. sent me up stairs to get from his bed a little package containing Bucke's letter of the 9th, a copy of

Baltimore Deutsche Correspondent containing a Whitman paragraph, which he could not read—and "a Childs' slip—and by the way, Horace, you will print that in full, won't you?—the Longfellow letter along with it?"

Thursday, June 13, 1889

7.55 P.M. The day having been clear, W. had his outing. But when I reached the house, though he had been out on the pavement, he was indoors, at the parlor window. Had spent a much better day than yesterday, and was correspondingly more communicative, therefore. I read W. letter of June 10th I had received from Will Carleton. Much interested and grateful. Thought we should send Carleton the Post. I showed proofs of photographs to W. He looked at them in the dim light for a long time. But he seemed inclined to dubiety. "I don't know," he said, "I am not much warmed to either: there seems little difference between them—a little more depth of tone in one—that is all. But the aspect of the thing—how does that strike you? To me it seems"—and here he worked his two hands as if to compress a mass—"as if all clumped up—clumped up!" Did he mean that this character-ized the original? He shook his head: "No—I do not think so —I was never conscious of it there." But however, "Let judgment wait—let me keep the proofs and examine them at ease, by daylight: then we'll see." Lincoln Eyre gave me his proposed but intercepted after-dinner speech today, but the room was so dark, W. thought it best not to attempt reading. "I'll wait till it takes its place," he said. When I had entered W. asked: "And how do things go today?" and when I said quietly: "Well—they go!" he laughed and said: "Good! and the tally for that is, I am here!" Spoke of his intention to send a copy of the birthday book to Stedman.

Somewhere, there chanced a cursory reference to the Nicolay-Hay excoriation of Chase in the current Century.

Upon this, W. indulged in a long monologue, which I only slightly interrupted with questions. "I am glad Hay and Nicolay are at him—handling him without gloves. I told Gilder so at the meeting the other night—told him to tell Hay that I accepted his statement of the affair. Shall tell Hay so myself if he comes here—Nicolay I could not: I would not know him if he was to step in the room this minute." It had always been his idea that "Chase was a bad, bad egg," and added, "I was on the ground at the time—knew the case well—there was a group of us at Washington faithful to Lincoln from first to last. O'Connor was one of them—and John Burroughs, too—though John never so vehement, hot, in his interest, as we were, while genuine and warm enough to be sure, and true as steel. I saw Chase—often: a handsome man in appearance, too—the finest-looking man of the lot,— figure, head all that—but nevertheless a bad, dangerous man. The abolitionists at that time were split up: some of them endorsed Lincoln, others accused him of temporizing, and called for a more radical policy—wished the engine driven at full speed, no matter what was on the road. I myself, coming in contact as I did with everybody, was right in the midst of a little group of inveterate abolitionists, never endorsing them or accepting their methods—though always an antislavery man—but there with them, rubbing up against them—hot abolitionists, which I never was myself." He therefore had every means of knowing the state of feeling. "I told Gilder that he might say to John Hay I could give him some very interesting and important matter on the subject now up. I have not read the piece carefully—the Century piece—but shall take it up again, now you speak of it, and do so, more at ease and, as I say, of malice prepense. J. T. Trowbridge—you have heard of him publicly: I knew him well. When the time came for Chase's proposed nomination, Trowbridge was sent for to come to Washington, there to write a life of Chase. Trowbridge always had a sort of personal friendliness for me—quite a warm liking. On coming to Washington he was induced for one reason or another to take up his residence with Chase—lived in his house. Happening, as I did then, to fall in with Trowbridge almost daily—meeting him for a couple of hours at a time—he knowing how I was interested in all things going—how curiously interested—it would not be thought surprising much was told then—much given out—which has today interest, importance, above all, veracity, which so little of what is called history really has." But Lincoln survived it all. "History has got a twist, somehow—has been on the side of the abolitionists. On this account much of what is true about Chase has never been told. But it should be told—I myself have been tempted to tell it. Think of the Lincoln of those days!—his inexhaustible patience—patience passing all the power of ordinary men to believe possible. Indeed, it seems to me, now I look back—now I survey the old road—years elapsed, and calm in age—it seems to me grand among all Lincoln's grand qualities—grandest of all, topping all the rest—noble in all the ages—was his patience, his long-waitingness, his suffering the last pang to be drawn, before he resented, spoke—and even resented as other men did not!" Imperishable such a man! And imperishable the America that could have had such a man at such a time. What other man would have fitted into that crisis? I asked, how of Lincoln's superb radicalism along with the composure? And W.: "Yes —it is an often-recurring thought—oh! how often and profoundly asked! Try to think of an America with Seward at the top there—or not that, but with Chase: Chase with the reins, driving principle, so-called, to death! To think of Chase in that place is to think of chaos come again—makes us shudder, and then warm up to realize what we escaped. But the people after all were wise—soon settled upon the unquestionability of Lincoln. All along the line of the big cities—New York, Philadelphia, Boston,—up in the great

Northwest, Detroit, Chicago, the big towns scattered there, the newspapers saw the true drift—oh! they were very cute!—and Lincoln was a conceded man. Chase was a bad type—in a sense a believer in a principle—but a believer in the sense only that marks the man who rushes into the Democratic party, the Republican party, makes a great hurrah about it, is extremely vehement—and ends, much of him, anyhow, in froth. Chase's self-esteem was enormous: he had all Sumner's self-esteem—which was big enough, Lord knows!—without those superb qualities which redeemed Sumner: an intense faith, unswerving courage, genuineness beyond suspicion, integrity. And Sumner was not the petty puerile man we knew Chase to be. It was the danger of that day that the government would fall into the hands of the extremists—of the abolitionists, perhaps, or of the Copperheads even, of whom there was a great following along the borders,—sometimes in the big cities north." Nor did W. credit the gifts for finance always attributed to Chase. "I think they are grossly exaggerated—made much too much of. From what I heard, from what I saw, felt, at the time, I little honored him even there. I happened, especially in the Treasury Department, to come in touch with some of the most skilled financiers—one in particular I remember—and I could never, therefore, accept even this phase of Chase's reputation as legitimate." And he smiled somewhat. "I have friends: some, who think my notions of Chase do me little credit—but do what I will, evidence against him only accumulates."

Gilchrist came in as we talked and was cordially greeted. W. called him "a pretty fellow" for never having sent over that Tribune, and he had to own up. Talked of a letter Gilchrist wrote to Tennyson describing the dinner. W. remarked: "I see Tennyson has been away—been away for several weeks"— and among things afterwards said (when G. spoke of an almost "morbid streak" in Tennyson),—"Herbert, there's something you fellows have over there which is quite peculiar to you—which Tennyson has quite markedly—something I should describe as sensitiveness of the cuticle; I do not mean this in the physical sense alone, or even chiefly." But Gilchrist thought Tennyson "tortuous"—found it difficult to find a word—the word. Said then, what a good W. would have done Tennyson had they ever met.

W. said to me suddenly: "By the way, Horace—you need not look in the Herald again—I got the poem back today. Look in the World instead." Said again: "No word with it—it was simply returned." He had addressed them "simply to the managing editor of the World." Directed me upstairs, to the foot of the bed, where he had laid out some papers, &c., for me. I left, Gilchrist still there.

Friday, June 14, 1889

7.50 P.M. W. sitting out of doors, in his chair. Was very cheerful, but not unusually so. After we had talked a while Harned came up, and after him, Gilchrist. The conversation was various and vigorous. Bonsall gave me the manuscript of his speech today. A rather severe reference therein to Tennyson which Bonsall was willing to cut out if we thought best. I spoke of it to W., who said, "I am free at once to discredit the story," adding: "Instead of being ostentatious, Tennyson is just the opposite." Saying, too, as to the title: "It is the old story—the old story of the fellows who don't like the cabbage: I don't care for the title, but that is no reason why the other fellow should not eat the cabbage if he wants to." But Tom argued that it involved more than that, W. readily conceding that such was the case. "I know—and I know I wouldn't care for it myself—to me Carlyle's treatment of such tenders was more admirable, more democratic, modern. But Alfred Tennyson did it for his family—he thinks a good deal of his family—his son, his wife, all." And after all, was not

Carlyle a democrat? "Yes indeed, a democrat of democrats—
one of the truest that ever lived. A raspiness in his democracy
at times, but true to his star, never deviating or having it
obscured."

Referred to Gilchrist's speech, of which he said mildly:
"I liked it very well—just as I said at the time—delivery
and content, both." Harned urged W. to take dinner with him
Sunday. It would be the last Sunday with his family all
together. They are going to the mountains. W. would not
"promise" but was "impelled to go." The day only could
definitely tell whether it was possible. Said: "I have a copy
of Harpers Weekly: it is the worst yet—has a paragraph
about the dinner, not more than an inch or two, with at least
one error to every line: takes the prize from all I have
known." He instanced several with great enjoyment. "These
are samples: it goes on so to the end."

Said as to the Morse head, the proofs of which I had
left last night: "I don't like it—don't like it at all. I don't
pretend to know what it is, but there's something there that
shouldn't be there. For one thing, it gives me a wedge-shaped
head—yet my head is not wedge-shaped—nor is the bust: if
anything, my head is rather chunky." Had we best try again?
"Perhaps we had; anyhow that does not please me." Directed
me to his room, had put the proofs in John Burroughs'
"Indoor Studies." "You must take the book along: you'll
want to use it—read it." "I had a bunch of notes from Hamlin
Garland today," he said, anent his mail—"he wished them
authenticated: I authenticated them and sent them back."
What were the notes? "Oh! of our talk together—views. I
don't know what he wanted to use them for, but he will use
them, and wished them seen by me before doing so."

W. in some way alluded again to the Herald's refusal of
his poem. Tom had not heard of this. "Why," he asked in
astonishment, "did they send it back?" And W. laughed:
"Yes, indeed: there's a new man on the throne there: the King

knows not Joseph longer." I had looked in the World but it had not appeared there today. Tom inquired: "Will they use it?" At which W.: "That's in suspenders! We'll wait and see! The Herald brings back one of the good stories of my dear Daddy: there was a man named Smith, or something, who ran off, owing a lot of money, among others to my father —perhaps a hundred dollars or so to him. When told of it— that he would lose with the rest, he didn't worry at all—simply replied: 'Never mind, I charged him a damned good price for it!' And so with the Herald—I charged it a damned good price for it! I sent off two little bits about the same time: one was promptly returned with a check—that was from the Century"—(he explained he meant "returned" in a broad sense of return) "the other returned rejected. After all, that's pretty good luck, one out of two!" Harned questioned him about subjects and titles, but W. curiously fenced off all direct or definite answers. "That World piece—it's only a little thing—it may not take at all" and about the other— "It is only a thumb-nail—about five lines in all." Harned lamented: "It will probably be a long time before appearing" at which W., with a smile: "Probably—the important thing is, I have the money for it!"

Talked of Garrison's speech—whether to publish it in extenso. W. said: "I should not advise that; publish what you yourself elect out of it." Gilchrist hoped soon "to have the pleasure" of "inviting some of" his friends to see his big painting. W. inquired after its subject, and when knowing it was a Cleopatra, remarked: "If the truth were known if such a person as Cleopatra ever existed." This raised an amused outcry: "You don't doubt that she existed?" To which he responded: "Oh no! I don't mean to question that; what I was going to say was, that if such a person as Cleopatra ever existed, it would be found that she was a bright, brilliant, vivacious little creature, quite different from all our pictures, our ideals, of her." He referred to David's Napoleon—described it vividly—put himself in attitude. "He pictured Napoleon crossing the Alps—on a shining war-horse, brandishing a sword—this way: it was terrible—it was all hell!" W. said again: "This picture took the ladies, even the gentlemen, of France by storm. But it was left to Delaroche to adjust history to truth. He had it hinted to him that this was not the true version—investigated—found that Napolean crossed the Alps, not on a snorting charger but on a lean, lank, quiet, composed, trusty mule; that he sought out an old guide—a stand-by there—probably as lank as the mule—a fellow resembling the pathfinders: you can still find a few of them in the West here—old, thin, wizened, but not too old to be alert, nimble. Equipped so, Delaroche proceeded to paint the real Napoleon. I knew the picture well—when I was a youngster it was brought to New York—a number of Delaroche's best pictures were brought here at that time: I can see Napoleon's figure now—it much inspired me—the cloak up on the neck—the head bent over—he seemed to be talking to the guide." And so the puzzle was, what was the real Cleopatra? "And even Jesus—who can show us the real Jesus—as Horace says, recovered from the myths?" He said finally: "The antique ideals of beauty were different from ours." Tom expostulated and W. defined: "Oh! I don't mean to say anything derogatory to modern men or women—only that the ideals are different." But then "surely" the ideal "of the modern woman—our modern ideals of what constitutes a pretty face,—are damnable!" And there was "the waspish waist" and "that abomination out of hell, the modern bustle" —&c. W.'s vigor was marked. We all shortly left and went up town together.

Saturday, June 15, 1889

7.55 P.M. It rained hard. W. sat at the open parlor window. Called out at once on seeing me, "Come right in!—here we are!" Said it had been "a dull day" and that the weather had prevented his going out. "And not a letter—at least no letter that is a letter: the autograph solicitors are always around."

He spoke of Hunt's photograph of the bust. "I am more and more confirmed in my dislike of it. That it is better than Frank's I should be willing to allow. The only way to do with such things is, to make a picture, to make a picture, to make a picture, to make a picture—then to make a picture again! Finally, the fact we are after will be developed; and only so: for it is a complicated problem, this, to get into a picture just what should be there. And I know the failure here is not because of any failure in the bust. I place an extraordinary value on the bust—if it can be done, want it done. For one thing, Hunt has failed to seize the amplitude of the bust: I don't know but that is the richest quality that inheres to it—its amplitude—its ample expression of poise, equanimity, power." Rather than use this as it was he would propose "the laughing philosopher"—and "by the way," had I written to Carey for permission to use the negative of that? I had not—had after all thought it best for W. to write himself. "I shall write a postal tomorrow." Suggested that I go myself to Hunt tomorrow and see to another trial of the bust. "If possible we ought to use it—and these men, these photographers, are generally willing to do and do and do and do again till they do!"

Said he intended "making every effort" to get up to Harned's tomorrow to dinner. Poem has not yet appeared in the World. W. equable. "Let it come or not!" Reference again to Bonsall's touch at Tennyson. W. declared: "I should advise its excision—advise that Harry cut it out entirely—not the name only, but the whole reference." And when he learned that Harry had invited our criticism he said: "That more than ever persuades me that I would have it altogether dropped. Tennyson is old, sensitive, my friend,—many reasons why this should not appear in such connection. Besides,

the story is wholly unconfirmed—altogether lacks the ring of
authenticity. I should not say that Harry was the man—but
some man has gone there, sustained a personal failure, and
then revenged himself. Probably the same ubiquitous American who knocked at Carlyle's door, which was opened by
Carlyle himself—asked, 'Is Mr. Carlyle at home?' And was
exclaimed at, 'No sir! Mr. Carlyle is not at home!'—and
had the door slammed in his face!" W. raised his voice into a
shrill—then laughed: "It is very good: I cannot forget how
O'Connor enjoyed telling it!"

Herbert having brought him the Tribune at last, W. today
read it. "It was certainly a very good report—and the
significant thing about it was its tone—an entire surprise,
knowing its connection. It flies in the face of the Tribune's
record—on the whole past." Thence somehow a reference to
Greeley, of whom W. talked freely: "I knew him very well—
oh yes! He was often in Washington—came to see me: would
talk freely—try to debate, raise questions, involve me. Many's
the chat we've had—many's—many's! Greeley was a contribution—a curious, idiocratic fellow—a considerable contribution, but he was not a great man—not nearly possessing greatness, as I believe. At that time—the early years of the war and
before,—he was the great panjandrum of his craft. By no
means a prepossessing man in body. Do you know Uncle Danny,
the ferry man—who stops on the street here and talks to me?
Well, Greeley was like him"—here W. pressed his stomach
with his fingers—"no belly—in Herbert's more vulgar but expressive phrase, no guts. At his best, not unlike Rudolphus
Bingham." Here W. spoke somewhat of Bingham. "He always
appeared to me a man bent with the hunger to do good—a man
not intellectual but struggling. And I have had Bingham talk
to me—oh yes! talk when I would have given a dollar in cash
to get away!" Back then to H. G. again: "Greeley was pale—
had no color in his eye, no color in his cheek, no color in his
hair. Greeley's great consuming trait—seizing and subordi-

nating all other traits—was his smartness—his ability to occupy the smart side of things, every time. It is the New England gift—almost all of them have it—it distinguished all of them—distinguishes—almost Emerson: from a severe analysis, even Emerson, but Emerson was free from it, I guess—I insist that he was. But in Greeley, the quality had possession to the full. And Greeley was bright—and a Jesuit, too—though not a Jesuit in any worst sense—any worst sense of the use of that term."

Speaking of a letter that took nine days to reach him from New York—"Yes—and it is not by any means the only case, either. Some fellow—I think in the New York office, too—seems to possess a persistent ignorance about me—sends my letters right and left, till finally they come here, not direct, but drifting." Spoke of the manly port of Julian Hawthorne: "I never saw the father, but have understood there was almost a grandeur in his build and mien."

Referred to Stepniak's "Underground Russia," which he had returned to me. "It is not the literary quality of the book which strikes me, but its inevitability—necessariness. And all these things come to wide-open ears. When we remember that till twenty or so years ago Russia was an unknown country—to us, mere blackness and mystery—such books have a great value. And for the light they throw on this Nihilistic movement more than anything else," he averred. "As to the 'form' of the book, as Gilder would speak of it—that does not occupy me." Did I suppose Stepniak had written it originally in English? "If so, I should say that would be another reason for giving it an extraordinary place—for it is certainly deftly handled. I found a letter from Stepniak in the Transcript—remember at the time intending to lay it aside for you. Generally I send the Transcript or the Critic or some paper or other to Mrs. O'Connor—send a paper daily, almost, and perhaps this has gone. The article was anent the Russian business." In order finally to settle about Bonsall's speech, W. thought my idea "good" that he should hear the speech first. Suddenly he said: "Don't you see it is clearing off? It is going to be a beautiful night! that is all gold there in the West!"

Sunday, June 16, 1889

W. came in at Harned's about one o'clock, Ed, of course, wheeling him. He got up the front steps with considerable difficulty, saying, "I am considerable more cumbersome than I thought I was," and afterwards, in being led to the dining room, joking: "I am not for getting prizes for agility —for foot-races—any longer!" He stayed several hours, and talked all along freely and vigorously, on all sorts of subjects. Rejoiced exceedingly in having the baby on his lap. As the boy played with his beard, he said: "Never mind—he is only trying to discover what kind of a critter I am—let him pull whatever he chooses." And he continued: "The dear babies! It is the Whitman trait to love women, babies, and cattle: that is a demonstrated feature. My mother used to tell us often about my father—that his love for the youngsters and for cattle was marvellous—simply marvellous: that often on returning from town he would load his wagon up with children he would pick indiscriminately up on the road." Was this love of cattle characteristic of his brother? "Oh yes! Characteristic of the whole breed!" Said he had been reading the papers. "Tom brought in the Tribune—I had the Press there." And as to Tom's portrait in the Press: "It was an affliction—wasn't it? The question comes up, was it not somebody else's picture in masquerade?" Gutekunst has argued with Harned to persuade W. to take a trip over to his galleries and submit for some special portraits. One suggested was colossal. W. not averse—may still consent. Said: "I suppose I have had at least a hundred and fifty taken—quite that many—perhaps a good many more. They would make a big gallery of themselves!"

Says that the baby "seems always to be wondering what

sort of a wild critter I am." At the table W. ate rather sparely, though taking a great delight in some late asparagus that was there. He drank joyantly—with his accustomed good humor. Said at one moment, when Tom spoke of Bucke's mixing Madeira and Champagne, "What a pity!" then explained, "I have a spice of wickedness in me—a vein that makes me rejoice to tell Bucke of my exploits with the wine now and then!" Discussed prohibition, anent the election Tuesday next. "Why not?" W. asked, "Why not let drink be free?" And to some arguments of Tom's that he listened to attentively: "Ah! I don't know but that clinches the whole case: and that is Libertad! and oh! for Libertad all is glory! I hold it dear, so dear!" The world of restricton was not the world for which he craved. We must not force our position: what grows, of its own innate necessities—"Well and good: but the policy that takes hostile possession of me—that I resist." Was very earnest, humorous and intense by turns. He doubted if the saloon would ever wholly disappear. Explained to one of the children's questions, how did he come to be called Walt?—"It was to distinguish me from my father originally and then the name held. 'Walt'—it is a good name, —to me! But Mr. Whitman does not surprise or startle me: I take quite naturally to that, too—though my friends, young and old—the real intimates—those, as I say it, of the inner circle,—all call me Walt—and there is no better way!"

One of his notable little expressions was this: "Oh! I hope that is the keystone of the arch of my teachings—allowing a place for every man's personality, idiosyncracy." He spoke again of "my good old friend Davezac" and explained his New York legislative sarcasm [I have recorded it]—and— "Oh! I have had the good fortune to fall in with the noblest fellows—not only Davezac, who was every way a high and genuine man—but Gurowsky, sharp and severe and wise among men—and then Flynn, too, my Irish friend, in some respects the grandest man I have personally come in contact with." Don't restrict men till they are the mere machines of law, but "give them freedom—all the freedom there is; if they violate rights, the statutes, snake 'em in then—but don't anticipate their sins."

Said some one had sent him "Willie Winter's pamphlet about the plays—the address delivered at the playhouse three or four months ago"—and he had "duteously looked it over." But Winter was "a poor, puny sort of a fellow—worthy of the New York crowd," which was "a mean one indeed at the best—not worthy of America—of its great future, its aspirations." And with reference to Edwin Booth (so much become an idol to Winter)—"To anyone who knew the father—saw him act—realized his power—Junius Brutus Booth,—Edwin, though he has parts and good high ones, is wholly and forever inadequate. Junius Brutus was the Homer, the Aschylus—Edwin is the Virgil, the Dryden,—is of a different type,—has no direct elemental touch."

I asked him about the report that the negro waitress who so effusively greeted him at the hall the night of the dinner had had a husband nursed by W. at Washington. He replied: "I don't know. Does she say so? I could not tell: every now and then a case turns up—some such claim is made: but with me, knowing so many instances—thousands, tens of thousands —special cases (only the few remembered) are swept seawards—no more met, or recognized if met." Referred to hospitals. "There was a hospital for the negroes down there, one at Culpepper, I think: and I was frequently there. I had no bars up against my freedom—always went whither I list. There was a special hospital for the treatment of venereal diseases—a place usually regarded as the most obnoxious of all—but I went there, too, and it was wonderfully well managed, with noble doctors and wise gentlemen at the very doorstone!"

I read W. and Tom the paragraph from Bonsall's speech, which hit at Tennyson's attitudinizing at a clubhouse window in London. W. was highly opposed to its use. "You see Harry," he said, "and tell him for me that it would not please me to have this go in—to have such a thing said in any pamphlet that discussed me. It is not true—it is its own refutation —it is a vulgar rumor, somehow caught up and given currency. I remember now that Harry once privately communicated that to me—I did not believe it then. The only thing I have heard of Tennyson at that point is, that he shies at attention—on the street, seeing a probable embarrassment of attention ahead, that he would turn off, using avoidance as his shield. But this!—this cannot be the truth. Then Tennyson has been so kind, so generous, towards me, this would be an ungracious return indeed!" I did not stay till W. departed. Had a mission in Philadelphia. The last thing he said to me, as we shook hands, was this: "Keep a sharp eye on the World: I have heard nothing of the poem yet!" W. regarded Herbert's eye with a great tenderness and intention. "Certainly," he said, "It is the most beautiful I have ever seen." I was at Hunt's in the forenoon, experimenting with the bust. It was much to W.'s pleasure that I did so. "We may hit it this time," he remarked, "and I should think Hunt's own judgment would be of importance." At dinner no strangers— Agnes there—the children—and Ed remained.

Monday, June 17, 1889

7.50 P.M. W. sitting indoors, at the window. We had our inevitable shower early in the evening. Temperature much milder in consequence. But in reply to my question, without at all enlarging, he said his condition was "only so-so." And he laughed: "No mail, either—at least, mail of importance. Of course, the autograph man: he comes up smiling whatever else fails!" I left the speech with Bonsall this morning with the request that he excise the objectionable paragraph, which he consented to do, averring, however: "But it is true, all the same!" But this W. says is "impossible." W. expressed his gladness that I had "so frankly indicated to Harry." I secured proofs of portraits from Hunt and left them with Walt. He said: "And I wrote to William Carey yesterday—a postal merely—asking if he, or Coxe, would assent that we use the negative for processing. It is a copyright picture—the copyright probably Coxe's. I described it as 'the laughing philosopher.' I don't know whether they'll know it by that name—it is a name I gave it. They had 'em numbered, but I have lost track of the numbers."

I received today three letters from abroad in re the dinner. One was from Dowden—quite full of meat, and the others (quite short) from Edward Carpenter and Pearsall Smith. I read all to Walt, who listened with the greatest interest. He remarked of Dowden's letter: "That will make a fine addition to the cluster—a wonderful, effective addition"— adding, after some remark I made, "It is a noble letter, indeed —and he is a noble letter, too, from top to toe!" Why was it Gilchrist seemed more to affect Rossetti than any of W.'s friends abroad? "I do not know—I cannot explain it. A few years ago, when John Burroughs was in Europe, he went over to Dublin and saw Dowden, whom he liked very much. Afterwards, at Herbert's instance, he consented, in London, to be taken to see Rossetti—spending an hour or so with him— and did not like him at all." W. was very affectionate in speaking of Carpenter's note. He consented that I use Carpenter's previous letter (to W.) except passage giving amount of draft, in the little book.

To my question whether John Burroughs was always as silent and subdued as when here last fall, W. said: "Oh no! John has always been a jolly good fellow—and full of heart." I told W. that Dave had in press an edition of Taylor's "Views Afoot." He asked quickly, "Has he had a snaking for that?" Then spoke freely of Taylor himself. "I met him— he came to see me—talked—but I never took to him, and

301

I shouldn't wonder but he saw it. Towards the last Taylor was not imposing—not good-looking: eating and drinking—beer, everlasting beer—was too much for him—spoiled him. Oh! when you saw him [1876] he had already declined in appearance: but he was a handsome man ten years before that—rather slender but well. As shown in Stedman's book Taylor is very flippy indeed."

I asked W. how Stedman had dealt with Cooper in that book? "I have not noticed," he replied, "but treated well, I guess. Everybody is treated somehow there—nobody is excluded. Cooper was a great light. Cooper, Bryant,—these were the two supremely good fellows, as good as any of any land or time—any! Cooper, Bryant, and the portrait painter, Charles Elliott, were the great American geniuses fifty years ago. Elliott—he was a big character, though nobody seems to know him, to have heard of him, to care for him. But surely there will come some time—I could not say when—an Elliott rebirth, when men will learn what a rich nature his was—what he contributed to the common stock out of it. Rebirth must come: such quality does not really die, though it may appear to." And then he talked in high estimate of Cooper. I alluded to Lounsbery's life of Cooper as "labored" and W. responded: "It is that—Lounsbery was not worthy of his subject. Cooper was a curious paradox—very hard to deal with—possessing great shining qualities—some harsh ones, too—perhaps in the direction of a too severe individualism if that can be; but breathing the open airs—never, never the odor of libraries! The life of Cooper has not yet been written. The time will come for it, without question. Cooper was one of the first-raters—had a vein of asperity which sort of cut him loose from the literary classes—perhaps preserved him—who knows?" On a reference to Whittier: "No one more than I could recognize and state the splendor of their light. I hold to the faith that, having all, we have room for all, glory in all." No sign of W.'s poem in World as yet.

Tuesday, June 18, 1889

7.50 P.M. W. sitting at the parlor window, reading Post. It was rather cool. Window was closed. No reply as yet from William Carey. "I thought perhaps you might use this picture in the little book, though, perhaps, it is not so appropriate." He had examined the pictures (proofs) made by Hunt of the bust. "I am not struck by them—neither one pleases me positively—but they do not offend me. You may use them if you choose—or one of them. Ed," he called out (Ed sat out towards the door), "Ed—go upstairs—on my bed you'll find a little package I laid out for Horace. Bring it down—it is a yellow book." And while Ed was on the errand: "I have written on the package what I wish to say." He had thus advised, in blue pencil: "Neither of these please me—but if either does I consent to your putting in the pamphlet—(the one marked 3 is most tolerable if preferable)"

I had a letter from Bucke today, and Ed brought one in for W. from the same source this evening. He read his aloud to me, I mine to him. He was much amused with Bucke's quoted comment on the pocket edition "Divine am I inside and out." Letter to me also today from Kennedy. This, too, I read to W. much to his interest and with the result of eliciting all sorts of quiet homely comment. Where Kennedy speaks of Rhys's "ineffably trashy" letters in the Transcript, W. would have it that I read again. "What does he call them?" And when he learned: "That is funny—very funny! Sloane and Ernest never can see together!" and would in neither way take sides. He spoke tenderly of Dowden's letter again. "I can see," he said, "why you should believe that this little book will have an importance: more and more, looking at it from others' shoes, I can see it myself."

I made but a flying trip in on him this time. He is "half-convinced, at least" that the World will not publish his poem. "But it has not come back—nor word of it either." Spoke somewhat of Gilder and "form" as stated in the birthday speech. But W. "took little interest in that at the time and still less now." But Gilder being there, and so hearty and warm and generous, had "touched" W. to "new reflections." I presumed, about Gilder, not form—though I did not ask him. The other day, when my sister Gussie stepped in (it was Sunday) to see him, he gave her an envelope thus inscribed—

The Fair Pilot of Loch Uribal.
One of my favorite stories
W. W.

and inside, some sheets torn from a magazine, on top of leaf, he had written: "I have read this little sketch three or four times—at intervals—sometimes when 'gloomy'—and every time it sets me up
"Walt Whitman"
it was "By an Idle Voyager"—
Said W.: "They copied my Johnstown poem into the Boston Pilot—O'Reilly's paper. It was that copy I gave to Herbert."

Wednesday, June 19, 1889

7.40 P.M. W. lay in-doors, on sofa. Had had his ride today, "and a good one" as he said. "We have a new place—are able to get to the very edge of the water there at Cooper Street now: and oh! it is a delicious going, resting—and the view over the waters—the big city there—the splashing ferryboats as they go!" It was along-shore at about that place I had learned to swim as a boy, and W. was greatly interested in my experiences as now recited. While I stayed there, I responded to a slight knock at the door and admitted a couple, man and woman, whom he gently greeted. "Oh! and the flower, too—the good flower!" He sat upright on the sofa deferentially. They invited him to stop in to see them (they were a

304

family he knew well). "We see you go past—you will come if you can?" But he: "I don't know: it is difficult for me to step out and up—it is a struggle. But it may be—it may be—I don't know but getting in and out, difficult as it is, would be the best thing for me." But although it was still solicited, he would give no promise—only say as they left: "It was good of you to come in: some day I may surprise you: but I can't say—I can't say!"

Said he had not yet received acknowledgment of book from Gilder, nor sent the intended copy to Stedman. I received a letter from Rudolf Schmidt today, and now I read it to W., who was greatly interested. "Our pamphlet, or book," he said, "threatens to be quite an affair—more and more threatens!" Handed me from his coat pocket the following letter received today from Wm. Carey:

Editorial Department
The Century Magazine
Union Square—New York

Walt Whitman Esq.
Camden N. J.

My dear Mr. Whitman:

Your postal has just come & I write to ask you for particulars before making the request of Mr. Cox.

Will you kindly let me know who it is wants the negative & for what purpose.

I was sorry not to be able to grasp your hand on your birthday.

Yours very truly,
William Carey

"I guess I'll have to let you do my correspondence if there is any, on this question. You take the letter—see what you can make of it." I said after having read: "What can I say except that we want to reproduce it by process, and that for the present anyhow, it is designed for private circulation, not for use in any book." To which W.: "Yes, you can say it that way

305

—for the present. I do not intend using it for a volume just now—I leave that question open, however. I can see, though, that your explanation to him will not deceive him." And he added: "You know—I have had 80 dollars or more from them—royalties. Once I wrote to Johnson—thinking there might be something wrong—and he called on Cox, but it was all right: Johnson said the advertisements of pictures for autographs were honestly put forth, in my interest."

Yesterday's election in Pennsylvania on the prohibition issue had vastly interested W., who asked me now: "Isn't it completely done for? Let me see—that is the third serious knock-down this year. Won't it subside now?" I had met a heated partisan today, who declared that "no Christian gentleman could but rue the day!" W. laughed outright and heartily. " 'Christian gentleman'! He is an unknown quantity, almost! There are few 'Christian gentlemen'—in fact, we do not know what a Christian gentleman is. Looking back over the past two hundred years, starting down in Spain, 'Christian gentlemen' have been rare indeed!—and fortunately for us, too! Now that is brought up in such a way, I am reminded of an expression of Felton's—C. C. Felton's—in one of his lectures on Greek literature—the best lecture of the lot, that on Homer: he started out with saying—rather slangily, perhaps, but in a way that was vastly expressive—'the great poet is a rare bird.' And so I should say indeed, 'the Christian gentleman' is a rare bird!—so rare he is never found at all!"

Thursday, June 20, 1889

7.45 P.M. W. was not at home on my first arrival. Had gone out, they told me, full two hours before. But shortly he came wheeling up, admonishing Ed promptly: "Get the book and the letter, Ed—and hurry up to the office: you have no time to spare!" Nor had he. "I" W. said, "will just stay here —out of doors—up against the house"—to which Ed wheeled the chair and left. We talked quite briskly together. W. said: "We have been down to the river again—and it was so fine!—so full!—the tide high and flowing strong! I look off across the water a long, long time—a long time! And there was just enough air stirring to take hold and refresh one!" Now they can get down to the edge of the wharf, he wants to go. We talked about the work of the day. I wrote to William Carey in the way W. had wished: and explaining now to him, he said, "That was right."

Gilchrist came up as we sat there talking. Reference having been made to John Burroughs and Poughkeepsie, Gilchrist spoke of "Po'kipsie" as an approved pronunciation and W. confirmed it. "That is the new way," said W., "and is coming to be the accepted way—rightly too: but I suppose some of the old codgers will still stick to the full word." Gilchrist gave an amusing account of Tennyson's pronunciation of Schuyl-kill. W. laughed heartily. "If he was to come here and get that off a few times, the local fellows would set down on him!" Current mis-pronunciations quoted—for one, asparagus. W. enlarged: "I know about this word—but now it has come to be pretty decently adjusted, even to the common conscious-ness: even the market men now say 'asparagus'—or at least compromise with 'sparagus.' I know, thirty or forty years ago it was everywhere 'asparrowgrass'—today it is aspar-agus." He asked again: "I wonder how Tennyson would pronounce 'Norridge.'" And he brought up the question— "And Lun'on, too—how about that?—how does that hold there?" Gilchrist explaining that it was a word so misused by rustics, farriers, &c. "Thames" as pronounced universally, was a puzzle to Walt. Gilchrist at first did not understand W.'s point, and asked: "But how would you pronounce it?" W. said: "'Temz,' of course? But certainly," he added, "It don't spell 'temz', whatever it does spell!" And in a humorous way he brought up the word "pumpkin," pronounced here, "punkin." "Why," he exclaimed, "everybody here says 'punkin'—even some who think themselves great 'punkins' too! I know it is not right, but sometimes a fellow is glad not to be right: he gets into the way of the locality, the people, allows their habits, phrases,—and better to do so, too! I have no doubt I often offend—often horror-strike people—in parlors —in all ways. Yet some of the nicest people I know say 'pumpkin'—make it plain-sailing."

Gilchrist remarked "the wonderful grit" of American women. I said, "They have more grit than stuff"—and both at once took in my idea. Was it, however, stuff or guts—the English phrase? W. laughed—said it was "guts"— a vulgar phrase "of course" in "the mock-modest, over-delicate, parlor society of America." He had on his best grey suit this evening and I remarked that he looked, if possible, unwontedly fine. He laughed and said, "Yes: now I suppose I am the good grey poet again! Well, I mainly wear the grey: but in the old times, down there in Washington, I used navy blue through the summers: that was in wartime."

Friday, June 21, 1889

7.40 P.M. Though away at the moment of my coming, W. was not long in making his appearance. Ed stood him up against the house and hurried away to the Post Office. W. himself was more than usually cordial, I thought, and talked at once. "We have come from the river again—were right down to the water's edge—lingered there a long time, breathing in the fresh air,—watching the boats, skies, city." But he added: "I have had a very bad day of it—very bad: but am better now, much better—though nothing to brag of yet." But whatever he may have wanted, he did not want in cheer.

He had had several visitors today. "Bonsall was here— Harry—and I gave him his copy of the big book." Had he promised him such a book? "Oh no! promised myself to give him one—that was all. I had made up my mind that Harry and Buckwalter should have copies—so as Harry was here, I thought he might just as well take it away with him. I thought, perhaps he had come to pay over that surplus of the dinner, but he said nothing about it, and of course I did not." W. laughed with great heartiness. "It is not my funeral, you know!" Then he said: "And there was a letter from Gilder today—a letter acknowledging the book. It contained nothing beyond an expression of his pleasure that I had sent it." He alluded also to another visitor: "I had a grand old man here to see me: his name was 'Lee'—spelled, L-E-I-G-H—and he was a genuine sample of a man. He came from Brooklyn—was one of the Old Brooklynites, who claim me as another of them. I felt almost ashamed to meet him: I had had a number of letters from those men there—never responded to one of them—not one, which was a churlish neglect, they had meant so well by me: such a wretch and scamp and scaramount I am! I have often taken to wondering lately, if my Quaker habit of waiting for the spirit or Socratic demon to move me before doing anything, was after all to be obeyed. But after one has gone through a long life and is at last at the finishing point, it is hard to change habits, so I suppose I shall go on as I have gone on to the end. I had waited for something to suggest an acknowledgment to these men, but that 'something' had never come into play. The old man begged me for a picture—and he said, too, picture with autograph. There was one picture up there which I had always thought wonderfully good—it was old—I do believe the only one I had, but I gave it to him—advised him to take it along, and included with it four or five others, all with my signature underneath. This special picture I had laid out to send to Doctor Bucke— I doubt if he has one: but now it is too late, and the old man is happy with it. He offered to pay for all I gave him, but I would not hear to it: I felt sure that that was little enough to do for him."

He had not yet been on the boat in his chair. "Sometime the spirit will move us, and on we will go!" Adding afterwards: "You see how much a Quaker I'll continue to the last!"

Spoke of having "read Mrs. Coates' poemet" in Lippincotts, but had no critical word for it. Some one had complained to him of Herbert Gilchrist's Englishism, but W. averred: "It never troubles me—did not that night of the dinner—never does in any way."

At Clifford's church on Sunday C. had read in part or all, "There Was A Child Went Forth." Several who were present have spoken to me of the effect produced. It was an interesting coincidence that just as we started to talk of it, a group of boys came up—each one awkwardly to shake hands with W., and one to linger near him for some time. Reverting to our talk, W. asked: "And how did they take it? Ah! it is interesting to hear it said they took to it. Why should they? There is really nothing in it at all—nothing at all."—he gave a sweep of his hand—"It is a mere looking-about at things. There was a child went forth! It is a sample, perhaps, of what calls forth Edward Emerson's criticism—a cataloguing of facts—nothing in it except perhaps a suggestion—nothing in it except what is to be credited to the reader himself—except what is stirred up in him." "But," I argued, "it is that very stirring-up which is important: that is the great and significant quality of all permanent literature. When Dr. Brinton argued with me that you gave us no definite philosophy, I admitted—no, he does not, but then I don't want that from him: he gives us the element of contact—and that is enough." W. turned to me as if greatly interested. "That is a good thing for me to hear you say. Curiously—or I should not say curiously, for it is natural enough for you to catch on to the truth of me: but I may say, happily, you take right hold there of the key-word to the book—the fact that lies nearest, dearest, to my heart. I do not teach a definite philosophy—I have no cocked and primed system—I but outline, suggest, hint—tell what I see—then each may make up the rest for himself. He who goes to my book expecting a cocked and primed philosophy, will depart utterly disappointed—and deserve to! I find anyhow that a great many of

my readers credit my writings with things that do not attach
to the writings themselves but to the persons who read them—
things they supply, bring with them." But was there not
suggestiveness, even though the writer did not study chiefly
or at all to impress or paint meanings? "Yes, there is that—the
suggestiveness of this beautiful evening—twilight—the trees
across the way there—the clouded northern sky—the river I
have just seen—the city beyond—all these give suggestion—
oh! suggestion how rich! But the idea that I must see all this,
and not be content to see it, tell of it as I see it, but must give it
an explanation!—that is not me—that is impossible! Yet I
am one who attaches great weight to Brinton's lucidity—his
knowing what he wants. No one more than I should delight
to have him here now, this minute, expatiating, objecting.
Bucke would be a good fellow for meeting the Professor on
that point. You must contrive when he comes down again, to
have them meet—then you must run the tide into this channel
and let them fight it out. The last thing the world needs is a cut
and dried philosophy, and the last man to announce a cut and
dried philosophy would be Walt Whitman. Why, boy, there's
just the secret of it—which you have always so well grasped:
including all philosophies, as I do, how could I nail myself
to any one, or single specimen—except it be this, only—that
my philosophy is to include all other philosophies." He was
quiet only an instant. "But after all it is a good thing for the
people to like that little poem. Whittier likes it better than
anything else I wrote those days—in fact, I don't know but it's
the only thing he likes it all."

As we sat there an old fellow, passing paused, greeted W.,
complained of ill-health. He suffered from insomnia—had
daily to take anesthetic drugs to induce sleep. As he walked
laboriously away, W. remarked: "It is a terrible affliction: if Dr. Bucke were here he would say, here is insanity—
here is the beginning of insanity!" He paused, shook his head
—"No—no—that may all be true, and yet something more
needs to be said. The best doctor is somehow doctor before he is

anything else—as the Methodist is Methodist, the Presbyterian Presbyterian, the Christian Christian—to me a more abhorrent state of mind! Yet I can realize the necessity that this should be just as it is—it is the working quality of the man's circumstances, his profession, it may be—a limit that adds to his efficiency!"

Saturday, June 22, 1889

7.50 P.M. W. sitting in front of the house. He had a strikingly positive blue gown on which at once attracted my eye and occasioned remark. He laughed. "It is so gay as to cause you to note it that quickly? I did not think it. It is a present from my sister, George's wife." Said he had just come back from his trip—"I have been to the river again—my first love—and best! We sat there a long time, cogitating, dreaming, loafing. It is quite a good deal cooler tonight—don't you think?" I received today the following letter from William Carey:

Editorial Department
The Century Magazine 21 June
Union Square New York 89

Dear Mr. Traubel:

I am sure that Mr. Cox will make no objection as the picture is for Mr. Whitman.

I feared the request might have come from some publisher who wanted to use the picture without paying for it.

When you get ready give your Photo Engraving Co a letter to Cox & he will lend them the negative I now send him your letter

Sincerely yours
William Carey

W. listened as I read it now, and was "much pleased," adding, "I was sure they would not object at all if they once knew the truth. I am glad you wrote as you did." Said as to his health: "I am better than yesterday—feel lighter, but then the day itself has been so fine, I have caught its color!"

Corning, whom I just met up the street, gave me the substance of a sermon of Minot Savage's in which Savage tried to indicate the difference between nature and artificiality in literature by putting Shakespeare at one end of the line, and Tupper and Whitman at the other. Relating this to Walt, he turned upon me direct a quizzing, half-smiling countenance: "Horace, what should you say of the critical faculty of a man who would class Tupper and Walt Whitman together?" And when I had finished an outburst of genuine feeling, he laughed gently—half-chidingly—nodding his head: "Yes, I thought so: that's just what I should have predicted you would say."

As the people went past, everybody, nearly, saluted W., and he everybody in return. An old watchman going past called him 'judge': to some ladies he freely expressed a recognition. To the baby in the coach it was—"Ah! my dear! You've come again!"—and to the constant stream of youngsters: "Well—how goes it with you now?" and "weren't you here with me yesterday?" I sketched for W. the "non-literary" passage among my notes for the book. He said: "Oh! that is very good! I don't know if there's anything I could wish more said than that!" I outlined my scheme of arrangement, to which he listened interestedly, putting in terse questions and finally saying: "I like it—like it all!" As to the general title page, he remarked: " 'Camden's Compliment to Walt Whitman' seems to me very good, as it did at first: I see no reason for wishing to change it: though, if a better should come to you or to any of the fellows, adopt it! You know, from the very first I did not approve of the idea of having a dinner, but the event itself sufficiently justified the plans."

Jenkins, of the American, returned my article on O'Connor as "too eulogistic." W. expressed disappointment, but comforted himself with saying: "It is about what should have been anticipated: what the Critic wants—what the American now seems to want—is—well, anything that is pale, colorless, vapid—and gets it mostly! It is characteristic of the whole New York crowd—for which, by the way, we ought to get up a name—some very expressive name—something that will hit them off at a blow. What could it be? And now I think it, am on it, I will tell you, I wrote to Gilder just today about my word 'Presidentiad'—told him to give my slip to Professor Whitney—isn't he the chief man there—the boss—on the Century dictionary?—told Gilder to give it to him or to his chief mate, whoever he might be. I wondered for a long time whether to say anything at all about it, but finally my anxiety got the better of me and along it went! It is certainly a much needed word, and as it happens, a word easily recognized, comprehended."

Here he suddenly got upon another subject. "I threaten to give you another commission. I want some of Thaddeus David's black ink and don't seem able to get it here in Camden at all. When I send Ed out first he brings me Thaddeus David's pale blue. It's as bad as it used to be when I sent Mary out a-searching for my socks. She could get everything in the world that I did not want,—get all the navy blue she wanted, but when it came to the thing I was hunting for, that was out of style! There must be enough old codgers like me, grounded in the past, to make it still worth while to make that ink. I suppose the old Thaddeus David is dead but there must be a son conducting the business. I always took to the ink—used it in Washington, in the departments. I have told you about my experiments, letting water run on it nearly a week without making it less decipherable." "That of itself would recommend it to me: it is a singular honesty in an ink. The rage for pale green is fashion—I can explain it no other way." Said he would write an order on Cox for negative and give it to me in the morning.

314

WITH WALT WHITMAN IN CAMDEN

Sunday, June 23, 1889

Down to W.'s before 9, but he was not up yet. I was hastening to Germantown, so after learning all was well, did not wait to see him. He had not given Ed for me as arranged, the note for Cox. I was in Germantown all day, going there of set purpose to display my manuscript to Clifford and have him criticise my plans. Did much through the day towards getting the book in shape. Mrs. Baldwin and J. H. C. argued that I should write to Edward Emerson about the foot-note disparagement of W. W. Did not get back in the evening in time to see W. Only day except the day of trip to Washington that I have not seen W. since his sickness.

Monday, June 24, 1889

7.49 P.M. A chill evening. W. sat at the open parlor window. I went down with Harned, who did not, however, stay through the whole of our conversation. W. wore his bright blue gown, and said: "I have just been out to my favorite companion—the river! But it is coolish this evening—one hugs a little closer to himself than usual!" I received a letter from Ingersoll today. After hearing it read, W. said: "That is just like the Colonel—always considerate of us! And that accuses me—will make me hurry along. For a great while I've been intending to send him a copy of the big book: now it must go, and at once!"

My mail today had also brought me letters from Rhys, Rolleston, Rossetti and William Morris. I sat near W. and read these aloud. He was greatly interested. At Rolleston's he exclaimed—"Oh the good warm fellow! Full of Irish—the true Irish—heartiness and bonhomie." To Rossetti's he commented "It is very noble—noble indeed!" Rhys sent me the poem celebrating W. of which Edward Carpenter had written. I shall use this in the book. His note read thus:

WITH WALT WHITMAN IN CAMDEN

From Ernest Rhys   To Horace L. Traubel
c/o Walter Scott: Camden,
                                    8th June '89

Dear Traubel,

In answer to your friendly announcement of the Birthday testimonial to Walt Whitman, perhaps the enclosed lines, inadequate & incomplete as they are, will form a better greeting than any I can frame afresh under pressure of the moment. The poet himself already possesses a copy, I believe, and will no doubt pardon one's still being something of a heretic in the matter of rhyme.

Believe me,

                              Very cordially yours
                              Ernest Rhys

But W. said—"I saw nothing of any poem: if he sent one, it surely went astray." And after I was all done my reading he remarked: "It is the wonderful genuineness of all that which touches me—and it is a wonderful genuineness—something entirely unprecedented. And I may add even to that and say, it is the wonderful genuineness of all that was drawn out that day—the whole prevailing tone of speech,—which took hold of me—assured me!"—"I was not sure about the dinner, but I hoped all would be well—and now all is well!"

On the table I found an envelope addressed to Cox, and in it this note:

                              Camden New Jersey
                              June 23 '89.

If convenient please give the bearer, for the Photo: Process Co: for me, the negative of the photo: my head (with hat) I call "the laughing philosopher"—to be carefully cared for & returned to you in a month or less.

                              Walt Whitman

Nearby was a card on which he had written. [This card missing] He said: "They have been there for a couple of days. But it was my fault you did not find 'em. I failed to tell Ed why I had placed them there." I had a letter from Kerr, of Unity, saying he would publish my O'Connor article, which I had sent him, in the next issue. "That is good news," said W., "and a few papers—say even a half-dozen or a dozen—ought to be engaged: we shall want to use them."

Clifford had counselled me to write Edward Emerson about the (to us) famous footnote. W. said thoughtfully: "I don't know—I should hardly expect any good of it—or even response. But then I am a great believer in every fellow's setting-to and doing what he feels he ought to do—following out the Quaker spirit; so if you must, you must! I can see no way to make it avail: If I wished to exaggerate, be extravagant, I should quote the scriptures, which say something about people going back to their idols. Or if I wished to be even more severe, I could refer to that other passage somewhere, in which the writer speaks about the pigs returning to the mire!"

Tuesday, June 25, 1889

7.40 P.M. W. at the window, as usual, and the evening very cool. He had been out, though for a brief space only. He felt and talked very well. He asked me: "How do you progress with your piece for the book? I wish you would let me see it before it goes to the printer: I think I should like to add something to it—little things that have more and more impressed me as I have thought the matter over." Was it something he desired to print as his own? "No—it could be put into the general piece—and there serve perhaps quite a place." Why should he not put them down now, independent of my article? "I could do that, of course—but can do it more efficiently under spur of reading what you have written. I prefer as a whole to let it go in on its merits and take its chances." Anything more definite than this he did not say.

I received today, a letter from Sarrazin, written from London. In it was a note added for W.'s private ear. The rest for publication.

> 67, George Street,
> Sutton Road,
> London, N. W.,
> June 12, 1889.

Dear Sir:—

Kindly excuse me for not having yet answered the letter by which you let me know that Walt Whitman's sixty-fifth birthday had just been celebrated in Camden. Your message reached me in London where I am spending a month and I should have liked writing to you immediately after receiving it, but my health is not always good and does not always let me do right away what I should like to do.

If I had been with you on the 31st of May last, here is in substance what I should have said and what sums up my opinion of the work of the noble poet:

Walt Whitman is, in my opinion, one of the only two living contemporaries—the other is Count Leo Tolstoi—to whom the word *apostle* can be applied. If I were to permit myself to make a comparison between these two so very great men, I should not hesitate to place Whitman one degree above Tolstoi. In spite of the evangelistic goodness of the latter, there remains in him too much pessimistic philosophy, and Whitman seems to me to have a larger and surer outlook. He is really the only one who has clearly seen that man is an indivisible fragment of the Universal Divinity, that the heart of a really pious person must prostrate itself without argument before the veneration of the Cosmos and, instead of getting lost in useless dissertations of the superiority of such and such a tradition, one religious dogma over another, it would be infinitely better to love and serve our equals. That is all the Divinity; he who loves his fellowmen loves God. This view of which Whitman has been in this century the practising apostle, this view will renovate the world.

WITH WALT WHITMAN IN CAMDEN

This, my dear Sir, is what I should have said, had I been this last 31st May among you: and then I should have raised in my turn my glass wishing a very long life to the august old man and assuring him of all my love.

Kindly convey, dear Sir, to all Walt Whitman's friends in Camden my very best regards and believe me

Most sincerely yours,
Gabriel Sarrazin
R. S. V. P.

I recently received a postal card from Walt Whitman himself. Would you kindly tell him that I have not yet answered him because I have not been well lately. I shall leave for Paris in a few days but I shall probably spend the whole summer in the country where I shall be more at ease.

Harrison Morris had translated the letter for me, it having been written in French. [Lacking this early translation, the one here given was made by Arthur W. L. Basy] W. was much pleased with the translation. "I should say, the fellow who Englished that, as I call it, ought to be able to do good work altogether." I asked: "How would it do to have Morris translate the Sarrazin essay and then get Curtz to print it?" W. seized on the notion at once. "A capital idea—only, would he? I have no doubt he could do it." And when I said, "Well, I shall suggest it to him," W. responded, "Do—and see what he has to say in regard to it." The letter itself struck deep into W. He made me read it several times—especially certain passages. His exclamation after I had finished was this: "Well—that's the Frenchman once more—once more comes out ahead, clear ahead. Isn't that the best letter yet?—the most clean-cut, the most direct, and to the purpose? And struck bravely out on new lines, too, don't you think?—not another has touched the same phase: what I call the religious phase—the cosmic. And see how he does it, too—the adroit Frenchman, through and through—the finesse superb: yet the man with a great deal more than adroitness, finesse, gifted as he is in these. See how he starts off, too—just that alone: no one else would have had the same thing suggested: a few simple words—'if I had been there in Camden, that day, that event, this is what I should have said,' &c;—and now, how delicate, how informal, that is, yet how close upon the mark!" And then he continued: "It is not be gainsaid—this man has said the best things yet about us—about Leaves of Grass grandesque things, and—though saying them always with the superb French polish, never drops into senility, weakness—is always giving evidence of vast reserve strength." And he said still again: "Yes, if Morris will translate the essay, I'll have it printed: tell him so." He had a great desire to see Sarrazin's "phiz,"—"and I am sure we shall, some day—perhaps not having to wait long for it, either!" And he continued: "That whole book of Sarrazin's would interest me—fill my knowledge of him with new light, stronger light. And I am very curious, too, knowing how he regards me, to know how he regards the others on his list there." He was much struck with Sarrazin's discovery of resemblances between him and Tolstoi: referred, in this connection, to my own repeated arguments in the same direction.

At one moment chancing to remark something about Lincoln Eyre's knowledge of the Italian language, W. remarked: "I must note that down, so he can avail me when I am in need. I have friends over there in Italy—they often send me papers—of course I can't read them—so here's a way out!" In talking of a description of the scene of the dinner W. said: "I am not at all sure but the Lord made me for a reporter, I seem to have the reporter faculty—rather accept it—just to state the bare facts of cases, then to stop, let them be. But I don't know—perhaps there's more than that to me,—more than that. But I have often run away with such a conceit." I happened to say to him that McKay had gone off to New York, at which—"Oh! if I had only known it, I should have sent a package of books in his charge. There are a number I have been ready to send there; but I guess I shall send all in care of Johnson—let him distribute them." I left the order for engraving with Brown today.

We discussed reading aloud. W. thought that "it arouses people—arouses the reader." Did it ever arouse him? "I could not say that it did—at least in any extreme sense. But I know I did my best reading when I was alone that way—off in the woods or on the shore. Long ago, when I was a young man, Coney Island was a favorite spot. At that time Coney Island had not the reputation it has now—it was then a desert island—nobody went there. Oh yes! when I read, it was in solitude, never in frequented places—except perhaps, Broadway, on the stage-coaches, where a little more noise more or less made no difference. Have you never tried it? You have heard of Legouve, the Frenchman, who wrote a book about the voice, &c.? There was a passage or more about Rachel—why it was she was so aroused when going to her room and reading aloud her plays, whatnot. Whether it was voice, manner, solitude, silence, what it was!" W. did not believe "the voice alone explains it, though that goes some way towards doing so." But "there are some who contend that no one can get a full or adequate idea of a poem till it is heard rendered aloud—the human voice to give it its free scope, ring!"—and "I don't know but there's a vast deal to be said to that effect."

Somehow we drifted into a reference to Savage again, when I read W. the following I had from Corning (date 23ᵈ, who was much aroused by the matter:—

413 Benson St June 23 / 89

Dear Mr Traubel

Mr Savage's words (p 228 in 'the Religion of Evolution') are these. "Human thought is one: that is, it is all alike the product of human brains, & differs only in quality and degree: do I therefore say that Newton's thought is on a level with & no better than a clown? Poetry is one: is therefore Shakespere no higher or more divine than Tupper or Walt Whitman?"

Somebody should mildly hint to Savage that he is not a master in literary discrimination. Truly yours

J Corning

W. remarked—"It is rather an extraordinary classification. Still we all know Savage carries very little weight—his cargo is very small and light—especially his critical faculty, as this indicates." I had told someone today, who asked me what I thought of it, that it was unmitigated stupidity,—that "whatever Walt Whitman is, he is nothing like Tupper—that he may be a fool but is not that kind of a fool!" W. laughed a great time when I told him this. "That is very good—very good: and surely true—no defect in the logic at all."

Discussing the artificial and natural himself, W. contended: "There's no difference between Homer and Virgil—oh no! —and yet there's every difference: there is, what is there?—nothing at all, people will say: but that nothing is everything—it is the whole gap between the fellow who sings because he is moved to, and the fellow who sets out deliberately to sing, and so sings!" Then he added: "I don't think you would agree to it, but I think Emerson has a good deal of Virgil in him—a big dash of him—a long tail: not that that's all. Emerson had enough in his own right to brace him forever: but Emerson was a good deal cultivated—though, Lord knows!—that's not to say much, for who is not cultivated? Of course I would not make an extreme charge against Emerson, because in him there's a whole world, independent of cultivation, that bubbles up, evolutes, is cast forth, naturally, superbly." As to Savage: "Shall we leave him to Ingersoll's sermon [?] article?" To which W. quickly responded: "No— he's not worthy of Bob—the Colonel deals with bigger game."

Wednesday, June 26, 1889

7.45 P.M. W. sitting in front of the house, in chair. The evening quite close. He had just been out on his daily trip. Difficulty getting to river, on account of mud, it having rained very hard today. Met somebody along the river line who asked him to go yachting. Did not absolutely refuse, saying: "I guess I'll take his address: that can't hurt, anyhow!" Has not yet been on ferryboat. Wore a pair of bright yellow-brown slippers. They made an odd contrast to the decided blue of the gown. I laughed and he, laughing too, remarked: "You must not laugh at my shoes—I am tremenjuously proud of them—tremenjuously—and should feel slighted if any fellow I knew went past and did not remark them!"

I had inquired after the ink today at Mann's and they did not have it—had no call for it. W. laughed when I told him I had still to proceed. "Yes—and it will be as hard to get suited in this as for me in my shirts. When I go to order my shirts, the man will say to me, with a mixture of compassionateness, superiority and disdain: 'Nobody wears such now, sir.' And then I tell him: 'Never mind—I wear them!—and he will still protest, 'but I'm sure they won't suit you if I make 'em!' and I say, still patiently, 'but they are just what I want and must have'—and again he goes on to excuse—and then I get mad and cry at him—'God damn you! What right have you to protest against my having what I want and will pay for?'—and the man hurries to the other side of the counter, evidently fearing me for some barbarian who needs be given lee-way!" I said to W., "Put on your red tie now, and you'll be in ball costume." But he protested: "I don't know about a tie: what tie? I have never come to a tie yet—perhaps a handkerchief to protect the neck, but that is all." I indicated the McKay picture. "Is there a tie in it?" he said, adding reflectively, "Well, if there is, it was one of the accidents—it was not in accord with the rule—sometimes perhaps worn to protect the throat."

Gilchrist had been in at W.'s after I left last night. W. "wondered" if H. G. was "to be here all the summer"—explaining—"He always speaks of work—work—as if he was working pretty hard." Committee in with 125 dollars surplus money of dinner today. W. said nothing to me about it this evening, and I did not inquire. In the west, running rapidly from southwest, were dark banks of clouds. I remarked their beauty, and W. responded: "I have been watching them for an hour—they are rarely beautiful—vast, deep, slatey masses, hurrying across the sky, chasing one another. See those now!—how they go and go, tireless and without number. It has always been one of my finer joys, to watch the varied, varying, ever-changing, inter-locking, cloud-shapes!" And of the evening in general: "It is rarely and supremely comforting, this evening—don't you think? The very dubiousness of things—the haziness, moisture—add to the fascination. But"—pointing above—"there's no more rain in those clouds—for the present." And a star or two shot bright gleams through the gaps, W. soliciting my attention to "the ravishingness" of the panorama.

Morris had very promptly today assented to the idea of translating the Sarrazin essay on Walt Whitman. W. himself greatly pleased and grateful. Morris had given me a more satisfying rendering of the Sarrazin letter, which now W. insisted I should sit down in front of the house and read again. He appeared more and more struck, and the passage which Sarrazin said would have been the matter of his speech had he attended the celebration W. had me read even more than deliberately, and with the minutest attention on his part. "I detect in it," he said, "a characteristic grandeur and power—just as in the essay itself." He thought this letter "a great acquisition" to the book.

As we sat talking an oldish, rather small man passed, saluting W. as if he knew him formally well. After he was beyond hearing, W. turned to me: "You have asked me about the old Booth? Junius Brutus Booth?—Well—that man there who just passed us would serve for him, except that Booth was more graceful in port and more distinguished in outward expression. Booth was a smallish man—though not small enough to seem stunted—rather well-built, as this man was. I did not know him personally—yet I saw him so often on the street as well as in the theatre, that I can almost claim to have known him as a person." I repeated to W. O'Connor's description of Booth, and W. assented: "Yes, that is essentially true: no one seeing him on the boards, would have called him a small man in any sense." John Gilbert, just dead the other day, W. never knew. "Of course I have seen him—and he must have been a noble fellow—everybody appears to have loved him." But the truth was "the actors are a noble set, anyhow"—and had always entered keenly into his "emotionality and affection." He had been offered benefits— "and they were generously offered, I know and realize fully" —and indeed—"I should esteem it a great triumph to have a clientele among the actors—and perhaps I have? Just now it would be hard to feel certain of it." "And then a benefit for me! That would crown all!"

Referred to review of Rolleston's new volume in Critic— of the Critic's "coldness"—in all respects lack of passion. W.: "That is Joe Gilder to the life—he thinks that being judicial. He has a couple of enthusiasms—for Lowell, for Holmes, for instance—but beyond these he is so much ice— so much marble." And among the Gilders, "Joe is the least— always the least!" Ed brought him some letters as we sat there. W. started to open them—then stopped. "No"—he said, "I won't now: it's too dark—and my eyes are no good anyhow!"

WITH WALT WHITMAN IN CAMDEN

Thursday, June 27, 1889

8 P.M. W. sat in front of the house. As he looked around, hearing my step, he exclaimed, "Oh! here is Horace coming—and with something in his hand which looks very like a bottle of ink for me!" And after we had shaken hands, he added, "So you got the ink? And it is the kind we were after?" Inspecting the label—seeing the inscription "steel pen" thereon—"That is the only thing about it which raises my suspicion" but turning the next instant to Mann's own label and adding—"But this is a guarantee!" Then he laughed. "And to show my faith in it, I will pay you for it forthwith!" doing so out of his pocket without delay.

Mr. Button, his next-door neighbor, came up the next instant—shook hands—said he was glad W. held himself up so well. To which W. responded: "So am I! I get along so-so—very well, considering all things." Then made a sudden break from this topic: "And today I had a splendid visitor—Horace here knows him—a splendid fellow—handsome, a typical American. He is a Boston man now—connected with the Herald there—is now on the way South. A young man—or not very young, either, probably thirty-one or along there—but young in spirit; and he is all ardor—has it in his bonnet that the world needs reforming—is a theosophist, Socialist, Anarchist,—yes, even Anarchist—I believe that word could be used; but oh! very ardent about it—ardent enough to touch even me, I do believe! He has been a good deal about in the world—has been for some years located with the Boston Herald: the paper now sends him down there. I think he is married—I know he is a man, way in to his backbone. He sat here with me today—said to me, 'I am going South: what have you got to say to me about it—what word to give me?' And so I responded with an expression often on the lips of an old Long-Islander I knew— 'I should say to you, Sylvester, only this—nothing but this' "—here W. raised his forefinger admonishingly—"hold your horses—hold your horses!" Here W. turned his finger my way, and said waggishly— "And that's for you, too!" Adding: "Sylvester [Baxter] thoroughly lives in the conviction that the world is to be saved by reforming it—that things are all end up now—that we threaten to go to the devil, the whole pack of us, if we don't make a turn." After Button had gone W. continued with me: "Sylvester was here half an hour—perhaps three-quarters. He is very enthusiastic about the South—goes to Kentucky and Tennessee—seems imbued with a faith that the South is the greater America—will one day awake to that fact—and I don't know but he's to some extent right. I knew many fellows from that section—from East Tennessee—and it was a pretty good race. One fellow out of all—and illiterate, too—I think I loved almost more than any other person I ever met. Sylvester told me that he saw very little of Kennedy—that Kennedy worked very hard through the day, then went home—so applied himself, week and week!" "And certainly, Horace, Sylvester is our man—I am sure of it—ain't you?—he belongs to us, we to him."

He referred to the money brought him yesterday. This item in connection therewith in Press this morning:

The committee of Camden citizens who had charge of the banquet recently tendered Walt Whitman, the poet, at Morgan's Hall, on his seventieth birthday, visited his house yesterday in a body. Geoffrey Buckwalter, the secretary of the committee, surprised the poet by handing him a bag that contained $125 in gold, the balance from the sale of the tickets after all expenses had been met. They also presented him with a nurse's chair for his use about the house.

I don't imagine W. was at all "surprised."—"They came together—three of 'em—Buckwalter, Ambler Armstrong, Derousse—and they left me a hundred and twenty-five dollars. This chair," tapping its arm, "was also paid for by the proceeds, they told me." And he added: "What an investment it was, too!—the best made since my sickness!" Dwelt upon "the rare beauty" of the evening—pointed to the swaying trees, the (at last) clear sky.

I wrote to Burroughs this forenoon, and to Stedman this evening. W. said: "I am glad—glad for both." And when I told him what I had said to Stedman, he exclaimed, "Oh! that is very good—I am especially satisfied to have you tell him that!" Adding: "Stedman is so genuine: and it is a peculiar fact, that Stedman, though not very far from being an old man, seems to get more ardent the older he grows. And Howells, too—why, Sylvester came right down from Howells —says he is on the right track—getting more radical, socialistic, all that"—though for the Socialism, W. did not know. But when I asked—"Don't you see why it is all the radicals like you—like Leaves of Grass? That going to most all books and literary men, they find so little life throbbing in them, whereas the life is the first and prevailing quality of L. of G.? They do not look for you to endorse their theories, but only to be alive and possess the big human spirit, which is always an ally." W. exclaimed: "Oh! that is a beautiful, pregnant thought, and that I could wish true!"

I looked over file of World today. No poem. Said W.: "No —I did not expect it. One of the letters Ed brought me last night while you were here was from Julius, and though he sent me the money for the first piece, he never mentioned the other. So in replying, I sent a fresh copy of the little poemet. Probably the other copy fell into the hands of someone in the office who never heard of me—this I sent addressed personally to Julius—the other was sent to the World. Or perhaps the other never got there—who knows?—it may have fallen into the charge of the post-office man who took a foreign letter addressed to me at 'Campden' to Pumptown—bright man, that, wasn't he?—damned fool! It was so simple, any idiot should have been able to judge for what place it was intended

—'Campden, New Jersey'—and seeing the foreign stamp alone should have helped it along, seeing how apt a stranger is to slip up that way. The letter is upstairs yet—I'll give it to you. It is very long and gushing—the writer or writeress—I think it is a woman—has let him or herself out pretty boldly. I've read it about half through—shall probably not get back to it again."

Kerr objected to my use of "sun-glown" as obsolete. W. said: "Let me commend you that you stick to it: I should do so in your case." I had done so. W. said: "I have a letter from Bucke in which he says he has heard from Sarrazin—that Sarrazin has been in London, goes back to Paris, will pass the summer in the country—much the same thing Sarrazin wrote you, except that Bucke mentions the place." I went upstairs to get the Sarrazin book for Morris. W. said: "I feel as though I ought to give Morris a book anyhow—and we'll do so yet." Adding "Tell him for me, to observe this in translating—that he get every word, sign,—every significant touch, —what not—down to the last turn, the final commas, periods. The quotations he need only indicate." I spoke of intending to write to Ingersoll of which he said: "Yes, do so—and give him my love." And of writing to Edward Emerson: "I don't think you'll make much by that—probably nothing at all. Edward Emerson is a bad egg—more and more I see evidence of that— and his sister, too." I spoke of him as "more respectable than his father"—at which W. laughed: "Yes—in that kind of respectability!" Then advised me: "When you see Burroughs next—broach this subject—he is an Emerson man—he will tell you lots and lots you'll like to know. I don't know how much John knew Emerson personally if at all, but spiritually he is an Emerson man."

Bill Duckett came up as I sat there. Had had a sister die. W. gave him 10 dollars. "I am more interested than you know, Bill," he said, "when you get settled in the city, write me how you like it, or come see me." And after Bill had gone, W.

spoke feelingly of the sudden death of the sister and explained the condition of things.

Friday, June 28, 1889

8 P.M. W. was out when I arrived, but shortly came along under Ed's charge. He did not appear well nor was he well. "I have had a very bad day of it," he explained, "very bad: in fact, a very bad yesterday, too—two days way down in the valley; but this evening I feel much changed and relieved." Several children came up, and for some time he kept his arms about two of them and held them there, even as he talked. As usual he asked of me: "What news?" and added—"And it has been quiet with me, too." Inside was a bundle on which he had pasted an inscription: "Two books: one for Frank Williams and one for Herbert Gilchrist." These were the pocketbooks, so much urged by me, which he had finally dedicated.

He suddenly remarked: "I got a letter and paper from Germany today—have them here." Went fumbling in his pocket—drew forth a blue envelope. "Perhaps your father will render it for me—the article. The letter is in English as it is. I shall want the paper back so I can send to Dr. Bucke, who is a German scholar. It is interesting to me to know what they think of us way over there. It comes from Berlin, which is a center, I suppose, an important center." I read the letter, which was addressed to "Mr. Walt Whitman, the Poet," and was as follows:

Dear Sir,
Dear Poet, Friend, and Master,
To celebrate your seventieth birthday, I your grateful and devoted admirer, have written some words of sympathy and congratulation, and published them in the issue of June 2nd of the paper I am editing just now, viz. the 'Deutsche Presse,' the official organ of the league of German authors (Deutschen Schriftsteller-Verband). I trust I may be able some day to devote to you and your work a serious essay better suited to do justice to your

genius than was possible in that aphoristic article. However, those few lines will at least serve as an unambiguous testimony of my deep and true devotion to you, and as it may give you pleasure to hear of an unknown German friend of yours, I take the liberty to send you that birthday paper, hoping you will look upon it with kind and indulgent eyes.

Ever yours sincerely and affectionately
Edward Bertz

W. remarked: "I am well aware of it, that my work has no currency in Germany. This letter is very warm, to be sure." Adding: "See what your father can make of it, if he will." I translated passages for him as he sat there, and he listened gravely, and thought them "probably significant of the whole article."

I had with me, a rough manuscript of my book matter, and read to him from it, here and there. He listened intently. At the "non-literary" passage he exclaimed, "Oh! that is very good—it is a great point—and a great thing to have somebody make it!" And to the closing paragraph exclaimed—"Strong! Noble!" I did not linger. Going down Federal Street I met Gilchrist and Harned; Gilchrist turned back and went to town with me. Harned and he had taken tea together. Gilchrist argued with me against the use of Morse's bust for frontispiece. I guess I made it plain, that, while open to counsel, I had fully determined upon using it, provided a good reproduction was secured. Gilchrist's line of argument did not impress me as broad and generous, while his manner was more or less offensive. He said W. was "self-willed," that "his judgment of a portrait was of no value whatever," that he "liked Morse's bust because it was the latest thing" and that I ought to defer "to competent judges that knew." He was sure the "Morse bust would not please the British readers," and I replied that in making up the volume I was not seeking to please anybody—that my plan was, the matter having been put in my charge, to give what I thought the most fitting record of the event. He spoke of Harned's approval of his position and I retorted that Harned had just dined with Gilchrist—that Harned had never before expressed such objection to me. The whole manner of Gilchrist's argument was supercilious. He raised the objection to having any portrait. But who supposes he would have objected if his wretched and untrue presentment of W. had been solicited?

Saturday, June 29, 1889

5 P.M. W. in very poor condition indeed today. Sat in the parlor when I came, fanning himself. The day quite warm. Said he had been experiencing one of his "very worst days." Looked haggard and weary. We talked only a little while. I had given Frank Williams his book today. When I described to W. his pleasure at receiving it, W. said: "Well—that, if nothing else, makes it worth while to give!" Talked about Gilchrist's onslaught on Morse's bust, but W. advised that we take no account of it. Corning came in while I was there, and we afterwards went off together. To C.'s hope that he would weather through the summer all right, W. said: "Oh! thanks! but it's all right either way! But I guess I will!" He called my attention to a bunch of wheat-stalks on the table. "A lady brought them in. And do you notice the delicious smell?" As usual he made no complaint whatever of his sickness, only saying that it "disqualified" him from all duties. "But in a little while we are going down to the river—Ed and I." I have not seen him in this condition for months. It raises my solicitude. As we left he took up a local paper—said he would try to read.

Sunday, June 30, 1889

7.50 P.M. W. was not at home on my coming, but in ten minutes or so was wheeled up by Ed. Though the evening was mild, he did not stay out of doors—came in instantly—said he was tired—had passed another very bad day, &c. Had been down to the river. I gave him my father's translation of the German article. He was "highly pleased to have it"—and said after some commendatory words of mine: "No doubt it is true. It is interesting and remarkable to know that the best criticisms of us nowadays are abroad—I think we can fairly say—all of them abroad. It is a fact to be duly noted— chewed upon."

Had read the papers today, but not with an absorbed interest. Had "an idea," he said, that perhaps a portion of this German article could be "appropriately used in the book." But he would have to read it first. Said his mails were "singularly destitute of news" nowadays. "Even Doctor, though writing, writes nothing of interest." Clifford, in his sermon this forenoon, made eloquent reference to "Song of Myself" as illustrating man's song of man and therefore song of God. W. thought that "a striking application—one after Clifford's usual vein"—&c. I stayed but briefly—long enough to know his condition, to deliver my own messages and get his. Then kissed him goodnight.

Monday, July 1, 1889

7.50 P.M. It has been a rainy close day, keeping W. well indoors. Sat in the parlor reading letters that had come in evening mail. Asked me: "And what of the day? What is the news?" And when I echoed his question, "Oh! I guess I am better—not much, but probably easier—at least this evening!" Today brought Unity, in which was the O'Connor article. I gave W. a dozen copies. "I am very glad to get 'em!" he exclaimed. "And by the way," he went on, "do you see Liberty? Did you get a copy today? There was a paragraph in it about O'Connor: Was it yours? Was it from you?" The paragraph to which he alluded was as follows:

William Douglas O'Connor, the author of the "Good Gray Poet," whom Liberty counted with pride among its warmest friends, is dead. The world of letters loses in him one of its grandest and most unique personalities. Mr. O'Connor was a student, a scholar, a passionate lover of art, and took no part in practical affairs. But the few short productions of his pen will yet be recognized as the ornament and glory of English polemical literature. Some day the conspiracy of the "paltry and venomous swarm" of literary hypocrites and prudes, poisoners and blackguards, will be put down by public intelligence, and then Mr. O'Connor's defense of Walt Whitman will be ranked higher than the "Provincial Letters."

W. said of it, "Anyhow, I thought it was yours, it had something of your ring in it. It is rather lofty, rather high, certainly strong. But I don't know—often I think whether after all, by and by given its due, O'Connor's name will not go down resonant in the centuries. I may be mistaken, that may be putting it too strong, but somehow I am led to make it a positive belief." And as to the complaint made against my piece that it was too strong, "Well, why should we not be strong in discussing a strong man? And especially with us— knowing him so well—how could strong words be avoided?" And then he asked, "Shall I send a paper to Mrs. O'Connor? I hear nothing at all from her, not a word—have not since that first letter after O'Connor's death—nor do I write to her, for that matter, but I send papers almost daily." He had not heard till I told him now of Tucker's severe sickness. "I read that first page—'On Picket Duty'—I am usually sure it is Tucker's own, and of course incisive."

By and by I told him I had "a letter from John," had just received it at the Post Office. Read to him, he all absorption.

West Park N. Y.
June 29—89

My dear Horace;

Was glad to hear from you & get a further word about the birthday dinner, etc. You say nothing specific about Walt; I hope he keeps well, I am always anxious about him when the hot weather comes on. Do make an effort to get him away to the shore, or the mountains. Of course he will resist, but he ought to know that the mere *change* would give him a lift & prolong his days. Let me know if something can not be done.

I wish I could suggest some likely names for your list of fond subscribers. I would like to add my own, but do not feel able this year. I should write to *Childs* & *Carnegie* & other rich & benevolent men—

If you learn anything definite about the death of O'Connor let me hear it. Tell me also if you think Walts chances good to pull through the summer.

I am very busy in my vineyards, but hope to find time to get off a week or so in July

If Walt could come here & occupy part of my old house with me, he could be as much at his ease as at home: he could bring Mrs Davis & his nurse & we could have a jolly time. See if he takes to the idea at all—

Sincerely yours
John Burroughs

(You could come too)

"Ah!" he exclaimed, "That would be to take the whole shanty! But then, the shanty isn't big altogether!" Then talked of "John's place on the Hudson," its "rare beauty" etc., and remarked, "He says nothing at all in that about the book—the pocket edition I sent him—nor has he written yet to me. I wonder if it reached him all right? I sent it off the same day with Gilder's, and Gilder I have heard from. I do not suppose it went astray, but I am never sure till I have had word of mouth, word of letter." Adding, "But when you write —you'll probably write within a few days—ask him about it." After a while when I came to go, and had kissed him good bye, I asked, "and what of John? What shall I tell him? Shall I say you'll come?" He laughed, "No—don't tell him that; but tell him we take his invitation at its true intent, not charily, not meanly, but as he knows we know how to take it! Tell him we are still about as we were, weathering it out—not consciously retreating—getting off to the river daily, there to sit perhaps for hours, reading some, writing some little, not spurning life but holding fast to it still." And as to John's health: "I hope it is better—indeed, I believe it must be. That is one of the things we never cease hoping for!" Referred to the German paper. "I like it very much, it is a little disconnected, but strong, evidently given out by a man who knows us. And the best of it is," here he laughed good-humoredly, "it helps the good cause along, and that of itself is a great deal." He thought the last paragraph might be used in the book.

I quoted to him a remark made to Mrs. Burleigh, by Prof. Giddings, of Bryn Mawr College, that Donnelly was a lunatic and ought to be incarcerated. W. remarked, "It is the old, old story: woe be to the man who believes in any doxy that is not mine—does not wear my stamp!" Then referred to Delia Bacon: "The sweetest, eloquentest, grandest woman, I think, that America has so far produced—a woman rare among women, rare among the rare. Romanesque,—beautiful, not after the ideals of the fashion plates, but after Greek ideals. A nature sweet, noble, sure, attracting when encountered in the right way. No, I never met her, but somehow I feel that I have known her, nevertheless, known her better, perhaps, than if meeting her—coming upon her, as it is understood—that breaker of charms too often—personally. Grasping her by knowledge of her life, by obicular, oracular, evidences. The very best, after all, as we often find." He dwelt upon her "beauty," and that "of all women in America so far she stands alone, in advance. Greater than Margaret Fuller—a larger type. I know of no such woman today. We have plenty of the intellectual, philanthropic, Christian Union, Woman's Christian Association sort of women, women of a weak, thin womanliness, but none to vie with her—none at all. Not that I have the least word to say against our women, except as

showing wherein they must change in the future of America."
—"It was not surprising Emerson helped Delia Bacon. She
was eminently attractive to serious-minded persons, always.
See how even Hawthorne sends out one of her books with a
note bearing his name, Hawthorne, so chary of lending name
or countenance to anything that savored of pretense. And she
was poor, of course, very unworldly, just in all ways such a
woman as was calculated to bring the whole literary pack down
on her, the orthodox, cruel, stately, dainty, over-fed literary
pack—worshiping tradition, unconscious of this day's honest
sunlight!"

As to O'Connor's "the brilliant knave, Macaulay" W. said:
"O'Connor was very violently set against Macaulay because
of his vilification, as William thought calumny of his idols—of
Bacon, for one—then of others. Macaulay was a brilliant sort
of a man—a Moncure Conway-ish man, if one may so say it—
though that would not exactly place him. Conway is by far
not so bright or big, though unveracious enough, to be sure.
Oh! the veracious man! how rare a creature he is! That is
where Emerson is the top of the heap, never a lapse in him
from his integrity, never an effort to be bright at the expense
of truth. Always the same serene, lovely spirit, moving about
smoothing away cares and worries!" And he thought further
that "John Stuart Mill must be such another man; a man
who could be himself, who could never be made to go with
the pack!" I said there were errors in O'Connor's book which I
had no doubt would not have escaped his eye had he examined
the proofs. W. assented, "That is true, I am sure. He was an
extraordinary keen man, on scent for errors—would spare
no pains—would roar and storm like a mad bull if crossed in
his work—even if having vital changes—necessary changes—
suggested to him. I never knew a man more vigilant."

As to our book, "I should say, leaded bourgeois would best
do the business. The matter will all go in, surely. It is wonderful how much of one's manuscript a few compact pages of

type will chaw up—consume—do away with: sometimes it is a terrible astonishment and ordeal for a poor writer to go through." We had found that out in our early days with November Boughs, the rapid disposal of copy of which "scared" him. Said the ink I brought him the other day was "just the thing—the very thing I wanted, at last."

Tuesday, July 2, 1889

8 P.M. W. sitting at the parlor window, reading papers. He had not been out today. Rain was prevalent—violent showers. Said, however, "I seem to be a bit better—not enough to boast of, but better!" He had read the Unity piece. "And I can easily say I like it better than ever—even better than in the manuscript. I have sent away seven or eight of the copies you left with me, one to Mrs. O'Connor, one to California, to Charles Eldridge there, one to Burroughs; did you send one to John? And there was another for Kennedy, then for Bucke —and Stedman ought to have one too: if you will send his, I won't worry about it. Stedman knew O'Connor well—yes, was intimate with him—and he would like to have this. By the way, the last number of the Book Buyer has a portrait of Stedman, a colorless sort of picture, a photo-engraving, perhaps." Was it anything like? "Yes—something—Stedman, with all the animation taken out, which is not Stedman at all. People generally, I should judge, would regard it as a great piece of work: I have my doubts."

At this he reached forward to the table. "See this—a picture of the baby"—taking from envelope—"Tom sends it down from the country. Perfect! Perfect! After all, Gutekunst is on the top of the heap, don't you think? There's no better picture than that!" I urged, "And you'll go soon to let him get you as he wishes?" To which—"I shall try. Someday when I feel in first-class condition I'll venture over—perhaps get a cab down here at the ferry." Then he ruminated,

"Nothing can be predicated of a photo—it hits if it hits, not otherwise. It seems true of all photos, that you can't start out to produce any certain effect: you must submit to circumstances!" At this, mention of Gilchrist's criticism of bust. W. said warmly, "I did not fall in love with the photo of the bust: I did not dislike it, but it did not warm me. But the bust itself? Oh! that was no humor in me: I think the bust a victory—that it has not been surpassed." As to G.'s feeling that W. "knew nothing about art" W. said laughingly: "Had he said that to me I should have acquiesced: I do not: that is an easy way over that point; but then I should have added, though it is true I know nothing about art, it is sufficient for me to know this:—I like it—I like the bust—it possesses me!" In this attitude "I could not yield," he said, "anymore than you could." "But at any rate," he went on with a smile, "this picture," picking up the baby again, "this picture is a great success. Tom don't write much—only enough to say he likes the place."

Explained that he had "sent a big book to Edward Bertz today," and further, "I addressed it to Potsdam, where it may find him or may not. Do you know the lay of Potsdam? How it stands, with reference to Berlin, for instance? I have no idea. Know it only in a dim uncertain way, chiefly for Frederick the Great's connection with it." Fumbled in his pocket, drew forth a crumpled envelope, addressed simply "Horace Traubel." "Take this," he said, "you may be able to use all or a portion of it in the book. The German piece is there—I have made some few changes in it." The envelope contained also the piece from the Post of last Thursday containing account of visit of testimonial committee to Whitman and payment to him of the money. He had interlined this report at one place to say: "he was averse to the public dinner at the outset, but said he should 'let the boys have their own way.'" He had likewise interlined the translation of the Bertz piece somewhat, but not markedly. "Whether you can use this depends, of course, upon how much space the general matter fills."

Morris had said to me today that Sarrazin was "extravagant." W. laughed to hear of it. "The word is just the one I should myself use—yes, extravagant—grandly extravagant—damned extravagant, like the sun that shines, the seas, nature's always liberal, spendthrifty self!" Proceeding then: "It is a good word—extravagant: Napoleon Bonaparte was extravagant: don't you remember the German general's protest: Napoleon was extravagant—he violated all the rules of war—'but—sir, don't he win his battles?' 'Yes, God damn 'im! he wins his battles—wins 'em!'—but violates all the rules of war in doing so!" And so of Sarrazin, "he gets there—tells his story: I don't know that we need trouble about his way of doing it!" Then, "Tell Morris to take his time: we can wait." I saw Dave today cudgeling over plate proofs of E. P. Gould's Whitman book. W., interested to know about it, made it matter for joking. "I do not feel at all responsible for it: I gave it lean support—so they cannot hold me, whatever the result. But wouldn't it be funny Horace, if the book should be a success—should sell? After our own experience, that would almost be irony: a funny result, surely!" I asked him for a copy of the first fold of the pocket edition, so I could get Bucke the copy he wished specially bound. W. promised to put it out. "And I'll put out a number," he said, "say 15 or 20 or even more. We can have them all made up. I am curious myself to see if I should not like them."

Asked me about Amiel. "I am resolved to keep a sharp eye for him," W. said, "I have seen hints of him here and there which have raised my curiosity." Inquired what was the "appearance of Tom's brother John?" And when I described him—"Oh! I think that's the fellow! There's somebody comes down on the wharf—has passed us a number of times while we sat there—goes out into the stream in a boat. Always accosts me pleasantly, in a way which says 'I know you well!' I set

him down as Tom's brother from the first." Frank he knows—
John very distantly, if at all. John rarely makes much of
the social life at Tom's.

Wednesday, July 3, 1889

7.45 P.M. Spent half an hour with W. He sat at the parlor
window, fanning himself, his legs braced against the table. It
was a close hour, as it had been all day, though the rain,
which had come in violent showers, seemed now suspended.
Already the din of explosives: a number of times in our talk
W. had to wait for volleys of fire-crackers to pass. From
Washington the signal service men this morning announced a
"muggy" day. W. remarked: "I guess this is it—I guess it is
'muggy'!"—"I do not, of course, get out such days as these—
we can no longer swim!" etc., etc. I called W.'s attention to a
postal I had received today from Yarros. He said promptly:
"You will do it? I hope you will." I wondered if Mrs. O'C.
would give me a few biographical dates? "Yes, I think she
will. Write to her about it. I wrote her yesterday—sent her a
postal, telling her about the paper. But if I were you I should
not wait to hear from her—commence at once: then if she sends
what you can use, weave it in. I am very glad you received
such a request, the mere request means a good deal to me, the
mere idea there is somebody who wants to know—some responsive souls, here and there, awake to the man." People
criticised my article for its applause—it was "too strong."
But W. reiterated, "It is much as if they should complain of
the attraction of gravitation, that it was too strong: when
pointed out its power, that they had never thought it in
that way—that they had never so seen it!" Then he said
reflectively, in a more quiet tone: "O'Connor was an outgrowth
of—was con amore with—the Elizabethan period in English
history, with the men, influences of that time, a growth out of
the tree—a limb—a noble issue, living, making a peculiar

record, suited to the environment, circumstances, men, of these modern times. It would be very happy for you to make use of biographical figures—data of that sort—but you could not get them from me, I have no head for them—could not supply them."

Speaking of the absurd protest of a bandmaster in Philadelphia against employment of Germans for public orchestration, W. laughed merrily, "I don't know why it may not as well happen soon that somebody arises to protest against foreign books, German music, Alfred Tennyson, yes—even the Bible! Isn't the Bible a foreign product? It would be perfectly consistent." Thereupon union with Canada entered discussion. Said he: "The older I grow, the broader, deeper, larger that word Solidarity is impressed on my convictions—Solidarity: where can one produce its substitute? To me, the largest word in human resources—the largest word in the catalogue—fullest of meaning, potential, all-inclusive." And then: "God save the bandmasters when such a word is at last proclaimed!—or perhaps bandmasters of this stripe will not exist under such a dispensation!" He labored with this for some time, then diverged, "The papers are making much of corruption in French politics—as though we had to go far to find corruption on this side! Another great affair in France just now seems to be the sale of Millet's pictures—the big picture, the 'Angelus'—which seems to have been bought by some one for about a hundred thousand dollars. Think of this, then think of Millet, Millet dead, his little children—or rather, not little, for they are grown up now, I suppose—his children and poor old wife finding it hard to make both ends meet, he dying off there in poverty—nothing in the world, they selling what remained—old paintings, sketches, for what they would fetch, the world fattening on his genius!" But "That is, as you say, 'the inevitable decree of the Fates'—it always happens— one has to do nothing but expect it!" Here he laughed again— "But there's no doubt the papers are full of it: between it and

342

President Harrison's appointment of Bill this or that to this or that office, the papers seem to be having a bothersome time of it!"

Asked me if I thought I could insert the whole of the matter he gave me in the envelope last night. Promised him to let him see MS. in a day or two. Suggested to him that a good capstone would be two or three lines—a poem—from him. I expected him to laugh that proposition out of countenance, or quietly say, "good! good!" and never refer to it again, but instead he declared, "I shall consider it—it is an idea—perhaps something will be suggested!" W. handed me a package from the table. "Here are the sheets," he said, "twenty of them, I shall have twenty copies of the book bound Dr. Bucke's way." On the package he had written, after addressing in corner to Oldach, the following:

> 20 *Autograph*
> *First Sheets* for Bindery
> for 20 copies L. of G.
>   bound in green morocco ordinary mode
>   (*without* the pocket book flap
>   trimmed close—full gilt)

Spoke of this as "purely an experiment," adding—"Perhaps I shall like it—perhaps not: I have no idea at all."

My niece had written in the course of a note to my sister, "There is a nasty dirty polecat prowling around here and nobody dares to try to catch it." W. laughed uproariously over my recital of this. "It's too good to keep!" he exclaimed, "and thoroughly like a child—an exquisite touch, which no grown-up person could have given!"

Thursday, July 4, 1889

11:30 A.M. Called in at W.'s, was there about half an hour. Had taken MS. of book along. Used his blue pencil for numbering pages. Discussed ways and means. He looked rather bad. Was in bathroom on my arrival, but came shortly over into his bedroom. But had forgotten glasses and said, "I shall have to ask you to get them for me." Characteristically, however, the Ledger, which he wished to go down stairs for Mrs. Davis, he went all the way across the room to find, then back again to the stairway to send flying down: would not accept my offer to do for him. Yet seemed very weak, and was. The night had been a bad one—the noise great. "One man our neighborhood is blessed with, lives right across the street. He went to bed early last evening so he could get up at 12 or 1 o'clock and keep the rest of us awake for the rest of the night, and he succeeded. And he or his boy—there the boy sits now—have been at it ever since." Across the way the unknowing boy, comfortably settled in a rocking chair on the pavement, was incessantly pitching exploding fire-crackers right and left. W. continued to fan himself. "There is a Mrs. Button next door, a poor old woman, she has been sick for years—is nothing now but sensation—as I am apt to describe it, is like a mass of sensitive jelly; yet there are a thousand and one tortures imposed on her because she cannot get away from these demons—is too old, too sick. They call this noise 'patriotism'—a queer patriotism it is, to my mind!"

Talking of the book, he said, "It should have an index: every good book owes its readers an index, but in this case I suppose it is impossible." Said he would let me have the MS. as I desired by 8 o'clock this evening. I must submit it to McKay tomorrow. A couple of foreign pamphlets of translations he had laid out for me to see. One, by the Italian Gamberale.[?] Prefatory note to this he said he had never read. "No one ever translated it for me—so of course I have no idea what is its purport." Should we have Lincoln Eyre render it into English? "I should like it so, if he could be led to do it freely." The other was French. Said W., "It is evidently by the young fellow to whom Sarrazin referred in one of his letters—dead now, I believe. We seem to be much whacked at abroad nowadays—for good or evil. Everybody is getting a word in on us, sweet or sour." Before I left he called my attention to a long sad letter from Mrs. O'Connor, then to a letter from Bucke, but of this last he said, "It is newsless—as most of Doctor's letters have been lately." I did not linger. He said, "I shall not look through this seriatim, but take it up as I can—as I am in the humor. It's a big bulk to read, but then, a sane wise rebel somewhere says, I don't have to—unless I choose."

7.50 P.M. It kept on raining all day. W. in the parlor, his fan again in hand. But now, at the last moment, comes perfect cloudlessness, the new moon, northwest wind, and a greatly moderated temperature. "Much cooler—don't you think?" W. at once inquired. It cleared up too late however for him to get out. "I was hoping the rain would continue—that it would rain all night." The noise had broken out afresh with the first clear half-hour. I wrote to Mrs. O'Connor this afternoon for data as to O'C. for use in Liberty article, as advised by W. He said: "I wrote to her yesterday. You probably will hear: it was right to ask." I wrote also to Kennedy, Morse, Garland and Brinton about our affair. W. asked, "And Burroughs—have you written to him yet? And did you ask him about the morocco book? if it arrived all right?" as I had, indeed. W. then pointed to a roll on the table—"There is your manuscript—you may take it along." Addressed in blue pencil—"Horace Traubel MS."—and pasted on an ink-written slip as follows

Suggestions
same sized page ab't as
"Specimen Days"
type Bourgeois leaded
run the letters, telegrams,
&c: the pages
—not block'd out
          pretty thick paper

On sketch of title page I had accidentally written "Camden's tribute" instead of "Compliment." He had made the change, and now said, "I don't like 'tribute'—I know there are people who use it, but to me it has a bastard sound—it never satisfies me." Commenting on the MS. in general—"As I promised, I did not go through the MS. seriatim—still I have gone through it. I said at the time of the dinner that I felt suffocated with sugar and honey and somehow I realize that feature ever more decidedly in reading this as it is collected together. But the matter itself, taken simply in chief, I like better and better the more I see of it—better far than in the hearing: it certainly has a good ring." As to my protests that this was a rally of friends, who did not come for analyses but for celebration, W. said—"Oh! I can realize that it was all just right just as it was—that it could not have been different. Indeed, I can say, what you already know, that it was all welcome to me—all— every word of it: and I know it came from the right spot and to the right spot. And anyhow, how O'Connor—our glorious O'Connor—would have revelled in the book you are getting out—the addresses, letters, all: but O'Connor is gone! As it is, John—Burroughs—Doctor and Kennedy—oh! they will be all eyes and ears! I can see them—anticipate their eagerness— even John's!" He would like to write a few lines to go on the title page, except that "I am averse to having to do with anything about myself that is so strong—so vehement—as that book has grown to be." He wondered if Sherman "would give us the whole mass of proofs at once—so we could get in touch at once with the ensemble—take in the whole area!" He explained—"I have made a few verbal suggestions in running over the MS., you will see them: but have left general matters wholly alone."

In the MS., (my portion) where I had written simply "Whitman's nurse, Edward Wilkins"—he suggested "Whitman's Canadian friend and nurse"—an admirable change, removing the servility implied by the first phrase. I had written of W.'s being "indebted" to the meeting "for at least a part of his present comfort"—the magnetism, etc. He considered it ought to be made much stronger (which I could not have known) so wrote instead of "comfort," "almost exhilaration"—another efficient record. In Harned's speech he proposed speaking of "army hospitals" instead of simply "hospitals," and "secession war" instead of "war," and "the person Walt Whitman" instead of "the man Walt Whitman"—certainly, this last, a radical improvement in musicalness; suggested also "His love for the aggregate race" instead of "for the whole race of man." In Gilder's speech he changed the order of the mention of "Cooper, Emerson, Whittier and Bryant" to "Cooper, Bryant, Emerson and Whittier"—a significant re-casting. No doubt, if he had been given more time to inspect he would have made other suggestions.

Friday, July 5, 1889

7.50 P.M. W. not home the moment of my call, so I sat down in the parlor, reading and waiting. Soon, however, he came along. I heard him say to Ed as the chair wheeled up to the door—"I guess I shall go right in." At which I hastened out and we greeted each other. His passage to his usual place at the parlor window decidedly laborious. I remarked, "You don't seem to gain any strength in the legs"—to which he responded, "No—none at all—nor anywhere else, for that matter: in fact, I am losing, especially in the legs, which grow worse and worse—are hardly any good at all any longer." But he had passed "a mitigated day," and spoke of the modified weather; while, "the Fourth over—and its noise—we have peace again." He dwelt with eloquent voice upon the aspect of the river. "The mere air this evening is a blessed thing to breathe in—but the river seemed rarely fine—I watched it as it flowed a long while, a long while." He asked me about some of the big buildings which he could descry from his position on the wharf—"the big buildings—all gone up since my day there—these two or three years past." He could see the tall towers, "vast marble and granite pinnacles," which were new to his eyes. My description appeared greatly to interest him, and he questioned me keenly in detail, as is his wont. Said Frank Williams was over today. "He came in only very briefly—just in to say goodby, almost: the kind of a visit a man appreciates when he is not feeling braggy." When I spoke of Williams as a good, genuine, almost boyish, fellow, W. responded, "Yes, that is Frank—every word of it!" He said again, "Frank appears to have come over in part to thank me for the book."

I had seen McKay today and Ferguson will do composition of the book. Dave will leave it absolutely in my hands to arrange. He goes away Monday, will be gone six weeks or so—goes as far west as Denver. I made it very clear that my control should be absolute, so far as matter and typographical make-up is concerned. Paper, printing and cover he will contract for himself or with me. I brought with me a proof of the bust reproduction. Lacked in effect. But W. looked at it a long and earnest while in the waning light, commenting, "Why, Horace—I like it very well—it seems to me well enough. Of course you know I didn't particularly love the photo—not that I altogether didn't like it—only, that it missed something that is in the bust itself—an exquisite something not to be defined. Still, I must say, I like this better than the photo print you brought me—much better: I should not reject it. And anyhow, I leave it all in your hands and Dave's." McKay will electro book after all—weighs all points and finds this dictated. W. said—"That puts quite a more effective light on things: I can see myself why it should seem advisable."

I saw Oldach and gave him order for the twenty books. Promised to let him have our old model copy as guide. Now spoke to W. of it and he sent me up stairs. "You'll find it easily," he said, "say I sat in my usual place up there—my chair turned this way"—wheeling his chair around—"it would be right in that place,"—pointing to a point on the floor—"under a pile of books." And despite the terrible confusion on the floor up stairs—a confusion much worse than usual—I really found the volume in exactly the position he had indicated to me. He has thumbed and marked the copy some. On one of the loose leaves he has written "Sample copy (first copy) from the printer and binder to show me everything is right—especially the putting in of the portraits at the right place—&c: &c:" "Seems all right" "Early June '89 W. W." Then at a later date he had added, given written confirmation to reports in these notes as to his disappointment as to one aspect of the birthday book—"the paper binding &c: satisfy me—the press-work (printing, ink, &c) *not*—sorry, very sorry for this, as in every other aspect it satisfies me & fills the bill—but this is a bad and important deficiency." All punctuated just as above.

"Herbert Gilchrist was over last evening after you left," said W., "but I did not see him—I had already gone up to bed." But not exactly in bed—for he sat up some half an hour after, reading.

Saturday, July 6, 1889

7.55 P.M. W. at window. Just in from his ride. Sat with feet planted against the table. As to health—"I suppose I am some better, though I have been bad enough all day." Sent Ed over to Dave's today for copies of Dr. Bucke's book. "There seems to be a demand for them!" I remarked, but he responded, "No demand—only that I have given away quite a number recently." Wrote a letter offering McKay the morocco book for 3 dollars per copy. Also inquired if he wished to take 25 copies at $2.50 now, as he needed money? But McKay did not. I saw Myrick today and gave him definite directions about the book. Will start his printers with it Monday morn-

ing. When I spoke of Myrick's good qualities—his readiness
—W. said, "That is a fine thing—a propitiating fact."
Then mention somehow of Oldach, his absolute knowledge of
binding—his intention to send one of his sons abroad to see
what could be seen in the great binderies of Europe. W. said—
"That is the meisterschaft business, as they call it—isn't it?"
Descanting then on its virtues: "Yes, not only good from the
trade side, but good for men to get off, see the world somewhat
—see what the world is up to. This much of virtue it has
however it may compare with our present system." He referred to "George Sand, Madame Dudevant"—he nearly always gives the name in full that way—"she treats of it in one
of her novels—if I remember right, treats it nobly." I said,
"And Goethe, in Wilhelm Meister." To which W. "Yes, 'tis
very good there, but not as good. Madame Dudevant's story
was an extra fine one—I read it—oh! what was its name? Its
subject matter is quite plain to me—the title is gone—'A
Journey Through France' or something like that was the
sub-title."

"I wonder," said W.—"that America—as would seem so
natural, so fittingly the case—does not raise a race of publishers the finest, the broadest, the world has so far seen—
publishers typical of our life here. Instead of having done
this so far—instead of having raised one such man—we have
had to get along with the most miserable, mean, tricky, cir-
cumscribed, hedged-in specimens the world has known—
specimens I doubt if the outside world can parallel." I said
"The Osgoods for example," and he laughingly—"Yes—they
are typical, undoubtedly—they are typical of the whole tribe."
I said something about the Critic notice this week of Burroughs' new book. W. said: "Yes—Joe Gilder is one of
them—I know Joe well and I can imagine what that review is.
The Critic, all our literary journals, are wanting in power
and warmth—to use Herbert's great and powerful word—
they lack 'guts.'" As to Osgood's again—"I have it from
O'Connor that their desertion of me was the beginning of their

downfall—he had it on good authority." Jennie Gilder was "more disposed our way, but she is making money—at least that is my supposition (there is no money on the Critic) and has more or less resigned her place on the Critic: that, at any rate, is my explanation."

Then mention of O'Connor's opinion of George Sand, at which W.—"O'Connor never had a chance to put forward his principles—his literary principles—yet he had principles and they were of the most remarkable character. How he could have written of Byron! And on the Shakespeare controversy, which he would consider the most important of all—even in that he has never printed his best things—never given the bottom reasons for his faith. And think of his knowledge of the Elizabethan cult—what he could have made of that! But though he has not printed these things, I know them—he has told them to me. For instance, this: when we would discuss the Shakespearean writings—particularly the dramas, I would sometimes speak of them as being the mouthpiece of feudalism and he would retort—'What of that? is it merely that do you think?' He held the ground that Shakespeare merely used to state the facts, plans, events, as they are, not to argue for them—make them more. And so would say at my mention of feudalism—'does it do feudalism any good to have it presented in such a habit, such terms, such an atmosphere?' For to O'Connor, Shakespeare did not introduce the villain because he believed in villains, but because he believed in nature: 'here the villains were and here they must be represented,' and I confess his reply always staggered me." As to O'Connor's great admiration for Byron—"It was natural with him—was a part of his nature. As to Byron's obscenity— "It seems to me to make its own case—that Byron deserves one great point to be made for him—this point, namely—that his alleged wickedness, queernesses are no more than the doctor's enumeration of diseases. The whole spirit of the persecution of Byron is the spirit of the town police—just as the spirit of the obscenity hunter anywhere (in mails and whatnot)—the spirit that will ignore all the gigantic evils—steal a way down to the shore—lay low—pull in a lot of little naked boys, there to take a bath—snake 'em in! It well pictures for me what is too commonly called the greatness and majesty of the law."

W. asked me—"Why should I not send Mrs. O'Connor's note to the Doctor? I generally write him Sundays. Is there any particular reason why I should refrain from enclosing this?" It seemed to me an odd question. He "found it difficult to decide." Returning to George Sand W. discredited "the frivolity of the French." I told him of the recent Labor Congress in Paris—that the French speakers were reported the most effective of all present—and solidly effective, too. He assented, "I can well believe it—it must be so: I never took any stock in the ordinary disposition to cry down French life. I have no doubt French life has much to teach us yet—and it has taught us plenty already, Lord knows! Every nation has its glories." W.'s condition one of weakness: "I would be a bad fellow to be in charge of a brigade now—or even a ferry-boat! I am over with the disposition to work—don't want to do anything at all." McKay made a remittance by mail to W. of 75 dollars. I sealed a contract with McKay today for royalty of 5 cents per copy beyond Harned's 25 copies to be given me absolutely.

Sunday, July 7, 1889

Coming from Philadelphia with Kemper,—between 5 and 6—near six—met W. at Third and Federal, he in his chair. We crossed the street: he saw and hailed us. We did not do much more at the time than shake hands with him, but he said to me, "on the fly"—"I have a letter from Dowden—I will show it to you—it is not much—he has received the book all right: his letter is very warm—very enthusiastic." Then, making some comment on the beautiful day, we started off, and he was wheeled along in his chair towards the river. Later on, very near 8, after our tea, we went down to the house, but he had not yet returned. However, it was not long before he came up. Sat out of doors. Talked freely. The day had "seized" him he said, "powerfully"—"this evening especially—and down by the river" but—"I wondered why so few were out sailing—there has been a good free breeze, and yet the yachts were few. I am sure that if I had my legs and a boat, it would be a day for me." And so to violate the Sabbath? He laughed —"No—I'd worship by it—worship with the elements—with the water, the sky, the shore." "Why," he said later on, "even the horse-cars will by and by run on Sundays: don't you believe it?"

I had been out to Germantown. Brought him from Clifford "Amiel's Journal." He was much pleased. "I've been keeping a sharp eye out for it: it is evidently a curious, if not great, book. Amiel was a Swiss—wasn't he? Perhaps with a spice of the French introduced: his name seems French. We'll see, now— what we get from it!" He said there was "something in the air this day that" you could "taste and smell—a delicious some- thing. I judge things not by taste alone but by smell—woods, for instance," and he spoke of "the New York Exposition— they had there thousands of woods—woods of all description— woods in their natural state—not even polished: and oh! the odors they threw out were sweeter than words can tell!" He had read the papers some today, and "some out of the books"— had in fact felt "a little on the mend" but not greatly—no strength coming, though some comfort. Talked some of Phila- delphia affairs. "I understand the Traction cars—the cable cars—come right down to the ferry now"—such matters.

Monday, July 8, 1889

8 P.M. W. was wheeled up by Ed the minute after I came. Was very cordial tonight—had a good color—and said that he

felt rather better—had been to the river, and "got from it the unusual enjoyment." A slight breeze stirred the trees opposite. He took off his hat—laid it on his lap. Said to me: "I have been reading Amiel—looked quite a good deal through the book today. But, Horace, he is not our man—not at all our man—I can see that at once. For one thing, he disbelieves in democracy, in progress—then, he is damnably pious—Oh! damnably pious!—and there is a sickliness in him, too—a thinness. I should not call him great—not in the slightest—nor do I think him the man for our modern world—not in any way. I can see that he should have an interest for the savant—but for us?—oh no! he is far, far, from being our man!" How had he come to wish for the book? "Oh! through hearing everybody crack it up!—the Critic, in the first place—then little paragraphs in the newspapers."

I had received a letter from Mrs. Costelloe. Sat here now and read to W., who was greatly interested and had me read some passages a second time. I asked,—"Shall it go in the book?"—knowing for myself that it would go in, and he quickly replied, "Oh yes! it is eminently fit—indefeasibly belongs there—'tis the message the woman brings: the woman's quickness, intuition—the woman's perfume—the woman's truth." And "particularly should it go in as coming from Mary Costelloe." I had a letter from Mrs. O'Connor today, also, one sentence of which was this—"I see by your article in Unity that you are disposed to treat very lightly Mr. O'Connor's Baconian theory." etc. If my article gave such an impression, it was one not intended. When I came to that point, reading to W., he interrupted—"No, that is a mistake, I did not read it that way—it did not so impress me." I then asked, "Don't you think it is by the Whitman letters he will be best remembered?" To which—"I do—decidedly; I think all his friends think the same thing, too." "Well," I responded, "that is all I meant to say—not that the other work has not importance too." W. hereupon—"So I supposed: Nellie has not rightly interpreted you." Adding—"William gave of his best in those letters—his best, quite aside from the general references to me. Glints of power and passion—of his knowledge of literature— sentences, paragraphs, graphically hinting what he would have done had he settled down to specific work in that line." At the point in which, discussing her affairs, she speaks of "the sad and humiliating developments," W. stopped me— "Humiliating? Does she use that word? How—what—'humili- ating'?" And when I was all through, he commented—"It is a sad letter."

A long letter from Garland to me today about W. W.'s condition. Although not reading him the letter there were a couple of points I referred to W. I told W. that in soliciting contributions to the nurse fund I had never put it on the ground of poverty but of necessity that a nurse should be kept and of the grace it would do W.'s friends in these last days to make it their own voluntary offering. W. said at once—"That was right—I approve that myself." To Gar- land's statement—"If I could state publicly that he was poor, that he did need money for running expenses (as I think he does)—and that his relatives and neighbors cannot or do not help him—then I could do something for him." W. quickly replied—"Horace—write to Garland—tell him it would not please me to have him make any statement in the public prints. Tell him I don't want him to discuss my Philadelphia and Camden friends." And as to Garland's question, what had become of the cottage money, etc., W. was equally quick to retort—"That was all fixed—understood—fully settled— long and long ago—it is a closed book—it is a question not again to be reopened." On the point of Garland's description of the hot and festering street and all that, W. only smiled, and without a word, pointed to the fine northern skies, and the trees swaying almost boisterously in the wind. It seemed like enough comment. By and by he said: "Hamlin does not under- stand." Then we let the matter drop.

W. questioned me curiously—"What do you hear of the fight—is there anything authentic—definite!"—having reference to Kilrain-Sullivan bout at New Orleans. And then he laughed at "the extraordinary spectacle of the nation aroused" over such a performance. But "all things have their place—this with other things."

Tuesday, July 9, 1889

7.50 P.M. W. at home, in the parlor, on the sofa. Had not been out today. The day clouded. "I have myself been under a cloud today—particularly this afternoon: even now it appears to hang over me." He fanned himself. Said he had felt "no disposition to go out, even if the day had been clear." I had a postal from Kennedy, speaking of a Sept. trip West, to St. Paul, with "stop-off" to see Bucke, if so to be managed. W. said, "Yes—why not? It is easily done. And Sloane would not regret or forget it." Said then: "You say he thanks you for papers I sent him? I don't remember recent papers at all. I sent a paper today to Bucke—one, also, to Mrs. O'Connor. Bucke still holds well up—writes often. In one of his recent letters he describes a jaunt he had with some others there—a fifteen-mile trip somewhere or other, and a good feed thrown into the bargain!"

I stayed but briefly. He seemed too wearied to do much talking. Ed described him as being "very weak all day" and asked me—"Don't you think he's getting thinner?" W. still avoids discussion of leaving Camden. I told him Harned thought the "Esopus" idea a good one to follow up, but W. merely asked, "Tom said that—did he?" Adding—"An so 'tis"—but did not follow it up. I look for him to mend quickly or to encounter some serious set-back before long.

Wednesday, July 10, 1889

Stopped in at W.'s on my way home (5.10) to leave one set of proofs of my piece for the book. He sat eating his meal—

fan in one hand. We talked little. He remarked, "I am glad you will leave it for an hour or two." Did not think he would get out today as it threatened rain. But he was in too bad a condition anyhow. His yesterday's discomfort persisted.

7.50 P.M. In at W.'s again. He lay on sofa in parlor, his cane on the floor, fan in hand, a chair nearby on which he rested his right arm. Talked very cheerily, however. Had not got out, as I expected. "Ed," he said, "are you there at the window?" and to Ed's "Yes," directed, "If you will go up stairs, up there on the landing, you'll find a little package— they are proofs for Horace: bring them down"—which Ed did. But he had found no material errors. Except for Johnston's name, "matters seemed mostly straight." Brown has promised (loosely) the picture for tomorrow. W. "glad." W. advised: "You must take care to give the topic of the toast a good size and shape: I hardly think lower case Italics will do—you should use caps—perhaps even caps pica." But, "I should not spread things out—I should keep both letters and speeches well together"—which was precisely my intention.

Asked me about Dave's trip West. "How far does he go?" And learning, to Denver, perhaps to take a season at Colorado Springs, W. remarked: "The springs are not wonderful—though fine and great: built up, I should say—wisely built up—but not initially striking, though Denver itself is a great town—or to be a great town—no doubt one of the greatest on the continent. Denver is bound to be one of the most wonderful of our city-growths—wonderful: she will always be a great cluster-point for the rich ores of the grand, limitless West—already has the finest smelting works in America: things all well done—the latest improvements— always looking ahead: and keen, strong, broad-backed men— America's best. The land about there is remarkable for its natural parks—there are numbers of them, fine, satisfying, Paradisaic, bits of reserve—the noblest the earth affords, often in what might be called a depression—the fountain of streams running there along into most fertile soils. Denver is phenomenal for its background—its ample background: not much of a river there, but a river that does. Denver has its own excuse for being—it is a center—a natural center—a rallying point: it is one of the great towns that had to be—as New Orleans, for instance." I laughed and said, "Yes, what would the Sullivan men have done without New Orleans?" W. laughing heartily also, "Oh! that is merely a fleeting, incidental matter. But New Orleans, not at all attractive in itself—not what would be called beautiful by an artistic eye—is yet a pure necessity: America, traffic—traffic even before the railroad; none the less since—ordained that a city was needed at just that precise point—a distributing center—a depot—and so this city grew, and so is likely to last for some time yet—last while the need lasts. Denver is just such a place; grew out of precisely the same condition." W. had heard somewhere of high buildings going up in the Kansan town. "I cannot see their necessity," he objected, "I can see how downtown in Philadelphia: how downtown in New York: such buildings would be advised—would become an imperative necessity; but in the West?—no, I cannot see it. One of the first points that takes hold on you as you go west is, that here is lots and lots and lots and lots and still lots beyond lots, of land, on which men may spread out as they choose—land limitless—miles and miles and miles and miles and miles—no end!"

He tried to name me one of the Western rivers—a Greek name—but it "failed" him. He laughed—"It was a terrible one." I put in—"Named by the drunken pedagogue who gave names to the New York towns?" He laughed—"Probably a relative: you mean the Ithaca, Utica, Troy man? I think so far as such names go, however, that the South beats us all hollow —look at Memphis—a fearful name—with no smack of the soil whatever—yet hundreds, thousands, like it!" The great Indian names "lost, like so many opportunities!" I referred to

McKay—my reference to him in the introduction—that some thought Dave's act in espousal of W. "merely a business act," but that I saw more than "business" in its effects, whatever Dave's motive. W. said, "That was right: it serves little good purpose to dive at such a thing microscopically—at anything: I don't know but every act—even acts accounted noble —may, at last analysis—in final origins—be found to be selfish. Is there not a great man—even one of our fellows— who says so?—seems to me so!" But "Dave at that time rescued us, whatever else is to be said—he appeared just in the nick of our trouble. That is not to be forgotten—we must not forget it!"

Thursday, July 11, 1889

8 P.M. Strolled down to W.'s with Harned. Found W. at house, sitting by the parlor window. Cordial enough,—extra glad to see Tom, who had not met him for several weeks (having been away)—questioning Tom much of the children, and remarking the "extra beauty" of the baby's photo T. had sent. But confessed he did not feel well. "I did not get out today"—this now the third day in succession. Was it hot enough for him? "Yes—hot enough—too damned hot!" I said I had just received a letter from Bucke. W. thereupon—"And so did I—by this evening's mail. Bucke has ordered me a tonic—I have been taking it—I am sure it contains strychnia: it does me good in general, but affects my head—also eyes and hearing—very decidedly. I have had trouble with my hearing for several months past—quite a decided loss of power": which I have noticed but hoped would be merely transitory.

Last night I had mentioned to W. that the printer wanted a paragraph added to my introduction, to run it over to the even page (18). W. asked now, "Have you filled up the blank? I have found a little copy for you." But when I told him I had, he relaxed—"Well—let it lay then"—though he promised it to me for any later exigency. "You should make speeches and letters solid," he counselled, and when I said I had examined and figured the whole matter over today and had ordered it so, he added—"That was wise." To some remark of Tom's about the importance of the book, W. assented, "Yes—so it seems—it evidently gets to be serious." Tom referred to the prospect of having Ingersoll's article on W. W. remarked, "Yes—let the Colonel go on: I can say to him with the Duchess in Richard, 'God prosper you in all your good intents!' " Here W. assumed quite an amused manner— quoted the whole passage, "It was spoken with a particular emphasis on the 'good' "—leaning forward and laughing heartily. "And Richard would respond that his 'intent' was the crown—and was not that 'good'? I can see the Duchess now as so often in my young days,—thrusting her head in at the flies." Thence telling of stories for nearly half an hour, W. as gay as either of us. "I remember clearly one of Samuel Lover's stories—I have told it to you? It was in one of his lectures—used as an illustration of ready wit. I suppose it must have been 40 or 50 years ago when I heard him: but his telling of it was an experience itself. A story of some one's falling overboard somewhere and being fished out—handing the Irishman a small coin—a sixpence, shilling, whatnot— the Irishman's scanning it, so"—W. indicating—"and the rescued man's question, 'Well—isn't it enough?'—then the cute reply—a blast in itself—'Ach, Soor—I was thinking as how I might have been overpaid!' Oh! the readiness of that Irish wit! How much we owe to it!" Tom told a sea of Galilee story which quite convulsed us all, with W.'s exclamation— "A retort excellent! A Roland for the others' Oliver!" Asked after Tom's affairs—if busy, etc.!—

W. not in good color. Has perceptibly lost flesh. Advised Tom to take "many trips: the mere change is good." But as for himself thinks he had best "stay quietly at home." To

Tom's remark that he thought W. gloried in the heat, W. shook his head, "Not such heat as this." Adding however—"it is not unpleasant tonight—indeed, this whole day has been bearable." Bucke inquires about his special morocco book, now being bound. Saw Brown today who says they had to make a second trial of the plate in N. Y.—but that the plate would be over Saturday. W. is quite favorable to having it used in our book if the Morse picture goes amiss, as is not unlikely to be the case. W. said strikingly at one point: "All that is good (and in fact all that is bad) in the English character rallies in its satisfiedness—its self-satisfiedness"—adding—"and yet I don't know if we can boast exemptions from the evil—if evil it be."

Friday, July 12, 1889

7.50 P.M. W. sitting at parlor window reading life of Cassius Clay. Asked me, "Did you ever know anything of Cas Clay?—ever see him, meet him?" Adding, "He was a great man in his day—must be a very old man now!" Looked very poorly. Deafness much increased. Nearly everything I said to him had to be repeated. Particularly fine as the day had been, he had not been out at all. To Mrs. Mapes, who came in and asked him how he was standing the hot weather, he replied, "Middling well—only middling well." I left with him the proof of Harned's speech, which he promised to look over before he went to bed, and "leave out in the hall," so I could secure it early in the morning, on my way to town. I wrote a short note to Bucke last evening. Told W. so. He said, "I had a letter from Doctor last evening, but so far have not felt impelled to answer it."

Gave W. some description of Hawthorne's picture of Lincoln printed by Fields in "Yesterdays with Authors." W. said: "I do not remember it: yes—bring it down. I should not wonder at any man mistaking Abe Lincoln the first two or

361

three years in Washington: it is very rarely anyhow that men come to know the really great fellows even when they are through, much less when they are in process of making. When men get their calipers out—then what? Nothing very wise, generally. Lincoln was not a specifically great man, as greatness runs in the average mind. He minds me most often of a captain—a great captain—chosen for a tempestuous voyage—everything against him—wind, tide, current, terrible odds—untried seas—balking courses: yet a man equal to all emergencies, never at a loss, quiet, composed, patient— oh how patient!—and coming out at the end, victor—no one in all history more victor! How could the average men know him?—how know Washington—even Grant?—any man of the first class?" And then he said fervently: "Reckoning how much we owe to the fact of Lincoln's presence at that day— his service—one is lost in wonder, what had become of our states, fallen into other hands!" Then vividly, with his usual simple touches: "But it was the average soldier, after all—the average soldier, north and south—who was the golden sword-blade of our war. I remember one man—a sort of teamster— driver of an ambulance. Off from Washington was what was called a convalescent department: I often rode out to it— whenever possible, rode outside, with the driver. There was one man among these who had known Lincoln in his early days —in the Springfield days—had worked in the principal store at Springfield, as clerk, helper, assistant, laborer, I don't know what. It was from him I learned many of my best things about Lincoln. Already at that time Lincoln was a man of some note—had a good home in Springfield—was married— ran things. He would come down to this store to buy. Oh! many's the little items of description this man imparted, how Lincoln appeared then—appeared in his purchasings, his buying this, his not buying that, why he felt he needed one thing, why not another: items, insignificant details, which the man soon understood were of an intense interest to me. This

362

man, occupying a place as teamster, was very subordinate—I don't know whether very poor, but certainly not getting much out of this work. I said to him one day, 'Don't you know that Abe Lincoln is big Injun now—that he could do almost anything for you—put you in almost any convenient position?' He answered at once, 'Yes, I do!' Then I urged, 'Well— why don't you go to see him then—why don't you call? Don't you think he would remember you?' 'Oh yes, he would.' 'Well, why don't you call, then?' I shall never forget the man's emphasis in replying—the tone of his voice—his look—it was a poem in itself. 'What—me call on him? Add to his burdens? —on a man worried from morning to night not only by his great cares but by applicants for this, applicants for that, applicants for the other thing? No indeed: I could never do it!' It was a flash out of heaven: the man was a hero to me at once: I was enthusiastic over my discovery. Did I never tell you of this before? It was typical of the common soldier—not uncommon in any sense: my experience has been full of just such noble consideration, tact, cute human feeling, as this."

W. spoke of O'Connor—of his novel and the short stories. " 'Harrington' was quite a big book—published by my Boston publishers—the publishers of Leaves of Grass—by Thayer and Eldridge. But it was by no means a pecuniary, a publisherial, success." Did the book give works of O'C.'s best qualities? "Yes—I think it did—it was full of vehemence, power. The book was instigated by the success of Harriet Beecher Stowe's 'Uncle Tom's Cabin.' Harrington was an ardent reformer—a young man, probably 30, 31, 32, 33 years—interested in all the new schemes, the fresh theories: a man of the kind you know well. There were passages in it— asides—diversions—of exquisite beauty—then passages of great power. The short stories did have a wonderful—a marked quality: there was one—'The Ghost'—probably the best of all. And another 'The Carpenter,' which certainly has a great emotional—I was going to say, overflow. Its subject an old man on the Maryland line with two sons, one of them belonging to the Northern—the other to the Southern—army—their re-union." I asked, "And the Carpenter: was that the father?" W. responded—"No—the Carpenter was a new-comer—a visitor—a happener-in: was meant, in fact—so I believe—for me, though drawn with O'Connor's vehement, impressive, Elizabethan pen—with exaggerated lines—not halting or lame at all in its testimony. I have not a copy here—but Bucke has one, I am sure. This story—I think it was this—was printed in the first number of Putnam's Magazine—the revised Putnam's—if I am not mistaken: they were very anxious, positive, about having something from O'Connor for the first issue, and so he gave them this. It was a long story: Putnam's, then, had, I suppose, as many or nearly as many, pages as the present Century: of these pages O'Connor's piece occupied 70." What sort of a volume did he suppose these stories would make, collected together now? "I don't know: would not like to say: there may be a preservative quality in them—I am inclined to believe there is: but a volume would be experimental."

He hears little from McKay about November Boughs. "I guess it did not sell—the usual fate!" Mrs. Davis came in and sat with us awhile. W. was very solicitous in inquiring after a woman next door, now much and dubiously sick, of consumption. From this went into general comment—gave hospital experiences—"hemorrhages of all parts of the system: oh! how much I have heard of these!" Despite evident discomfort of condition, the thought of the war, of O'Connor, aroused vigorous speech in him. Memory of old things still strong. Spoke of George Stafford—his physical trouble.

Saturday, July 13, 1889

7.50 P.M. W. sitting at the parlor window. Again, had not been out. In shirt sleeves—looked fine—fanned himself from time to time—then would take out his knife—play with the blade of it. I left with him proofs of Grey's, Harned's, Gilchrist's, Williams' and Clifford's speeches. Said he had had a letter from Burroughs today. "He tells me he has got the book—then that he is going away—that his address for a while will be Hobart. I sent the letter off to Doctor at once. John spoke of the dinner—said he would have been down here except that a return of his insomnia—about two weeks of it— badly tried, distressed him." I said, "It is just as well he did not come. Had he come we should not have had that letter." W. smiled—"I see! And as I always say, everything is right—and if John did not come, it was best so." "But," W. went on, after a short silence, "that insomnia—that baffles me—I do not see its inciting cause in John: he was always a wise man with his body—never squandered it. In fact, his later years have been his best years. It is very clear to me that in going to New York, John, gaining much, lost a great deal— lost irretrievably. John's place by nature would seem to have been from the first out of doors: his best books are the early ones—'Wake Robin,' others. But John was never satisfied to remain out of doors—to view field-life—report it. He always had a hankering after problems, explanations, metaphysicalisms—to me an obvious weakening. I never disguised from him or from anybody that I thought it a bad investment. It is true he did this work itself remarkably well— contributed inestimable discoveries, all that—said novel and inviting things: but to me none of it, whatever value it had, had the best value of the man. And yet I know that in criticism he had written superbly—for instance, has said some of the best things said by anyone about Carlyle." I protested the, to me, natural greater importance John's critical work had, and that "certainly his work—whatever touching—has been always noble and unusual." W. at once said, "You are right—of course mine is the [severe] view—he deserves your statement—and your statement belongs right at this point, too. Then it is true, I have certain knowledge of Mrs. O'Connor and Burroughs—of both—which—while I am not privileged to disclose them, or would not, tend to illuminate their characters—to explain many things inexplicable otherwise." He alluded here to "John's house" and "the Hudson country in general"—its "malarial tendencies." I said, "If it is malarial, it is good you did not go there to spend the summer." W. hereupon, "Oh! I do not mean to say that it is all charged with the evil—only that it has a tinge of it: for instance, that it is not by any means as good a place for me to be in as this south Jersey country—these sixty or eighty miles up from the Cape. Not as advisable a place, in fact, as New York City itself—built mainly on rock, sand—in the sea air, practically. Good sand, such as distinguishes our parts here—poor enough from the standpoint of tillage, but sanitarily excellent." And again, "John's fault is then, metaphysics as Burns' was, literary criticism. You remember there came a time to Burns when he imagined he was called upon to put estimates on writers, books. And of course he made a bad mess of it. Sort of realized it himself, only that he never got out of it, the snake having bitten him!"

At this juncture he said suddenly: "By the way, speaking of Mrs. O'Connor—Doctor's last letter was written in a terrible strain: he proposes to me that, Mrs. O'Connor having no place her own now—nothing to do—that we somehow set up a bargain—that she keep house for me—that we go into alliance, get spliced. I wrote the Doctor at once, explaining why I thought it impossible, or at least unlikely. As I feel now, I see no way but the way I am pursuing. It is, I know, impossible to tell what will occur. It is very probable—probable that before long—death will cut the knot—settle the intricacies now so baffling. But if death does not come at once—if I eke out for some time longer, an existence like this, or a worse, as is likely, which is needless [Oh! the tone in which he said this!], it is not impossible other considerations will have to be allowed. Doctor says the impression has got abroad that I am not rightly cared for—that I live in squalor—litter—all that. But what a mistake all that is! As for the litter—that is of my own choosing: I need not have that except as I elect to have it—I could have anything different. And I am sure—notwithstanding Hamlin Garland's fear, I am most blessed in my Camden friends: who more blessed in friends? I consider myself nothing but fortunate in having had you all about me—such faithfulness, loyalty! And in the house here, Mrs. Davis, the boys, Eddy—all are kind, attentive, serve me!" "I know all this solicitude starts right—that it is natural—that it really comes of honest affection: only, they don't know all things—do not rightly realize our condition." W. said again: "The attempt to unite the life out in nature—the life of the woods, of the fields, of the rivers—with what is called the intellectual life—often with the metaphysical tinge —is always bad—always."

Sunday, July 14, 1889

7.55 P.M. W. in bathroom when I arrived, but shortly out. I asked, standing upstairs, "Up or down?"—he replying—"Down, of course" and so struggled down, Ed in front of him, and W. saying—"You there Ed? I suppose you'll catch me if I fall?—though I doubt if you can catch a good 200 lbs., which I believe I still weigh, in spite of my emaciation." But he got down and into his chair in the parlor and neither of us touched him. Has been better today, though not decidedly so— not enough so to get out. But digestion very poor—has to hasten it every two or three days.

He had examined the proofs I left with him yesterday and put them together for me on the parlor table. He said of Clifford's address—"It is a wonderful piece of Transcenden-tal, Emersonian work! 'Tis Transcendentalism all the way through!" He took what I thought an erroneous meaning out of C.'s reference to Emerson—"Clifford is wrong in one thing," he said, "Emerson never took it back—never retracted his endorsement; or, I should not say endorsement—that perhaps is not the word—but he certainly never budged an inch—there is nothing to show it and everything to show the charge of it false." I said, "I do not read it that way: to me he seems to say—Emerson did not retract, but if he did, then alas! for prophet's faithfulness to prophet! Meaning that even if he did, it would make little difference." Said W.: "Well—I am sorry it is not clearer: I am certainly eligible to be deceived by it if it means that. It is a pity to have the general public get it that way, too: the general public, you know, wants everything explicit: we know well enough by long experience—you know, I know—that if there are 301 different ways of interpreting a passage—300 right, 1 wrong—the great mass will hit upon that wrong interpretation, insist upon it, dogmatize." "Even the intelligent public goes off in this way—and it is to be supposed that anybody who reads this book will be intelligent—that the book has no attractions otherwise." He added laughingly then, when referring to those who close all controversy by saying "that is a difference of opinion"—"That is a very prevalent fashion, especially in America, when a fellow gets completely stumped, he takes refuge in that—'It is a difference of opinion!'" Said he knew Gilder had had an aversion—"an extreme aversion"—to being set down for a toast and yet it was a toast—if not that, what? But of course such a thing is not debatable—it is as if a fellow tells you he don't like turnips, potatoes—you don't argue the point, he don't like them! That's enough, that's conclusive."

I told him I had orders for two big books, for the Lychenheim boys. W. queried, "Hebrews?" then to my affirmative response: "If I keep on in this way I shall by and by have a Hebrew clientage—and I do not see why I should not—I see every reason why I should: for am I not a Biblical fellow myself—born and bred in Hebrewism—the old forerunners, teachers, prophets?" And he said still again: "And all my

Hebrew friends are turning out to be among the young—you would call that an omen, wouldn't you?" He talked regretfully of not getting out, still his voice and whole air was more inspiring—much stronger—than any day for a week. Not out since last Sunday.

Monday, July 15, 1889

7.50 P.M. W. in parlor, but as the afternoon had turned very cool, he had pulled down the window sash and sat there with his blue gown closely folded about him. I had not been there but a little while before Frank and Tom Harned came up and in. W. talked freely. To Frank's question as to his health, he said, "Oh! I get along middling—I guess I can say I am middling." Afterwards addressing Tom—"The weather has taken a fine change—I am sure I enjoy it: I have been hoping we would have a week of it, now it has given us a taste!" But again, had not been out in his chair. I brought him proof from Brown of the "laughing philosopher" picture, now photo-engraved. W. seemed to take much pleasure out of contemplating it. He said, "I cannot see it well, but it appears all right." Here he laughed heartily—held it out from him some distance—"What a fat old duffer of a story-teller it is, too!"

Talk developed towards Millet, then the "L'Angelus." W. said, "I thought I saw the original of that at Quincy Shaw's, up in Massachusetts, years ago—but I guess I didn't—probably saw a copy, or a copy of a copy, as often is the case." He admitted the greatness of Millet's "most famous picture," but insisted—"There is one of Millet's pictures—not so well known—I have seen it—which seems to me the gem of his creations—at least, of such as I have known. The plot of it was simply this—a girl going home with the cows of an evening—a small stream running lazily along—the cattle tempted forward to the water, mildly drinking. I can conceive of nothing more directly encountered in nature than this piece—its simplicity, its grand treatment, the atmosphere, the time of day: not a break in the power of its statement. I looked at it long and long—was fascinated—fastened to it—could hardly leave it at all. This picture more than any other to my judgment confirmed Millet—justified his position, heroism—assured his future."

In reading proof of Gilchrist's speech W. had put a question mark upon the use of "prosperity" in the sentence reading —"The prosperity of this occasion" etc. Gilchrist very positively to me reasserted the word, whereat W. laughed—"Let it go in, then—I shall not object—I claim no authority—if it is a fit word for his use, let it be used! As I have often said, 'This is not my funeral: let the cortege proceed!'" But he has made verbal suggestions to all hands which have been wisely adopted. Read him from Unity a description of Morse's preparing bust of George Eliot. W. said fervently, "Well—I hope his work is such as to justify that ardent paragraph!" Stayed but briefly after the Harneds left. Happy to find W. improved.

Tuesday, July 16, 1889

7.55 P.M. W. not at home when I arrived. Out at last—the first time in nearly 10 days. Soon returned. Did not sit out of doors, as sometimes. In immediately—though it was a painful job getting him in. His legs very palpably are losing power. Seemed cheerful. Expressed rejoicing at getting to the river. "It was a grand trip—a grand evening, too. And I am better, I believe—surely better." Said of the portrait I left last evening—"Yes indeed—it will do—it seems to me a success—I suppose 'tis as good as could be done with such means." And when I asked what he would do with it, he responded, "For the present, nothing—except perhaps to have a few printed for my friends." Would it be well to ask Cox's consent to use it in our book? The bust reproduction did not satisfy me. But W. said, "Let us stick to the bust: why not?" He said he probably enjoyed the engraving of the bust more than I did. "I must get my copy of 'Mr. Donnelly's Reviewers'," he remarked later on, "get it from Tom and sent it off to John Burroughs, who says he has not seen it: Mrs. O'Connor evidently not having sent him a copy."

Further: "I had a paper—an Open Court, as it is called—from Kennedy today, in which is an article called, 'Carlyle's Religion' or 'The Religion of Carlyle' or something of that sort. I have read it: it contributes nothing essentially new—is not long—not weighty. I know Moncure is slippery—that one must have a care what to accept from him. But it seems to me that in this case there exist almost indubitable marks of authenticity: at least I have been so impressed in looking it over. He has had the sagacity here not to interpose any—or to interpose very few remarks of his own. He reports, simply: tells his story on others' lips—goes to work legitimately, so that the record means a record such as we read of great generals, public men—quick, wise, pat sayings, which, whether actually uttered—sworn to—or not, at least make interesting reading." He had received copies of Poet-Lore for June and July. "There was a paragraph there—towards the last—a sort of Critic note, though larger—describing the dinner. 'Tis not signed—makes no important additions. The magazine seems to be edited by two women: what do you know about them?"

Had inscribed the two Lychenheim books, which he sent me upstairs for. Had authentically endorsed the package thus—

Two Books ($6 each)
Two Copies *Complete Works* Walt Whitman
1889
per Horace Traubel
Camden

and in corner had pasted one of the curious Curtz labels to indicate contents more fully. Always makes up packages in this explicit way. In the volumes had written the names of the purchasers and "from the author July 16 1889." Not a mark of punctuation either in inside or outside inscriptions.

Wednesday, July 17, 1889

Down at W.'s about 4.45. He lay on bed in his room—his eyes open—his look rather vacant: seemed a little startled by my entrance. Fan in his hand. Was passing through a bad day. I stayed but a few minutes. Was "in passage" to Logan, to take tea with the Fels'. Said his head troubled him. I had a letter from a Chicago friend of Salter's enclosing check for complete Whitman like Salter's. I wrote back saying that such a book was not to be secured now, but that copies identical with it except for the cover I could readily secure for him: further, that I held his check subject to his directions. I told W. who said, "You did just right—did just what I should have done under the circumstances." Informed me that Gilchrist had just been in "for a few minutes."

Thursday, July 18, 1889

8.10 P.M. Had gone down with T. B. Harned. W. out but came along in chair shortly. He seemed better. Shook hands— his hand cold. To Tom's question, how he was, he responded at some length, hitting at the Doctors as he went along. "I think I feel middling—but not more than that. I think I can best describe my condition by saying I feel dull—that I am afflicted with a terrible inertia—almost a fatal inertia. For instance, I like every day to take a bath—make it my rule, nearly—particularly in this weather: it betters me in various ways. Yet do you know it is the hardest thing before I can bring myself to go to the bathroom and turn the spigot—just as if it waited for some superior power to take hold of me and push me bodily to the task. I attribute this—not chiefly to the weather, but to a drug I received from Dr. Bucke a couple of weeks ago and have taken every day since—which I stopped today. This drug did save me from the deathliness I had suffered—from the frightful caving-in-ness that possessed me —but in doing this it afflicted my head—set it into a whirl— deadened it. I don't think any of the doctors—the best doctors—have arrived at my doctrine yet—that each person who comes to be treated, has to be treated as a person, not as a member of a class. I remember one of my first doctors—in Washington—a very good, brave, bright man he was, too— when he heard that I ailed, that I mattered, he said to me, 'Oh! I can easily set that right!' 'How Doctor?' I asked, 'with what?' 'Quinine!' he answered. So I took quinine—and what did it do but set my head spinning, this way"—indicating —"like a wheel. And I took it—kept on taking it—for 2 or 3 days—and the more I took it the more I wheeled. And then I stopped. And it has almost always been so—I may say, always so, without the 'almost.' Drugs, for me, always defeat the best purposes: always, always. All the Doctors have rec- commended to me, quinine, quinine: but no—quinine, nor any drug—serves me badly, I do best by wholly avoiding them. I can see how in emergencies—in stress—they might be made to act, but not otherwise. I find that the drugs always exces- sively affect me—almost violently—that my nature seems set against them. It is true, that the drugs may effect the end for which they are applied, but I find they effect more, too—so much more, that the balance of good is on the wrong side— that I come out minus."

Asked Tom for "Mr. Donnelly's Reviewers" to send to Burroughs. Talked of the book. "It is true I read everything that is written by William O'Connor with great absorption— to me, it is all a great ship under full sail, grandly sailing whatever seas—William's writing always this. But this Shakespeare-Bacon-Cipher business is not a great question— is not vastly important: so that, anything in the way of going through a big book like Donnelly's would be out of the possible. O'Connor himself was not altogether satisfied with Donnelly—I may say, he was even displeased—though later on, as I have reason to suppose from what he said to you—'that he had met Donnelly, thought him honest and expected new revelations still'—that he was mollified, at least to some extent. It was always a pretense of the Bacon-Shakespeare fellows that they yet held a card—that there was still a card to be played—a crusher—that behind all revealed, there was a revelation of revelations yet to come which would clear the air. But it has not come—O'Connor was always conscious of it—conscious of it as a weakness. And yet William has said to me here—written me, too—as if himself convinced there was something, if not undiscovered, at least undivulged. To me, it is a curious question—do these fellows still stick to their notions? Is this still their game? I have seen no retraction of it—no turn-about—which, if so, is significant. I do not see new revelations—doubt even if there are any—if any more will ever be discovered. I am sure all that is known now I have known for years and years and years." But whatever the truth "the question is primarily of literary, not human interest." Here W. laughed roundly—asked Tom: "Tom—what is the celebrated Woodstock will case?"— meaning "Comstock." T. confessing ignorance, W., thereupon going on with the greatest unction—enjoying it hugely, "There was a curious question brought up in the court—an insanity question: a Doctor there, an expert, so-called, was asked if he thought all poets insane,—and he answered that generally he did. They questioned him—he admitted he thought Walt Whitman insane—even Milton. Then some one went at it again—this time was Shakespeare insane?" W. laughed heartily here—"Oh! his answer was very good—very rich!—and would make, O what a text for an article in the papers! He struggled out of the question by saying very deliberately, 'Well—from what I have heard I should consider Shakespeare as having rather a superior mind.'" W. asked,

WITH WALT WHITMAN IN CAMDEN

"What do you think of that, Tom: isn't that a curio? I think it has been a long time since I heard anything so funny as that!" (The paper account herewith shows how closely W. followed it from memory)

INSANITY EXPERTS

*Some Amusing Opinions
in a Will Case.*

[SPECIAL TO THE PUBLIC LEDGER]

NEW YORK, JULY 17.—Some rather surprising evidence was given by the insanity experts in the Comstock will case this afternoon. Dr. William R. Birdsall, a visiting physician at the Bellevue Hospital, expressed the opinion that certain letters in evidence betrayed the writer's insanity, giving as one reason for his opinion certain poetical tendencies which the letters displayed, and he was then asked if he considered all poets insane.

"Well, not exactly," he replied, "but I do decidedly when I find that this poetry is not logical. I think Walt Whitman is insane."

"How about Milton?"

"Well, I think Milton was insane."

"And Shakespeare?"

"Well," answered the witness deliberately, "from what I have heard I should consider Shakespeare as having rather a superior mind."

Dr. Charles Dana, a lecturer on insanity at the New York College and one of the specialists at Bellevue Hospital on brain diseases, was also called as an expert witness. He said he differed in a few particulars from Dr. Birdsall, but, in general, agreed with him.

375

Tom quoted from Shakespeare, "The lunatic, the lover and the poet," etc, etc. and W. exclaimed, "And that is one of the grandest bits, too—Shakespeare's or Bacon's!"

At this moment came strains of song from the Methodist church at the corner. Tom went into a ridiculous description of a class meeting, W. throwing in a mock sentence now and then: T. then of demoralization in churches—especially in camp-meetings—said at close, "But I suppose that is putting it too strong!" W. responded, "I don't know, Tom—I guess not—not a bit too strong. I think Swedenborg was right when he said there was a close connection—a very close connection—between the state we call religious ecstacy and the desire to copulate. I find Swedenborg confirmed in all my experience. It is a peculiar discovery. It was Burns—Whittier's friend Burns—who said in a couple of lines of one of his poems, I'd rather cause the birth of one than the death of 20! And that would be my doctrine, too!" I laughingly twitted W., "You always get one in on Whittier's friendship for Burns." Responded he, "I don't know—but Whittier sticks steadily by Burns, and I don't know that it's the best thing he ever did!"

I had a postal from Clifford today confirming my interpretation of his Emerson passage but suggesting and permitting change to make it more definite. W. said, "Well—let it go in as he has it, if he has it as he wants it." Saying afterwards when Tom spoke of Dr. Emerson as "le petit," "No, let us not say that"—though saying fervently when Tom said, "Emerson never retracted anything—in his whole life had never done so"—"That is the right view to take of it—he never retracted a word—not a word—not by word, not by sign—in no way!" Spoke of a letter he had had from Tom Donaldson. "He said at the end of it—it was a very small concern—only 3 lines or so—'The money is all right.' What he means by that I don't know. He said also that he would be over in a day or two—but he has never come." W. not yet prepared to say what to do with "laughing philosopher" portrait. "You may tell Brown that it perfectly pleases me— and I am willing to pay for it, too, whenever you say." He gave Ed his watch saying, "Take this up to the watchman's— the damned thing has stopped again. Let him tell you what is the matter with it."

Friday, July 19, 1889

7.50 P.M. W. in parlor at window. It rained hard, which he remarked. "Wasn't it long acoming?" he asked. "At least— plain enough that it was to come, but long making up its mind?" Ed came in after awhile and sat at the other window. Some reference being made to eyesight, W. exclaimed, "Well—that's my case exactly—I am getting worse and worse fixed—so that by and by my sight will be altogether gone." I protested, "But having flung the Doctor's medicine away you'll be strong again?" Whereupon: "I have stopped it, and feel better, but really think, however, it may have had its good effect: except that we must not forget there's no way under heaven to give me my youth back again." I repeated Ingersoll's picture of the youngster tugging at the grey-beard's sleeve at the table of life and indicating that the time had come, etc. W. laughingly: "So that is the Colonel's: it is very good—very worth the telling!" Adding after a pause, "And true, too: oh! I do not complain,"—looking at me—and he does not.

Said, "I got 'Mr. Donnelly's Reviewers' from Tom and sent it to John Burroughs today." Added, "And I had a long letter from Charles Eldridge, who writes from San Francisco. He says he is at a desk again—is Internal Revenue Collector for the district covered by California, Oregon, perhaps one or two other states. Charles is a Republican— probably got left in Cleveland's term—now on deck again." And in speaking of Grace Channing and one of the women out there who was deaf, W. said, "And she is greatly to be envied in her deafness, too. I have told her so, often, but she always looked very glum about it, saying to me, "Ah! Walt—if you knew what it was—really realized it—you would never say that!" Then: "But I am getting to know what it is! All my faculties seem to be settling down into a masterly incompetency, dullness." Harned goes off to the country tomorrow again and W. thought, "There must be something fascinating about that lay of country to make him so eager." I suggested, "The baby, for one thing"—whereat he laughed— "Sure enough—I had not thought of it!"

Gilchrist sent me the letter from Hallam Tennyson, acknowledging for his father G.'s letter about the banquet. G. thought we could use simply the phrase "All congratulations," which occurs in the letter, but W. urged, "Use it all—don't garble it—though remaining very careful not to claim more for it than the law allows. Tennyson is very conservative— almost squeamish, I might say—writes little or nothing— would no doubt resent us if we made too much of this note— made it mean what it does not." I had read the whole note to W. I expressed willingness to use all if G. would consent. Ed went upstairs, got me a postal, which I wrote to G. as I sat there. W. said of Tennyson, "He don't write much any more— in the first place, because he can't—then because it is not in his disposition to do so. I think Hallam does some—or a good deal—of his correspondence. There was a time when Alfred's wife wrote for him, but that is past now: she is sick, ailing, must be old, spends a good part of her time sofa-ed, confined—and I am told Alfred is everything to her that is noble, tender, quiet, brave, devoted—all that nobility, tenderness, bravery, devotion, mean! Have you never noticed how these men are backed by women—how fortunate they have been?— Gladstone, now—Disraeli, Tennyson, others: and see what an age they live to! I remember, Pearsall Smith spoke of this to me, remarked that the caretaking was more notable in

England than here." But W. instanced even here the longevity of literary men: "Emerson, Bryant, Longfellow—even Whittier, though Whittier has been frail all his life. Yes indeed, Whittier has been more than temperate, I should say— even abstemious—and that has saved him. I easily picture Bryant in his old days—the last 15 or 20 years of his life, always the long beard, the bald head, the shaggy brows,— though with a sallow complexion. John Swinton used to call him 'a cadaver.' That was John's word, and I suppose Bryant justified it—nevertheless I liked him. In his old days I think Bryant shied at loneliness—liked to be about—to meet friends—to be entertained, an altogether opposite frame of mind from that which had previously prevailed in him— ordered his life." Even Lowell was "well along in life— though ruddy and fat and healthy enough." And W. W.'s age, too, "is getting along, I must admit for myself." Referred to Bright, Carlyle and others.

I left proofs of title page and his own speech and Rhys' poem with him. He would examine them tomorrow. Had not been out today. W. said: "We ought not invite the carpers— ought not to deliberately put ourselves in the way of the carper." And then retracted with a laugh: "But what do we care for the carpers? They will carp anyhow, whatever we do! All we can do is to do the best thing in ourselves!" Gilchrist had addressed a letter to me (written in Phila.) to "Camden, New Jersey, U. S. A." W. laughed—"That is thoroughly characteristic of Herbert—I can see him in it!" W. laughingly asked me at one point: "How is it, Horace— are we America? In Canada I was always astonished to hear people speak of us as Americans—as if they were not as really American as we were." I said, "Ask Ed." W. thereupon, "How is it Eddy?" W. then went on: "Of course there is no difference at all—we all acknowledge it—and yet we go on calling ourselves exclusively American at somebody else's expense. Why not all American—the Canadian, the Mexican,

379

the Panamanian, the Nicaraguan—what-not!" Adding: "It affords an astonishing instance of how corruptions get legitimized—gain currency—become orthodox and are defended."

Saturday, July 20, 1889

7.55 P.M. W. sat in parlor in his shirt sleeves. Had not been out. "I've had a bad day—a devil of a bad day," he reported, "though now I am much easier and more nearly myself again." The day has been quite warm, though not excessively so. Mrs. Davis had been sitting talking with him; she now withdrew. "Ed has been to the post office—just came back," said W., asking, "Did I tell you of Burroughs' letter the other day? Ah! Yes! I have such a bad memory nowadays I put no faith in it. Did I tell you that John said anything about receiving the Unity? I sent him a copy—but now I don't remember if he said anything about receiving it: yet he should have acknowledged it." W. said further, "I do not in the least share Mrs. O'Connor's interpretation of the article—I don't think it at all justified: to me what you said is not only perfectly clear but perfectly true. Oh! the great O'Connor! How these Elizabethan fellows would have rejoiced to have had him with them! would have gathered about—listened—quickly recognized him as one of them—his great information—his grand famous speech!" This reminded me of the accompanying piece out of today's Times (Phila.) reviewing O'C.'s "Mr. Donnelly's Reviewers," which I read to W., partly at the window, then, as it grew dark, by gaslight which I secured. He exclaimed at the lines I had marked: "he was the only man who was positively known to have read Delia Bacon's book." "That's a lie, to start with—and all because the writer wanted to be sharp—epigrammatic; for the sake of the epigram he played truth false. But that is quite an ordinary trick of the author!" And after I was done: "Well—that don't amount to much, does it? It is very light! No one but William ever read

Delia Bacon's book? How about me, then, don't I count? I read it, read it all, cover to cover—and what is more, read it with greatest interest—and knew others who read it too and thought the reading worth while!"

I bought a copy of Bucke's Whitman today to give to Mrs. Fels. W. said, "It is a good book—it has my cordial regard right through. The book is guilty, like the dinner, of being too honeyish—is open to the same accusation—but apart from that has a distinct value. I think a good point is its sympathy. Victor Hugo or somebody else—the saying is just as good by whomever said—has said that a book ought always to be reviewed by friendly hands. Well, Doctor's book reviews me at friendly hands. But of this I should still say—be bold, be bold, be not too damned bold!—for one may err in friendliness, too. I should advise, commence to read me in November Boughs. Here I am found, not going back on the past, gently hinting all that has been claimed in Leaves of Grass—approaching the world we might say through its own media—in a Backward Glance defining myself, yet doing so, while positively, affably. As I have considered, this more and more has loomed up, asserted itself, as the wisest road. While it may strike you as peculiar, I may say it almost assumes the shape of a conviction with me." I said, "For a man who would take you up out of violent opposition, I might try to steer and advise, but I find that in a person who takes you up freely and open, his own instincts always find him right." To which: "Oh! that is a keen, profound judgment!—and it must be true—has all the ring of truth!" Asked me again of "my Jew constituency"—the young fellows, etc.—and said, "It does me proud to think they listen and share me! Who knows but after all the youth are my natural friends?"

Letter from Gilchrist who said he would be "pleased" to consent to the use of Tennyson letter in full. He asked if there could be objection. W. inquired, "Objection where? Over the water? Oh! I guess not: I should not for a minute hesitate to use it on that account." The proof I had left him last night he had laid on parlor table for me, but as I brought him proofs of some of the letters he said, "I'll keep both till tomorrow—then send 'em up to you by Ed—say at four or a little after." He "liked" the way his speech was set up. I suggested, "I should like to state that it is printed verbatim from your own slip." He asked, "Why?" And after my reply: "Oh! that they may know about it 60 years hence." "Well—do it if you choose—or perhaps I can give you a line for it: we'll see!" He laughed—"I won't criticise things in general— I'll be like Christy's man—I won't give it—I won't give it up —I won't have anything to do with it!"

Spoke of nationalities, lengthily. "I believe 'the poor in a loomp are bad!' just as Tennyson puts it—by poor, meaning human nature generally: and of course not [actually] all bad or mainly bad, but bad, bad! And yet in the average human nature—in the so-called ordinary man,—what decorous, gentle, affable, [kindly] manners are often seen— what persons developing!—I can see it almost day to day. And this among Americans more markedly than any others —certainly with a great and grave advance over European personalities. I suppose England contains the best specimens to be found abroad—but even England, how far short of our achievement! It is coming into the bone and marrow of the race—our race: we know it in the men North, South, East, West: any Maurice Buckeian, any Walt Whitmanian man, travelling America, getting en rapport with its civilization, its great average personalities, readily gives a cordial recognition to this precious quality. Herbert Gilchrist, Ernest Rhys, Edward Carpenter, are three who have actually spoken of it to me—three out of the many. And even these, seeing much though they did, fell far short of seeing what they might have seen—or, as I may better put it, what was to be seen." And this, W. was sure, would "go from more to more" till the grandeur of the nature had "testified of itself."

"How grand and good," exclaimed W., "it is to have a philosophy that includes all!—how inspiring to look at a man like O'Connor, so vehement, yet so catholic! It is as though we had got in touch with nature's profoundest, her largest, her last lesson, what we call mystery! William was a book-man—not an inch of him clear of the charge—but a book man after the most elemental sort, knowing the abstract book, [divining] its human purpose, meaning."

I was in to see Oldach today and he promises the morocco books without fail next week, though not specifying a day. Saw Brown too—told him portrait was O.K.

Sunday, July 21, 1889

Did not see W. at all today: was out of town—at Logan. But he went over some proof for me and sent it up to the house by Ed in the course of the afternoon. Though Sarrazin wrote his letter which I am using from London, W. wished it indicated in some way that S. was Parisian, etc. Also, as he had it much at heart—seemed a little concerned lest Herbert Gilchrist and I would "garble" the Tennyson letter—I let him arrange it to suit himself—and it proved to suit me perfectly. I have noted in the past week that he was a little twitted that I would not adopt some of his suggestions, but always comforted himself with saying, "It's not my funeral, but yours:" once laughingly saying—"If we do go on this way, it will prove a funeral!"

Monday, July 22, 1889

7.50 P.M. W. out on my arrival—had gone to the river between 6 and 7. Soon, however, he came up in his chair and hurried Ed up to the post office with several papers (no letters). Remained outside in his chair. We talked full half an hour. Said he felt "more comfortable but not stronger," but he certainly looked well (for him). "I sent a paper to John Burroughs today," W. remarked, "it was the Transcript—Boston Transcript—contained a notice of his last book." I alluded to Clifford's question whether (as found in proof of my article) two t's were necessary in "basketted." W. said: "I should not wonder but that the question was valid—but if it were my case I should not crack my skull to fix it—indeed, I doubt if it could be said that the t was wrong—only that it was unnecessary." Adding, "But it is very likely that an etiquettical litterateur—a pedagogue—would make a fight on the question." This raised another subject, connected. Burroughs, in the banquet letter, speaking of the American character, said: "We lack mass, inertia, and therefore, power." Contrasting with this W.'s possession of those qualities. W. said: "I am inclined to question that use of the word—and yet, provided a result is had, provided we can clearly take hold of a writer's intention, I rarely quarrel with peculiar manipulation of the language. I have always associated inertia with what is dull, sluggish, I may say dead: whether John discusses me with it don't worry me at all—it is not that—the question whether the quality would be considered a virtue or not don't enter." It seemed to me the word was wisely used, and I told W. my idea of it: but he still persisted: "It is a word that has been used to express a lack of verve—a lack of fire: it does not fully or even friendlily recommend itself to me." I judged from his tone, etc., that he would have desired J. B. to use a word of more definite purpose. But I did not agree.

I gave him a proof of the first page of letters again—and this, a couple of hours later in the evening, he returned (marked) to me, by Ed. He said as we sat together: "I particularly wished another proof to see how 'Paris' was worked in there at Sarrazin's name: it seems to me it ought to be generally known that he hails from Paris. Indeed, it is one of the great features of the book—you have said this yourself in your introduction—that all countries contribute, and this ought to be clearly signified. Besides, I—I, as a non-personal person—as Walt Whitman—I am immensely pleased with Sarrazin's adhesion—with his whole attitude—his enthusiasm: for he is a Frenchman of Frenchmen—a typical Frenchman—not the Frenchman we are told so much about—the Frenchman of etiquetteries, veneer, polish—but a Parisian of highest quality—of firm, lasting fibre—a Parisian the type in whom we will look for the best democrat, the perfect man." A political change of postmasters in Camden. W. remarked: "I shall regret it for several reasons—the principle is bad, in the first place—then I shall lose my carrier, who is a very good fellow. But then," he continued, "letter-carriers always seem a picked class—always seem of the best sort—only the best seem to gravitate to that business." I had received a letter from the Chicago man advising me to send the book anyhow. Gave W. check (with money from the Lychenheim boys) and he promised to send the book tomorrow. W. spoke of the beauty of the evening—"its unalloyed beauty—almost phenomenal." Mrs. Davis handed him a bag of mint-candy and he at once gave me a stick. "You favor it?" he asked, and then dilated like a child on his own fancy for it. Hearing that we had read Whitman some at Logan yesterday, he laughingly remarked —"You must have been prospered, having so good a cause!"

Tuesday, July 23, 1889

7.55 P.M. W. had just returned from his trip to the shore. Appeared well and talked well. But still avers that he "gains no strength." Complained of the heat of the day—at least, laughed over it—though had not thought it at all severe. At one point in our talk, when I spoke of "going up town," he said, "I wish I could say I would go with you!" I responded, "I wish you could!" He thereupon: "The worst thing with an old man when he is sick is that he sees nothing ahead—that for him, is nothing but reverse, down-hill. A young fellow, when he is sick—when he is poor—when he is troubled—has everything before him, but a man old, quite old, who has been badly whacked, as I have, has but to wait and expect an end!" I put in—"But a man of 70 is sure he has had his seventy years, whereas the young man has no assurance that he will have his!" W. laughed at first—then said soberly: "I don't know—he is sure if he has had 'em—but 70 empty years, what are they?" Added, however: "Did I ever quote you my favorite couplet? I've no doubt I have."—but he had not— "It reads something like this—

> 'Over the past not God himself has power,
> 'For what has been has been, and I have had my hour!'

It has a Drydenish sound—yet is very noble and grand." I said, "It is almost Shakespearean." He then: "It is, for loftiness—but too mellifluous for Shakespeare. It's true, it might be said, too grand for Dryden,—but then somehow these fellows can often catch up with the finest lines. But we know Shakespeare never encouraged mere beauty. I have no distinct idea at all where my couplet is from—nor of the words of the couplet itself—except that it has a grand tone."

Gilder's proof not returned to me yet. Said W.: "But the matter is in pretty good shape as it is? How much Gilder improves on contact—don't you think? It is not always the way, sometimes our disappointment in people—in meeting them— is keen. Gilder is always very cute—sometimes a great deal too cute. But, as you say, he is the man for the place—no doubt ably managing the magazine. Gilder was Holland's assistant. I think it was through Gilder's [illegible] that the Century took its great step forward in illustrations: this is my impression, just come upon me—or returned, perhaps, as told to me long ago. Certainly the Century in this respect has achieved wonders." As to "Topics of the Times," W. remarked: "I never read them—hardly look at them." Saying however that "so far as I have looked into them, Curtis and Howells, in Harpers, are of another stripe."

Alluded to a letter he had received today from Bucke. "He tells me of books he is reading—one of Renan's, for instance: let me see—oh yes!—some sort of a history of the Israelites; and then there was another—but I cannot recall it now. Bucke is a great reader—he is a good pick out of the typical English leisurely man of power. He has a good library—choked with valuable matter. I remember it well—would sometimes saunter in there myself—a big table in the middle of the room. Bucke reads both German and French—but most affects the German. Is a great Goethean, for example—reads a good deal in 'Faust'—thinks it among modern poems, the best, or almost that." W.'s ways very simple—several times children passed us as we sat there, each time he would stop talking—regard them lovingly and ejaculate something—an "Eh" or "Oh" but one full of significant music. When Uncle Danny, the garrulous old ferryman, came up, however, W., while kind to him, said very little and succeeded in freezing him off. Says his hearing still "perseveres in its badness." When I asked him—"What shall we do with 'the laughing philosopher'?" He laughed and answered—"I have not decided—let it go a day or two yet."

Wednesday, July 24, 1889

8 P.M. As usual, W. was not at home at the moment of my arrival, though coming soon after. I sat on the step and waited for him. Upon reaching home he hurried Ed off to the P.O. rapidly with a letter and some papers, but the hour was too late for receipt of mail, and he seemed a little disappointed that it was so. But Ed reminded him—"You know, we're always late now," and W. resigned himself, saying like a child, bound to comfort himself with something—"It was very fine down at the river, anyhow—we had a long, happy, inspiring

stay!" I did not stay long this evening. W. "wondered,"
among other things, "if the man, Edward Bertz, there in
Potsdam," had "yet received his book?"—though when I
inquired, W. himself did "not know whether" he had "sent
him the big book or the pocket edition"—excusing himself
with the explanation, "That's the treacherous sort of a
memory I have to deal with nowadays."

I received Gilder's proof-sheets back today, with a letter
from Marion, Mass., dated 23ᵈ July—in which he said—

Horace L. Traubel
Camden N. J.

My dear Mr. Traubel,
You will be alarmed at my corrections. But they are absolutely
necessary & you must let me pay for the proof changes—My
"involved style!" evidently isn't adapted to the reporter's uses—
The changes are to make clear what I said & not to add new ideas.
I saw by some of the papers that I was reported as saying that
W. W. surpassed all modern poets—including Tennyson—in
form—a manifest absurdity. What I thought I was saying was
that his style is unique & beautiful in itself; that it is admirable &
that no one—not even Tennyson can successfully imitate it. In the
proof I have omitted Tennyson because although it has been said
that it was W. he was imitating in some recent experiments, it is by
no means sure that this is so. I send on another page the passage
written out in case the printer is stuck. I *must* see a revise of this.
Please send it to me here. Surely accuracy is better than speed, is
it not, in a case like this.
You can direct to Julian Hawthorne care of Mr. Wᵐ Carey
Century Magazine
33 East 17ᵗʰ St. N. Y

Yours sincerely
R W Gilder

W. was much interested, but said little, though remarking,
when I told him that Gilder had cut out his little colloquy with

W. W. about "form"—"Did you say so?" etc. W. said: "I regret such a cut: that struck me as one of the best passages in the book; anyhow, there was no reason—at least, none to me —why it should be sliced out. Besides, I should have maintained the integrity of the speech—kept it mainly as it was: it seemed to me all right—or nearly right—as it is. Gilder has so blackened that with corrections, I think myself it might just as well be set up anew!" He did not object to G.'s cut of his reference to Tennyson, though admitting it was not "necessary" to excise it, as was "undoubtedly the case with Bonsall's."

W. spoke of Gilchrist: "He was over last night but only for a little while: he always comes so late!" I had letter from Bush (Lachine Locks) today in which he inquired where he could get a good photo of W. W. thereupon—"Why—we must give him one—he deserves it: he must have one and a good one!" Gets home from shore later nights now than of old. Lingers by the shore.

Thursday, July 25, 1889

7.55 P.M. Again I had to wait till W. had returned from his chair-voyaging. But tonight he had provided for one thing— came home by way of P.O. and got his mail, which he always is pained to miss. I had a letter from Bucke, saying: "I must be away all day tomorrow in Sarnia, at Pardee's funeral—tell W. that Pardee passed away quietly at noon yesterday. It is well—his mind had been completely gone for weeks—did not know a single soul—could not speak a word—absolute eclipse." I asked W. if he had heard from Bucke recently? "Oh yes! a letter within a day or two." "Did he say anything in it of Pardee?" "No—why?" Then I explained as above. W. exclaimed, "Oh! I had heard nothing of that. Poor Pardee! Gone at last!" Then added, "Yes—he has been here to see me —I have met him: he was what you would have called a brainy man—a man of parts, intellectuality. He at one time occupied a position of importance under the government up there—as I understood, had weight in counsel—was a man rare in his way. And now he is passed away! Nor was he old, either—probably 60—if older, not much above it. Poor Pardee! It is the end of the drama, for him!" Several times last year Bucke wrote me that it was singular, his three closest friends—O'Connor, Whitman, Pardee—down with like afflictions—and W. expected then to be the first to go. But first O'Connor, now Pardee, and still W. is in one sense whole and sound and gives us hope.

When I asked him if he had looked up a picture for Bush yet he exclaimed—"O! bless my heart! I never thought of it at all, the whole day through. That's a good sample of my memory these days. And yet he must have it—it or something; for I want to prove to him that he is remembered!" I sent Gilder his "revise" today. W. remarked: "It was a horrible sight to look upon—wasn't it? And yet I know an author's temptation always to do likewise—I myself, for one—I am always tempted to put in, take out, change. Though, having been a printer myself, I have what may be called an anticipatory eye—know pretty well as I write how a thing will turn up in the type—appear—take form. But in spite of that, I remember how, years ago, I used to wish for the privilege for myself—the privilege to alter—even extensively. But various things have intervened—the doubt if I would better it if I did go at it again—the thought of the printer—such considerations!"

Then: "That reminds me—I have a mission for you—a commission: I want you to buy something for me. Eddy," turning to Ed, who sat on the step next me—"Ed, go into the parlor—you will find a little bit of a package there on a table—near it a big card—bring me both." Which Ed did—W. thereupon continuing, "They are pens. I want some of the big pens—Esterbrook's: I know you can find them—they come on a card—a dozen of them—with a holder along." It was Ester-

brook's "Mammoth," of which I took due note. He added—
"The old army passes were written with enormous big pens,
sometimes: have you never seen one? I must hunt one up and
give it to you. They were written immense—a letter an inch
high often—intended to be read at night—by light of lamp,
lantern, candle, what-not—anything. Yes, they were often
forged—but not forged as much as you would suppose: the
fellows grew to be very cute in detecting forgeries. Oh! how
the past comes back, even by such a little memory as that!"

Habberton in town recently—Ferguson printing a book of
his. Had he been over? "No—you remember, I don't know
Habberton personally: I am told he is very friendly to me, to
Leaves of Grass—even warmly so—but I have never met him."
W. wrote on the sheet that he gave me containing sample
(old) pen: "Get me a card of, (or any other way) this kind
pens W. W."

Friday, July 26, 1889

7.50 P.M. Rained slightly. W. at parlor window. Had not
been out. Found his deafness no better—hears very defec-
tively, now—having to ask so much repetition. Said of his
condition: "Till this evening, my day has been very poor—a
poor one indeed. Now I am better." Then—"And I have had
little news today—a letter from Bucke—that is all. Doctor
says little more than that he is just back from Sarnia, where he
had gone to attend Pardee's funeral. Poor Pardee! His fever is
done for at last!" I had found him the pens today. When I
displayed the card, he exclaimed, as he put on the glasses—
"Just the thing! It is a replica—it is a revival. What could
better satisfy a man than to be satisfied?" Then he asked—
"Where did you get them?" "At Murphy's." "Oh! I supposed as much. I wonder if that is the same old, old firm of
great stationers?" As it was—and, "I wonder if the old
Murphy's—the father's, grandfather's—sons, grandsons—

branched off to New York? It is an Irish family: I knew Murphys in New York 30 or 40 years ago—famous men in their line—stationers." He was going to insist that I take pay for the pens. I said, "No—I will take a copy of the little green Passage to India instead for Mrs. Fels—I want a copy"—but he still insisted—"Well—take both—I want you to take both —this must have been an absolute outlay of 30 or 40 cents." But as I was stubborn too, he had to relax, promising to lay Mrs. Fels' book out for me tomorrow.

Speaking of Emerson I said to W. that I was thinking out for myself a letter to write to Edward Emerson about that footnote. He still insisted that I would get no reply. I retorted —"I'll bet I can write a letter to which he will have to reply: I won't knock him down—I won't write in that mood: but he will have to answer me in some way." He laughed somewhat. "Well —I should not advise against you—it—I am always in favor of having a fellow do what he is strongly bent on doing— what comes to him as a duty; what he feels he must do, that by all odds he is bound to do—bound. That has been my course from the first—to write what I must write—not hesitatingly but decisively—and will be, I'm sure. But we have enemies and enemies. I find there are opponents of Leaves of Grass with reasons and without reasons: some without reasons who have not a leg to stand upon, men who, like a row of defective houses, no one of which could stand alone—any wind, any un-usual disturbance would ruin them—but which, braced one by the other, very well hold their heads up. I am very much afraid Edward Emerson is one of such a dozen. The literary classes, so-called, are prone to be so—to be stiff, unyielding, to despise: many in Boston—certainly—mostly the whole gang in New York." I protested, "Philadelphia has no literary class, in fact, but Boker and Furness, its two real men, are friendly towards you—both of them." W. "That is so—I realize that, too—and it hits deep. I really consider them friendly—nobly generous."

Remarked further along, "I have been reading Amiel again —that is, reading him in my way: taking him up casually— from time to time—his 'Journal Intime.' But I found no change from my first impression. It is very introspective— very full of sin—of looking sinwards—a depressing book, in fact." I asked: "Don't you think, then, it is a bad book for you to read?" "Yes—I do—it is depressing—it gives no relief." I passed the conversation to another book: "My friend Johnston today came in and left with me Bellamy's 'Looking Backward': how would it suit you to read that?" He lighted up instantly —"Excellently well—oh! excellently. I have been recommended by quite a dozen—and a dozen of the best fellows— my fellows, friends—to read it." We discussed social tendencies. I referred then to Nationalist Organ in Boston, W., after I had described its purport, saying: "Well—let 'em whack away—let 'em be heard—anarchist—socialist—what-not: the world has, therefore needs them all. And whatever, I am sure I shall like at least to look at that book, whenever you may bring it down." To Bush's so-frequent use of the "we"— including his wife in nearly all his good words for W., W. said tonight—"Good for him! And good for the wife: that is what it should be. I have often felt, my good luck with the women has been phenomenal!" Spoke of Heine: "Although by birth a German, he was to all intents and purpose, French— possessed of the French lightness of touch, yet not flippantly superficial either: he was rather a sampler of the true—the grander—French."

Saturday, July 27, 1889

8 P.M. W. in bathroom when I came. Sat in the parlor with Ed till W. came down, which he did shortly. Ed explained that W. had another of his attacks of indigestion—had not had a passage for 4 or 5 days; but would not take medicine, arguing it did more harm than good—afflicted his head. W. himself was

not confident in treating of his health. Did not get out today—
partly because of the cloudiness but mainly because of his
weak condition. "Nothing further from Doctor," he said, "and
little other news, in fact. Buckwalter was in to see me today.
The purpose of his visit being, to press me to make that visit
to Gutekunst. He was very urgent—insisted, almost—said he
would see to having me taken there and brought back, which
is very important, as I know and you know: a fellow with such
locomotive inability as mine has to be well attended to. Much
of my reason for going would be, the weather, my condition,
the ease of transportation—this probably best secured
through Geiss, the old hackman there at the ferry, who knows
how to handle me—has handled me often—and well. But then
after all that is considered, the previous question arises—why
go at all? What's the good of it? It would be quite a serious
job—and haven't I had enough pictures—more than enough
—taken? And many of 'em good ones, too?" This reminded
him of a package he had there on the table for me marked in
blue pencil "Passage to India and three pictures W W"—
which he picked up and handed to me. "Here is your book,—
your 'Passage to India'—and three pictures—you can send
them to Bush—all or any of them."

I had an inquiring postal from Clifford today about the
big book—some one up there at Farmington desired a copy. I
spoke of it to W., who replied: "And that makes me think—
I ought to send something to Clifford himself: he sent me the
Amiel book to read—I ought to show a sense of the obligation."
And so he was very specific in getting C.'s address, whether to
write it simply J. H. Clifford, or spell out the "John" or
precede all by Reverend, which of course I advised against.
He added: "I thought to send him it and have him read—the
Mazzini book—you know the book I have there? It is, in my
eyes, a valuable volume—peculiarly valuable, unique,—I
might almost call it sweet—for two at least of its essays—
essays on Byron and Goethe: Oh! they have an exquisite

subtlety. I knew these essays as many as forty—at least 30—years ago—and through all these years, as then, they have attracted, held, fascinated, absorbed me. Mazzini could write a good English, too—so I am told—though writing mainly in Italian and having it rendered into English. His personality was a rarely beautiful one—grand—unusual, and Clifford could not miss him." Would simply addressing at Farmington do? "I shall send it—or let you send it—just as comes up as most convenient and easy—fits in with my mood." "Was Clifford there for a long stay?" he asked again. And then of the nature of the country, etc. And when I got up to go after a while he again said, "We'll send the book—either you or I."

I sent him the Bellamy book by Ed last evening. He now said of it: "I have looked at it: it is a curious and interesting— I was going to say, perplexing—volume, but knowing so little of it yet, I ought not to say anything about it." I repeated to him a "personal" from the last number of Current Literature: "Walt Whitman says that the greatest pleasure of his old age has been in reperusing the novels of Charles Dickens." He looked at me in amused astonishment: "Does he? That's news to me! I was a reader of Dickens from the first—liked his books—Nicholas Nickleby, Oliver Twist, others: but a dweller-upon, an enthuser, a make-mucher of, I never was—never—am not today. And you know, today I don't read him at all! But that is the interviewer through and through—the paragrapher: delegated to fill a certain space, he sits down in the Moncure Conwayish manner, decides upon what would interest the public, and so puts that down as history. But history! Pscha! I think of what old Doctor Johnson once wisely said—I think it was him: the Doctor thinking that a fellow can well measure out how much credit he is bound to give history by remembering how many lies are told of him, and go on record as facts. I know there are interviewer exceptions—that often there's a framework legitimate enough for the story—making it probable, anyhow, that what is related is true. But generally, the capacity of an interviewer for not getting the facts of the case into his narrative is extraordinary—surpasses all belief."

Debate on royal grants in Parliament yesterday resulted in support of the crown by a vote of 398 to 116. W. had "followed the debate with a great interest" and now said to me about it—"It struck me not as victory but defeat for the crown. I was reminded of a story—a saying—I think drawn out during our Revolutionary War—that a few more victories like that for the enemy will make us great guns. And so the Queen's enemies will be great guns if these signs continue. There seem to be several reports about her—one that she is a hunks—a hoarder, miser, getting a sovereign and taking good care to keep it; then others say this is not true—that she is just the opposite. But I incline to believe the first story nearer the truth." As to the Prince of Wales—"He is pictured as a jolly, affable sort of a dog—a bon vivant—though with how much justice I could not tell. This has raised what I suppose is a great question to Englishmen, these children of the children—this third generation!" I am to leave for him in the morning the proof-sheets of speeches of Gilder, Hawthorne, Bonsall, Garland, Eyre, and he will examine, suggest, and return to my house by Ed, if I do not get back from the country in time to see him (I am going to Mrs. Fels' at Logan). I must return same to Myrick on Monday.

Sunday, July 28, 1889

Did not see W., but left at his house in the early forenoon the proofs I had promised. Also with these the Bush pictures. A note along, asking if he would not endorse one of the pictures. He had not done so in case of any one of the three. Late in night, when I got home, he had sent me pictures all autographed (the 1855 steel—the Gutekunst phototype—the complete works frontispiece). Also sent Mazzini book for me

to send Clifford, with this note written in blue pencil on back
of one of the proofsheets:

"Say to Clifford I send the Mazzini book more especially for the
'Byron and Goethe' piece tho' the whole Vol is interesting—I
shall want it returned, but am in no hurry

"W W"

His suggestions on proofsheets were very light. Wondered,
should we not write "Harry" instead of "Henry" L. Bonsall?
But B. always prints himself Henry. The one essay particularly spoken of in the Mazzini book is heavily marked by W.

Monday, July 29, 1889

7.55 P.M. W. at parlor window. Had not been out. "Not
extra well," he reported. It has been a very hot day. Read him
a letter I had today from Brinton, (Geneva). The passage
following—

It gave me especial pleasure to learn that our national poet's
70th birthday had been celebrated in so successful a manner, and
that he himself is feeling at least no worse in health than when I
left, and is, as ever, and as he must ever be, so firm and so serene in
soul. When I was at Parma, I saw a picture by Murillo, one of the
greatest of that greatest of masters, representing Job in his direst
affliction, lone, naked, deserted, his potsherd in his hand, but looking up to heaven with an utter faith, that I have seen in no other
painting, and that, as I told Mrs. Brinton, I could parallel in
nothing else than in those lines of Whitman's on Columbus—

"Poor, old and paralyzed,
"My God, I thank thee."

I am certain that in these noble words the poet has expressed the
calmness in affliction which is his own, and though I cannot share
in the faith which it breathes, I honor and admire any disposition
of mind which lifts the man above his fate.

Seemed greatly to touch him. "That is very fine—fine indeed!"
Harned (came to town today) had a letter from Burroughs,
in which B. questioned the importance of the W. memorial
volume. W. remarked: "Neither John nor I may like to confess
it, but it is true, nevertheless, that in the last 12 years or so
there has a great change come over him—the literati have
seriously affected him. It is the Emersonianism in John—the
spirit that starts out to gather all it can of others, that gives
an ear to everything. It is partly a result of John's body, the
corpus, John physically. By instinct he is sound, but his body
militates against him. I remember this was so when I first
knew him. But this pessimism—this insomnia—is a quantity
not to be accounted for, inexplicable; except you start out
with the hereditary sense of the man—the ancestry—and
trace it from that, which is the real fact at last. For instance,
in that Bacon controversy: John never took an intense interest
—in spite of himself he was inclined towards the literary
position. There are consciences and consciences—a moral
conscience, an aesthetic conscience—all that—but these are
quite different from that conscience of which Elias Hicks so
often spoke—the conscience of consciences,—that conscience
which ordered the largest measure of fact—that penetrating,
fibrous, spinal quality which over-arches all. The literary
conscience is a leaning, a surrender—sacrifices itself to other
consciences, and here it is John has been touched. It is the
spirit of Emersonianism, which is the spirit of culture, of
knowledge, of elegance. Not that Emerson had it in the least,
but that Emersonianism leads straight to it, and it is dangerous, Horace—dangerous from the start—it is a playing with
fire. O'Connor never changed in spirit—to the last he was
what he had been." As to J. B.'s criticism of the book, W.
protested: "John is wrong: even to me—certainly to our
group—to our earnest fellows—it is plain that here was a sign
of progress—an evolution. There was Gilder's speech: I did
not object to his changes—the whole speech reads well and it

is quite radical enough and now this puts us right at a point showing the importance of the book—that it has an importance for here is Gilder applauding at the very point at which the Philistines have long stormed. I do not object that he cut out the little colloquy, because he substantially inserts it anyhow in the text—yet it might have remained and been a good addition—fit well in the place." Buckwalter thought Gilder "finicky," but W. declared—"anyhow, he is radical enough for us here."

I met Buckwalter today. Among other things he told me W. had once a couple of years ago promised Bonsall to carefully search L. of G. for a certain sort of errors or unfortunate repetitions, lapses from art, etc. W. said very positively: "That sounds very doubtful—I know nothing about it—especially the part of it, that I went down to Harry and excused myself, saying I was too sick. That alone would stamp the story, is not me. You see, Horace, that is the way history is written. I should say, this story is not only essentially wrong, but wrong in detail. I am but a fragment, anyhow—Leaves of Grass is a modality of but fragments. If I should attempt to perfect it, I am afraid the result would be as with Balzac's proof sheets, that they caused the whole matter to be set up again! Why, it would be a hell-of-a job!" And he added—"You see how it is: the little a man says is often made a world of, and stretched wholly in the wrong direction, too: this, undoubtedly, if it arose in anything, arose in something quite different from what is reported."

He had read the proofs I left him yesterday carefully. "And do you know, boy, that speech of Lincoln Eyre's is one of the best—I do believe as good as any—especially the way he speaks of democracy—delivering stern blows, defined, undeniably strong and to the point. I don't know how the excellence of that escaped me before, but it did." Said he: "I guess you are right about 'Henry L. Bonsall.'" I had explained. Spoke of the little book again "It is a step forward: I could easily say that if the book involved another: then why not now?" I sent off the Mazzini book to Clifford and pictures to Mrs. Bush today. W. said as to Bush's inquiry which was the best W. W. edition for him to buy: "Tell him the big book: that is complete, authorized—that is the book." Then reverting to Bonsall W. exclaimed: "How foolish it would be for me to make such a promise! The book Leaves of Grass as it stands now is the book as it will stand in the future if it stands at all. I shall substantially never touch it again: it must go, make its way, be what it may be, just as it exists now—nothing added, practically—nothing taken off!" "I look upon L. of G. as it now stands as the final version, utterance—the last pledge, statement." W. spoke of Canada: some one had lately taken a trip—been enthusiastic—W. thereupon, "Yes—I do not wonder: it is full of scenic surprises: among other features, has a thousand little lakes, from a mile to 5 miles in length, which are not found in the maps, but are of wonderful beauty and interest." Speaks of having "the laughing philosopher" cut narrowed. "As it is now, it will not go into any of my books." Eventually he proposes to use it in Leaves of Grass. Was interested to know if negative had been returned to Cox yet. I told him the negative had not after all been used. Having to reduce the picture, it was found easier to do so on the print.

Tuesday, July 30, 1889

On my way out of town, stopped in to see Whitman at 5, and found him eating his dinner. A hot, clouded, much-raining day. He sat in his bedroom: his meal rather meagre, but even as it was, "more than I care to eat"—some things wholly untouched, a fan in his right hand,—his left used for knife and fork, etc. He had prepared a superscription for the Morse picture, of which he said as often before, "I am satisfied with it, though not in love with it: it will do." Did not look well. Said he had spent a bad day, altogether. No news. I did not linger. Ed informed me W. was extremely feeble the day through—had been quite sick, lethargic, early in the day.

Wednesday, July 31, 1889

7.45 P.M. W. sitting with Ed in parlor. Hard rains again today, so he was again robbed of his outing. Speaking to him of check for Brown, for engraving, he said: "Is it 13 dollars? Isn't that more than the others? I wonder if he is going to make up on that for the cut we didn't take?" Which I thought an unfair remark and told him so, whereat he said: "I guess you are right. I can give you either the check or cash tomorrow." Asked me how I got along with the book. Suggested several details. "I always leave my title-page till the last and always keep a full set of proof-pages as I go along. It has always been my habit to do so: I have found it a very good way." W. had a cold: voice not at all clear and hearing very bad: had me repeat a great deal in our conversation. Asked me about my country trip last night—of the great rains and how I traversed them, interpolating his peculiar ejaculations.

He said here—"Tom was in—come about an hour ago. He told me about John's letter—just about what you told me." Adding after a pause, "I don't know where to address John now—whether at Hobart or somewhere else. That is his brother's place—off there in Delaware County—Berwyn— something like that. A land grand and fine from the scenic side—and for its fresh sweet air—but probably not fertile, in the farm-sense—in crops—wheat—what not. I, too, was a land-owner once—oh! long long ago. Did you never know it? Why, yes—it was so: I had a farm—have it yet, for all I know, but guess not. It was a gift—I never saw it—never followed it up—some wild wooded land somewhere off there to the west. It must have been as good as thirty years ago—but I suppose it has now reverted." I laughed, "How?" Whereat he added, "Oh! I never paid a cent of tax on it—never inquired about it—never took the slightest interest. It came to me in the early years of Leaves of Grass—even at that time Leaves of Grass had an admirer—a disciple. He was a rich old man—a New-York-City man and with a grand port, too—grey-bearded—fine head and body—I can see him now. But I have lost sight of him—he must have been dead long ago—long ago—and his gift to me no doubt is lost—now in other hands." He then spoke of country air generally. I described some old experiences in the mountains about Bushkill—the great vistas—particularly the rivers. W. then, "Yes—I can see them all—all: I can take in the whole picture. To one who knows as I do what it all means, it is always painful to come back into the cities—the streets—the stinking reeking streets —Mickle Street—sluttish gutters—women with hair a-flying —dust-brooms clouding the streets—confinement—the air shut off. Oh! I know with the most knowing what you have described. And I know best of all the rivers—the grand, sweeping, curving, gently undulating rivers. Oh! the memories of rivers—the Hudson—the Ohio—the Mississippi! It would be hard to put into a word the charms of the Mississippi: they are distinctive, undoubted—do not consist in what is called beauty—which, for instance, would be picked out as essentially the wonders of the Hudson—consist rather in amplitude, power, force,—a lazy muddy water-course, immense in sweep —in its various wanderings. The Hudson is quite another critter—the neatest, sweetest, most delicate, clearest, cleanest, river in the world. Not sluttish—not a trace of it and I think I am pretty familiar with it—at least as it was—for the matter of 200 miles or so, which is about the whole story. The beginnings of the Delaware are scattered all through southern New York—delicate threads finally making way to union and power. Rivers! Oh the rivers! When you described the Delaware as you saw it from that mountain-top—the fields and hills about it—the placid flowingness—I was there—I saw it all—I felt the odor of it steal about me, envelope me!" He talked in this strain for some time, as if his whole heart was in every word.

Thursday, August 1, 1889

7.45 P.M. W. sitting at window, as usual—in parlor. Rain still prevailing—an unwonted session. W. laughingly asked me: "Are you going to bring us this kind of weather every night?" Of course had not been out today. I brought him 10 of the 20 copies of the morocco book without flap—opening package and displaying one to him in the half-darkness. He at once pounced on the pictures and the fact that Oldach had not strictly followed his directions,—given more margin at bottom than top—"An idea which I much fancy." Told me to take a copy, but promised to give me tomorrow, in exchange for it another, inscribed. I gave him Oldach's bills. He handed me envelope containing $13.00 for Brown. "I forgot all about his name," he exclaimed, "my usual habit—nowadays!"

Morris had brought me in the first part of Sarrazin's piece, fully translated. I gave to W., who was very particular to ask: "Do you think he finds it a good deal bigger job than he calculated for? Should we ask him to continue?" Adding, however, that he "hoped not" and was "appetized now to see it all." I told him Morris had said Sarrazin understood W. W., though he was "extravagant" and "high-falutin." W. laughed: "Yes—I suppose he is high-falutin!—and so is God-Almighty! God Almighty is very high-falutin! All his ways, globes, habits—high-falutin! I suppose in all our millions of population—our 80 millions—teeming, spreading—there are not a dozen men—not a dozen, even—who realize—really realize,—realize in the sense of absolutely picturing, nearing, participating in it—vibrating, pulsing—that this earth we inhabit is whirling about in space at the rate of thousands of miles a minute—going on in a hell of a way: that this earth is but one of a cluster of earths—these clusters of clusters of clusters again—and all again, again, again, circulating, whirling about a central system, fact, principle—movement everywhere incessant immense, overwhelming. Now—I doubt if there are a dozen men who really sketch that to themselves —perceive, embrace, what it means—comprehend in the midst of what a high-falutin extravagant creation we live, exist. And yet things go on and on—keeping up their high-falutin course!" He thought "the literary fellows, like Morris, Gilder, all look too much at conventional things—at the usual order: they lack and do not understand in others, vigor—vigor. Yet there is a brave penetration about Sarrazin which beats anything heretofore—is better than Maurice Bucke's, better than John Burroughs', better than Wm. O'Connor's—the largest, most liberal investigation so far, particularly in what he says of evil—of evil, not for itself but as an essential of the orbic system—the cosmos. There has been no such word spoken elsewhere. No—it is not astonishing in Sarrazin as a Frenchman, for Sarrazin is not Continental Frenchman—continental this or that—but continental, elemental, having the intuitive, native, original cognitions. High-falutin, natural—he may have been. How Voltaire ridiculed Shakespeare as a barbarian. The story is told of him—it is not very nice—and I don't know if authentic—that someone protested—'but he is natural even if barbaric'—to which it is said Voltaire replied, slapping his back-side, so"—indicating—" 'So is this natural, but I don't make a display of it!' This was the rock on which Stedman split once—long ago—but he has come out of that—come bravely. It is a point—a greatest point—I always declare for many of the fellows—or fellows like Stedman and Morris particularly: the power of getting on—of moving out—of overcoming themselves with themselves—it is the Emersonianism of it all—of our time: I used to feel—feel now—that of all points in Emerson, that was finest by which he taught men how to escape Emersonianism itself: Emersonianism against Emersonianism. Emerson was cultured—generations of culture were in him—but he was more, too—he was a superb gift to our time—abundant in native powers."

He said at one moment with respect to the book: "I think Tom is right—I don't think it ought to be a dunghill, for everything to be dumped in it that happens to be laying around. That is what I thought in connection with the 'pudding-head' business: I know the expression was mine—that O'Connor uses it as mine, there in the letter—and though I should not for general reasons have objected to what I said of Ingersoll going into the book—there are particular reasons why it is best out—this for one of them." But as for those who had believed "he wanted to take the Colonel down," W. responded, "That is a great mistake: I aimed at nothing of the sort: I think too much of the Colonel for that. It probably is true that I was a great deal more vehement years ago than I am now—Oh! I know I was! In my old days I take on the usual privilege of years—to go slow, to be less vehement, to trust more to quiet, to composure."

He had got a portrait from Garland today and spoke to me of it. "It is very good—it shows him up in good style." I said, "Garland is a good-looking man, but the handsomest of all your friends is Edward Carpenter." To which he fervently responded—"That he is! That he is! I have thought it myself!" He knew I was getting up the O'Connor article for Liberty and gave me "counsel" of things well to be said. When I said, "I have anticipated you in some of that—it is already said," he responded, "Good—good—emphasize the point that O'Connor was a scholar—every inch of him—but a scholar after his own kind—after the real kind: a hail fellow to the Elizabethan men, yet one in himself purely American, using his great accumulations for living purposes." At one moment he exclaimed, "There is the little speech of Eyre's—why, he takes the bull right by the horns: means democracy, says democracy—seems to take easy hold of what I hope is ever and ever the point of my teaching—if teaching there is—

405

democracy, freedom, unity, universality, inclusion! I like that speech more and more, it is small, but it covers the whole ground."

After going out, as I passed the window, W. leaned forward —called me—"Horace—I should like you to take Ed here, to the opera. It is to be my treat. I should like him to see 'Fra Diavolo' and 'The Bohemian Girl'—especially the latter—the latter first. I see Castle is there with that troupe—still singing, singing." Asked me if Castle was "any good" any more—and upon my negative, "Well I supposed not, as a singer—but 15 or 20 years ago, when he was in his prime he was prime indeed. They were his halcyon days—I saw him often. In the rollicky characters, his abandon was great—a thing to be studied and pleased with." So I promised to go with Ed and he was satisfied. Then a final "goodnight"!

Friday, August 2, 1889

7.30 P.M. Went to W.'s earlier than usual, having to go to town, to Old Man's Home. W. asked where I was going and who to see and asked—"Will you be going again?" Adding, "Then I will get you up a bundle of papers to take with you next time." Not out yet, the stormy weather still persisting. Looks rather thin and worn. But is cheerful. Voice strong and vibrating. Worst time always the forenoon—best, this. I did not stay long. Shortly went up to P.O. with Ed. W. had sent Dr. Bucke 2 copies of morocco book last bound. I asked jokingly, "Did you send him the bill?" Whereat he exclaimed —"A bill? No indeed—I should be ashamed to send him a bill!" Was very anxious to have Ed find out if he had put the requisite amount of postage on. As to the books, "they pleased me very well—very well indeed." Wrote in a copy for me while I stayed. I left page proof with him of the Bertz translation and reprint of circular announcing the celebration. Would "probably look over them tomorrow." Saw Billstein today and his reply was, yes, he could print well on cardboard. W. thereupon—"I will get you up an order so you can go see him early next week—size of card, etc." Will probably get some of the McKay pictures also so struck off. I paid Brown his bill today, and left the cut with Billstein, subject to further explanation. Notice of expiration of insurance on the 8th came today.

Asked me if I had seen The Century—"and the picture of Tennyson there?" And when I spoke of pain in Tennyson's face, W.—"That did not so much strike me, tho' I can see it is there, but the picture itself—oh! isn't it grand? Tennyson is a very old man, well towards the 90—and we must expect age in his face. What engaged me was the picture as a piece of noble workmanship. Did you notice his nose—what a tremendous nose he has! And yet it appears essential—the more you look at it!" Spoke of burden of taxation and laughed about his "farm," on which he had never paid a cent. "The wise old Franklin thought taxes very sure—and they are, doubtless, but taxes and that farm, while I held it or seemed to hold it— for I never really had anything to do with it—certainly never saw it—had very little to do with each other." Referred to Burroughs once as "inclined of late days to be pessimistic." Of "Looking Backward"—"I am looking through it: I can't say I am ravished with it: but it has a certain sort of interest."

Saturday, August 3, 1889

7.45 P.M. Another day of confinement: rain plentiful and this evening dark clouds still floating overhead. W. in parlor. Ed out. Said he had gone over proofs today, but if I "did not need them" I had best leave them till tomorrow. "They are up stairs, on the foot of the bed—with them the bust, with what I should suggest to go along with it." I sent proof of bust to Morse today, asking if he approved. W. said: "Don't close all the pages of the book out—I have one—perhaps a couple—

to add at the end." But when I questioned him, what?—he replied: "I don't know myself—it is all in a nebulous condition—state: what it will be, come to, I could not say—but most likely something."

Hereupon I read him a note received from Buxton Forman, to which he said, after listening intently and having parts read a second time—murmuring much over the reference to him as a prophet—"That is very bold—he makes long strokes: but I suppose you are right—it ought to go in if it can." After a pause adding—"I want to say to you, Horace, too, how much I like Harrison Morris' rendering of Sarrazin—it seems to me good—very good; besides, it is just what I want—exactly—a close rendering—verbal. You know, I consider Sarrazin's piece our Koh-i-noor—unsurpassed—the very topmost, wonderful for its daring, its explicitness. Oh! I think there is a marvellous lightness of touch in parts of it that, in the French, must be delicious, appetizing, beyond our alien conceptions. It is Forman's excuse, too—that to fellows who have encountered so much of the 'I dare not, wait upon I would' spirit, as we have, it is refreshing to come upon such a positive declaration." He felt "more strongly than ever" that the Sarrazin should be published. "How I don't just know. Not in the Camden papers, of course, but somewhere. I have been thinking, in the Home Journal—that they would give us their columns. Not that I could expect to get it all in one number, but to have it run two or three weeks. Still," he said deliberately, "we had better go slow about it—say nothing about it now—let it hang, work in us, gestate, find finally its own undeniable result. That is my habit—they call it my procrastination—it has always been my habit. And while my friends always declare that I have lost much by it—my best opportunities, even—I feel for myself that I have gained, too—that in some large sense it has been the making of me—has been me, in fact. Now, take this little book of ours, for instance—how good it was not to hurry it! If you had followed my original notion—which has not been my notion since—and had got it out at once, within a few days—its distinctiveness, much that does now distinguish it, and will, would have been utterly lost—utterly."

I spoke of Clifford's minister friend True, at Farmington, who wished a copy of the big book but seemed staggered at its price. W. said he would let T. have one for 4 dollars and the expressage or postage. "That is my price to Dave, and this man shall have the like favor." Then he said, "And when you write to Clifford again tell him that when he is done with the Mazzini book, instead of sending it here he send it to Kennedy. Of course he is to take his time—to read it only as he can—I do not press him. I shall have Kennedy send it again to Dr. Bucke." I queried, "And he back to you? I hope so—for I should like to read the essay myself." To which—"Oh yes! He will send it back—that is the idea—and of course you shall have it as long as you wish. I want the book here by me—in a sense it is a household book. Of course that essay is the particular piece I am after. Mazzini's great ideal was the collective— to me that seems very significant—collective democracy, as opposed, or as complementing, our individual—or as we call it, individualistic, democracy. And there is a great deal to be said on that side, to be sure. I often question myself—being such an individualist—if I have not made too little of it—but I guess not—I guess that is all provided for—I have great faith that the tendency of things in our modern life will take good care of that. And yet it is a point to be well considered— even I grant it. Mazzini's was a great and lofty spirit, an off-set in his philosophy as it were, to his friend, Carlyle, who was confirmed in other ways, as I am. I had a picture of him— have it yet, I guess. I think him one of the most significant and suggestive characters of our century. A fanatic in some respects—very religious, too—I doubt if there has been or is such another devoted man on the planet. This particular essay, which I so much admire, has peculiar and marvellous qualities. Oh! take for instance, Macaulay: he was nothing like Macaulay. Macaulay was a brilliant pyrotechnical master of verbal melody, but Mazzini dealt in essences—went right to the fountainhead. And there was verbal felicity, grandeur, too. Oh! Did I never tell you of the way he opens that essay? I always thought it a splendid description—and yet it is not long —takes only about a page or less of the little Walter Scott book. He says the idea of the thing was first suggested to him in the Alps—I think it a place called Jurra, or by some such name. A storm was coming on—overhead and sailing across the sky were clouds—dark ponderous masses—everything portending a storm—the elements all of a rage—hell abroad and loose—the forerunners everywhere of one of those terrific Alpine storms, greater even than our Western storms which are so violent—of which we make so much. In the midst of all the turmoil he sees a falcon, ascending, ascending, riding on the storm—rising, rising"—W. gesticulated and his voice was eloquent and deep—"with each increased gale seeming to go higher and higher—regarding everything with a fearless, defying eye—up and up and up—the storm meanwhile nearing and nearing—the bird never afraid, never shrinking, never losing control—up—up—up—till at last it is gone into the clouds, into the heavens, God-embraced, safe, grandly self-subserved. Then he tells of a stork there on the hills—he not afraid either—how he gathered one leg in, folded it about— how he looked up, out, calmly, not greatly curious, but taking in everything. So he goes on—taking little space to tell it, yet giving us one of the grandest of figures—the very grandest. Of course telling it a thousand times better than I can. As you see, the falcon was Byron, the stork Goethe. It was a vivid lightning-touch—the rare insight of a rare nature—a flash from a master."

I received a letter from Mrs. Bush today which I read to W., who was pleased that the pictures had arrived safely. Also referred to a Boston Advertiser account of a visit to Emerson (see Current Literature July or August) and Emerson's evident mental weakness. W. said—"It sounds very like. But I don't think in those days any of Emerson's friends—Sanborn, his family, the neighbors—ever trespassed much upon him—asked him to write anything—imposed upon his reserve —the retirement of his spirit—beautiful it was, too!" And he asked by and by, as we still continued of Emerson—"How do you stand about that letter to Edward Emerson—is it yet done? Do you persist in it still?" And again—"Well, if you do, I am inclined to let it rest in your hands—if there should be any controversy, to let you manage it—as no doubt you can. But there are some things in which I should post you in case you go on—several. I don't know but it would be best for me to make memoranda for you, or have you bring your pencil and take it down yourself—so as best to secure you in case you cross each other. I don't know but I'll find you right away O'Connor's letter—you knew it? He wrote a letter or letters to the Tribune—got into some controversy there with the Rev. Chadwick, of Brooklyn. O'Connor had made much of the Emerson letter and Chadwick retorted, 'Yes—but he took that back; considerations of purity, etc., etc., etc., induced its withdrawal.' Then O'Connor replied to that and Rev. Chadwick to O'Connor—there were several letters on both sides, I think, and it was quite heated." I laughed and said: "I have the Rev. Chadwick on record in quite another way on the book." W. thereupon: "Yes, I know. I have met him—years ago, in Brooklyn—perhaps several times—and my impression of him then was what it is now—that he is one of the men who lets I dare not wait upon I would—inclined Leaves-of-Grassward but hesitates in his inclinations: but not alone quite distinguishingly with Unitarians in general—especially ministers—but all, really—and Liberals—who have the best inclinations but in spite of an emancipation in one sense, still have an eye on respectability, so-called." I interposed—"How O'Connor would play with Edward Emerson's 'or words to that effect' if he were here!" W. responding laughingly—

"Yes he would: it would be a sight to dwell upon: he would play Edward sick with it. And it was a dirty paragraph, anyhow, making the best of it—unwarranted, lugged-in, untrue."

Sunday, August 4, 1889

Did not see Whitman today, but he went over proof-sheets I left with him and sent them up to my house by Ed. Made some funny corrections (?) in German headline to Bertz's piece. Sent along proof of bust with suggestion that it be thus superscribed—

> *Print f'm plaster head*
> WALT WHITMAN *in old age*
> *By S H Morse f'm life*

and around it all very minute description of arrangement and type he would suggest. Had tied all these together in a little package and written description of contents on outside. Had prepared size of card with minute instructions for Billstein.

* (print 200 copies each card)—size of this white paper *this sized card*—
card not very thick,—you are to *adhere to this sized card through all the prints* (as you will have several)
Use yr own judgment ab't color and other technicalties—make a *good job* of course
print the ¾ standing figure same—(same sized card)
(They are all (will be 6 or 7 or 8 of them) to be collected together & put in a very handsome strong proper-sized mail envelope label'd in gilt, & sold as *pictures from life of W W*—
(perhaps made in a small album)

Had hit upon an idea, he said, of printing and mounting pictures—6 or 8—handsomely enveloping them, and selling as "portraits from life of Walt Whitman."

Monday, August 5, 1889

7.45 P.M. Pouring rain. W. still confined. Sat at open window, with cloak thrown broadly to protect his right side. But he appeared happy: joked about the persistent storms. Wished to know at once—"What do you bring new?"—his usual question. Ed was just going out the door. How would he like to go to the Opera Wednesday, to see "Chimes of Normandy"? W. said: "I guess that is a good one, tho' I have never seen it—they say it is—it holds its own, anyway, which is a sort of evidence. Yes, go, Ed!" So it was so arranged. This to be W.'s "treat" as he said again. Morris Lychenheim is to go along.

W. said: "I had a letter from Dr. Bucke today—a short one—but it was in the usual strain—nothing novel is in the wind there just now. And by the way, I had a postal from Mrs. O'Connor—from North Perry—something of that sort —in Maine, where she is now, staying with some old lady, a friend. I sent her off a bundle of papers today—quite a bundle. Among others, I also sent off a postal to Gilder." Was it about the speech? "Oh no!—about the Tennyson picture in the current Century—that's all—and a grand picture it is, too: I like it more and more—even as a piece of work merely it is notable. Who is T. Johnson, the engraver?—can you tell me anything about him?" And he reflected—"And so Tennyson's 80th Birthday is right here, within a few days! 'Tis a grand life—and many years!" At this instant he looked across the room at the Eakins picture which hung in a peculiar half-light, from the gas in the hall. I saw the direction of his gaze; said: "Tom likes that immensely—would like to see an engraving of it." W. remarked: "Eakins makes few or no inquiries after it. I should judge it was a wonderful piece of work—the work of a master. And so you think it one phase of me, do you? I always say, too—not only is it good as art, but

413

as nature—it is a portrait." And this recalled Gilchrist's dislike of the picture, of which W. knew, and he added—"Herbert participates in that fault of all Englishmen, and some Americans" here he laughed—"certainly some—of thinking he knows all about everything—that everything is centered in him"—and he laughed again. "But it is an amiable fault: let 'em have it, all for themselves: it's their own burden, not ours!"

I read him the following letter from Gilder received today.

Editorial   Department
The Century Magazine
Union Square—New York

Aug. 2—1889.

My dear Mr. Traubel,

Thanks for the suggestion about O'Connor—& regrets that we have not room for what you suggest.

Let me say that my feeling about Whitman is such that I would not dishonor him by letting a report be printed which did not accurately represent my thought concerning him, so far as it was expressed at the dinner. Some things were omitted, some unconscious changes made by the short hand reporter,—& it seemed to me just to Whitman to read the proofs with an idea of actually presenting the thoughts I was endeavoring at the dinner to express. As they stand they will doubtless be charged with extravagance—but at least this is essentially what I said & what I am prepared to defend, without the addition of new ideas, or illustrations, & *to my mind without modification of meaning or difference of opinion.*

Will you please read this sentence to W. W. & any one else interested.

Sincerely
R. W. Gilder

W. asked at first, "What does he mean—what is his object in writing that?" And when I said—"Probably for those who,

being present, might notice phraseal changes in the print"
etc., to which he nodded assent. "I suppose that will be the
reason. I can see no other. But to me no such criticism as he
fears seems possible—not at all. I read it with greatest care
and it seemed to me all right, though the reporter's version
was also very good, I thought. It is always supposed that a
speaker should be given the privilege of putting himself in
good printed shape: and this speech surely is very significant
and remarkable—coming as it does from New York, right
from the cluster of those there who are most engaged in throwing salt water, acid, on our glistening fame. And what he says
of the form of Leaves of Grass—that is the most remarkable
of all—hearing such a thing from such a source, one almost
begins to feel a confidence—a confidence that the book after all
contains something." I put in—"But the young—they will
take you up: I read Leaves of Grass to a group yesterday—
and they were all intensely interested." He asked: "So you
really think they took hold? Well, if the future is secure—we
can surely afford to trouble ourselves little about the present!"
And as to the signs right and left of coming over,—"Yes—it
is as I told you the best point in most of these fellows—their
power to get on—to shake off obstructions: give 'em enough
time and enough rope and they surely will get there!"

Promised to give me a signed portrait of some kind for
Mrs. Fels. Said he had had "a long letter from the Berlin man
—from Edward Bertz—and it was written in English. He
writes a wonderful English—almost idiomatic—but all that is
explained when he tells me as he does, that he spent several
years in this country—three, I think—and as many in England—indeed, wrote a book in English, once. He alludes frequently to that novel—English—that he spoke of in the other
letter—'Phryza' "—(spelling it out)—"or something of that
sort, wasn't it? The novel seems more than ordinarily given up
to discussion—parts of it to us—and warmly, too—I don't
know who by,—forget—but I was going to suggest that you

keep a sharp eye about for the book—a very sharp eye—and see what it all amounts to, signifies anyhow." "Bertz got all the books I sent him—Leaves of Grass, Specimen Days, Dr. Bucke's book—and he says he takes them all in—can immediately use them—as he proposes some sort of essay now, before long, treating us." I brought him samples of cardboard from Billstein. Which would he have for the pictures? He laughed "I'll keep the boards till tomorrow and tell you. But I don't know for what good—he knows what to use—and it will all amount to the same thing in the end. I find that these fellows always have good reasons, or arguments, for doing as they choose anyhow, after you have made your own careful choice. In all my experience I have never met a man who didn't pursue his own pleasure against mine. At least, it is so in this country—and I don't know but here's the characteristic difference between our own workmen and workmen abroad." Spoke of "fine paragraph" in our quotation from Bertz in the book—passage touching love and affection. Said of book: "If you will give me all the sheets, after you have them in good shape—all but the title-page—then I will see what I see— perhaps have a line to add." I said—"Yes—I have a blank page near the front, back of 'contents,' which you may consecrate." He laughed—"Consecrate? Well—we'll see: let us get the ensemble—the book entire—in our noodles, then wait for the last stroke." Asked me—"Gilder did not make extensive changes in his second proof?" And when I said, "No," he responded, "Then I can see no cause for his anxiety—none at all: the speech was well as the short-hand man had it—was well as Gilder fixed it: I am satisfied either way."

Tuesday, August 6, 1889

5 P.M. W. had not yet had dinner. Sat in bedroom, reading paper. Ed brought in meal just as I was leaving after staying 10 to 15 minutes. Said that he had been out. "I was over to

Gutekunst's today—Buckwalter came here for me—so I went. I suppose I was 2 hours or so—probably a little more than that—in the voyage. An hour and a half, I should say, at Gutekunst's. We had a swell carriage—a fine strong affair. And I saw all the ferry boys at last—they came to me. But the ride was wearisome—it tried my head severely—though in a little while after I got there I had recovered. But I guess it would not do for me to go in at the city on high tide—in the full swim—no! I am past that. Everything looked familiar, everything full of power—even poise—the buildings all so wholesome and handsome. But they did not ride me about much,—we went direct—came back direct." In reply to various questions from me, he said: "Yes—I suppose the pictures were a success—I inferred as much from what he said—one he took very big. I told him to prepare to give me a liberal number of copies. I thought to get a couple for Dr. Bucke and one for Tom and one for Buckwalter and one for you—if not others—but he said he didn't know that he could allow me many—as they were very hard and costly to produce—as I suppose they are. But he promised me that of the smaller ones he would not raise the same objection. I wanted the big ones badly—especially for you fellows—but it probably won't be a go. Anyhow, we must submit. Since getting back I have been alarmed for one thing. Gutekunst took a picture of Buckwalter awhile ago—I saw it—and I suppose it is regarded as a superlative piece of work, as it is,—but all smoothed off. What do you think—is there danger he will smooth me off that way? I am just on the point of telling him to give me the result just as occurs, not as fixed and patched up. What do you think—shall I write? I suppose Buckwalter's picture would be considered ideal—indeed, it is good—but to my taste, it falls short of the natural—or goes beyond it, if a man could say it that way."

Had made his selection of card, putting with samples this memoranda:

417

I prefer the white card
(thickest of all "samples")
marked * in the little book

"Of course," he said to me, "I wish the white: I am going to
get up a whole packet of pictures." But he was doubtful about
the November Boughs picture—"I noticed it looked rubbed—
different. So Brown thought it had been spoiled, did he? I
shouldn't wonder." Had laid out a phototype Gutekunst picture for Mrs. Fels, and signed with his blue pencil. Gave me a
copy of Hobby Horse Guild (July) containing a paragraph
about banquet with his speech in full. He said: "I never look
at it but its old-fashionedness strikes me: its noble old-
fashionedness: for that is a noble piece of work—of printing
—of paper—types—all that. Take it and see what you can
make of it."

"The day started off grandly," he said, "cool—inspiring—
dilating: but now it grows hot again." I asked him if he
thought he would go to the river this night—the first absolutely clear afternoon for a week. But he shook his head. "It
is doubtful—I have already had a trip today which quite tried
me." He added, "There was no preconcerted plan for going
over today—Buckwalter came early, inquired, I was pretty
well, we went." W. looked pretty well—his color good—in
spite of weariness. I stayed but briefly. But he inquired of
various things. Had I heard of the Liberty piece? And he
rather raised his eyes at Gilder's explanation that he had not
"room" for a couple of pages on O'Connor. "The best of these
fellows are not distinctively our men." Lamented in his
resigned, good-natured way that he could not go with me into
the country—I being on my way to Logan. Asked—"Have
you more proof for me?" Was "very happy" that I had found
space in which to add letters (or parts of letters) from
Brinton and Forman.

WITH WALT WHITMAN IN CAMDEN

Wednesday, August 7, 1889

6.50 P.M. Went down with Morris Lychenheim, intending to pick Ed up and go to opera together. W. in his bedroom when we arrived. We talked there about 20 minutes. He very courteously showed L. to a seat and remembered the book he had signed for him. At one point asked, "So you came down to take Ed along?" Then spoke of operas—of this one "The Chimes of Normandy," he "knew nothing" and asked, "Can you tell me about it?" Adding, "Somehow, nobody can tell me!" But we should get a book of "the scheme." "In my opera days, I always took care to get a libretto the day before, then took care to leave it at home on the day itself!" Spoke somewhat of "Lucia." Had he seen it? "O yes! many a time! And once at least with the finest, superbest Edgardo, the tenor fellow, that ever was, probably—with Bettini, grand of the grand!" Of "The Chimes"—"I suppose the plot is the usual one—love, a little romance, difficulties—then all comes out right!" Alluded to Castle with considerable affection—"he plays, I see—and who else, do you know?" I digressed to Salvini—his coming in the Fall. "The real Salvini?" he inquired, "the father?" And on my saying "yes" and saying I wished he might see him, he looked dubious. "Not in the afternoon?" I asked. But he dissented: "I don't like afternoon performances—never did—they seem very impropitious." Then —"But I cannot say I even have the desire any more: the time for that is gone: Emerson's poem is wonderful good—you cannot bring the shells home to your room or the sound of the sea or the skies—nor I my old days, my youth, my forty years ago, any more!" But I argued—"Salvini is your man—he is elemental!" To which—"Yes, I believe he is—from all I can understand he deserves what you say of him: he is a great— perhaps the greatest—Shakespearean interpreter." I joked at that—"Willie Winter wouldn't allow that." And W. spoke up instantly—"The devil with Willie Winter! What does he know? He knows nothing! He is one of the fellows possessed of the old armors, costumes, what not—but of the spirit that habited them—the beating heart, the pulsing blood, he knows nothing—cannot even dream!"

Lychenheim spoke to W. about reading "Song of the Open Road," and W. asked quickly, "Well—could you get along with it? Was it plain sailing? Did you get stuck in it?" L. replying with a vulgarism which caused laughter—that he was "stuck" *on* it! This opera was W.'s treat—he had given Ed a dollar to pay the way. In spite of his weariness, had gone out a while yesterday—towards the City Hall, the outskirts, not to the river: only a short trip. Not out at all today, though he said, "I do believe the trip to the city did me good instead of harm." We did not stay beyond our time. Ed says that on the way to Philadelphia with Buckwalter yesterday W. scarcely said a word till he got over there, when he asked abruptly, "Who are these pictures to belong to?"

Ed gives a good description of the sharper who the other day came to W. pretending to have money from distant friends which he would deposit in bank. Sent word to W. on arrival that he had "Good news." W. would not pay him the $5 he asked for expenses. Fellow called several times on various pretenses, W. saying he was willing to pay when money was assured. He must have half accepted, half suspected, the story—fingered a check but would not accede. By and by sent Ed up to bank and found the whole matter cooked. The sharper asked who attended to W.'s affairs. Ed gave him my address but of course he did not come to see me. W. himself very philosophical over it, said, "This is not the first time I have been played with—I could show you a string so long—" indicating about a yard with his hands. And there is a good deal of dry humor in him. "I thought we were going to have a good time for a good while to come—now we must have a good time on 5 dollars." The five dollars keenly withheld. Spoke to me of the carriage Buckwalter got the other day as "got from a friend who furnished it as a 'for-God's-sake' job!" I left orders with Billstein today for portraits—would furnish proof tomorrow evening. Lychenheim sent W. back by Ed a book of the play.

Thursday, August 8, 1889

5 P.M. Stopped in on the way from city to leave proof of picture with him. W. in bedroom. Said instantly on seeing it, "That satisfies me—I like that"—and requested me to write them a postal at once to that effect. Brought him also the 10 copies additional of pocket edition from Oldach, which he had me pack away in a box for him. Left proof of last 2 pages of book with him—those containing telegrams and "postscript" letters of Forman and Brinton. Said quickly—"I like their arrangement considerably—oh! thoroughly." Would read and return to me. One of his first questions was, "Well—how was the opera and how was Castle?" "Oh! Was he still fat? handsome? easy? genial? The same man!—the same man! And there is still some voice left? A glimpse of the old times? I thought so!—it must have been! His voice used to have a wonderful magnetic quality." He had said to us yesterday, "It seems as if the people would listen to some of these old favorites —even favorites who now are all broken up—as long as they will consent to appear." Now he added to me—"Ed seemed to enjoy it greatly—I had hoped for him to see Fra Diavolo or The Bohemian Girl, but this will do." I did not linger. Went home to supper—promised him to be back again.

7.50 P.M. W. now just back from his trip to the river. Evening beautiful. Was out of doors in chair. But after shaking hands with me he said, "I am just going in," thereupon rising and with Ed's assistance going up the steps. He called back, "Come along—come along Horace, come and sit in the parlor, here by the window." So we were thus together for half an hour. Spoke of opera again. "Ed seems to take it as one of the treats of his life—he has been full of it all day. It is a light opera? Fra Diavolo is light, though not farcical: full of delightful byplay as they call it—and good tunes, melody, all that." Had read proofs. Took them out of his pocket. Referring to closing phrase of Brinton's letter [see notes for Monday, July 29th] he asked, "Brinton don't take much stock in the immortality business, does he?" Inquiring further—"What is his position?—or has he none?" Adding some fine words of affection—"I always hold him high in the list of men who ought to be heard." As to inserting the letters from Forman and Brinton: "I suppose you will have it your way—will insist that they are important: as I suppose they are if anything in the book is important." Again—"Bucke writes me that he got the pocket editions I sent him"—he said editions, plural—"and he is pleased—I might almost say extravagantly pleased—with them." Harrison Morris is nearly done with translation of the second part of the Sarrazin article. W.: "I am glad he gets along with it—glad he don't find it too much for him." Was curious to know why we did not take 25 cent seats for opera. "Tom tells me even he takes the 25-centers!" Said of the piece twice sent to the World—"You mean the 'here, you, the Paris Exposition poem?'" laughing —"Oh! I have never had a word about it—not a word. I have given it up." Told him of my postal from Yarros that the O'Connor piece would be published in the next number of Liberty. "Good! Good!" he exclaimed, "that's the best news! and now, we'll get plenty of papers, won't we? I shall want a number all for myself, for home and abroad—for I have quite a number to whom to send—who must not be missed!"

I spoke of patent opera-glass machine in opera house—drop ten cents in a slot, turn a screw, and lo!, an aperture appears and in it a glass. W. inquired, "But what's to prevent a fellow from not returning the glass when the affair is over?" And then we talked of human nature generally. W. insisted, "Even in the way of operas, the average human critter is bad—bad." Then—"I know you will consider that strange doctrine from me, but I more and more come to perceive it." Spoke then of the growth of parks—whether Camden should have them. "It has no Old Man's Home?" he inquired—"but it has a Children's Home, which is going a good way—a half a loaf is better than no bread. But as to the parks, I have wondered—wondered. What do you know about the Diamond Cottage park here? It always seemed very rich, suggestive, to me, but that was some time ago." I spoke of Camden as "extending rapidly and becoming a big town," to which he quietly said, "Yes—an ever larger and larger congregation of maggots—human maggots." I laughed aloud; then he added, "Of course, that is the sarcastic view—the extreme sarcasm of it—but in a sense it is strictly true. It seems to me there never was a time in the history of the world when the underflowing currents of life—the beating pulse of social idealism, was so low, so vile, so dirty, so mean. Never, never! Certainly, in our social life all is villainy and dollars and cents—it is rotten to the core—men grasping, grasping, toiling, fighting, full of venom and bitterness—and for what?—for what high purpose?" And to protests—"Yes—I see—there is a great deal more to be said—you are right, too—give the crises and the men do appear. For myself, I think that if the soldier boy himself had not proved what he proved—North, South, East, West—all of them—the plain every-day men—I should still go a-begging for my evidence. The state of society—of our society—at this stage—is deplorable—deplorable beyond words." But when I said, "I disagree—I believe the great currents, the permanent tendencies, in humanity, are all healthy,"—he put in fervently, "That is nobly said—that summons us back—back to origins, deeper meanings." Said "Gilchrist was over last night, but he brought no news." Asking him if he would authorize me to renew insurance on sheets, now run out, he said: "Yes—I authorize you to do with it, just what you consider the right thing in the matter."

Friday, August 9, 1889

7.45 P.M. W. at parlor window. There had just been a tremendous rain, with thunder and lightning. He had kept by the open window through it all. But had not been well today. "It has been a poorly time with me—a poorly time. But now I am relieved." News? that is his invariable question. What had I brought? On his own part said, "Buckwalter has been in again—but he did not sit down—was only here very briefly." Said at one moment: "More and more do I see that it is with the young man, the young woman,—that there lies the future of Leaves of Grass—that its real constituency will be these newer personalities." I interposed—"Is not that what I have often argued?" He nodded assent. "I know you have argued it—often—but I have been slow to take it up—slow to admit it—giving in only gradually—though now it would seem surely. Look at such fellows as Richard Watson Gilder, Julian Hawthorne—others—what tremendous strides they have taken! There has been, for us, no more significant events of late days." The picture of Garland, which did not particularly strike me, W. liked very much. "As you look at it more and more, you will take it in: though considerably—too considerably—smoothed off, it is very just, apt." I renewed our insurance today for 6 months—W. acquiescent. "I wished to leave that entirely with you," he said. Asked about the book. "It must now be nearly done. When you have proofs of the whole mass—except, of course, the title-page—I want to see it—want you to bring it down to me—leave with me a day or two. I have wished for about a page—will no doubt have something to say myself—but cannot make up my mind exactly what till I see it in its entirety—the ensemble—so as to take in its full measure." I told him I had reserved a page next "contents" and opposite his speech, clean at the front. "Well—that might do—though I had it rather in mind to come in at the very last —the final page or so. Is there nothing you can swing about so as to achieve this?" When I said "No"—he added—"Well— I'll see just how it appeals to me." I asked, "Can't you make up something that would fitly fill such a page?" "Perhaps I can: but till I see the sheets, I cannot say, even to myself. I always keep to my own method—to write as moved to write, and what: and what depends upon the moment."

I had a letter from Morse today, in which he said the proof of bust looked "quite Whitmanish"—though pleasantly saying he had no doubt Gilchrist was more than half right about its defects. But W. still "believes in the bust." Morse likewise wrote: "I hear Julia Ward Howe's daughter, who resides here, is a liker of W. and his books. I shall probably see her in the Fall." W. took this as confirming what he had said—"of the youth—the younger generation—of America." Complained of our mail-facilities. "The books I send seem more promptly delivered abroad than at home: I have sent a book as far as Potsdam—another into the wilds of Ireland—another to France—to Paris—from there to be forwarded way off into county districts—always, too, for only the 40 cents postage that is required of me here—and yet in every case the book went quickly and was quickly acknowledged. In England especially they seem to take pride in their mail carriage—and I do not wonder: they deliver everywhere—no man has to go-a-searching for his own." "I have sent some papers off to North Perry, to Mrs. O'Connor, again. And how about your friend —the old man—the old man out there in the Home? Did you say, you go tomorrow again to see him?" And when I had replied affirmatively—"Well—I surely must make up a bundle for him. What are his proclivities, is he religious? Serious? Did you say he was Scotch? Tell me his name, too," all of which he repeated quite deliberately after me, even spelling the name. "I always delight in this: so many papers come—and somebody there is always to enjoy them." Asked me then: "I had an old friend out there in the Home— Mr. Cane: did your man know him? Ask about it. He died recently—just last week." Would make me up a bundle for tomorrow. Quite laughingly, he said of someone who had thought he "would be damned for his heresies"—"I am glad to hear it! Glad to hear it! It is a good thing to be dealt positively with, somehow: and the company on the road will be large." But in a more serious vein, "And yet that is a queer notion— don't you think? As if we needed to be damned anymore than to be the vermin many of us are at times!"

Saturday, August 10, 1889

7.40 P.M. W. just returning from his evening's trip. Went in doors at once, and sat by the parlor window. Called my attention to the package he had laid out and addressed to my old man friend. Had name all right. "They are drifts of things," he said, "currents, cross-currents, eddies, out of the flow of affairs: probably will interest the old man—some of them, anyhow. Give them to him with my love." Package very liberal—magazines, etc. "The weather tonight," he said, "is uncertain—in the balance, rather. And affairs the world over are like the weather—murmurs, mutterings, suggestions, threatenings—but nothing more: of great events, shorn, unprovoked." I asked him if he had finished with Bellamy? He assented, "Yes—at least, enough. I do not think I shall look at it again. But I have been glad of the chance—if for nothing else, for Sylvester Baxter's sake: Sylvester was ardent about it when he was here—ardent and he is a noble fellow—and one wants"—as if, by his tone, to say he would please S. B. When I see Garland and Baxter and others—of differing schools— trying to engage W. W., and see how sweetly he listens, reads and yet waives all special teachings aside as of great importance but not chiefly his, I am prepared to see aright W.'s antagonism of some of my own notions which seem in line with his teaching and should, one would think, have his endorsement. I asked now, "But don't you think it well to know what all the world is agitated about?" And he responded, "Yes indeed—I do: and I pursue that plan myself: there are some drawbacks to it, but I think one very rarely goes far without finding out what it is—what particular point—the public finds of moment in such a volume. But I have by no means read this volume through—no—not at all."

I left with him proof sheet which he promised to send up to the house tomorrow if I did not call. I am going out of town. I showed Harrison Morris, Gilder's letter today, and he called it cowardly. W. asked, "Did he say that? I hardly come to such an idea myself. It never impressed you that way, did it?" Morris thought W.'s question to G. in the midst of the speech "one of the keenest things on record—it nailed him"—and regretted that G. cut it out, as I had. But W. himself would say nothing on the point when I repeated it to him. The trouble with hearing continues. W. remarks also that "I shall not see you another year"—having reference to his sight, which he says is badly failing him, and which breaks sadly on his reading hours.

Sunday, August 11, 1889

I was out of town all day. Did not return till late in the evening. W. had kept his promise—sent proof sheet up to house for me by Ed. No comment.

Monday, August 12, 1889

7.55 P.M. W. at parlor window, hat on. "Yes," he said, to my question, "Yes, I have been out—down to the river: and how beautiful—oh! how beautiful!—it was there tonight!

These have been rare days anyhow—these last two: and such thoughts, recollections, they raise in one!" But his health today had "not been extra good." I brought him a bundle of pictures printed by Billstein. "Oh!" he exclaimed—"is he that far along? I had no idea he would steal that quickly on us! We must move along. I started to get the other pictures ready today—even to writing directions." Intended having the steel 1855 picture used. Was curious to know if "we could not best tie our envelopes with floss—I think it is floss. It is a fine, silky, broad, tape or something: they used it in Washington in the old days—used it round special documents sent to the big nibbses, dons—foreign diplomats, state fellows, others. I like it; we must hunt it up; I should think any of the big stationers would have it."

I gave him copy of Christian Register containing reprint of part of preface of Renan's "History of the People of Israel." "Yes indeed," he said, putting it in his side pocket, "I am glad to have it: I have heard a good deal about the book—a good deal, and all good." Of Renan's autobiography—"I know nothing: if I ever heard about it, all memory of it is now fled —but I guess I never heard. Did you say this was the Christian Register? Oh yes! I know it, to be sure!" Then after a pause, he asked me, "Have you seen the Critic this week?" Adding further—"Among the book reviews was one of another Russian book—a book by a man named Brandes [Georg Brandes, "Impressions of Russia"]. How do you pronounce it?—I see! It appears to be an extensive volume and the review itself has a vast charm—rouses in me a great curiosity to see the book. Though not a very great one, either—for nowadays—these later days—I have no ambition to tackle big books—take a great plunge—start out for a long swim. But this book seems to have a peculiar fascination perhaps in part the fascination of the Russian character itself." I interrupted —"And they seem to bring forth some of the biggest men." W. responding—"That they do—a literature in some respects

428

the greatest—but all of it, as the Frenchman says—yes, all of it, all of it—soaked in pessimism. Not the notion, perhaps, that the world is all going to the bad, absolutely, but that things are in a bad way, need repairing. The Russian is a marvellous character—I watch it very closely, wonderingly—regard it as bread in the making—dough not yet in its final shape—the dish, however, proceeding!" But the "pessimism" was "possibly a result of conditions—at least so in part. Russia seems to suffer from what afflicts—seems to afflict—all governments, organisms, institutions in our day—peculation, fraud, hypocrisy, humbuggery, cant, outrage—Russia, surely, and I don't know but all of 'em." I laughed at his vehemence, and said, "But there's enough virtue in the universe to bear us all on," to which he responded, "Oh! I believe that, too—enough for all—all. Underneath this surface—underneath this forbiddingness—underneath the drift—is the great sea, still deep as it ever was, still sound, still fortifying, sustaining, washing clean!" "The integuments of national character are always markedly interesting—to me full of attraction. It must have been ten years ago, I met Russians—a number of them—at Mrs. Gilchrist's. She lived here at that time—on 22ᵈ street, north—far up—it must have been near where you went to the opera. There was a Russian vessel came up into the harbor about then—several of her crew got in the habit of stopping at Mrs. Gilchrist's—so of course I met them, benefited, enjoyed. One was young—fell in love with one of her daughters—even proposed marriage, which was declined. But he was a fine interesting character anyway, and a great field for me, from which I plucked much!"

I asked W. if he had read the Lounger account of the doctor's evidence, and he said—"Yes—and I think the Lounger must be Jo-Jo Gilder. But what is Jo coming to? As he tells the story there it is quite different from the Ledger's and takes quite another tone—loses all its humor, in fact. As we read it first, what the fellow said of Shakespeare,—his way of saying it,—had quite an unmistakable flavor of humor. 'Twas very funny—at least to me—and I am sure I made no mistake." The Lounger in the Critic for Aug. 10, 1889, writes:

If we find a man questioning the sanity of the man of imagination, we may put him down as himself unbalanced. I should have very serious scruples about calling in, to attend anyone whose life I valued, the "expert" called to testify for the contestant in a recent will case, who testified that the testator was demented because she was a poet in a small way.

[The following paragraph in smaller type.]

He based his opinion partly on the fact that Miss C—— had occasionally written poetry. He thought that all poets were insane, more or less. Milton and Walt Whitman, he always thought were insane. From all he had heard of Shakespeare, however, he believed he was a man of considerable ability.

After desultory talk on matters connected with our work he remarked: "The Press is full of this elixir of life business. Not one day, but all days lately. And its accounts seem to be written up by some one interested in borrowing the discovery." As to Brown-Sequard, he said—"He is a sensationalist in medicine—a man of great ability, to be sure, but rated by good judges, by the best doctors I have known, as a man of schemes, sensations." I asked if he was in Washington during war times? W. said: "I do not think so—I never heard of it— I am sure I should have remembered it had he been there. At least, I am certain he was not there in any public capacity— connected in any way with Lincoln. This business seems more or less of the sorcerer sort—of a kind with Cagliostro, in France, in the last century, and previous to that, way back, with Paracelsus. Dr. Hammond has written about it—he is one of the big surgeons—he gets furious, in a rage,—because somebody accuses him of believing in the elixir. The point seems to be, that it is a tonic—a tide-overer, one may say. Some one sent me a paper—a Transcript—maybe it was Kennedy—with a long article on the subject from a Dr. Palen"—

spelling his name. I spoke of "humbug"—and W. said then—
"Yes, it is from that standpoint Palen writes. It was an
interesting article: I sent it at once to Dr. Bucke." When I
asked him if he was going to try the Elixir, he laughed
heartily. "The river is my elixir," he finally said—"and such."
But the subject "interests me—the papers are full of it—so
of course we discuss it."

Tuesday, August 13, 1889

5 P.M. In at W.'s for about 15 minutes on way to Logan. He
sat at window in his bedroom, reading paper. Did not seem
particularly well, nor was he well. Was waiting for his dinner,
which Ed shortly brought up—after which he was to go out in
his chair. The day somewhat clouded, though no storm.
Showed me the Gutekunst portraits. "They are here at last" he
said—"see"—pointing under a chair, where they lay together
—3 of them—2 quite large—one medium—even the last much
larger than cabinets. W. was palpably disappointed in them.
The small one was the best of the 3—more rugged, less
touched up. I looked at them—he at me. "Well," he said—
"What of 'em?" I only returned—"Do you like them?"
Whereat he smiled. "You—you: what do you think of them?"
"In the smaller" I said—"no smile at all—no smilingness:
different from all pictures of you heretofore." "Can it be?"
he asked—"no suspicion of it at all?" The big pictures I at
once dissented from—both position and finish. Then he was
free to speak. "It is that exactly—the finish: They are
touched up—touched up to perdition's point: I wrote him
about it—not to do it—as you know,—but I suppose he got
my postal too late. No—no—I suppose he didn't wish to—
probably—evidently—took his own way—thought it best. The
faces have been badly tampered with—the eyes have been
palpably tampered with—palpably. And the curls—see
them!" He had no doubt "they are finished in the highest style

431

of the art—as art is generally understood." But then, "highest is low, sometimes, to the other fellow"—and he was the other fellow in this case.

Called my attention to a copy of Poet-Lore which he picked up off the floor. "Take this," he said, "there is a piece there about O'Connor's book—I don't know who by—there are no marks of authorship in it. But it will interest you. After you are done with it, we must send it up to Dr. Bucke." Also called my attention to another pamphlet—about Rudolf Schmidt—written or sent by Rosenberg (referred to in Schmidt's letter in Whitman birthday book). Said: "I'll have you take this to your father—see what he can make of it." He had forgotten—I told him—that it was Danish, therefore of doubtful meaning to my father. Exclaimed—"That's so! It never struck me: now I can well see the difficulties. I must wait for some other to help me out." Asked me after news. Also about portraits. Those I brought him last evening he said— "pleased me much—I am perfectly satisfied with them." Has been studying up a list of portraits to go in his packages. A bit of brown paper on a pile of books on the floor contained a list of about a dozen.

Wednesday, August 14, 1889

5.30 P.M. W. in his room. Had finished his late dinner. Looked well—in color; his eye, too, clearer than often. Asked: "Is it not very hot"—fanning himself—"hotter, in fact, in the last hour?" Called my attention to absence of one of Gutekunst photos. "I sent the small one back—approved that—at least more nearly approved than the others." I said: "Then you think my instinct was right? You would say nothing yesterday"—to which—"Yes—perfectly right—unmistakably. Of the three, the little picture was decidedly the best. Those two there"—pointing—"are all touched out of character—not good anyhow of themselves. I suppose he thinks he had good reason for them, but to me they are not clear." Adding—"I shall get you one if I can—be glad to. I sent Gutekunst a copy of the big book today—sent it as a present." Asked after "news"—what had I "done with the printers today"—etc. I asked him if he had arranged the other plates for me, for printing, at which he exclaimed—"There! I knew there was something: I have frittered the whole day away—several days, in fact—doing nothing—and here this might just as well have been attended to. But my memory! my memory!" I laughed at his manner, and remarked—"Well—it makes no difference—if you are not in a hurry, they are not in a hurry." But he did not accept the solace, responding seriously: "No— no—but that is not the way for me to look at it—in a sense I am in a hurry—one day to all of us—to all of us—" (I could read in his tone the underlying "to me")—"there comes the closing of the doors—the entrances—the exits—so that one may pass no more out or in—so that if there's something to do, it is well for a fellow to do it—to do it without pause." Therefore—"I think I should stir myself: I have this work in view— must perfect, achieve it!"

Asked me about my work at the bank. Then—"It has often been a wonder to me, how great the volume of business—how little the fraud—very little. How do they defend themselves against fraud? I knew a fellow in the mint at New York who would count his coin quick as lightning—yet in the very act detect counterfeits—chuck a counterfeit out so"—indicating with a throw of the hand. "I asked him how he knew it—he said he couldn't tell—and I guess he couldn't—it was an instinct— long accumulations, delicateness, of experience, now residing in the very fingertips." But—"Business is a wonderful complexity, anyhow a marvellous establishment. I realize its grand inherencies—how much it means,—what it requires. Of course we can't do much but wonder at it—rather wonder than explain. I often think of myself—a living person—sitting here now—at 71 years—bridged across experiences, dangers, not to be computed. What a wonder it is—living still—living still —coming here out of the stages of babyhood. What more helpless creature is on this whole orb than the newborn baby —yet I am here, held on and on—from that stage and stage, stage, stage since. Is it not a wonder—a wonder? In my periods of trouble—when I am sleepless—lie awake thinking, thinking, of things I ought not to think about at all—am flustrated —worried. Then I recover by centering all attention on the starry system—the orbs, globes—the vast spaces—the perpetual, perpetual, perpetual flux and flow—method, inevitability, dependability of the cosmos. It excites wonder, reverence, composure—I am always rendered back to myself." How sweet his voice! And gesture, look, were full of grace and expression.

I asked him if he had read the Renan piece. "Yes—that is, looked through it. But you don't want to take it away with you today? I should like to take a more thorough look. It impressed me, as I read it—sort of this way—with something I had often experienced before—: that it seems to be the inevitable result with scholars to magnify the influence of special nations in history—Greece, Rome, Judah. At least, Greece, Rome—and I am glad to see that Renan adds Judah: though that, too, only widens the list a little." I said—"It struck me at once, that such a selection of nations was not ours—not democratic." Whereupon W. said: "You are right—it is not —not at all. It is true it comes partly of the Hebrew notion of an elect people. But what is Christianity itself—Judaism— but full and full and full again of Orientalism—Oriental influences?" I remarked, how in modern days, especially with the Buddhistic Cult was Christianity seen to be allied—and W., "Yes—it is truly wonderful—to me beautiful, signifying so much!" Asked: "And Renan—he is of Jewish stock? It has often caused me to think, how much of the great French literature—of French greatness—comes of Hebraic sources—the German, too, for the matter of that!" I picked up from the floor a piece of paper to which was pinned various newspaper clippings, scraps of writing, etc.—marked—"Hospital notes"—and asked him "What's this?" Before taking it he said, putting on his glasses: "I suppose something or other I have needed some day and not found: as with so much of my stuff, spirited away at the moment I most asked it. You know," he said—waving his hand down towards the litter on the floor—"I live here in a ruin of debris—a ruin of ruins. This piece was probably a bit I wanted very bad the time I wrote up the Century article about the hospitals. Sometimes things I know very well I possess, turning up after a piece is printed, sold, paid for—make me almost mad—as near mad as I could get over such a matter." Then with a laugh—"But I suppose all this is a necessary part of the critter—of this critter, anyhow!"

He fanned himself as he talked. His shutters were thrown half open: rarely so. Suddenly he added:—"We were talking of Buddha—Hindustan: I found something in the paper this morning—which bears upon that." Reached back to a package of manuscript and took from it an old envelope on which he had pasted an extract preceded by this:

?/add this to supplement "Nov. Boughs" in additional notes abt Elias Hicks———fr'm Phila: Press Aug: 14 '89

I pin a copy of the matter to this sheet, taken from my own Press,

A MISSIONARY HERO

WASHINGTON, AUG. 13.—The Department of State has received from the legation at Peking, China, under date of July 3, an account of the death and extraordinary life work of the Rev. J. Crossett, an independent American missionary in China. His career appears to have been a very remarkable one, characterized by absolute self-devotion. He died on

435

board the steamer El Dorado, en
route from Shanghai to Tientsin, on
June 21. He leaves a widow, living
at Schuylersville, N. Y. In speaking
of Mr. Crossett, Minister Denby
couples his name with that of Father
Damien, the French missionary, who
lately died on the Island of Molonkai
[sic].
[*The first paragraph only, is given
above.*]

W. said: "It is from the Press. The Ledger published a fuller
account of the man, but the Ledger belonged to Warrie down
stairs, so I used this. I don't know if you are interested in such
things, but to me they tell a great story—oh! a great story.
And Father Damien, too—the devoted man! These things take
you back to the early days of Christianity—the early days of
anything, everything—days of purity." I mentioned the
Unitarian missionary in Japan, and W. laughed heartily.
"That is as if we sent 'em over dead men," he said. "But these
Catholic missionaries: these are the men—these of all who go,
go most effectively. And this man was very broad—steeped in
humanities, liberalities!" Tried to find me "Looking Backward," but it was nowhere to be seen. "Never mind—I shall
hunt it up—it will turn up—and at the same time Amiel. I
am through with it now."

Thursday, August 15, 1889

5.45 P.M. W. sitting in bedroom. Just had his dinner. It
was clouded: did not know if to go out would be advisable. I
returned him the missionary piece. He was very communicative about it. "It seems to me this presents the outline of an
ideal personality—nobly great and fine, Christ-like, other-
like. I suppose there's somewhere a good deal to go along with
this—facts, experiences—but as it stands, here was a typical

436

man." Then he laughed and when I looked at him, referred to Unitarian missionary to Japan. "It forcibly reminds us of Carlyle, preaching silence in 30 or 40 volumes or more!"

Had read in the morning's papers, accounts of the shooting of Judge Terry in the west.

> [*Opening paragraph of long news-paper account*]—:
> LATHROP, CAL., AUG. 14.—Ex-Judge David S. Terry, was shot and killed by Deputy United States Marshal David Nagle at the breakfast table in the Depot Hotel this morning. The shooting was caused by an assault made by Terry upon Justice Stephen J. Field, of the United States Supreme Court.

Said to me with considerable vim: "I have looked into it all—looked carefully—at least into the newspaper accounts. I know there is much more to be said than is found in these accounts—more than on the surface: that there are 3 or 4 years there to be accounted for—bitter years, maybe—eventful. But nevertheless the story—its pertinent points, hints, suggestions—is clear to me as it stands. It seems to me the assertion of the majesty of the judiciary—that whether right or wrong—it is not particular—the judges—the panoply—must be sacred—sacred. I confess, I like it—I like the act, approve it: it is one of the few violent deeds, out of the hurrying, crowding, record of newspaper horrors, which commends itself as a moral benefit. It is in fact, the declaration of our government—a declaration much needed in the face of desperadoes, now getting to be many and many,—the declaration of our government that from this day forth the judiciary shall not be slapped in the face—shall be backed by all the power that resides in the arm of the state. Personally, I am always slow to say any word for violent settlement: this you know: but this case is out of the common run—far out. I think we have in the main been very fortunate in our judiciary—almost all the way through—men chiefly incorruptible. Often enough wrong-seeing—but that never to be helped. That deputy—will they do anything with him? I think not—how could they?—what? He was a dead shot—a prompt man—in fact that was the place for a prompt man—for no other. The great significance of the event to me was in the stern determination of the government to protect the Justice at all hazards—that, barring all else—aside from all other knowledge to come —is, to me, its continental significance." So he talked, very vigorously. Yet he had had "a very bad day indeed—without a break, till the afternoon." W. gave me money for insurance, renewing for 6 mos. Returned to me Amiel and "Looking Backward"—which he had found yesterday after I left and laid out for me. Said: "Gilchrist was over last night—stayed during the rain" but "brought nothing new."

Friday, August 16, 1889

7.55 p.m. W. at parlor window. Had not been out at all today. "We did not go—I have been sick all day—am sick now—feeling bad indeed." Put his hand up to his head. "It's here—here: the strange mugginess, inertia, soreness." I left with W. a letter from Clifford, containing a portrait of Dr. True, at Farmington, and ordering book. W. wished to keep "for a day or so." Would "send book directly to Clifford." Left with him likewise sheets complete now but for title pages, of birthday book. I spoke to him of filling up blank page between "contents" and his own speech. He inquired: "So you think it would be the thing? Not inappropriate?—not out of the way?" And to my assent—"Well—I'll examine this as it stands—see what it suggests—see what comes of it: perhaps a page, perhaps nothing. I can well understand there should be no impropriety in it. Just now, however, I can say nothing." Then he asked: "Is Dave home? I got an order for a copy of the big book from him or someone there who writes much like him—received it just today." But McKay is not yet returned.

"And now," he asked, "how about the meeting last night—the George meeting? I see a suggestion of its value in the papers—that the papers give it good mention—some even long." Questioned me closely for details—"the scene, who was there—tell me." I had seen Gilchrist. W. thought it "probably of more than artistic interest to Herbert." Gave him insurance receipt, which he folded up and put in his pocket. He had laid out for me the profile plate for the complete works, which I was to get printed at Billstein's. Ingram in to see him today. "He stayed 20 minutes or so."

Saturday, August 17, 1889

7.55 P.M. Went to W.'s with Lychenheim. Sat in parlor, and talked for 25 minutes. W. in very good humor, and talked freely, though saying he did not feel extra well. His hearing bad. I asked him six or seven times in the course of our talk if he had got out in the early evening, and not till I was about to go did I get an answer. "No—it is too cool—isn't it? We did not get out." Said: "The Odenheimer girls have been in: you know them? Lou Odenheimer? They brought me tiger-lilies—leopard lilies, they called them—and how curious a flower it is—how subtle, beautiful—graceful! Do you know anything about them?" I spoke of the wild lily—and he said, "I know nothing about them—at least, don't remember them. Perhaps years and years ago I may have known, but I doubt—I doubt. How more than ordinarily involved, curious, this flower seems! I have examined it."

Handed me Clifford's letter, and said he had sent the book off—"addressed it to Clifford himself." I said—"You certainly have a constituency, if you could but reach it." He laughed and responded—"That's the point—to reach it. I don't believe Dave is the man to do it—perhaps no publisher is. To reach it: that brings in the story of the old woman," he said—adding explanatorily—"she insisted, every woman born, man born, had his or her mate, somewhere—if they could but find out where! I suppose that should be the whole matter of life—the whole story: to find the mate, the environment—what to be,—then, adjustment!" Still we talked about constituency, and to my various remarks he rejoined: "There may be—there may be: the natural thing to do would be for me to go about myself—go from city to city—New York, Chicago, St. Louis—take quarters—locate for a few days, weeks—see the publishers—sell: whack about, solicit, bargain myself." Then after a pause: "But of course that is impossible now—all out of the question. I can hardly go upstairs now without assistance—never without fatigue, danger. So, going away is not even to be considered." And yet—"I do not suppose I should complain—I ought to be thankful I am here—that I am listened to at all—as the boys said, when I was young there in New York, have got my hookers in." As to any big constituency—"That is altogether doubtful—doubtful!"

I inquired of him if he had looked over the proof sheets—he then: "Yes: that is to say, I am reading—have got well along. I have read your description—then along into the speeches as far as Hamlin Harland's"—he always says, Harland—"and it has struck me—the wonderful continuity of the thing—that all these fellows—writing, talking away—talked, wrote, without crossing each other." Had he yet written me the page I asked? "No—nor do I think I will: at least, it don't come to me now as if I should." But—"I will let it simmer—let it simmer—then see what results." I asked if he saw any impropriety in the insertion of the circular announcing the celebration. He shook his head—"No—I thought it integral—as really an important part of the affair." He said further—"I did not think it necessary to write—I find on rereading your introduction that you have said about all I should have

440

suggested—written." I asked, "Then you are satisfied with that?" "Oh yes! perfectly—perfectly; it seems thorough, inclusive, conclusive." But then he went on: "I was going to suggest something that came to me today—how do you think Dave would regard the proposition to add the Sarrazin piece as a supplement to your little book? Would it be proper? Would it be in place there?" And as to the blank page I held for him—"I was going to advise that it be given to a Whitman forecast—dates of birth, writing, and so on, so on." I replied that I had not thought of that myself, therefore could not answer his question—"How does it strike you?"

As we talked, a couple went past. W. regarded them quietly. "Thank you!" he said, more as if to them, than to us. "It is so good to have them look in here that way—the young man, the girl, together!" Billstein had closed up today by the time I got to his shop. Hence we are delayed in ordering. Morris brought me today a copy of circular of the Deerfield "Summer School of History and Romance" in the program of which Charlotte Fiske Bates was announced to speak of "Walt Whitman's Works." W. said: "I knew nothing about it: it is news to me." Inside was printed a poem from George B. Bartlett, I think of Concord—one verse of which read:

Walt Whitman stands a boulder grand in senses more than one,
And graceful lady tries to rub the spots from off the sun,
But stars should shine with light divine down from the cloudless
*   skies,*
And books read best for which no friend needs to apologise.

I had forgotten to bring the circular along with me, but repeated this in part from memory, and W. laughed heartily.

Sunday, August 18, 1889

Did not see W. this day—I was out of town, at Logan. But learned his sick spell continued. Yet he went out, to the shore in the evening—stayed there a long time, "drinking in the scene—the quiet—the peace superb." Weather beautiful and mild. His present spell not caused by atmospheric severity.

Monday, August 19, 1889

7.45 P.M. W. in parlor at window. Had not been out, though the weather was beautiful. When I asked him how he was, he responded, "Bad—bad: I am now passing through a bad period. Digestion is poor—poor indeed—I am in a bad way: belly, bladder, catarrh—my brain, physical brain—all are in discomfortableation." I laughed at this struggling last word, and he looked at me and laughed too. Ed says he has shown great signs of weakness for days—especially this morning, on first being aroused: could hardly sit up at the first, on edge of the bed. W. said: "I have read all the sheets, now—all of 'em—and I like 'em, too—like 'em all." And to my questions as to how the book wore on him, he said assuringly— "Well, well!—I am fully satisfied with it!" He had not of course written anything for the blank page today—was too unwell. "It has now been for three or four days I have suffered this," he said "and it is not on account of the weather this time either: these last days have been as beautiful, comfortable, peaceful as could be." I ordered 70th year and profile cuts printed at Billstein's today. W. asked: "I shall not need to send any word?—to see a proof? I'll risk it, anyhow: at the worst it's not a matter of life and death." Left with him proof sheet of "Contents" and the School of History and Romance circular. As to the first—"I will tell you what I think, if you ask it" and to the latter—"It will be a curiosity to me, if no more." McKay comes back to town Tuesday of next week.

I described to W. our long walk to Logan on Saturday after leaving him. He was much pleased. "Spell me that young man's name again," he said—"I have known it, but it escapes me again and again." And after I had done so—"Ah! And he is reserved, isn't he? quiet? said very little while he was here." I said "Song of the Open Road"—seemed so far most to have struck L.'s fancy. W. said: "Ah! That was the one William Swinton most affected—most read. You know about William Swinton? He was John's brother—a good fellow—always had the good sense to like me!"—with a laugh. Was he as radical as John? "Oh yes! but on a higher plane: not so much interested in figures, politicalisms, what-not, but essentially radical—in his dislike for conventionalisms, laws, forms, restrictions, as radical as any of us." Went into a description of Swinton's career—his going South first. "He was a teacher. He often came over to see me when he was in New York—was always an espouser of Leaves of Grass: and his wife too: a fine, large, splendid, handsome woman—mother of children—for William when he went to New York from the South took to raising a family." "The wife was my friend—I was proud of her—and they had good babies—how I loved them! William went west—to Oakland—taught there in the college—was Professor of something or other. Afterwards, he got the conviction that our then present school books were poor fossils—that the time had come to abolish them. So he set to, on this principle: that history should not be a matter wholly of the far past but of the near past—constructed on this principle histories not giving exclusive place to Revolutionary events but recognizing the importance of our rebellion, for instance —modern incidents, proceedings, lives. These books were probably a great success. He came to New York, fell in with the big publishers, made writing school-books his vocation." Here W. turned quickly to me. "But does all this interest you at all? I was going right on to give you a history of his life— sketch—outline." And at my assent he did go on for some time. Asked me for close particulars as to the Boston trouble— then—"Aside from that, William has been very successful— struck his true vein, worked it well." Referred then to the

Swintons, Hinton, Linton—symphonically "all radicals—all Leaves of Grass men." Warmly of Linton: "He is somewhat hypochondriac by temperament, but warm, noble—a radical of radicals, too. He has been here—I don't know but in this very house, to see me—always faithful. You know about his wife? She was the woman over there in England who writes novels, essays. I don't know if they had a divorce,—she still bears his name—but they broke up in a devil of a row. But whatever, Linton is what they call a royal good fellow—true to the bone."

Tuesday, August 20, 1889

4.50 P.M. W. in his bedroom, by the window, reading. Took him the second part of the Sarrazin translation from Morris. He said: "I had an idea it was in four parts, not three"—as it was in fact—a preface, then three parts. Said as to his health —"I am still poorly: these are hard days for me." Gave me back proofs, and sheets of book—saying of the latter: "I am entirely done with them: they greatly satisfy me—though I don't know that I am the one they were made to satisfy!" I referred to the gentleman in charge of Maine Historical Society—his request a long time ago for a piece of W.'s manuscript for the Maine Collection. W. said: "I shall give you something for him—it seems to me I should: it is not the usual autographic request—not one that should be slighted." Then as to paragraph in current Critic, describing autographs held by Aldrich, of Iowa—among them one from W. to Wm. Rossetti, W. said: "Yes—a newspaper wrapper—something or other like that. That is a very hungry man—Aldrich. He has been here—has had autograph, what-not. But is never satisfied—is always crying for more and more."

The Lounger in The Critic for Aug. 17, 1889, writes:

Mr. W. M. Rossetti, the distinguished literary critic, distinguished also as the brother of Dante Gabriel and Christina G.

Rossetti, has sent to Mr. Charles Aldrich of Webster City, Iowa, many letters and scraps of letters, postcards, etc., bearing the signatures of more or less well-known English writers and artists of today . . . . the rather abrupt chirography of John Morley appears in a one-page note, and Walt Whitman's clearly outlined letters on a newspaper wrapper addressed to W. M. Rossetti at "5 Endsleigh Gardens, Euston Road, London, N.W."

"I am glad to see you spell Shakspere the short way," he remarked—spelling it—"it is always my way—has something in the look of it I like." Spoke of Bartlett's poem on the circular of Deerfield School—laughed heartily: "He seems to say, 'have nothing to do with this critter—monster—he is a dangerous one—it's safer not to touch him.' "

Wednesday, August 21, 1889

5.20 P.M. W. in bedroom. Had just finished dinner. Sat at the middle window, glasses on, a fan in his right hand, a copy of the Post (Camden) in his left. It has been a very hot day. W. did not get out at all yesterday, nor has he yet expressed any intention of going out today. As to his health, said: "I am still as I was—no improvement—no let up."

I asked him if he had read the Sarrazin manuscript I left yesterday. "Yes—and it thoroughly satisfies me—thoroughly." Was he taking good care of it? He looked at me and nodded his head. "Yes—indeed—it is there" pointing to the table—reaching forward a little while after and taking it up. He had enclosed it in cardboard and written its substance on the outside. Opened it and asked me particularly as to Morris' name—had again got him mixed with Charles Morris. Wrote Morris' name carefully inside on a sheet of paper. Then, as he slowly tied the matter up again: "I consider this an important comment—in some respects the most important comment yet made on Leaves of Grass—comment in the high sense—not the American sense, not as critics un-

445

derstand comment here, but in the sense of the writer who, like Sarrazin, not only discusses a stated personality but makes that discussion an opportunity for the expression of his own thoughts of things—the orbs—worlds—men on the earth." He referred to Morris' feeling that Gilder's letter was cowardly: "It does not strike me that way—I gather no such impression. Yet I can see! I can see! It may be true that my question to Gilder had something to do with it—for here, truly, at last, it is down explicitly, definitely, without a peradventure—down in a way not to be evaded. And what is most significant, it is an espousal at a point which has been the battleground for a long, long time—form, shape, method. I do not worry over such things—I always heed the Doctor's caution. I can well see how necessary it is they all should be —but I, who know the long story of Leaves of Grass—the things said of me as a writer—said of me as a man—can best of all appreciate Gilder—his position—what his presence with us that night signified, signifies. For it was surprising—the most surprising thing of the day—that he should have come down here at all. Then there is a delicacy in his position— think of it: like Emerson, he is at the center of the Literary crowd—pushing, clamoring about him is the baffling, battling, poisonous army of writers—and he must withstand them. And of this piece itself—when they come to read it—they will be struck with horror—will cry out, 'Well—here is Gilder advocating that hell of a man—advocating Walt Whitman!— enough of Gilder!' " He struck his fist down on the arm of the chair, laughed heartily after this explosion of good-natured energy—and went on: "But this conflict—this continual pushing, nagging, discussing,—is no doubt necessary—I do not worry over it. Abstain not from physical reasons alone but from other reasons—see these circumstances as inherencies, inevitabilities—not only not to be avoided but not desirable to be avoided."

I left with him a book of essays by Frenchmen on Frenchmen—one by Claretie on Hugo. "I have no doubt they will interest me greatly." Then he reached to the table—handed me 1st Annual report of N. Y. Institute for Artist-Artisans, inscribed autographically—"To the '*American*' Poet Walt Whitman with the Compliments of Jno Ward Stimson Supt" —"Does such a thing interest you?" he asked, "take it along —put it in your pocket, if it does." We talked over matters of our work. Billstein promises us profile and 70th year portraits Friday. I showed W. a card announcement of Mrs. Baldwin's School—he calling it "a handsome piece of printing —I like to look at it." Commenting then on type development.

Thursday, August 22, 1889

7.40 P.M. Went to W.'s with Mrs. Fels, Jennie May, and my sister Agnes. W. sitting in the parlor, in his usual position at the window. I went in first—he greeted me—then saw and recognized Aggie—said: "How are you, my dear?" And then: "And who are the other girls you have with you?" At once invited all to be seated—turned to me—"Horace, I guess I'll get you"—stopping here long enough to fumble in his pocket for a match—"to light the gas out there—there in the entry-way"—which I did. He at once entered into conversation with the girls—seemed more animated than I had known him for weeks. Yet he said he was "poorly" and that he had not ventured out today. The girls had brought him flowers, which he greatly cherished—had me go back to the kitchen and get a mug and water to hold them—then put them right in front of him on the table. They had brought him some pears, too, which by and by were referred to—fine samples of the fruit over which he expressed a great pleasure—saying finally: "Well—I shall take the mellow one for breakfast, anyhow— although I must be very careful what I eat nowadays." The talk was of a general character, of course. He seemed unusually willing to benefit the girls. I asked him if he had seen a portrait of Lincoln made by Wyatt Eaton in 1877, and he said he thought he had not—adding: "Oh! Lincoln! No one can know better than I the preciousness of that gift to the age, to America! But we have never had a portrait of Lincoln— perhaps not the man to paint it. Charley Elliott, perhaps, though he never tried it of course. Carpenter painted Lincoln, after a sense, but an absolutely good picture—no—we have not had it." I referred to the usual first judgment on Lincoln as to his ungainliness—W. saying: "Yes—I know! and that's enough for me!" Turning away from the subject, then.

I asked W. if he had seen Charles DeKay's article in Sept. number of the Magazine of Art on "George Fuller, Painter"? And he at once said no. It was given to extended comparison of Fuller and Whitman. W. repeated me: "An article in the Magazine of Art on George Fuller in which Walt Whitman is greatly implicated?"—as he often does to make sure he understands the questioner. First he asked us: "And who was George Fuller? Tell me about him?" And after I had run into some little description, he assented: "True enough—I must have known him—I can recall, now you speak of him— open the subject." Quite humorously spoke of DeKay—asking me initially: "You know about DeKay—who he is? He is Mrs. Gilder's brother" turning laughingly to Aggie and Mrs. Fels who sat at his left—"and he has written big volumes of poetry—or rhyme—what-not—fine gilt-edged affairs, pro- duced unexceptionally. He has money, I believe—is rich, or what they call well-off, anyhow. DeKay is now abroad—has been sent over to write up Irish matters—in some such capac- ity, as I understand it, as that in which George Kennan was sent to Siberia." I objected—"But he has not Kennan's ability!" W. then quickly: "No indeed—no ability at all, I should say. He has been thrown up much as many writers are, by connections or propitious circumstances." "And yet," he added, "John Burroughs thinks he sees something in DeKay, and John is not a man easily captured, deceived." He ex- pressed no curiosity to see the piece.

Aggie had explained to W. that she was now living off in the country, loafing—he wondering if she did this "as the pigs and chickens do." They "wished" they could have him on their porch, etc.—but he said protestingly: "My great hankering heretofore has been to get out where nobody else is —to get away from groups, from company. But the great thing for one to do when he is used up, is to go out to nature— throw yourself in her arms—submit to her destinies. Many years ago I passed some time down on Timber Creek." They did not know where this was—questioned him—he respond- ing: "Oh! it is down here a little ways—a matter of 8 or 10 miles or so—near Kirkwood—Kirkwood is on the railroad. My friends the Staffords lived away from the town—had a farm. They were quite a family—farm folks—father, mother, children, boys and girls." He paused—then: "It was six months or so after I came to these parts—I was in a poor way —a sad plight—had been doctoring a good deal. Now I ceased all that—simply gave myself over to nature. Have you ever thought how much is in the negative quality of nature—the negative—the simply loafing, doing nothing, worrying about nothing, living out of doors and getting fresh air, plenty of sleep—letting everything else take care of itself?" He al- luded to the "cat-birdy" quality of the life down there—how "native" it seemed to him—of "the insect life—life of birds, animals, clouds, rivers." How much it had done for him "how much it will do for anyone." I asked him if he had heard any- thing of a celebration of Tennyson's birthday, and he said: "No—have you?" Then remarked: "Herbert Gilchrist was over last night—we spoke of the well-preservedness of the big men over there—of how much more marked is their vigor, old age, power to work: and we concluded it was in this, that they were all well-groomed—that they all had wives—oh! wonders of women!—or sometimes sisters—or, as it happened, valets —miracles of valets—who made it their whole business to preserve them, watch them—habits, what they ate, drank, wore. We take no such care of ourselves here—the American people have not hit upon that conviction yet. Not at all." He suddenly asked me: "Have you ever had anything to do with circus men—any intimacies?" and on my shaking my head: "Well—I have—particularly years ago—in younger years. I remember when I was quite a boy I knew a circus company in which there was an old horse—I think 22 years old—who yet would go into the ring—perform prodigies. I asked his keeper how it was—how he could explain it, and his answer was, that this horse was given extraordinary care—that no man in Brooklyn or New York was so well guarded, cared-for, as this fine animal—groomed, curried, rested, watched, unweariedly, constantly. This is the explanation, I think, of the fellows over there—Gladstone, who had his wife; and Brougham—do you know about him?—and Disraeli, with his wife, too—and many—many." "There is Harrison, now," he continued, "careful enough to shake off the cares of office, but likely to founder on the other rock—rich dinners, entertainment" etc.—and when I spoke of Harrison's "insignificance" W. added: "Insignificant indeed!—to me, the most insignificant—perhaps the only really insignificant man—in the long line of our Presidents. Let me predict this—that as long as Harrison remains in office, the aura of the Presidency will give him prominence—be his saviour—but after that—oh! what will be his oblivion!—utter!" And as to Cleveland's simple tastes: "Yes—so I have heard—and it is a gratifying exception. Simple as a child, I hear." Americans he thought "worked like the devil till they were all worked out"—though sometimes he "envied them." Spoke of his brothers as exceptional. "There is Jeff, in the west—was at St. Louis for a number of years—constructed and managed the waterworks there till a political trouble of some sort came and threw him out. Why, he works and works—and George, too, up here at Burlington—both of them big hearty preserved fellows—George working, I was going to say, not only like a house afire, as the story goes, but like half a dozen houses afire!"

Turned to me with the question: "By the way, Horace—speaking of Tennyson—did you know the editor of the North American Review had invited me to write him an article of about 3000 words about Tennyson?" "Well, will you do it?" "Oh! I don't know! That remains to be seen!" Aggie seemed surprised at the limit, whereupon W. said: "Yes, Aggie—that's the way they do it nowadays—these publishers have it down very fine—so many words to a line—so many lines to a page. Why, a few years ago, when I was writing for the Review, I could tell just about how much space a page of my writing would take up, was quite an adept." I remarked: "It would be more interesting to have the editor of the North American Review write Tennyson to write about Walt Whitman!" W. laughed: "He would do it!—I have no doubt he would do it!—but then, like the lawyer, he would charge 'em a devil of a price! The story is that the publisher of the Youth's Companion asked Tennyson if he would write them a poem—and he assented, on condition they paid him his price, which was a thousand dollars. And they took it—paid him—and I am told it was about the dullest piece he ever printed—no doubt taken out of his scrapbook, where he has many more like it!" I joked: "There was a time when they would not have you at any price." To which he responded: "Ah Horace! And I am not sure that time is yet past—at least with some of them!"

Thus freely he talked. At one moment: "I have no news—no letters from known persons—though letters, of course, from unknown—from friend, family—but not a word from John." Then again: "It reminds me of my favorite story—the story of the Dutchman—a miller—who would say, 'Vell, vat do I care for vere die veat comes from, so it is good?' " W.'s power to tell this dialect story good in spirit but poor in twang. It was mightily interesting at the moment we were going—the three girls there in a group bidding him good-by—he reaching forward out of his chair—taking Miss May's hand with his right, saying, "goodby my dear"—and saluting the others with his left—his head thrown as he did so in the full strength of the light from the hallway: a sight I shall never forget— and the tone of his voice inexpressibly tender and conciliating. Said also to the girls—"It was good of you to come." I lingered a few minutes before my departure— asked him if he would not give me a Whitman forecast for p. 4—and he said immediately: "Yes—of course—I have already commenced such a thing: I will let you have it at once." Kissed him goodby—he held my hand warmly—said "Goodnight boy—goodnight! We'll meet again!"—and so I left. A memorable night: the flowers, fruit, girls, seemed to conspire for his joy, peace and power: for certainly his speech was strangely strong in the face of his present suffering.

Friday, August 23, 1889

7.45 P.M. It rained very hard this afternoon and evening. W. of course in-doors—in the parlor. Had been talking with Warren, who had brought some fish home from one of the engineers on the road. Mrs. Davis brought them in, a candle in one hand. W. leaned over and regarded them: "Oh! the beautiful fish! Why—they are the most beautiful I most ever did see!" Adding: "They have had their last swim—poor fellows! I sympathize with them!" And after Mrs. Davis had gone and my exclamation: "How beautiful in their own element!" He went on: "Beautiful even on the stalls in the markets! But in their own element, oh! how more beautiful— beautiful!" I spoke of his visitors last night: "They took it as a great treat," I said, to which W.: "Not a greater treat than I to have them come!" Then he asked me for the names of Mrs. Fels and Miss May. I told him they had been reading Bucke's book most of the morning. He remarked: "Bucke's book is a good deal like the birthday book—has everything in common with it—is all sugar and honey—don't make enough of the other side of the critter—and there is another side, as all you—all my friends, well enough know. If it was not that I am old, weak, toppling, full of defections—if I had some of the vigor of other days—I should rise up, fear this praise, to be applauded in this way, think it dangerous. But as it is, I think I am safe—that this but goes to offset the extreme antipathy I have had to encounter." I put in: "It is of more significance to have this youthful endorsement than any other." W. affirming: "So it is! So it is! And these girls too—the girls! And you say they read Leaves of Grass?"

I asked him about DeKay's piece—if he would not like to see it? He replied: "I suppose I might just as well—bring it down." And when I said: "It is non-committal—he commits himself to nothing," W. affirmed quickly: "No doubt—no doubt: that is the New York crowd—that is their sign, by what known: the attitude supercilious, one-eye-glassed which fits the literary dandy: without color, holding aloof from the crowds, from facts, appeals." Then after a pause: "But do you know, Horace, it more and more seems to me that that is the finale of Emersonianism—that this is always and inevitably, its result?" To my demur, explaining: "I know that is the harsh view—that there is another. But I do not throw it out as a finality, only as a suggestion, a hint, a possibility— something for you to prick with your pin. Emersonianism seems to lead to this—don't commit yourself, don't surrender to anything, don't be decoyed: it matters little—all is a fraud anyhow—so look out, be on your guard, lest too much is deferred!" Then he said, quietly: "It is hardly known of Tennyson abroad, that though he has written the most polished—perfect—poetry of our era, he himself is not at all like that—Tennyson the person—that he is rugged, crude, even coarse in a sense—would say a thousand things—use words, folk-phrases—which would shock and shock society, so-called—not nasty words, but vigorous words, native"— yet of this the whole world shrank. I asked W. if he had read

the Hugo piece in the little book I had left. "Yes, indeed—
and how interesting it is!" The conversational sayings of
Hugo there quoted had particularly attracted him. I touched
on O'Connor's delight in Hugo's Shakspere. W. then: "Yes
—and for good reasons. I shared the feelings—I felt it one of
the best of Hugo's published books." Somehow referred to
Lowell. I described Clifford's early distaste. W. then: "I can
well understand. And O'Connor, too—he had a powerful dislike—powerful. John Burroughs was worst of all—he realized
a sort of venom towards Lowell. But I think John has got
over that now. He has got over a good many of his dislikes—
and I don't know but his likes, too." I quoted Burroughs'
saying to me, in his inclusion of literary men at large: "Whitman is the man for America—Matthew Arnold for England."
W. asked: "They are his own words? They sound it—and
they are indexical—they tell the story. It is the later story of
John's life—what some would call his evolution, I suppose,
but I don't know."

He took from his pocket an envelope marked "Autobiographic note (to go in one page)" and handed it to me. "This
is the manuscript you wanted for that page—I guess it will
serve." This practically completes the book. I spoke of having
read "Song of the Rolling Earth" aloud in my room—of the
delight it gave me. He commented: "I can comprehend—
there is a mysterious, wonderful, quality in the human voice
which no plummet has yet sounded—to which literature has
not done any sort of justice—as it could not, I suppose.
There is a wonderful passage in Legouve's book on the voice
which relates an experience of Rachel—I think it was her—
and I must have you see the book. It is about here somewhere
among my trash and would serve well for you to know. I often
say to the elocution fellows, that in spite of all their study, the
deepest deep of all they have not yet sounded. There is the
consciousness of abounding presence in a fine organ—a superb
voice—I have known some—Alboni's 40 years ago—the mag-

nificent contralto. Among speakers—Cash Clay's, John P. Hale's, and, I have heard, Tennyson's: have you been told? In Tennyson it is a factor that has not been sufficiently dwelt upon—hardly alluded to—a monotonous grandeur, I have heard—profound power, music. And there are some women who have it—have it to a marvellous extent." I spoke of Salvini—W. said: "I have never heard him." I suggested: "How would you like it for us to arrange to have him come over to see you in the fall, while he plays here?" To which he replied: "Who knows? If I am still floating about here when the fall comes, it might be—it might be!" Alluding to Garrison's speech in the book: "Some of them say it is obscure—that nothing can be made of it—but I think I not only see something there, but something quite worth while."

Saturday, August 24, 1889

7.50 P.M. W. in parlor. Again had not ventured out. The sky dubious, somewhat—his condition more so. But he was cheerful. I left with him proof of his "autobiographic note," which he promised to send up to my house tomorrow by Ed. I am to be out of town till late in the night. Asked me quickly: "How about the Magazine of Art? Did you bring it along?" And when I said I had forgotten, he laughed heartily. "Well— we will try not to grieve about it." I said: "Let Ed get it of my mother when he goes up to the house"—to which—"That's so —that will do—though you must acquit me" turning around to face me—"of any worry for it!" While we sat there a ring of the bell took me to the door and I admitted a young fellow, a reporter of the Post. In the dark as he entered the parlor, W., who frankly extended his hand, asked: "Who is it?" and after he had learned: "Oh! I see: sit down. And how is Harry?" The visitor said he was passing by—saw W. at the window— thought he would step in and inquire. W. let out one of his expressive "Ohs!" Then he was asked: "And how are you?"

To this he responded: "Oh! still afloat—still on the surface."
Turning the matter then by his own question: "And how is
the Post?" The talk then desultory—a little about Harry
Bonsall. W. remarked, as we discussed printing in general—
its "mysteries" etc.: "Yes: and I think the best part of the
Press is its extra sheet. Now, take this morning's paper—
the extra contained some stuff that interested me more than
anything in a newspaper for a long time—a series of letters
from workingmen—Americans—gone abroad—gone to study
industrial conditions there—the Paris Exposition—feasted,
royally received, investigating everywhere. There was a letter
among them from Julian Hawthorne—so good, I read it carefully from end to end. They promise us more of these letters.
I was so drawn to them—they seemed so significant—I took
my scissors—cut them out—and shall try to keep them, if I
can—if they don't get mislaid and buried, like so much of my
material. Keep these, then add the others to them when they
appear." The visitor asked W. what he knew about Bill Nye.
W. responded: "Nothing—I have never met him. I have very
little liking for deliberate wits—for men who start out, with
malice prepense, to be funny—just as I should distrust
deliberate pathos—the fellow who sets out to be serious, to
shed tears, or make others."

I told W. after the visitor was gone that I was going to read
"A Song of the Rolling Earth" to a group tomorrow. He said:
"God prosper you in all your good intents!" I asked: "Is not
that good?" He then: "Is it?" We talked some about the
general understanding of Leaves of Grass. W. said again
that he was "in the hands of the youth of America." By and by,
on hurrying away, I met our reporter visitor down the street.
He said to me: "The old man is not very comfortable."
"No." "Why don't he get up and stir around?" I said something about his sickness. The man looked at me dubiously—
quizzically: "Ain't he lazy—ain't that his principal complaint?" This fellow had worked at Harry Bonsall's elbow

and for this! It takes a long time for fame to get rightly adjusted in the minds of some people. When I told him of W.'s paralysis, the fellow exclaimed: "Well—I had no idea—no idea at all!" And he added: "The old man is quite a famous man, ain't he? I suppose one of our best poets—Holmes, Whittier and Whitman I suppose are the best now, eh?" I laughed in a mild sort of way and shortly slid off. There was small fruit on this stem if any!

Sunday, August 25, 1889

I was out of town all day but W. did as announced—sent Ed up with proof—to which he had added the last paragraph commencing "a long stretch of illness"—and counselling on margin—"let me see another proof" and proposing to take out lines if not condensed enough for one page. On envelope had written—"get the 'Magazine of Art' from Mrs. T. Horace forgot it last night"—which Ed had done.

Monday, August 26, 1889

7.50 P.M. W. at parlor window, in darkness. Had not been out. "I don't get out much nowadays"—nor—"am I much better, if any. I have been the same today—am the same still." I left with him the second proof of his autobiographic note. He will examine it tomorrow. The matter, by squeezing, went in entire. W.: "I am glad—generally, I like a regular page— but in a case of this kind, rather than run a line or two over or cut it out, I would run a little into the margin." Took up a couple of big fat envelopes from the table. "These," he said, "are for you to take—one for you, one for Harrison Morris— Harrison is his name, didn't you say? I was looking through some of my scraps today—these were some of the results—I thought you would perhaps like them—like to see them, anyhow: if you do not—if they are nothing—you are not far from the fire!" Remarked: "I have not got far in the DeKay piece—you knew I sent Ed for the magazine yesterday? I have skimmed over it—but heavy, heavy! DeKay is always of the heavy sort—never attracts—never holds. He is a man of quite ordinary capacity." He spoke of having read in the papers this morning Ingersoll's oration on Horace Seaver. "Who is Horace Seaver—or was he?" W. asked, "at least, what were his special traits?—for in a way I have known him. He was not a marked man especially, was he? This address of the Colonel's is very beautiful—I was going to say also, ornate—and perhaps ornate is the word, or a word—and I do not know but he intends it to be so. Or is this the natural man, the man just as he inwardly is—the fine personality outgiven?" seeming to be debating his judgment with himself. I ordered 200 copies of the steel plate on cards uniform with the process pictures today. Should have all the heads so far ordered this week. We commented on the beautiful evening— "the cold just come up—a good deal of it within an hour"— the wind blowing high from the northwest. He had wrapped his gown about him closely. "I feel secure—quite secure— though it is a sudden turn of cold."

Letter to me from Mrs. O'Connor today:

North Perry, Maine
August 23ᵈ 1889

Dear Mr. Traubel—

I have long wanted to thank you for your very kind letter of July 15, but I became so ill that I have been obliged to curtail every note & letter that was not a necessity, & so now at this late day I have again read your touching and good letter. I am glad of all the words I get from Walt by means of the newspapers, & now & then a postal.

With very sincere regards to you, my friend,

Yours cordially,
Ellen M. O'Connor

W. said: "I am sure I sent the Poet-Lore either to her or to Doctor with instructions to forward to her—whichever." "And as to the Critic, I sent that to Washington at the time—it must be there now. I study to send her all such things I have here which I think will be of particular interest—all—all. Am sending papers every few days." Then: "You write to her and tell her this—tell it just as I say it here—to this effect."

Read him also a letter from Clifford, acknowledging receipt of book and interestingly saying of Dr. True:

Farmington, Me., Aug. 24, 1889.

My dear Traubel:

Here is postal note for the doctor's book—$4.00. Book came all right by Walt's own complete and legible directing. The old doctor is delighted. He did not know Walt but had long meant to, as he was so well abused. Yesterday he [illegible] me and showed that he had already entered in and supped with the great soul. "None ever like *him!*" he said.

Did the photo. come all right? I hope Uncle Sam brings it safely back, as 'tis borrowed from a *valuer.*

Another week & my days here will be about [illegible] again. Shall probably start back Sept. 1, calling by the way, & be at Gtn. on the 8ᵗʰ. Hope *soon* to see you. I see Barrows *has* that poor sermon. But one care for it have I, to let publishing show that 'twas not necessarily (& offensively) "personal"—my absolution for the rest must be granted by you & other good ones.

All well—Charlotte better. Hilda the whole town's delight, so it seems.

And I am *ever yours*
J. H. Clifford

Love to Walt
Thank him for liberal terms to my doctor.

W. exclaimed: "Good! Good! So we are to understand that he took some hold at once?" Clifford's little passage drew from him as I read the exclamation: "Ah! fine!"

459

Had written Morris' and my own names on the big envelopes, on the former's giving "respects and thanks," with the Sarrazin labor in view. My envelope contained such matter as this and Morris' much the same, including however, Future of Poetry from old North American Review sheets. Morris tells me the Sarrazin piece is after all an introduction and four parts—one part, however, mainly extracts. Has this done and is wrestling with the last. Wants proofs for revise in case W. decides to publish.

Tuesday, August 27, 1889

4.50 P.M. W. in room—had just finished his dinner. The weather today continued delightfully cool. I asked him how he felt and he replied—"Much better"—and when I spoke of the weather as inducing it, possibly, he said—"I am more apt to say, my begetting—I rest nearly everything upon that!" But "however—I feel better—which is the important point."

I showed him title-page as at last approved. He regarded it carefully. "I like it—yes;—I liked the other, too, in fact—but I can say the same of this—and if you like this, then is the end reached. I give you the same privilege I demand for myself—the privilege of believing that in my own affairs, in yours, I, you, are the man essential to be satisfied. With me satisfied, you satisfied, the world must be satisfied." He laughed—"This might be called a gospel of conceit—but hardly!"

Spoke of the Gutekunst photos. "Yes—the young man came over with them Saturday—Saturday morning. Then came back in the afternoon to say that Gutekunst wished them back again—hoped I had sent none away—intended copyrighting them. I returned a message by the man, but doubt if he carried it faithfully—he did not look as if he could—advised that none but the one be copyrighted—that I cared nothing for those others—gave them no value—but thought this one of the best I have had. Don't you think it was? I had intended sending one on to Bucke—told him I had a large picture but thought perhaps it would be dangerous to trust it to the mail—breakage was so frequent. And he has written me—it is in the letter there—" pointing to a letter stuck in the string about a bundle on the table—"he explained that one of his men was making a sort of tour of the states—that he could stop here—could take it along home with him." W. added—"I suppose now he may come along any day—I may have to send him to Gutekunst for it. He is a man I know well—Ed knows, too—have met. Dick Flynn—ain't it a good name? Comes easy from the tongue! I like to run it over, it trips along so easily! He is a gardener up there at the Asylum—a modest, reticent sort of fellow, disinclined to self. I remember I praised him once or twice up there, and he resented it—did not like it at all—sort of drew himself up— so I did not venture often on that line. He would say, when I spoke of something he had wisely done—planting, digging, whatnot—that it was no credit to him—that he was only working, only making a living: though it was true he liked, loved, his work! We got along very well—indeed I got along well with all the fellows there—they seemed to like me—I them." I asked, "don't you think you're eligible to get along with men?" to which promptly—"Yes—I think I am— thoroughly so." Was it because of looking up to their strength, etc.? "No—that only in part—rather, my liking for the fellows who delve in the soil—work at first hand—a tendency towards things of the earth, earthy, as they say." "Oh!" he said again, "I am sure I shall enjoy Flynn's visit, if he comes—just the sight of him—the remembrance he will bring—brings—of past years!"

Bought book from him for Mrs. Herbert Putnam, Alta, Iowa (through Mrs. Fels)—complete—which he gave me for 4 dollars, and endorsed with her name. When I asked W. for this endorsement, he exclaimed—"Oh! My hands are all over honey—honey"—and washed them as I waited. Then as he put the cork in and lead foil over top of bottle, he added— "How delicately they do these things, nowadays—see how it fits—and cheap, too. So well put together that even an ant could not get a slick inside—or a pismire, a fly!" Also sold her copy of Bucke's book for 1 dollar, saying of this last, however—"We must not make a practice of selling these, however: morally, we must not do it. This, of course, is not a regular sale, but Dave gives them to me very cheap only that I may make a profit out of them." "But we must not be squeamish—we more than make this up to Dave in other ways." I will express the books west.

Returned to comment on picture: "I must send my message to Gutekunst by written note—when I thank him—then he will understand." Returned me proof of his "autobiographic note"—called my attention to a change, "Only one—perhaps one most people would consider immaterial—yet it is well to be accurate." In the paragraph "1865 to '7'"—had changed "till '74" to "till well on in '73"—"which makes it about the true thing—a point well to observe where one can."

Had written on proof and on envelope containing it and inside had carefully wrapped the quarter up in a slip containing an inscription. "I like to treat the boys well—they always do me. And then these sheets—I wish to send 'em away—some of 'em. Is the same darkey boy taking the proofs who worked for us on November Boughs?"

"I have been thinking of Poet-Lore today—now I am sure I mailed it direct to Mrs. O'Connor last Saturday. You had better tell her that—or no doubt she has the magazine itself by this time." Returned me "French celebrities"—remarking the "great interest" of the volume—"True, it is not heavy— but it attracts one—perhaps by that very fact." Looked very well—his color better than for weeks. Lying on chair was a package which he had endorsed as "favorite" pieces for "spouting"—as he put it—his own piece among them "A Voice Out of the Sea." He said: "I was a great spouter in my early days—even later on—had my favorite pieces—these among them. I picked them up here the other day and bundled them together. Yes, 'A Voice Out of the Sea,' my own piece was one—one of many. I always enjoyed saying it—saying it to the winds, the waters, the noisy streets—on stage-coaches. And one has love for the sound of his own voice—somehow it's always magnetic." Told him I was going out to the Old Man's Home this evening. Had he papers to send? Would make me up a bundle. I then left, to come back later on.

7.35 P.M. W. was just being helped into the house by Ed—had been out at last. When he sat down in parlor and I asked him how he enjoyed his outing, he responded warmly— "Oh—much—much!—it was the best of all—clear, invigorating—I am much helped by it!" Morris had been very grateful for W.'s remembrance of him, and W. now said: "I had no idea he would care so much—no idea he would care at all! So he was pleased—pleased? So am I, then!" Had read the following paragraph in today's Press and commented indignantly on it:

Colonel Ingersoll's address at the funeral of his friend, the late Horace Seaver, on Sunday, in Boston, was eloquent and beautiful, but there was no perfume in the flowers of its rhetoric, no warmth in the rays of its brilliancy, no comfort in its awkward philosophy. It was an apotheosis of the doctrine of Doubt, an exaltation of the creed of Nothingness, containing neither sympathy nor hope, promising nothing, believing nothing, hoping for nothing to the dead or living. It was a fervid rhetorical outline of the strange, empty religion which begins with an If and ends with a But—the religion of self-boastful ignorance and indifference, which has Doubt for its spirit and intellectual husks for its sustenance.

"That is by one of the smart men—the smart man—of the editorial clique—a supercilious know-nothing who thinks he can best please the world by denouncing its heterodoxies—by making every man who is any way heterodox to feel the blow of his club: and indeed, society is, in a way, pleased with that. But I often question myself if we—if I myself, for one—make enough allowance for the swelling and swelling and swelling and rising tide of radicalism of our time—radicalism everywhere, overflowing churches, states, institutions everywhere. Whether after all an absolute majority of the millions of people now in this America—our America—is not radical, more or less, knowing or unknowing? That is what reconciles me—us—to such paragraphs as this in the Press."

He had made me up the package for Mr. Montgomerie, and remarked: "It is not as careful a selection as I should have made had I been given more time, but I hope it will do. I have never seen the old man, but I wish you would tell him Walt Whitman sends his love." He spoke of the Phila. papers. "Yes —the Ledger—it is the best. In the newspaper way—the daily paper way—the Ledger is about as much as is good for a man." At one moment, speaking of the radicalism, I said, "But things are all right—I never miss that conviction at all. How could any man in fact live without it?" To which W. said quickly, "That is really so—how could he? I should think it would at least take all comfort, happiness, content, out of his living, working. I liked so much the serenity, the deepening peace, with which Marcus Antoninus—Epictetus, too—the great Epictetus!—regarded life—always insisting, 'O Nature! What is good for thee is good for me, too—sound and necessary'—or to that effect—grand, wholesome, inspiring convictions!" Asked me if Morris had not a middle name—then said: "For a year or so there I addressed Bucke as 'Dr. R. M.'—but now I drop all prefixes but the 'Doctor'—which seems sufficient. I am not a believer in superfluities of speech, writing. And these letters go just as well. I suppose the fellows up there must by this time know pretty well anyhow who I am looking for when letters marked 'Walt Whitman' come up there—would know without looking up Doctor's name."

Wednesday, August 28, 1889

7.50 P.M. W. down stairs, in the parlor, but had not been out. Appeared well and said he felt "reasonably well." I had with me a dozen copies of his Autobiographic note. Wished to send some of them away at once. I inquired if he had yet heard from John Burroughs? "Yes—just today—and he carefully avoids saying a word—Oh! so carefully! as if by study!—saying a word about the book, whether he got it or not, and so forth. He does, however, speak of 'Mr. Donnelly's Reviewers.'" I asked, "He is not a Baconian?" "No—oh no!—but I do not think he is anti in an extreme sense—his mind is not fortressed here against assault—nor in anything that I know—he welcomes hearing. But he has his opinions, cognitions—some strongly held—as that about Carlyle, for instance, in which he is bold, tenacious. He is rather favorably impressed with this book, if anything—at least that is the idea with which his letter impressed me. I do not remember his exact words, but he says something like this—that he regrets the 'irruptive' tendencies of the book—some unfortunate temper towards the critics—." I asked if he had ever known J. B. and W. D. O'C. to have the Bacon matter out together. He shook his head—"No—I guess not." I said again, "I don't think John changed in his personal feelings towards O'C., but he certainly shrank from his emphasis." To which W., "Yes—that was plain enough—plain enough: he feared, as we have just been saying, O'Connor's 'irruptive' influence, tendency. However caused, however regretted, painful, what-not, the John Burroughs who wrote the early books—who was convinced, who commanded—is not the John Burroughs we know now. The old John Burroughs is much thawed out—much melted. And I must confess, it is all inexplicable to me—

465

even to me—that to me, who perhaps should know him and
do know him better than any other—even to me, it is a
mystery, inexplicable, a baffling quantity." "John says in
his letter he has left his family at Hobart—he himself is
settled at West Park again." I said to W.: "O'Connor, as I
saw him sick there nearly at the end of his life, was the same
man in mental strength and courage as when he wrote the
Good Grey Poet—but Burroughs, as he came here last Fall,
was by no means the Burroughs of the books—not of complaint, I know, but of plaint—and his letters to you and to me
confirm this." W. fervently—"It is a striking contrast—I can
see it all—all, and it is justified by what we know—these
inexplicable later years." And when I added something about
J. B.'s "lovable personality" W. acquiesced: "Yes—that is
so, too—that will never change."

W. spoke of Stedman as "effusive—effusive, glowing, flow-
ing-out—as they say the Frenchmen do—though with rather
doubtful truth at times, of individuals. But I have always had
an affection for him. I have met his embezzling son—a handsome fellow, I believe. Arthur, the other son, whom I have
met also, helps the father." Spoke of the Modjeska-Booth
troupe for the Fall. W. had met Modjeska. "She is a fascinating, bright woman. I have never see her act—saw her at
Gilder's, in New York—handsome, agreeable, magnetic." Alluding to his family—"We all kept slaves then on Long
Island—up to the early part of this century—in it. Not I,
for I only came in at the very last—saw only a few samples of
it. The legislature then had passed some graduated emancipation bill—something of that sort. There was considerable
feeling at the time—all were not agreed in favor of it—but my
folks were emancipationists. It was to cover a term of years—
finally, however, there came some decree of absolute emancipation—though I do not know that it was needed, for towards
the end there was a sudden release all around, as is apt to be the
case in matters we know must take a stated course any-

how—tension is relaxed, the hold taken off." Spoke of Long
Island—of Bryant's home—"a beautiful place—somewhat
cliffy—rather cliffy: of old it was called Mosquito Cove, but
when the wealthy New Yorkers came along there with their
handsome stately villas, Mosquito Cove had a plain rude
sound, which they changed to Roslyn." "There's no sign of
Liberty yet," W. remarked, "no copies for me—and you?
not you either? What can have come of it?"

Thursday, August 29, 1889

5.40 P.M. W. in his bed-room, looking very well and saying
"I feel very well—well for me." No word, he said, from
Gutekunst yet. I took him sample copies of medallion and
70th year pictures, which he enjoyed. "They satisfy me—
came up well." Will get the whole body of copies tomorrow.
Was he going to use the bust picture in this collection? "O
yes! that is what I intend—and with just that inscription I
put on your proof-copy"—"I want 200 copies of that, too—
you may order them any time." Did he intend putting any
superscription on the other pictures? "I have not decided yet
—perhaps—perhaps not—I should not wonder."

He was greatly amused over some ignoramus' serious remark
to me the other day—"So you know Walt Whitman? I heard
so. They say he is a writer of dirty books? Is he? I shouldn't
wonder but it was true." W. remarking—"The world at large
might suppose I am sensitive—would not like to hear such
stories—and sure enough there have been plenty such—about
the books, about me personally. But there are three or four of
my very most intimate friends—those nearest, best understanding me—who thoroughly realize that my disposition is
to hear all—the worst word that is said—the ignorantest—
whatever. That there's nothing, in fact, I should so regret as
not to know how affairs are regarded. For I know—never hide
from myself—how much is to be said on the other side—

467

antagonistically—however cherished our own notions are." Was solicitous to know from me—"So the medallion picture still pleases you? You still like it as much as you did? I find myself that I like the bust picture better as I go along." Then he laughed and pointed to the cards near by which I had brought him. "Why in the world do the printers—like the tailors—always pursue their own way, regardless of what others want or of what is best? I can never get them to print my pictures as I want them—with an inclination towards the top of the page—certainly the way more striking to the eye. But a printer is much the same—always puts in his dashes, superfluities—which he thinks pretty or necessary"— then with a laugh—"which I as always strike out!" I read him a letter I received from Bush today. He thought it "admirably easy and direct." Bush may be on next month. Quite curiously asked me—"Well—does the book get along well? I guess it will be a success." I said, "Your two pages of it will be, anyhow." To which—"Ah! more than that—more than that, if anything—and something it must be!"

Friday, August 30, 1889

4.50 P.M. W. in his room, eating dinner. I had intended staying but a few minutes—went in merely with the bundle of pictures I had secured from Billstein (medallion and 70th year), but W. was in many respects so inquisitive—talked so freely between bites, that I stayed half an hour. Talked somewhat about the Gutekunst photo. Copy of it—sample—on chair, face down. I took it in my hands. On face had endorsed in ink with his name, and on reverse lead-pencilled his opinion, describing day as "sunny" and Buckwalter and Ed as his companions—and that he greatly enjoyed the three hours. I looked at the picture a long time and he at me. "It still impresses you favorably?" he asked, and on my acquiesence—"So me, too. I think it one of the best—the very best. Curiously, yes, even the coat is fine, natural—the creases, fold, texture, all there—

I conceit I can even see the color!" I said, "Doctor Bucke will love this." But he looked doubtful—"I don't know—the Doctor is very whimsical—it would be hard to say what will please him. But then we may declare, whether he likes it or no, that it's good—good: its goodness, excellence is inherent." He had sent Ed over for some this morning, and got them. The copy he had written over was a sample. A number of the card photos were on the floor. He said he cared little for them. The fine version contained the history of the past year or two—for that I liked it—all the pain and doubt and the rugged fight against both. "Doctor's is on the road now," he explained—Flynn came in the other evening and took it away in his arms.

As we sat there talking, my eye lighted on a manuscript sheet on the floor—which I picked up—found it an early draft of "Yonnondio." He asked—"What is it? Let me see!" And when he had got it in his hands—"Yes—I remember. Didn't you want a piece from me for some-one? Who was it?" I named our man—Bryant, of the Maine Historical Society. "Oh yes! Now I recall it. How would it do to give him this?" The sheet much trodden—rumpled—stained—no doubt long thrown about there—since publication several years ago. W. took his big pen, wrote a headline for it—"Yonnondio"—and off in the corner—

"printed in book
"first in 'Critic' "

and handed it to me. "If you will, then—send that to him." This has lain over since last year. Aroused talk of "Yonnondio"— the word—as I said—"full of music and meaning even in itself" to which W. fervently—"It is! it is! Oh! I have felt it all! So often a word, a sign, more than all attempted explication—all!" Adding: "My use of the word has been contested. Did I ever tell you about the queer old fellow who wrote me several years ago—at the time I printed the piece— saying no Indian significance attached to it—that I had gone all wrong? Yet I am sure of my correctness. There never yet was an Indian name that did not mean so much, then more, and more, and more—then more beyond that. For the word 'Mannahatta' I believe I have the best authority ever was, Judge Furman, in Brooklyn—and Jeremiah Mason. I doubt if better philologists—knowers of the Indian tongues—ever existed than these men. I knew them well—many years ago. How this word clung and clung!" As to gutteral Indian dialects, W. said—"That is a great deal fiction—just as the fiction of the Russian tongue—yet what is finer than this?—where we say Russia—the Russian himself says Roo-see-a—soft —melodious, fine." "You know I very fondly use Manna-hatta—I doubt if anybody ever used it as advisedly as I have done. Do you know what Mannahatta means? The Indians use the word to indicate a plot of ground, an island, about which the waters flow—keep up a devil of a swirl, whirl, ebullition—have a hell of a time. To me it is all meaning and music!" W. had thoughtfully laid out on one of his chairs for me, a proof copy of "Robert Burns as Poet and Person." "Take this," he said, "to Peter Montgomerie—perhaps it would interest him—or even you by the way." He did not get out last evening, but thought he might this.

Saturday, August 31, 1889

7.45 P.M. Went down to W.'s with Jacob Lychenheim. W. in front of door, on chair—Harned sitting on step talking to him. Had just returned from trip to the river. Looked in fine condition and talked well. We stayed nearly an hour, and he discussed various matters with great vim. Spoke of his work. Had he written anything lately? Harned asked, and W. re-sponded, "O yes! several things—the Century has one piece—two pieces. One piece on my 71st year—a proof came of it today—it probably will go into the November number—only seven or eight or so lines. And you saw the Inness picture the other day?" turning to me—"Don't you remember it? 'The Valley of the Shadow of Death'? The most surprising thing of all—the Harper's wrote for a piece to that. And so I sat right down and did it—did it the other day. It was not a long job—it was quite easily done—and a third of it—the first third—I cut wholly out. Just as I was folding it up, the thought struck me that I was not satisfied with it—with that part and so I cut it off the sheet—let it start with the other—sent the mutilated piece. And in a couple of days comes the pay for it—so all is now done on that!" He had called my attention to the Inness picture several days ago—asked me—"What do you think of that? It is by Inness: Do you know anything about Inness? What? Tell me." Harned now asked him if he had yet written the Tennyson piece for the North American Review? But he answered quickly—"No—not a word of it—nor shall I. I have no such intention. I have said all I want to say—should say—about Tennyson. There is nothing I could add to that." I asked—"Why not Tennyson write about Walt Whitman?" He laughed. "No—that involves another question—that would not do. For one thing, Tennyson has never written about his contemporaries and I have. Then Tennyson is in England. And there are plenty of better reasons than either." Added, "Herbert Gilchrist thinks I already think too much of Tennyson—have written too much about him—made too much of him, but I do not—have not the slightest suspicion of it myself." Harned spoke of T.'s "Lordship humbug" but W. retorted—"Oh—that does not matter—don't disturb me in the slightest—I make no account of it whatever." Tom said what he loved in W. was his consistency, whereas Tennyson, etc.—to which W., "Who knows, Tom, but he is as consistent as I am? Back of the formal, stately, Tennyson, anyhow, there is the great, rude, rugged Saxon Tennyson. It is true Tennyson is the poet of parlors—of our topmost civilization, so-called—of the infinite graceries —all that. Why is he that? It is not easily told. He is that,

because—well, because!"—ending with a laugh. "Then besides, I feel no call to write of Tennyson—no call—no inner
command." But he ought to, Tom argued—whereat W.—
laughingly—"No—that is not so, Tom. Did you ever hear
the story of the woman, who asked her neighbor to return her
her borrowed tubs? The neighbor replied that it was impossible, and for several reasons, which she gave—'In the
first place I never received any tub from you,—in the second
you never had a tub to send me, in the third I never had a
tub myself'—and so on through half a dozen explications.
And it is so with me, Tom: I never had the tub—nor did the
North American"—and he ended it in a slight but hearty
laugh.

Reference to the London strike. "Yes indeed—it is extensive—it has great ramifications. It is wonderful, the great
internal, industrial troubles of the nations in these later
days—in England—over the Continent. I call them intestinal
troubles. I don't know but they're in America, too—but
then I am in the habit of saying of America that she has such
a big belly that she can easily take care of them all." He was
silent a moment, then resuming: "Mrs. Gilchrist happened
very often to say to me, speaking of turbulent, revolutionary,
other, tendencies of our time, that we were 'going somewhere,'
and I suppose the sour old irascible Carlyle would say, 'yes,
going somewhere—going to hell, all of us!'" Spoke of Huxley's debate with Wace and others—Harned enthusiastic—
W. saying: "He is great man—this Huxley. A man, I
should say, who, on these questions, plows deep deep, below
even Colonel Ingersoll." Adding—"Oh yes! for us—these
stories, fables, legends, of the orthodox, were settled long
ago—long ago. Myths, piled on myths—then myths again.
But as to accepting them literally—oh! how could we? They
have an importance—had a necessity—their place in the line
could not be questioned—a quality like the evanescent tint of
a sunset sky, of the fish that swims the waters—here—gone—

but actual, oh! how actual!" Tom gave an amusing rendering
of Huxley's discussion of the Gadarean swine story. Was it a
moral action in Jesus, to so destroy another man's swine, etc.
W. laughed tremendously—turned jokingly to Tom: "In
New Jersey, Tom—in any one of our States here—wouldn't
that be an actionable offense?" And to Tom's "Yes indeed!"—
"And even in England, I suppose—even in the Archbishop's
own country!"

Referred again to the Gutekunst picture and to my copy
of it. "I shall put it in good shape for you!" he said. W.
quoted in effect Kant's "Two things in the Universe strike me
with awe—the starry spaces above, the law of Duty within"—
I gave him this, he saying—"No doubt that's the phrase—
I was blundering towards it—a grand and efficient statement."
Then he turned questioningly to me—"But how do you explain
it, Horace—how?—that in my old days, I more and more
make morality so called take a back seat—relegate it—
subordinate it? Take it away with you—carry it in your cap—
don't attempt to answer me now, but when you come again—
then!" Tom invited him to dinner tomorrow. W. said—"I may
—to get a drink! But for the eating—well, you know how all
the Doctors caution me about that." And as to the champagne
—"Have you the same—the same you had—good as ever
was?" And to T.'s assent—"Well—there is no better to that
best. As in the story of the peach—the man—Sidney Smith
was it?—who said, God no doubt could have made a better
fruit, but no doubt God never had." Finally—"Well—Tom—
probably I shall come—did you say one-half after one?
Well—if I can—if I feel so—I shall come!"

W. said as to Ingersoll: "There is a young writer for the
press there in New York—someone—a friend of mine, I
believe—who gives Ingersoll first quality in poetry. How
does that strike you? No doubt it is at least in part true."
Harned told a story of Beecher—how at the time of his
trial, in a company a young lady had asked a gentleman

473

present, "Do you think Mr. Beecher is guilty?" and got for reply "Guilty of what?" W. laughingly saying, "Surely that was a poser." Then adding—"I have heard a good story of Beecher himself. They were discussing the nude in art—a young lady asked him—perhaps an old—a lady, anyhow—woman—'Now don't you, Mr. Beecher, consider so and so indecent?'—mentioning some statue. Beecher replied: 'I must confess, Madame, I do not think it indecent,—but I think your question indecent.'—which was one of the best I ever heard." Harned quoted words or lines from "In Memoriam" W. exclaiming as he listened—"Splendid! Splendid! There's nothing to beat it!"

Harrison Morris put the question today—Would it be pleasant to W. to have him discuss the Sarrazin essay in the American? W. said of it: "Oh! let him fire away. We have put ourselves in the way of the public, to be whacked at, pecked at—investigated, and so we must welcome all comers—all!" Said he had seen by the papers that Talcott Williams was back in town. Alluded to fact that the Williams' had money. "It is queer how the folks lose their money, get more, fall down, are set up again. John Swinton and his wife had a fortune left to them—an old uncle, somebody, died: John thought he had a call to start a paper—put his money in it—then duly lost—in a year was poor as poor—then came another fortune—even more—which now he has, I believe."

Sunday and Monday, September 1–2, 1889

Did not see W. at all. I was out of town—at Logan: Monday was the first celebration of Labor Day in Pennsylvania.

In last evening's talk, Harned said to W.: "Brinton wrote a note to Horace in which he took up a difference with you—said he did not share your belief in immortality." W. laughed. "Did he? Then all the worse for him! But Brinton is a clear-headed man of science—I value what he says. As to immortality—well—well"—and so he ended.

Morris had given me the conclusion of his Sarrazin translation.

Tuesday, September 3, 1889

7.45 P.M. W. in parlor—had been in but a few minutes from outing towards the river. Reached out his hand for me. "Where have you been? We missed you much," he said. Then, to my questions, answered, "Yes—since you were here I have been reasonably well—as well as I have a right to expect to be. On Sunday I was up at Tom's, dinner-time." And did he eat? "Oh no! but I made it up on the champagne, which did me a deal of good—oh! a deal!" Then went over such events as he thought would interest me. "There was a letter from the Doctor—from Bucke. He has got the picture—Flynn duly reached London—and Doctor likes it much—likes it much—is even enthusiastic over it—thinks it the picture of the future. And I have had a nice letter from Nellie O'Connor, too, in which she says she is very grateful to you. She has Poet Lore—it came at last—but she says she knows nothing about the Critic—does not believe it ever arrived. Yet I am sure I sent it. She mentions some number of the Critic—July 8th, June 8th—in which she was told Lowell has something to say about William. But that is a mistake, I think—I should have seen it if it had been there." And as to Lowell and W. W., W. laughed—"We long ago decided that we were not to fraternize." "Now it is Holmes' 80 years," W. said, "they have been celebrating that—there were quite a number of accounts of it in the papers. How the fellows are getting along!—and Tupper, too." Here I laughed and said, as he looked round at me, "Yes—that other representative, with you, of the artificial in poetry"—whereupon he laughed heartily. "Yes—that's so! Poor Savage! Bright idea! I wonder if

475

he comes about many ideas as bright as that? They must be a burden." Here a mention of the Sarrazin piece—W. remarking: "I have read it—and Morris' letter, too. I liked the first part of the translation much better than the last—there was a freshness about it. But it has been very generous in Morris to persevere with it—and his letter is flattering and kind." I expressed my liking for a translation not so literal—one more bathed in the spirit—and W. said—"I see—I see how justified you are in the preference." And when I further said, "It would be hard or impossible for a distinctively literary man to render a man like Sarrazin," he answered—"You are right —it is impossible, in any strict sense." Adding—"Morris says in his note he would like to have the sheets back, for possible slips. You can take them to him any day—it might be well. If we should conclude to publish it, it would be but justice to him."

I told him of Jake Lychenheim's removal to the country— and his desire to have from W.'s hands (and to pay for) a picture, to hang up in his room. W. at once said: "Yes indeed—he should have one—have it without pay." But I said he was anxious to pay. W. however—"No—I should prefer to give him a little token—say the McKay picture, with my name on it—wouldn't that do?" Finally saying—"And he shall have it tomorrow, if you wish. I'll make it up for you. The boys must be humored—Oh! we all love the boys!" Asked me: "Do you think you could find me an envelope-maker, somewhere? I must have an envelope for my pictures— a good strong capacious white envelope—capacious, for the pictures are quite large. I have the memorandum, specification —all made out for you to take any time you choose." Asked me about proofs of book. I got plate proofs today. Sent Gilder's off at once. He said: "I want 200 of the bust pictures printed— and would it not be well to let the same superscription there go through the entire printing—for me, for the book? It needs some explanation."

476

So we talked—and by and by Tom and Frank Harned came in and were heartily greeted. Tom asked him how he had fared from Sunday's champagne and he said—"Good! Good! Felt all the better for it—always do, Tom!" And to the question "Are you now out of the Doctor's hands?" he laughed heartily and responded—"I hope I was never in—was I ever in?" Tom inquired after the Gutekunst pictures—W. saying—"They are upstairs, tucked away somewhere or other. If you wish it, I'll go and hunt 'em up"—offering to rise from his seat, but on Tom's protest, leaned back again. Harned asked if the pictures were a success. "I understood one of them was," he said, upon which W. remarked: "I suppose they all were, in a way—in fact would be considered very fine—in their smoothification—the quality that never pleases me. There is one which I call an eminent success—which makes it worth while to make the trial." He said of Anna's picture— "Beauty—beauty! I should say, almost the most beautiful I have ever known." Gilchrist also came along by and by. All hands then settled down, and it was 9.15 before we were all departed, Frank having gone first. W. was very talkative and vigorous. Harned had asked Gilchrist how he was progressing with his Cleopatra picture—and he reported, "Well." W. asked, "What is the story you wish to tell—or don't you want to tell it now?" and again—"Is she aboard anything?" and still again—"In order to represent the craft, you must have had to go into a devil of a search after information—ships, what-not—of those times." Gilchrist explained his counsel from Murray (London)—on the question of habiliment—how much less was luxury a part of Cleopatra's make-up than might be supposed. W. said: "Yes—that is generally the case: when we get at the truth of a thing finally, we are always impressed with what a devil of a plain matter it all was."

Reference to the London strike—to Burns, who leads it, and is a great admirer of W. W. Then of free trade. Gilchrist spoke of how rapid movement would be when once our working-men here got over their British scare—dwelt upon the English workingmen's greater friendliness for America. W. exclaimed —"But Herbert, there's great good reason for this: your men over there look here out of their necessity—they must: America is their forerunner—without America they would be without a foot to stand on—would not be justified in their own claims—would, as it were, be without an anchor—at sea in all this radicalism of modern days! I have been reading today again those workingmen letters in the Press—they interest me beyond any other thing of late. But I have a suspicion—it is especially strong a suspicion today—that the Press tampers with the letters—cuts out any information which militates towards free trade. You know," he said vigorously, "they're a villainous bigoted set!" And to a reference to Talcott Williams—"I have known Talcott Williams now ten years—in a sense intimately—and I should say that at heart—at heart, I say, for he may be unconscious of it himself, as happens—he is a free-trader." W. is always contemptuous of the Press—but spares T. W. "America has settled, will settle, many problems for the British workingmen—your workingmen know that well. Not, of course, that there's nothing to be said on the other side too." Frank quoted something reported as said by Carnegie the other day—that the tariff is no longer helping the iron business of Pennsylvania. This led to discussion of Carnegie. W. said to some deprecating remark, "Look out—you fellows"—laughingly—"Carnegie paid a handsome price for a seat at my lecture, and I won't hear him abused!" At another moment he remarked—to do so or so "is like writing of literature—the literature of our time—and leaving Carlyle out—without Carlyle there would be no literature." And as we sat there and discussed labor, etc., he was quiet for a while—finally rising from his chair, taking his cane—slowly going to the door—stood in the doorway, his back to us—his face turned—the light of the gas playing with his hair—body bent (grand!): "Don't you fellows be too quick to dismiss Carnegie—take in the whole man—think of what Carlyle was with all his sourness, irascibility, scolding—the grandeur and glory of our time—but for whom the literature of an age would have been a blank!" And he had said again to my offers of help: "No—all keep your places—I am going off only for a minute—I'll be back again." And so into the hallway and laboriously upstairs— nobody following him. Shortly returning, with the Gutekunst picture, himself turning up the gas in the hall and saying, "Here it is, Tom" etc. Gilchrist did not like it—complained of the monotony of color etc., and got into debate with W. on the point as he said that "photography is not art," that it was rather science and that he would rather have an indifferent oil than a fine photo etc. W. admitted that "of course color, warmth, all that, is inestimable" and would "always yield painting its value"—but he still said: "I should not myself, Herbert, allow such a sweeping classification. Indeed, what is art? Is it one thing or all things? I think, all—the Italian laborer on the street, the woman with her child, the curbstones out here—all is for art. No—no—we must not be too quick— even science cannot spare art—this art. The human expression is so fleeting—so quick—coming and going—all aids are welcome." G. somewhat misunderstood W. at this point, thinking he had said this as derogatory to photography, but he had not, as he afterwards explained. Talk on both sides greatly interesting. W. said: "Bucke counts that the best picture yet —says that is the picture which will go down to the future." But this was combatted and W. made no fight for the idea himself beyond saying—"I take it to be a first-rater—one of the best, anyhow."

The talk was variously in this strain till we departed. W. had said to me before the others came: "I have a letter from Pearsall Smith, the father. He is off—I think in Surrey— has distinguished neighbors—Tyndall on one side, Tennyson on the other." And, among other things—"and still no sign from Liberty! Have you?" Said to me also, "Tom should now get a picture of little Tom. He's a great institution—he's not to be slighted."

Wednesday, September 4, 1889

7.38 P.M. W. sitting in front of the house. Just back from his chairing. "I got to the river tonight," he said, "and how gloriously everything appeared. Look at the evening now," waving his arm—skywards—"a glow everwhere." I said "Yes—'the transparent and shadowy night.'" And he smiled and repeated, "The grand night! The beautiful night!" Then after a pause: "It will be the finest of the year—now for two months, the mild, gentle days—season above seasons!" Off toward south-east the moon—"How it fills the night! I suppose it will last now till 3 or 4 of the morning." I told him I was going out to the country for a walk. "I quite 'enviges' you," he said, laughingly. "Never a word," he said, "from the World poem. I cannot understand it. The embarrassing point is, the uncertainty: if it was not for that, if they had only sent it back, I should try it somewhere else—should not wonder but I'll do it anyway." I commented—the Register made quite warm reference to Holmes' 80th birthday—gave it editorial first place—but significantly had never mentioned the recent W. W. celebration. W. laughed, and said, "Well?" And went on—"The Unitarians are still in the uncertain stage—they are not sure of themselves—feel they cannot afford to be ungenteel." And that "Japanese missionary business" on the part of Unitarians, which had always aroused his laughter, came up for more questions.

A man in the Bank much resembling Lincoln in figure—I called W.'s attention thereto—referring to the man's gravity. W. then: "Yes—I should say that at first sight Lincoln would impress one with his gravity, seriosity. But Lincoln the man was not basically serious—at least, not to the point of seriosity: he was rather cheery—cheery is just the word." As to Lincoln's laugh: "I do not remember that as remarkable, but I remember his cheer, his story-telling—always the good story well told. His ways were beautiful and simple—how well I knew them, watched them! He delighted in simplicity, ruggedness, naturalness, straightforward nativity—in plain habits, clear thinking, doing. And he was the same man in all relationships—for instance, to the boys—the messenger boys —who came often, he would put his hands on their shoulders— say, 'My son, is there an answer?' or 'Sit down there, my son,' something in that way, with a radiant kindliness, humanity— in a natural tone, as if out of a great heart. Though not slangy—not slangy at all—Lincoln was in current with our average life—a great, great presence, in our age, our land." Reference here to Arnold's notion that Lincoln lacked "distinction"—what did he mean by the word? "I do not know, except that I might say of this as of many things that Arnold says—that it is a recoil upon himself. Matthew Arnold was not in the abstract sense a damned fool, but with respect to the modern—to America—he was the damnedest of damned fools—a total ignoramus—knew nothing at all. I know Arnold was not alone in this ignorance—even Americans have been slow enough to take in the modern-America. The last 15 years have found Lincoln up—quite the thing—but in those early days, how few there were to measure the man! O'Connor, always, and from the first—and my claim always belongs and there was the curious great Russian Count of whom I have often spoken to you—Gurowski—he was enthusiastic—a keen, profound judge of men. It was curious—in those times— whenever the Count went to the White House he took his hat off. He was a queer fellow—disliked, for one thing, to be questioned—in that respect resembled me closely. But I once inquired of him, 'Count'—I always called him Count— 'Count—why is it you always take your hat off when you go

to the President?' He asked me, 'Do I?' and when I had
questioned him further—'Why yes! so I do!—and yet I
never knew I did. I cannot tell why I did—only that something or other commanded me to!' And it is of this influence
that Lincoln partakes—partook." I interpolated a story of
the difference in millhands—the native American always
speaking to the Boss with hat on, foreigners deferentially
with hats off. W. laughed heartily! "It is a good story," he
said—"you must consider it is a great possession—as it is: I
should say that was something to note—to jot down."

At the near corner from W.'s house (4th St) they are
planting an electric light pole. Said W. amusedly: "Little shall
I care for it—I always did shrink both from getting into a
great light and from being a great light." "Yet," I put in,
"did not some anyhow contend he was a light?" To which—
"Yes: the sort of light that says, Beware!" Spoke of Phila.
papers—and of the New York papers of his early life. "I like
the Ledger very well." "In those first times, over in New York,
I read the Herald, generally." Detailed ages and precedence
of papers. When referring to the Times he explained—"It
was in the War I wrote for the Times—wrote letters from
Washington." Were these letters signed? "Yes—most of 'em.
I signed them, when signed at all, with my last name—Whitman—Whitman alone! At least—I think so—though the flush
of those times is past—I find much that then ensued getting—
if it has not long been—hazy, misty, doubtful." "Indeed, it
was through these letters mostly at this time that I was able
to go along at Washington. Raymond made no bones of
paying 50 dollars for a letter he liked."

W. sent Ed upstairs to get me memoranda of Envelope for
pictures. Several papers enclosed in envelope inscribed

"Send me a sample proof first
& tell me how much price for 100
    "   "   "   "   150
    "   "   "   "   200

make large envelopes
<u>White</u> <u>or</u> <u>light</u> handsome
    cream colored—or some
    handsome light color what
    they call undecided color,
    light blue light rose or
    something of that kind
    —<u>strong</u> <u>and</u> <u>first</u> <u>class</u> in
    <u>material</u> <u>and</u> <u>appearance</u>—
Size on the piece of brown paper
    enclosed mark'd *
Style—with a handsome eyelet
    —bag-form'd (as sample herewith)
    (intended to be tied, bound by a string
    of floss silk)
    (the intention of the envelope is to hold
    (to be sent by mail, or otherwise) 8 or
    10 cards, pictures—want a handsome
    job—envelopes will be printed on
    —must be pretty <u>strong</u> <u>paper</u>—Some
    will go in the European or California
    mail)"

inside a white sheet containing directions copied above—a tough brown sheet for size and a square envelope (a Book-News envelope) with eyelet drawn. "Eylet here" W. had written above it—and elsewhere on the envelope: "This is not the size—is sent as sample (bag-fashioned envelope) I want something and handsome and strong—to go through wear and tumbling and the mail and across the sea"—

W. said: "I want to tie them up with the floss—don't they call it floss? or have I gone wrong in the name? It is a fine substitute for the ordinary red tape of the law—in Washington put about all state documents to their Nobbses—the tony diplomats, whatnot. A sort of silk tape about a quarter of an inch in width—yellow was my color—I used to get it—took delight in every opportunity for using it—made opportunities!" Then—

483

"I guess you'll find our man. See what can be made out of our necessity."

Thursday, September 5, 1889

7.55 P.M. Went down to W.'s with Joe Fels. W. in parlor, —utter darkness—no light even in the hallway: Ed, however, coming along by and by and lighting the latter. W. very cordial—bade us take seats. I knew he had been out—Aggie and Mrs. Fels had met him in his chair on their way from town. W. said—"Yes—I was out—down to the river. I met the girls—Aggie—her friend. What a panorama is this night—oh! the wonder of it!" The moon splendidly shining—getting now nearly full. W. inquired: "What of the President?"—who is now in this neighborhood commemorating the founding of Log College—the first Presbyterian College in this country. "I suppose his speech was not in the afternoon papers?" Fels, happening to say he didn't think much of Harrison, W. said, "Nor do I—he is a poor affair altogether." But he inquired—"What would you call the principal points of objection in him?" Fels thereupon explaining, among other things comparing Harrison to Hayes. Here W. demurred. "I should not agree to that—I have a larger opinion of Hayes—he is to me an indisputably better man. He took a trip over the West and South while he was President. I was West at the time—sick—in a poor way, but I remember what enjoyment I got out of his speeches. It was said by some, they were wanting in dignity—but they were not. I thought them much to the point—simple—direct—full of suggestiveness. And he was so ready, too—willing at any call to speak. These things seemed to me to indicate a significance in the man."

I took him the steel prints, and a paper I had received from Bush containing an account of his departure from the works at Lachine Locks. W. took them with his "Thanks! Thanks!" and "I shall enjoy both, I know." I had made inquiries and found an envelope man, but had not gone to him yet. "You will see him tomorrow, I suppose?" queried W. Referred to dock laborer's strike in London. "I see by later tidings that the bosses are inclined to give in, and I am glad for it. It would seem to be a dispute in which nearly everybody, outside of the bosses themselves, believe the men were justified—that their demands were just. There seems to have been a great fear that somehow violence would result—but they had worked against that appeal—Burns wielding his influence. The point now is, given this point, will they insist upon more and more—make matters worse?" "The great strength of that agitation in England seems to be in the leaders—the remarkable men at the head—men of wide knowledge, solidity, keen faculties." He had heard of great acceptance of the George theory in England: "If it keeps on, this thing will get fashionable—then it's all up with it!" We talked faith—would not the world stand all? I expressed absolute belief. W. said: "That is, you mean that things are and remain all right in proceeding? That no radicalism can spoil it? I guess there is no doubt but the laws that govern the planets—the atmospheric, meteoric influences—will persist according to their own inherencies but whether some of these human things deflect, stray"—here he stopped, as if with a question. I said: "After the George theory, something else. After Emerson, who was a bear in his day, Walt Whitman, and after Walt Whitman, another." W. lighted up—"Yes—Emerson was a dragon in his day—perhaps still,—and so we will go on and on." Fels spoke of Ruskin letters he had seen while in England—denouncing railroads, etc. W. spoke energetically: "Without the railroads, where would our civilization be? Certainly we could ask, where would America be? America in fact could not be. In Ruskin's own corner-lot bit of a country, coaches might still serve, in a way, but in an America—any country continental in its territory, aspirations,—the railroad belongs—has its place. But Ruskin's appeal has its justification, too. In a time when we are beset everywhere by what is called progress, the spirit of progress, civilization, radicalism, railroads, machinery, it may be well to have men like Carlyle, Ruskin, to strike the alarm—to warn us not to go too far."

As we sat there talking, Gilchrist came in—and confused in the darkness was unable to find a seat till fumbling upon the wheeling chair. He sat down in this with some comment on its comfort—W. exclaiming—"Yes, Herbert—we're ahead of you in chairs!" H. acquiescing—and W., striking the arm of the chair he sat in and saying, "I want to send a couple of chairs like this to England when Herbert goes—send one to Tennyson and one to Wm. Rossetti." Discussing then chairs—his preference for the cane—"it has an ample, beautiful look," he said. Gilchrist dined with Talcott Williams last evening. Williams had intended coming over to see Walt—had he come? No. We talked of public men. I asked W. as to Lincoln's complexion. He said, "Not a bad one—rugged—much made up—wholly—of open-air, out-of-doors." Then of Southern men: "Cadavers—complexion of a most remarkable stripe—yet lasting and lasting into 70 years as often as others of us." Instanced Alexander Stephens—called him "a mere bag of bones." "Yet he had endurance, and became an old man." Had he known Oliver P. Morton? It seemed he had. "Morton's lameness came from paralysis—he always impressed me as a man of handsome port—strong—at least, that he had been such." And we discussed Morton's extreme partisanship. W. said: "Morton was in politics the type of what we find in religion—the men who are all Presbyterian, all Methodist. But I do not know that now we need such men. We have specifically now entered into a period of peace, of quiet." Though the Lincolns were not plenty now—"We must remember there is no call for them, nor should I wish there might be. I, for one, have no wish to have new events like those old." I urged for Morton that he was to be judged with reference to the events that had made him extreme, and W. allowed, "That is so—I should not disagree there: then I should go on and say, how like a godsend it was that at that time such a man as Lincoln was here on the stage and availed of: a man of universal grasp—no sign of narrowness, of exclusion, anywhere exuded." But "our era, now, since the war, tends to the development of commonplace men." I objected, in politics but not elsewhere—instancing even more important work was elsewhere being done—Henry George, etc. And he granted—"That is a happy idea—an idea to follow out: I should not be surprised to find it an answer." "But with men like Stephens and Morton in mind—and these others South—and others still to be named—it would seem as if our fellows would have to voice some of our notions of what constitutes beauty—personal beauty—health —wholesomeness—all that." Talked of Bob Lincoln—Gilchrist of his popularity in England. W. said: "I have met him a few times—was always more or less impressed. He seemed a true man after his own kind—but true rather by negative qualities than in the way of his father—yet something of his father in him, too. Did I ever tell you what my good Doctor—a very wise man there in Washington—used to tell me? That the body by 4/5 part existed by virtue of its negative qualities? It is a remarkable idea at first blush, but can be found to hold water."

Having referred to the Strand, London—W. was curious to get at a description—in which he was gratified by Gilchrist and Fels in turn. The origin of the name discussed—then reference to Indian names—their beauty,—W. affirming— "It is all so: no one has better reason for believing it than I." We instanced near-by names—Tulpehocken, Wingohocking, others.

Friday, September 6, 1889

7.55 P.M. W. alone, in the parlor. It had showered in the early evening: therefore, he did not go out. I stayed till about 9—Harned coming in after I had been there some time, and W.

487

engaging us both in vigorous conversation. Asked him if he had read the Bush piece—but: "No—it is still in the pocket of the coat I wore yesterday—I think it was laziness kept me from looking it up—that and nothing else or less." Nor had he looked up the steel prints—"did not open the package." In fact: "I had quite a bad day today—and it has been very hot, hasn't it? Now I am easier: this last hour or so has mildened things up considerably." We got on the subject of Indian names again—I had met with one today—"Kokendaugua"—which he much enjoyed. "It is as you say, something quite distinct and recognizable that they bear through which the Indian names appeal to us. They are totally genuine—we could say of them what Gilder said of my poetry—that they stand specifically alone—are not to be imitated—not to be manufactured." "There is nothing in all language, ancient or modern, so significant—so individual—so of a class—as these names. I have often threatened myself to make a collection of them—I don't know for what purpose or if for any—but have never done so."

They had discussed at Harned's last Sunday a point made in Gould's pamphlet, "Frankenstein"—that there was no such thing as an insane asylum in China. Tom said he had confirmed it. W. said now: "Yes I thought then and say again, I think that the most extraordinary, significant fact, statement, of all." And he added in the course of a discussion of the importance of Christianity: "I think the first five centuries of Christianity very precious and necessary to the history of humanity. It came as a protest against a too great leaning in one direction—a too great tendency—exclusive tendency—towards militaryism: among the Greeks to mere beauty. In an era which could acknowledge nothing but the military virtues—which, high as they are, are not by any means the highest—it came, filled great niches, wide gaps—furnished a purifying, freshening of the race. I should say of it as I might of our Rebellion here in America: our Rebellion confirmed, justified, explicated America: Christianity confirmed, justified, explicated humanity. I refer more particularly to the Christianity of earlier days—the first five centuries—before the split into Methodists, Presbyterians, theological conceits; then to what Hicks saw in it, Parker, men of that stripe, large-seeing." And he added: "Of course the orthodoxy of our day represents a revolting spectacle—an organization persistence of the so-called religious spasms of the commoner masses of the people, the lowest, most horrible ideals to be conceived. In our day the time had come to put down the brakes, and the brakes are being put down—put down very effectually. All the fellows of any value put the brakes down—all of them: among my personal friends I know of no exception whatever." "The miracles" he said, "will do for the Marines, but today they are a poor meal which everybody else refuses." As to the Gladstone-Huxley controversy: "Gladstone amounts to very little in that anyhow" and as to Dr. Furness' belief in the resurrection—"Well—we may say of that what I so often say of criticism—if it don't prove the resurrection, it at least proves certain things about the Doctor!" The Rev. Mr. May had once taken a very radical ground in church here as to birth—or at least confirmation—of conscience in Christianity. But W. shook his head: "No—that is as if we should say, there were no brave men, or only half brave men, before Jesus—before Christianity—an evident absurdity, arrogance." Tom asked him: "Are you still as firmly pantheistic as you were in the earlier poems?" And he at once replied: "Yes indeed, Tom—if anything more and more so!" "But how do you make that consistent with the immortality of identity?" "You think it conflicts then? It don't seem so to me." "But how can you prove it?" W. laughed. "I cannot prove it—I only believe it—feel it. And then you know, Tom, I'm an indifferent prover of anything. Even my dear mother long ago saw that, for she said to me there were two things I could never do and was never intended

489

to do: I could not controvert, I could not explain! That is as much true now as ever it was!" Here he said: "I was reading the Sarrazin piece over again today. He makes a good deal of that point—the point of the pantheism. And every time I read that piece I grow in my perception of the capaciousness, amplitude, of the man. I don't think there ever was anybody writing of us who more boldly—as boldly—grappled with what I may call our theory—theory is not a good word, but it is safe for us to use it here between each other—theory of evil—of good. He goes at it with a strange, wonderful daring —as needs—for it is a weighty charge and needs to be met weightily. Sarrazin says in effect—there have been many writers who have gone so far as to declare for evil a purpose as manure, as a fertilizing, force in human character, but it has remained to our century and to America to erect evil and good upon equal pedestals and read in them an equal purpose. To that effect, not in those words. We must certainly get the piece published somewhere. I see there is a new magazine starting—the Transatlantic—devoted to reprint of the greater essays of foreign reviews. I thought to try that: we'll see."

He promised to read the autobiographic page once more before I returned the plate proofs, but—"I am sure there's no change whatever to be made." Harned referred to Gilchrist's distaste for the Gutekunst portrait. W. remarking: "Oh! we have gone over all that before—that is an old notion of Herbert's, but in spite of him, that is a great portrait, indeed, I incline to agree with Doctor Bucke—that that is the portrait of the future"—Tom dissenting but W. insisting: "Well—you are welcome to your opinion, Tom—I believe it will go down, perhaps as the best of all." Alluded to the Smiths—"I have been sending Pearsall something every day, almost, for a week past—papers, what-not—addressing them to Surrey—Haslemere." Tom asked at one point: "How about Mrs. Costelloe's religious opinion—is she radical?" W. crying out in a laughing way: "That's a pretty question for you to ask, Tom—she's as radical as any one of us!" But how could

she stand Costelloe's Catholicism? "Oh! well enough: you
know she's a thorough Leaves-of-Grass-ian—has no bigotries,
no exclusions." But how about Costelloe—how could he suffer
the great difference? W. again quaintly: "Oh! he's a woman's-
rightser—I am sure: I think I was told by some one that all
that was gone over. You know, I like Costelloe myself—like
him a great deal—he has been here—we have talked together. But of the Smiths, I think Alice is the most American
—the most democratic—best calculated to measure Leaves of
Grass. She is coming to America soon—next month, I believe—
and you will meet her. Oh! she is handsome, too—the finest
specimen of womanhood I know—almost!"—"Alice does not
take naturally to the English—she has a word for them—I
forget it now—muggs—something of that sort—something to
express insignificance." I sent the manuscript of Yonnondio
to the Library of the Maine Historical Society today.

Saturday, September 7, 1889

7.38 P.M. W. in his usual place in parlor. Had been out.
Felt "right well today." Said: "I read the autobiographic
note over today. Was there any particular passage in it—or
word—which you thought wrong—to be patched?" I asked
if he was annoyed by the great noise of the cars. "No," he
said, "there's nothing in the world a man easier gets used to
than just such a noise." There was a parrot in the room—on
the machine—and on the wall a bird cage. W. laughed when
I commented. "Yes," he assented, "we need but a snake—then
our menagerie will be complete." Laughed on hearing that
his portrait was used on a cigar label. "Who knows but by and
by we'll give a name to some new brand pop-corn or the like?
I remember what fun we had a long time ago over the Jenny
Lind pop-corn." As we talked a man passed the window—a
child with him—seemed to hesitate—then came back. W. had
regarded him carefully. Finally reached his hand out. "Ah!
Tillman—it's you, is it? And this is the boy? It has been a long

time since I saw you—oh! years! And the boy!—how grown! He was a little fellow then. Come up here, boy—let me see you—shake hands with you"—as he did—the boy coming up over the cellar-door—W. reached out, kissed him. "Oh! you dear little boy!" and as the boy was sliding away: "See here, little boy—tell your mother Walt Whitman sends her his love." And to Tillman himself: "And you, Tillman—take my love to the ferry boys—tell them I hope to see them before long. I have not so far been on the boats—but my time is near —my time is near!"

Liberty at last turned up today and contained the O'Connor article. W. quickly said to me after I came: "I got Liberty— I have read the article: and I like it very much—it is strong and fine. Now how about copies? Shall I write for them or will you? I want several—one for Bucke—one for Charles Eldridge—others." And then added: "I think I had better give you Mrs. O'Connor's letter to read—the letter that came the other day." I found on reading that it had a reference to me which he did not wish to repeat. I read him a letter received from Morse today (dated the 3d). W. greatly interested—at many points solicited re-reading—particularly where Morse speaks of his wanderings among the poor of the city. "Fine— fine!—Good!" "I have read the Sarrazin piece again today— the whole of it at one reading—and it impresses me more than ever. It seems, the first part is better rendered than the last— the last sounds a little as if done in haste, without the necessary care." "But," he added slowly, "after all, what seems want of care may come from the literalness of the translation—and for the literalness I am responsible—for I sent him word, the more literal the better." Then he asked: "I wonder if in the French they have an equivalent for our word 'children'? Morris translates a word, infants—evidently an inclusive term. I should not wonder but infants in the French covers all that we mean by the word children, and more. After all,— deducting for all charges against its music, what-not—I should not wonder but the English tongue is the richest in possibilities of expression—potential for the most varied combinations, beauties, wonders, of speech!"

Spoke of Harrison as "a great phu-phu! A thin enough sample of a thin enough type!" As to the Log Cabin speech it was "a lost opportunity" but "no more lost than all of Harrison's opportunities." Referring to Gilchrist's "Cleopatra" W. remarked: "I wonder if he lets anybody see it? I suppose not. I am anxious to have Herbert all right. It seems to have a tide character, water character—current character—seems to be a-float, to depict a large expanse of water." As to his succeeding better with that than with the portrait of W., W. remarked: "I hope he will—think he will: it is more in the line of his abilities, tastes, training." Asked me if there would be advertisements in the book. He had thought "It might be a good thing" to advertise "all the Whitman books there together." Clifford preaching tomorrow, for the first time. W. said: "Give him my love." A young Unitarian minister from Cambridge preaches in Camden tomorrow. Dines with Harned. When H. proposed to bring him in, W. said: "Yes bring him along—we want to question him!" Returning to matters of translation, we discussed literalness and freedom. I contended—in repeating a man's spoken words, we should try to give his manner too—the manner being essential—and so in translating.

Sunday, September 8, 1889

Did not see W. I spent the day at Logan and Germantown. But learned he had passed a good day and got his outing,— "the good hour by the river."

Monday, September 9, 1889

5.00 P.M. W. eating his dinner. Was very cordial, and talked heartily, keeping right on, however, with his eating. McKay had showed me a letter from Angus, in Glasgow, who sent on a copy of the original edition L. of G. and 2 Burns vols—wishing W. W.'s signature on title pages of all. Told McK. W. would no doubt refuse to write in the Burns, so I did not carry them to Camden. W. was, as I supposed, willing to sign L. of G.—did so while I waited. "But those others," he said, "no—I should have no way to explain it." I said I thought the request absurd. W.: "Yes—rather; I suppose the man had a clearly-defined reason, but whatever the reason, it was a reason for him, not me. I object to signing everything —here, there, everywhere, right and left—anyhow." And he added—as he turned the L. of G. volume over and over and scanned it—"I wonder at its voyage—where it has been all this time—where he got hold of it." I had with me a copy of the Forum containing Gosse's "What is a Great Poet." W. said: "No—I don't think I have read it—entire, anyhow. You did not lend it to me, did you? You may leave this if you choose—I think I should like to take a close look at it. A fellow likes to know, if no more! Gosse is a type of the modern man of letters—much-knowing, sharp witted, critical, cold,—bitten with the notion that to be smart is to be deep— able to assume wit. Shakespeare was beginner in that field— but Shakespeare was more—this was in him but a tint, a spice, a subordinate phase entirely."

I returned him Mrs. O'Connor's letter, asking, "Don't you think it genuine and good?" He replying, "Yes indeed," and going on to say—"It is a New England letter—characteristically, dipped in New England air. Mrs. O'Connor is always that. The typical New Englander is always discussing his own affairs—the last trouble, sickness, complaint—all that— lugging it forward at all times, into any company." I asked: "And so you make that criticism on the letter?" He laughing and saying: "I mention no names—I give you an observation —you can make of it what you wish. Now, that was peculiarly absent from William—though of course he was not New Englander alone—rather Irish, English. But I was going to say, he had a remarkable shrinking from any temptation to pose, to discuss, even mention, himself—an abstention in him that I never quite appreciated—expecially in his last days, when that was just what I wanted, to have him talk about himself. But William was first of all cheerful—kept up to the last a devil of an interest, energy, in things at large—in all his letters." Suddenly then, after a pause: "And I want to tell you, I like your piece, oh! very much—very much— more and more! It has a wonderful quality—is itself O'Connorish. And the tact of it!—I like that most of all! That is a quality in which the French excel—finesse it is called—what we name tact: a right disposition of tints, colors,—recognizing fine distinctions. You certainly caught that essence—for you say what you say, pause, go on, just as one would suppose nature herself to divide her action. No doubt the French are masters there—no one sees it, bathes in it—more enjoyably than I do. But then, while we miss that, is there not something to compensate for it? Sarrazin speaks of America—that she gives him the barbaric lyrism of the Hebrews—how fine that! And I, for one, am content with that—the rest I am willing to let go! I think a subdued sarcasm lurks in the phrase—or perhaps not, though I think I see it there. An old wharf, the decayed, rotted, soaked, beams, pilings: the debris: the grass-grown—mossy endings, surfaces—oh! they appeal to me most of all. Many, many, many years ago—in New York—up towards Harlem—Mott Haven—there was an old wharf on which I spent some of the happiest hours of my life. An old, dilapidated, ruining, breaking, wharf there, with sea-weed— sea-drift—caught in its sharp corners: and a slight whiff of salt air—just enough for a reminder—and the flowing waters —on and on—and the boats—craft—of all sorts. Oh! it is the surpassing remembrance—barbaric lyrism!" He laughed when I mentioned Zola in connection with French "delicacy, finesse—an exquisite play"—his own phrase objected. "Yes— even Zola: it seems to me, if we could read Zola in the vernacular—as Frenchmen, continentals—we would penetrate to the truth of this charge—would see that Zola is only treating of life as a physician treats disease. To the general it's nothing but a question of guts, stains, blood, wounds, horror, pain, nastiness, smut: but not so to the chemist, the surgeon, the doctor—not so—not so. Rather something far higher, finer. The time will come—is already here for some—when all these things will be treated so—will enter in that way upon our conversation—even in parlors—among the sexes. Not to be lugged in, or made nasty, but so dealt with when necessity introduces. Then, perhaps, we will see that Zola is justified—that he was advanced, not retrograde." Then he continued: "Dave told you about the book salesman—the Porter and Coates man—who spoke of me—asked Dave if he was still selling the works of that whore-house poet?" And he laughed: "It has been a frequent charge—I have heard it often and often —more often than you know, but this man I guess did not mean it seriously—rather tried it on Dave as a piece of wit." I suggested: "Agnes Repplierish"—and he: "Yes—only she would use politer phrases."

Spoke about article in Press by Melville Phillips—"God and Immortality"—a review of Renan's writing under that head. "Was it good? I felt too stuffy to undertake it yesterday, but laid it aside, to look at later on. There it is on the chair now"—indicating. W. then said: "Tom was in and took one of the big portraits—he liked it—so I let him have it. I intended one of the big ones for him if they turned out well, but they did not, so I dropped the idea of it—thought to let him have one of the smaller—and Buckwalter the same—but now he has made his own choice." I have been reading Burroughs' new book and said: "He thinks highly of Arnold— more highly than I imagined." W. assenting: "Yes—John has changed some: every man is more or less sensitive to his environment, and John's environment has of late years been the New York crowd." And again he referred to Burroughs:

"I think Emerson rides his high horse once in a while—and he does—and Carlyle: and no man but may do so to advantage!" Told me that "Tom took the Sarrazin piece along with him," and asked: "Don't the city begin to show new signs of life?" Asked me, too, about Clifford—the sermon yesterday, how he looked, &c. Called my attention to a book in which there was a portrait of Tennyson, with his big hat. I said: "There's something in it like you!" but he shook his head: "Something, perhaps: but something too much of the Yankee for me." Knowing I was to go as secretary of a meeting this evening, he laughed and said first: "God help you!" Then: "Emerson used to say in respect to material things, that we should act just as if they were real—and I would give you the same advice now!" Returned me the Magazine of Art containing DeKay's paper. Commented on Fuller's portrait as that of "a strong man—rather a noble face." Then asked: "Have you ever seen a full-figure picture of Millet? I was going to say I have one here, but I have not, I guess. I have seen one, however—and it represents a rather Germanic type: indeed, Millet seems to have looked much as your father—short, thick, solid,—a thinker."

Tuesday, September 10, 1889

7.40 P.M. W. in parlor. It has been a frightfully stormy day. W., after greeting us, at once spoke of it with [Harrison] Morris. "I think we will learn tomorrow that along the coast it has blown much more even than here." This caused M.'s reference to the Johnstown disaster, occurring in the very hours of the banquet and which W. called "most dreadful hours." Lincoln Eyre had had a brother out there. Morris described—and W. said, inquiringly: "He circumvented the flood, then, somehow, did he?" Frank Williams' wife is at Atlantic City—communication cut off—W. saying: "Yes, I read in this night's paper that they're in the way of being flooded." I sat on the sofa in the shadow of the room—Morris taking position at W.'s side on a chair, which W. always keeps near to use the back as a rest for his arm. W. had at once on our entrance insisted on having a light—"Oh my, we must have one! We always do for visitors!" And when several matches "flashed in the pan" as I said,—he laughed and said: "Matches are not always what we expect of them"—which Morris took to be a good joke. I let them do the talking mainly alone, putting in a word only now and then, or when W. addressed me, as he did several times, once with the usual query: "What have you been doing today?" Morris asked him about the Sarrazin article and W. said of the translation: "I liked it very much and sent word to you by Horace." And to questionings, said of Sarrazin himself: "He is indeed expert, penetrating: he seems to have exploited us all in the spirit which we should ourselves demand—in the spirit of our highest claims, in fact." "That's Heine's canon," he went on, "Heine says that to examine a thing critically—by just methods—the point is, to inquire of a writer—What's his spirit? What's his aim? Has he accomplished himself that way—his way? Not, has he done it some other way, but that way—not the way of some other, but the way of his own choice. That, precisely, Sarrazin has done. There's a new school in Paris, of which Sarrazin is one—very catholic—very Hegelian—including all—thoroughly tolerating—acknowledging other places than Paris, other men than Parisians. Among the old fellows, even so great a man as Victor Hugo seemed to start out with the assumption that there was no city in the world but Paris. But these new men have come to the conclusion—the conviction, in fact—and a deep conviction it is—that there is a wider audience, a vaster area of action, of big guns, populaces, ideals, what-not." And then he asked Morris: "Is Sarrazin's criticism of the other writers as free and trenchant—strong, noble—as this?" And he said as to Morris' dealing with the French: "I think you do well to get well ingratiated—to well ingratiate yourself—with modern writers—modern Frenchmen. There's quite a difference in their handwork—the old, the new schools. In the modern writers you find new vigors, habits, modes. I don't know what it is—I don't know how it could be indicated—but it is a marked change. It's quite a difference like that a stranger encounters—a Frenchman—in reading Carlyle's books— Carlyle's peculiarities—idiosyncrasies, they may be called,— of style."

Morris gave quite a circumstantial account of a French novel he had been reading. W. listened intently—said: "Yes— yes—I see it, I think." And then remarked as to realism: "Millet, the painter, had a saying—I think there was a good deal in it, applying to all these days—I can't repeat it in the French—but he signified—you have a right to deal with any subject, if you deal with it in a high mood—deal with it worthily. And that is very profound: to me it has always seemed as if that enclosed the whole story—saying that, all is said." Morris repeated a saying of Frank Williams': "It's the drapery that causes all the trouble"—and W. laughed greatly at this. "That's very good," he said. "Somebody says —some very witty Frenchman, I think—on a nude statue— even the most perfect—put a lady's bonnet—and the whole subject at once becomes strange, perhaps vulgar. It is really funny why—none of us can tell why—and yet I think everybody will tumble to it." I told him a story I had heard of Eakins—of a girl model who had appeared before the class, nude, with a bracelet on—Eakins, thereupon, in anger, seizing the bracelet and throwing it on the floor. W. enjoying it: "It was just like Eakins—and oh! a great point is in it, too!" I asked if Harned had brought his young minister in on Sunday, and W. said: "Yes—he brought him in. He is an Englishman, and I could see the mark of the young minister: but I liked his way—his atmosphere."

Morris referred to Concord—his own visits there. W. assented: "Yes, I liked it—it is very pretty—New England, though, is full of just such places—Jamaica Plain, Roxbury —all these places—the Highlands, as they call one of them." And when M. referred to what he supposed were changes in Concord—"I guess the main lay of things is the same"—and as to a picnicing ground instituted at or near Walden Pond— "That to me would add nothing." The Thoreau cairn of stones: "That was there when I paid my visit—I carried a big stone—a stone as big as my head—and threw it on—we all did. But I have heard that it did not grow much—the pyramid is much as it was. Some one told me something of the sort, that it was not in good form to go on such pilgrimages—but at that time—we men—2, 3 or 4 of us—went, carried stones— rocks, they call them out West—threw them on." And he questioned Morris about Emerson's burial place: "You went up to it?—saw the stone?—found it white? White quartz, eh? Very pretty? No inscription? No monument of any kind?" Morris told him a story he had from Hamilton Gibson—of a twig, or limb, from the pine-tree over-arching the grave falling in his presence right across the stone—that he remembered Emerson's fondness for the pine—accepted it as of poetic significance—and took the limb home as memorial. W. called it "very fine and touching." As to Sleepy Hollow: "I've been there, but not many times—Emerson, you know, has died since then—Thoreau, Hawthorne, I think, and Thoreau's brother—and quite a number of celebrities, famous ones—lie there."

Morris inquired if W. did not think well of Julian Hawthorn's speech at the banquet? "Yes—I thought it good"— but ran off from that particular matter by asking: "Do you see Julian's letters in the Press?—the labor letters there? They're wonderful good"—talking at considerable length then on the subject. "There are 3 or 4 fellows writing those letters—they're all good—I read them all with care. They're the only newspaper things I read with care nowadays. They have such a natural flavor—unspoiled—have the attraction I always find in simple recitals—a sort of word-of-mouth manner—as if the men sat here and told us what they eat, do, where go, how act, so on." Morris suggested: "They give the American point of view." And W. assented: "Yes, a good deal that. One thing I get from it that I learn also from other sources—that although we are a great country—in machinery, territory, institutions, wealth, progress, yet there's a world— I spoke of the new school of Frenchmen, for instance—a world of other men, measures, industries, greatnesses, than ours, still to be accounted for—a world in many ways superior, in all ways wonderful. We are great in machinery, in cuteness, in intuition, in labor-saving-ness—everything in that direction. Then after that there's another thing"—and in speaking of the work of mechanics abroad—"at the last point they seem to surpass us—do it by an impalpable something—something in the feel in which they get ahead of us." And again: "We're not only ahead but behind the mark." And as to the cutlery business: "We equal them in much—probably go ahead— but we don't equal them in the touch—the last finish—of something—of razors. That touch, that is the thing—the thing not to be acquired. In one of his letters Julian says that men who give that last finish were not new men, but men of fathers in the same line, and their fathers, again—an inherited delicacy, aptitude—like a sailor—born on the sea." And to Morris' expression of American self-congratulation: "That kind of thought or boastful consideration is not needed so much as the kind of things these fellows are giving us." And he told the story of the Long Island man and his expression "hold your horses," with great zest—and averred: "We ought to adopt it in our America"—adding—"We need not indulge in brag and wind over our abilities, which God knows are great enough: there are other spots smiled on by the Almighty. These letters not only read well but are well—not ephemeral— make a deep cut, notch. Probably they will be collected—they are but beginning. I have been waiting to see Talcott Williams —I fear the letters are cut—the high protection editors probably cannot stomach all they would naturally contain. Yet these are the very things we want—without them we have the doctor who leaves out of a great case the very necessary warnings. I am not certain of that, but have the suspicion. They seem to have gone there with the determination to see the truth—tell the truth—they are almost as faithful as a mirror. They are wonderful in modern literature—wonderfully good even in point of literary style. Julian Hawthorne's letters you would expect to be so, but these others are almost equally good. All these exquisite modifications and correctivenesses—little shades of new meaning, foreign, unsuspected,—that we didn't know—these are the things we have to learn. This matter is astonishing—certainly a hit—is consistent with the modern spirit—the democratic spirit. With the principle of free communication added to inform, refine, we inaugurate a new era, gain ports long needed—all the ports needed." And so he discussed the subject, even more fully than I indicate.

Pointing to some apples on the table: "I have had visitors, some girls—and they brought lots of things—apples, pears, flowers. I have gorged the pears—I am weak on pears." As to coming down stairs (W. having gone up and said to us: "Don't move—I'm only going for a minute or so"—going to his room, walking about there for something—coming immediately down): "I am pretty thoroughly disabled—I often sit here—come here for the change." Then he spoke of "the curious and remarkable specimen of humanity out at our hospital here"—a man "paralyzed completely below the neck—yet keeping up a show of cheer if not cheer itself." And as to Morris' laughing reference to Brown-Sequard's Elixir: "There is no such thing as an elixir of life"—but the mind cure, "that is a very important part of the materia medica"—Morris laughing wildly at this sally. W. then told the story of the Englishman whom a doctor had treated by a thermometer—the doctor having put it in the patient's mouth to find the temperature—"the patient at once felt better— the imagination so acting upon him. So the doctor treated him regularly that way, with the result, that in a time the patient declared himself entirely cured." Morris gave W. some account of Furness' explanation of the miracles, which W. called "a mumbo-jumbo sort of business."

We finally sauntered off, W. asking: "And what is the programme for the rest of the night?" I sat back on the sofa most of the time, taking notes in a little book. Several times W. asked me: "Where are you boy? Where are you Horace?" —Morris sitting in such a way as to interrupt the vision. W. altogether in good voice. Severe as the weather is, it does not appear to break him in any respect. Morris was highly elated over the talk which he called the best he had ever had with W. I walked through the storm to the ferry with Morris, when we parted. Gilchrist had told M. today he expected to be over, but the violence of the storm evidently deterred him.

Wednesday, September 11, 1889

5.45 P.M. W. in his bed-room—had just finished his dinner. Reading Camden daily papers. The terrific storm continues. He referred to it rather seriously: "There is still no word from the shore. Oh! it is to be hoped that there will be no more Johnstown disasters—one is enough for a century! Camden has its deficiencies, which are plain enough: but it also has its efficiencies: it seems situated beyond the perturbation of tides, storms, water-spouts." I instanced the cyclone of 2 years ago— but he shook his head: "Even than that, for after all, that was not very serious—not nearly so serious as might have been." I described the river to him, and he remarked: "I should like to see it—I must try to find a way to get down there. If I could but get a look-out point!" I spoke of the railroad front—he then: "I suppose that is the point from which to see it. I should soon know about it—should know at once, like an editor his manuscript—whether it would do or not!"

I brought him envelope samples, and he was very happy in them, saying at once on handling them: "Yes, they will do— he caught my idea exactly." And when I said the maker was a German—"That accounts for it—intuitively penetrates." Adding—"I shall look at them at my leisure. And what about the cost?" At first saying—"That seems high enough" and after—"But no doubt it's the price we'd have to pay any-where." I delivered books to McKay today. W. said: "Yes— and I received a note from Dave in which he enclosed another from someone else, asking permission to use some of my pieces in a reading-book—which I readily granted, of course." He had pasted the signature of the letter on his post-card as the address, because he could not fully make it out. Called my attention to it. Asked me: "Is Morris unusually gay and happy? He sort of struck me so—and yet one can't tell except by long contact—often not even then. He is thoroughly Ameri-can—quick, pushy, wide-awake—very cheery. I like him quite a good deal."

Pointed to Forum on table. "I have read the Gosse piece— read it all, even carefully. It seems something this way—as if he had invited you to a swell meal—you had gone—found a fine table, plenty of dishes—knives, forks, spoons, silver,— but nothing to eat, or if anything to eat, very little but tastes —'not enough to swear by.' That was a great Long Island phrase in my early days. It is dangerous for a man like Gosse, having so little butter, to attempt to spread it over so much bread—it comes up very thin. I never heard that expression 'to swear by' in literature, though it may be there—but have found it among people I knew. It seems to mean nothing of itself, yet has a something—one can smell something in it— or perhaps that is a weakness of mine," with a laugh— "that smelling business. There was one of my English critics

who dwelt upon the prominence I give to the sense of smell—
gave it first place, as he said. I seem to get the sense of smell
first. Have you noticed anything of that sort? I have not—
am not at all conscious of it"—and referring to W.'s "the
smell of an armpit" etc.—"I don't think that could have been
the objection—the point of criticism—he urges it quite seriously." W. said further of Gosse: "He is the cheapest of
present essay writers over there in England. It has been a
long time since I tasted such a poor mess of stuff in a magazine.
It is as if the editor had written him—the tide is on now—the
public is awake—here are 50 dollars for a piece on such and
such a subject: and then he sat down and eked it out. It
sounds very much as if it had that for an inspiration and no
more."

Thursday, September 12, 1889

7.30 P.M. With W. about 20 minutes. Harned came in,
returning the Sarrazin and Liberty pieces, which W. had
loaned him. W. very well, though saying jokingly to H.: "I
took a nip of the sherry today—felt a little depressed and
took that to off-set the depression." Harned expressed pleasure
in the photo W. had given him and W. remarked: "It is well
our tastes for pictures are like our tastes for food—very
various. That enables all to get suited, because results are very
various, God knows!" Remarked concerning Dr. Brinton's
inquiries after him by me—"Tell him I am still above the
surface—still afloat—that I am not yet engulfed: though I
don't know but we'll all be engulfed if this rain perseveres."
As we sat there Harry Fritzinger came in, rubber-suited and
W. bent forward for a kiss, which was given. He then indicated
us in the dark: "Harry, this is Mr. Harned and Horace."

He had got the envelope ready for me, inscribing such
instructions as he thought necessary. "It is just the thing—
the man took hold like an inspiration." Though he had not

yet inscribed my picture he said: "It is ready at any time you choose to take it." Spoke of where Morris had translated Sarrazin "infirmary"—"When he meant hospital, no doubt. I changed it to hospital in the manuscript. Made very few changes indeed—this one of them." And he added: "I should imagine there were various words that would need such attention on closer scrutiny. This is one of the drawbacks of literal translation—still, I am the responsible man this time." "Talcott Williams was here to see me today—stayed, I suppose, half an hour or so. He looks well—talks well." Had he made the inquiry about the Press labor letters? "Well I declare! I forgot all about it—it never struck me till this moment! That's a sample of the way my memory works nowadays!"

Friday, September 13, 1889

7.35 P.M. Storm clearing, though not entirely abated. W. not out this evening. In parlor when I came. Ed came in shortly and sat with us. W. had sent Ed over last evening to see "The Bohemian Girl." Wished very much for him "to know what it is"—paid his way. Said to me very quickly after my coming: "I have had visitors today—several. I suppose you can't guess who one of them could be?" And to my doubting—"It was the man Arnold, from England—Edwin Arnold, author of 'Light of Asia'—you know of him?" He explained: "He was a hearty, jovial, fine sample of a middle-aged man. He stayed with me from three quarters of an hour to an hour. We talked quite a good deal. Oh yes! he was very flattering—said a great many eulogistic things—like most all of 'em nowadays. I liked the style of the man very much. He came in a carriage. Ed—who was the man with him in the carriage?" Ed said: "Only the driver. He told me he had a daughter 18 years old." W. asked Ed to repeat the sentence, then asked me: "You have read his book? I don't know whether I have or not—but I have it here, I am sure—someone gave it to me. His visit was only in transit—he goes back to New York at once—then across to San Francisco—then to Japan and the East Indies." "At least, that is as I understood him," he added. And then he told me of his other visitor: "An actor—and a hearty fellow, too—Hanson, I think was his name. Their company is now in the city—have 'A Possible Case'—a play of some sort, of which I know nothing."

As to someone who had objected to W.'s plain speaking of sexuality he said tonight: "There is that side to the case, too. The world is not ready to be thrown from the nag it has been astride these ten thousand years. It is a matter of slow growth, in which a man's whole patience is exercised." Asked me: "What's a 'hustler?'" and laughed. "Hustler" a new vulgarism for a busy man. W.: "I thought that must have been its meaning, but I did not know." I alluded to the expressions: "Get a gait on you"—"get a move on you," and they amused him. "They are very suggestive—they don't lump at all."

There was a reference to Ouida. "I have never read any of her novels." I recounted a group I had heard, in indecent language, debating her indecency, so-called, and arguing for her suppression. W. said: "I can understand all that—I have encountered the like of it from the start. In our New York boarding house—a house in which I boarded many years ago—there was an old darkey who had a child—quite a comely, pretty child, too. The darkey was very pious—a Methodist, I suppose, or whatever—I overheard her screaming one morning to the youngster—'You won't, won't you? You won't go to prayers! Well—I'll learn you, Goddamn you! I'll show you, you Goddamned little bitch, if you won't mind me!' That is an incident in kind, don't you think? The world has much to be forgiven it!—and me, too!" Spoke somewhat of Gilder's speech again. "I thought it well enough as it was at the start, but he thought not apparently." Called my attention (though it was not needed, the room so fragrant) to a cluster of woodbine on the table. "What a flavor it brings in of the woods!" Keeps up well, in spite of weather.

Saturday, September 14, 1889

7.50 P.M. I went to W.'s and sat with him some time alone, talking. By and by Harned came in, bringing Morehouse, the Unitarian preacher, with him. Though W. expressed himself as having had "a poorly day," he entered quite animatedly into the talk, and surely displayed a vigor that surpassed our own. At some mention of the Pope's official denunciation of Bruno, W. exclaimed: "Science is not in this age to be submissively slapped in the face. Nothing is so dear to the heart of science as the fact, sense, of its freedom. Bruno is the love of every discoverer. It was with him as it was with Galileo. They are no more to be extirpated by a papal bull than is a comet. Especially here in America do we resent such interference. Yet I am free to say, I glory in all that transpires—glory in this—glory that they seek to vaunt themselves as they do—for it gives us a chance to show them where we stand—show them who can strike the hardest blow. My surprise is, not that they feel it or say it among themselves, but that they are damned fools enough to rush into print with such gammon."

Harned mischievously questioned W.: "Are you not the friend of Unitarians, Walt?" For the instant W. misunderstood him—supposed he asked, "Are you a Unitarian?" "No—Tom—I don't know why I should ask or accept the name." But when T. explained, added: "O yes, that—why not? I am the friend of all. It was the Hegelian idea, principle, that all are needed—that all are part of the whole—and so I should insist, all belong in their places—none can be dismissed—Catholic, Quaker, Mormon, Freethinker—even the Unitarian! I cannot be this or that, but I can recognize this or that. I know of no school in this, our day,—not Gladstone's, Henry George's, any other—who offers anything adequate—anything that would land us at the goal, any more than the present system. We old fogies, in the absence of fire, health, solace ourselves with clinging to what is—with not making ventures any longer. Yet I like the sects—I feel of them as a doctor [does] of pimples on the face—it is better for them to come out than to be hidden underneath the exterior—a hundred percent better. Pimples are a thing we can fight, but insidious hidden processes defy battle." And again: "A great city—London, for instance—would typify our present condition—the prevailing tone, what-not—of our civilization—the religious aspect: London is not made up of one man but of several millions of men—so our universe—so religions. Some people see a decadence in the present troubles—what I call our intestinal troubles but then we do not—do not believe in decadence. It was Mrs. Gilchrist's favorite expression—when she looked out on this surging seething man—that we were all going somewhere—not only that, but somewhere good. And I believe it." "It is true there is plenty of bad in the human critter—we all agree to it—he is a bad lot, as Tennyson's farmer puts it—but that is not the whole of him: he is not all or only what Carlyle paints him." Harned quoted Emerson, to the effect that to find a man trustworthy, you must trust him. W. said fervently: "That's it—that's the whole story. It's the story over again of my woman friend in Washington who complained that whereas her sister, who distrusted nobody, had no locks and keys for drawers, no mysteries, no securities, was never robbed, she, who was so careful, padlocked and keyed everything, was careful of all her goings and comings, was continually losing,—being robbed, taken advantage of." Again: "After all, I wish well to all reformers. And besides, there's no danger of a dearth of them in our age—our age, on the contrary is full of Henry Georges, temperance, other reformers—all with panaceas. And for an old fogy like me to doubt a little can do no harm. There is an embarrassment of riches in reform."

W. spoke of Arnold's visit and added: "Why, Tom—Jim

Scovel was in today—with him another reporter—a Press man. I did not think much of this Press man. Generally, I like these fellows, but this time is an exception. Yet he was a handsome sort of fellow—straight, well-dressed, used to moving in conventional society—evidently had been about in the world. I never knew Jim to look so well—he tells me he is now writing, altogether—probably for some of the big New York papers,—and well-paid. He said he was under instructions to find out all he could about Edwin Arnold's—I suppose it is *Sir* Edwin Arnold's—visit to America. I told him Arnold had been here—how fresh, hearty, tanned,—how English he was. Arnold is a great globe-trotter—seems to be moving about and about. My main objection to him, if objection at all, would be, that he is too eulogistic—too flattering. He was very frank in his expression of his own view with respect to Leaves of Grass—of his decided friendliness—of his particular friends' friendliness over there. Indeed, though not saying so directly, he did speak indirectly as if one of his purposes in coming was to boom me—to give me unmistakable evidence how he stood—and I think he did. He is a comfortable looking man—a man of the sort I should like occasionally for a neighbor. He brought me a message from his daughter— she did not come, but wished to be remembered. I had an inclination to open up the theme—the tremendous theme—of Hindu poetry,—scriptures—Buddhism—but did not— thought it inadvisable then—and so not a word was said of that on either side. Ah Tom! it does one good to have even Jim come in—he is so cheery, chirpy!"

I had received a note from Symonds today, and before the others came in had started to read it to W. It was this:

Am Hof
Davos Platz
Switzerland
Sept. 3, 1889

Dear Sir

Owing to circumstances connected with the fact that I inhabit
one house at Venice in the spring & another here at Davos in the
summer, your letter of May 24 has only just reached me—too
late, I very much fear, to be of any use.

Never the less, I enclose what may be styled an expression of
my [creed] with regard to that noble (& here is rightly named,)
grand old man.

Whether it would in any way have suited the scheme of the
pamphlet which you wrote me was to appear after the celebration
of May 31, I do not know.

But it has at least the merit of sincerity & of careful consideration. I took thought before I set on paper what will perhaps to
many persons who have read my books, appear an exaggerated
expression of my intellectual and moral obligations to Walt
Whitman.

Will you, if you are in personal relations with him, convey to
him my hearty though belated congratulations? And pray
believe me to be cordially & in all good comradeship yours

John Addington Symonds—

P.S. I cannot read your signature distinctly. Therefore, in order
to avoid miscarriage, I have cut it from the foot of your letter &
pasted it upon the envelope of this.

Enclosed was the piece which I shall use in the book. In the
midst of my reading, the others entering, W. suggested I
begin over again, which I did. All were highly gratified,
though W. himself said little concerning it except that "it
ought certainly go in the book."

Tom invited him around to dinner tomorrow. He would not
promise that but said: "I'll come if the spirit is on" and at

Tom's mention of wine—"Oh yes! the wine certainly—that is always a necessary part of the coming!" Had sent Harned some clippings and so forth. "I am glad you cared for them, Tom—I thought you would like certainly to keep that address—and while I was in the way I sent other things." Interrupted himself in the midst of his talk on evolution, etc. "But I must not expatiate any longer on that theme. Take what I have said for the last 15 minutes and apply it for yourselves: a man goes on and on talking with less and less sense, sometimes."

Index

INDEX

Bryant (Maine Historical Society), 469

Bryant, William Cullen: Whitman on, 117, 118; description of, 379; home of, 467; mentioned, 87, 239, 302, 336

Bucke, Richard Maurice: on Dickens, 6, 22; mention of letters from, 12, 25, 58, 66, 84, 85, 104, 111, 147, 413, 422; Whitman on, 36; as friend of Forman, 87; on Whitman's going to hospital, 91, 99, 138; on Arnold, 117; opinion of Harrison, 123; keeps Whitman letters, 129; on Hartmann affair, 136; on O'Connor's death, 163; advises Whitman to find a cottage, 181; Whitman's reaction to advice of, 182; letter from, 218; effect of dinners on Whitman, 219; as an individual, 265; on wine drinking, 298; on Whitman's joining Mrs. O'Connor, 366, 367; as reader, 387; Pardee's funeral, 389, 390; Whitman compares with Sarrazin, 404; whimsicality, 469; on Gutekunst picture, 479; mentioned, 42, 80, 129, 133, 149, 154, 168, 186, 188, 191, 195, 198, 201, 214, 232, 237, 241, 246, 252, 262, 264, 269, 270, 273, 275, 285, 303, 309, 311, 329, 330, 333, 338, 343, 345, 346, 349, 352, 356, 359, 361, 364, 381, 382, 391, 394, 406, 409, 490, 492

Buckwalter, Geoffrey: takes Whitman to Gutekunst, 394, 417, 418, 420, 421; mentioned, 45, 51, 139, 146, 156, 246, 251, 257, 258, 309, 327, 399, 424, 460, 496

Bülow, Hans von, 79, 97

Burroughs, John: on Whitman, 51, 91; on beauty, 130; on O'Connor, 163, 179, 465; letter from, 212, 335; on Stedman, 213; on his testimonial letter, 254; Whitman on, 301, 365; as Emersonian, 329; contrasts Whitman with America, 384; questions memorial volume, 398; Whitman compares with Sarrazin, 404; on DeKay, 448; on Whitman and Matthew Arnold, 454, 496, 497; mentioned, 60, 164, 168, 187, 247, 283, 287, 307, 328, 338, 371, 377, 380, 384, 401

—*Fresh Fields,* 56; *Indoor Studies,* 282, 291; *Literary Fame,* 232; *Looking Backward,* 407, 436, 438; *Wake Robin,* 365

Bush, H. D., 155, 257, 389, 390, 393, 396, 400, 410, 468, 484, 488

Button, Mr., 326

Button, Mrs., 192, 344

Byron, George Gordon: O'Connor on, 351; Mazzini on, 394; mentioned, 127, 129, 410

Cabot, James Elliot, 96

Cagliostro, Alessandro di, 430

Camden Daily Post, 32

Cane, Mr., 426

Carey, William: holds pictures of Whitman, 261; letter from, 312; mentioned, 268, 274, 278, 301, 303, 305, 307, 388

Carleton, Will: visit from, 72; mentioned, 73, 98, 100, 107, 147, 286

Carlyle, Dr. John, 74

Carlyle, Thomas: as inspiration for *Democratic Vistas,* 135, 204; mentioned, 168, 290, 291, 295, 365, 371, 379, 409, 437, 465, 472, 478, 479, 486, 497, 499, 509

Carnegie, Andrew, 335, 478

Carnot, Marie François Sadi, 151

Carpenter, Edward: letter from, 255, 256; handsomeness of, 405; mentioned, 197, 222, 234, 235, 241, 242, 249, 264, 301, 315, 382, 448

—"Our Parish and Our Duke," 109

Carpenter, Frank, 226

Castelar y Ripoll, Emilio, 214

Castle, 419, 421

Cattell, Prof. James McK., 245

Cauffman, 98

The Century Magazine: Whitman sends piece to, 261, 280, 364; mentioned, 292, 388, 407, 435, 470

Chadwick, John White, 411

Chambers, Julius, 196, 224, 228, 250, 255, 264, 266, 269, 283, 328

Channing, Grace, 378

Channing, William Ellery, 188

Chase, Salmon P., 287, 288, 289

Chicago Journal, 246

INDEX

Childs, George W., 3, 211, 222, 234, 286, 335
Childs, Josiah, 6
Christian Register, 428
Christy's Minstrels, 382
Clarke, Louis Gaylord, 41
Clay, Cassius, 361
Cleveland, Grover: Whitman on, 65; Gilder on, 255; mentioned, 202, 205, 214
Clifford, Charlotte, 6, 22
Clifford, John Herbert: sends Swinburne ode, 44; profit-sharing book, 64; on Stedman, 98; Whitman's opinion of, 99; his testimonial speech, 203, 214, 217, 248, 249, 251, 365; on Edward Emerson, 252; on *There Was A Child Went Forth,* 310; *Song of Myself* in sermon, 333; his transcendentalism, 367; on Traubel's interpretation of Emerson passage, 376; mentioned, 5, 27, 94, 101, 108, 143, 155, 196, 200, 228, 229, 232, 236, 244, 246, 248, 250, 258, 269, 280, 315, 317, 353, 384, 394, 395, 409, 438, 447, 455, 459, 493, 497
Coates, Edward H., 8, 73
Cockrill, Colonel, 196, 236, 242
Coleridge, Samuel Taylor, 129
Comstock case, 374, 375
Conway, Moncure D.: compared with Hartmann, 38; distrust of, 39, 40; opinion of, 337; mentioned, 371, 395
Cook (of the *Herald*), 266
Cooper, James Fenimore, 239
Corning, J. Leonard: letter from, 321; mentioned, 224, 225, 313, 332
Costelloe, B. F. C., 77, 491
Costelloe, Mary Smith: Whitman on, 54, 78; mentioned, 56, 142, 159, 209, 222, 354, 490, 491
The Courier, 165, 278
Cox, George C., 261, 301, 305, 306, 312, 314, 315, 371
The Critic: on Whittier, 87; on Whitman, 132, 135
Crosset, Rev. J., 436
Curley, John, 66, 120
Current Literature: untrue Dickens story, 395; mentioned, 125, 126, 255, 262

Curtis, George William, 72, 231, 245
Curtz, Henry, 244, 245, 279, 319

Damien, Father, 436
Dana, Charles A., 375
The Danmark, 16, 20, 23, 26, 51, 54, 59, 66, 73, 74, 75
Dante, 74
Darwin, Charles, 75
D'Avezac, 76, 298
Davis, Mary, 16, 64, 104, 106, 262, 282, 380, 385
David, Jacques Louis, 30
David, Thaddeus, 314
Davidson, Thomas: lectures on Aquinas, 4, Bonaventura, 30, 54, Savanarola, 105; opinion of Dante, 74; mentioned, 7
DeKay, Charles, 184, 185, 448, 453, 458
Depew, Chauncey: his joke, 108; Whitman on oration of, 111
Derousse, 327
Deutsche Press, 330
Dickens, Charles, 6, 21, 396
Diderot, Denis, 136
Disraeli, Benjamin, 73, 450, 378
Donaldson, Thomas, 20, 198, 271, 278, 279, 376
Donnelly, Ignatius, 336
Dowden, Edward: edited Whitman poems, 91; Whitman on letter from, 301; mentioned, 222, 256, 303, 352
Doyle, Peter, 228
Drinkard, Dr. William B., 225, 487
Dryden, John, 386
Duckett, William, 82, 329

Eakins, Thomas, 413, 499
Eaton, Wyatt: Whitman on article of, 123, 124; portrait of Lincoln, 448
Eldridge, Charles W.: O'Connor authority, 177; mentioned, 338, 377, 492
Eliot, George, 105
Elliott, Charles, 302, 448
Ely, Prof. Richard T., 13
Emerson, Edward: Whitman on, 96, 232; on Whitman, 172; motto of his book, 222; gives father's opinion of Whitman, 411, 412; mentioned, 62,

515

INDEX

516

INDEX

INDEX

INDEX

INDEX

520

INDEX

INDEX

Wanamaker, John, 13
Wannemacher's Band, 20
Warner, John DeWitt, 56
Washington, George: described, 61, 62, 93, 94; mentioned, 228, 362
Watts, 210
West, Forrest, 189
Whitall, Hannah (Mrs. Robert Pearsall Smith), 52, 53
White, Frances Emily, 39, 40
White, Richard Grant, 283
White, Z. L., 101
Whitman Club, 35, 38
Whitman, George, 232, 450
Whitman, Louisa Orr (Mrs. George) 262, 312
Whitman, Thomas Jefferson (Jeff), 247, 255, 264, 450
Whitman, Mrs. Louisa Van Velsor, 489
Whitman, Walt: out-doors, 2, 169, 170, 175; on the *Press,* 3; stage fright, 4; labor agitation, 14, 16, 485; free trade, 14, 20, 478; portraits of, 15, 19, 73, 132, 148; *Dombey and Son,* 22; Linton, Wm. J., 22, 185, 444; socialism and anarchism, 22, 275, 393; on farewells, 28; agitation, 29; annexation of Lower California, 33; responsibility on own writing, 37; on journalism, 37, 69; conscience in newspaper men, 41; Cox photo, 42; New England speech, 45; New York harbor, 47; satisfaction in his work, 50, 460; evangelism, 53; Scandinavians, 54; Inquisition, 55; his gentleness, 59; on political appointments, 61, 62; American art publications, 62; on Sunday, 64, 65, 137; Sarony photo, 64, 81, 87; newspaper policy, 67, 482; sea rescue story, 70, 71; faith in human nature, 74; spiritual endowment of modern man, 75; prohibition, 75, 210, 298; original men, 76; America's greatness, 77; clerical writing, 77, 78; musical performances, 79; lost or stolen things, 82; Gutekunst photo, 82, 417; on hospital life, 84, 85, 91, 95; Pictures of: on collecting, 86, 412, 428; advice to young doctors,

88; medicine, 89; on Washington, D. C., 89; flying machines, 92; disorderliness, 92; the military, 93; foreign editions, 94; on critics, 96; Keyword of literature, 97; enemies, 105; endorsements, 109; Vereshtchagin photo, 118, 126, 171; presence, 130; on office-seeking, 130; Western writing, 131; art, literature, and science of the period, 134; penalty of notoriety, 137; his chair, 140, 144, 167; finances, 142, 355; slang, 143, 194; sports, 145; birthday reception, 146, 157, 163, 248, 249, 251; quality of printing, 153; physical condition, 156, 427, 442; book design, 157; on babies, 160, 224, 297; with children, 173, 202; the voice, 174, 463; letters in, 180; New York literary crowd, 184, 203, 217, 314, 392, 453; meetings, 194; women, 196, 206; single tax theory, 197; flowers, 201, 208, 209; function of books, 203; endorsers of him, 208; on abolition, 208, 287; certainty of events, 209; prices of his books, 211; electric lights, 216; Morse photo, 217; equality of women, 218; on dinners and drinking, 219; acceptance of all men, 227; on pathfounders, 238; communion, 253; serenity, 259, 464; the big book, 260; *the laughing philosopher,* 261, 263, 377, 387, 400, 689; American enterprise, 264; Seattle, Washington, 271, 272; Denver, Colorado, 272, 357, 358; *The Ledger,* 273; land holding, 275, 276; on good and bad, 276; slavery, 276; Morse bust, 281, 291; Hunt photo, 294, 300, 301, 303; freedom, 298; hospital work, 299; Christian gentlemen, 306; pronunciation, 307; suggestiveness, 310, 311; philosophy, 311; *Presidentiad,* 314; letter to Cox, 316; reading aloud, 321; the artificial and the natural, 322; solidarity, 342; *Camden's Compliment,* 347, 399, 400, 440; Greek names of American cities, 358; New Orleans, 358; selfish motives of man, 359; good

INDEX

intent, 360; tact in common man, 363; Hudson River country, 366; on his squalor, 367; public interpretation of his books, 368; Hebrews, 368, 369; inertia, 372, 373; drugs, 373; deafness, 378; care of important men, 378, 449, 450; Americans, 379, 380; longevity, 379, 400; understanding his writing, 381; on revising, 390; opponents of *Leaves of Grass*, 392; literary conscience, 398; Bacon controversy, 398; on Canada, 400; organizing a book, 401; rivers, 402; the universe, 404; Emersonianism, 404; Englishmen, 414; trip to Gutekunst's, 417; opera, 419; approached by sharper, 420; evil in average man, 423; state of society, 423; mail delivery, 425; method of writing, 425; Russians, 429; Elixir of Life, 430, 431; description of, 431; procrastination, 433; nations in history, 434; protecting Justice, 437, 438; on promoting himself, 440; submitting to nature, 449; human voice, 455; on radicalism, 464, 478; emancipation, 466; dirty books, 467; Indian words, 469, 470, 487, 488; composed piece, 471; the turbulent times, 472; art, 479; Unitarians, 480; Christianity, 488, 489; orthodoxy, 489; English language, 493; finesse, 495; the French, 495; Eakins photo, 499; New England visited, 500; greatness of America and other countries, 501; modern communication, 502; trust in mankind, 509

—comments on people: Alcott, Amos Bronson, 103, 104; Amiel, 354; Bacon, Delia, 336; Baxter, Sylvester, 327; Booth, Junius Brutus, 151, 299, 325; Booth, Edwin, 299; Brinton, Daniel G., 15, 311, 422; Bryant, William Cullen, 117, 118, 379; Bucke, Dr. Richard Maurice, 36, 182, 381, 452; Burroughs, John, 109, 301, 365, 366, 398, 460, 465; Byron, George Gordon, 351; Carlyle, Thomas, 204, 479; Chase, Salmon P., 287, 288, 289; Cleopatra, 293; Cleve-

land, S. Grover, 114; Clifford, John H., 99; Conway, Moncure, 40; Cooper, James Fenimore, 302; Dante, 74; Elliott, Charles, 302; Emerson, Edward, 176, 178, 232; Emerson, Ralph Waldo, 103, 104, 119, 233, 238, 322, 379; Emerson, Mrs. and daughter, 179, 238; Garland, Hamlin, 268; Gilder, Joseph, 325; Gilder, Richard W., 185, 415, 427; Gilchrist, Herbert, 12, 30, 150, 220, 240; Gilchrist, Mrs. Anne, 14, 150; Gosse, Edmund, 504, 505; Grant, Ulysses S., 30, 31, 61, 62; Greeley, Horace, 295; Gutekunst, F., 338; Harrison, Benjamin, 114, 450; Hartmann, Sadakichi, 35, 39, 107, 207; Hinton, Richard, 41, 42; Ingersoll, Robert G., 187, 284, 285; Jackson, Andrew, 17; Jefferson, Thomas, 30, 31, 61, 62; Jesus, 17, 18; Lafayette, Marquis de, 29, 30, 31, 93; Lee, Robert E., 31, 94; Lincoln, Abraham, 30, 31, 361, 362, 363, 448, 480, 481, 482; Linton, Wm J., 22, 185, 444; Longfellow, Henry Wadsworth, 379; Lounsbery, Thomas R., 302; Lowell, James Russell, 114; McKay, 2, 3; Mazzini, Giuseppe, 395, 397, 409, 410; Millet, Jean F., 369; 499; Morris, Harrison, 476; Morse, Sidney, 27; Napoleon, 293; O'Connor, W. D., 36, 163, 334, 341, 354, 355, 363, 364, 380, 405, 465, 466, 494, 495; O'Connor, Mrs. Ellen, 494; Ossian, 257, 258; Phillips, Wendell, 275; Potter, Bishop, 115; Rice, Allen Thorndike, 191, 193; Sarrazin, 319, 340, 385, 404, 490, 498; Smith, Robert Pearsall, 52, 53, 54; Stedman, Edmund C., 34, 35, 36, 58, 69, 99, 188, 328, 466; Stevenson, Hannah, 200; Stoddard, Richard H., 184; Sumner, Charles, 289; Swedenborg, E., 376; Swinton, William, 443; Taylor, 301, 302; Tennyson, Alfred, 5, 21, 290, 378, 407, 453, 471, 472; Tolstoi, Count Leo, 101; Turgeneff, Ivan, 101; Trollope, Anthony, 215; Tupper, 313; Washington, George, 61, 62, 93, 94; Whitman, George,

INDEX